Latent Variable and Latent Structure Models

QUANTITATIVE METHODOLOGY SERIES
Methodology for Business and Management

George A. Marcoulides, Series Editor

The purpose of this series is to present methodological techniques to investigators and students from all functional areas of business, although individuals from other disciplines will also find the series useful. Each volume in the series will focus on a specific method (e.g., Data Envelopment Analysis, Factor Analysis, Multilevel Analysis, Structural Equation Modeling). The goal is to provide an understanding and working knowledge of each method with a minimum of mathematical derivations.

Proposals are invited from all interested authors. Each proposal should consist of the following: (i) a brief description of the volume's focus and intended market, (ii) a table of contents with an outline of each chapter, and (iii) a curriculum vita. Materials may be sent to Dr. George A. Marcoulides, Department of Management Science, California State University, Fullerton, CA 92634.

Marcoulides • Modern Methods for Business Research

Duncan/Duncan/Strycker/Li/Alpert • An Introduction to Latent Variable Growth Curve Modeling: Concepts, Issues, and Applications

Heck/Thomas • An Introduction to Multilevel Modeling Techniques

Marcoulides/Moustaki • Latent Variable and Latent Structure Models

Hox • Multilevel Analysis: Techniques and Applications

Latent Variable
and Latent Structure Models

Edited by

George A. Marcoulides
California State University, Fullerton

Irini Moustaki
London School of Economics and Political Science

LAWRENCE ERLBAUM ASSOCIATES, PUBLISHERS
2002   Mahwah, New Jersey   London

Lawrence Erlbaum Associates, Inc., Publishers
10 Industrial Avenue
Mahwah, NJ 07430

Cover design by Kathryn Houghtaling Lacey

Library of Congress Cataloging-in-Publication Data

Latent variable and latent structure models / edited by George A.
    Marcoulides, Irini Moustaki.
        p. cm. — (Quantitative methodology series)
    Includes bibliographical references and indexes.
ISBN 0-8058-4046-X (alk. paper)
1. Latent structure analysis. 2. Latent variables.   I. Marcoulides,
    George A.   II. Moustaki, Irini.   III. Series.
QA278.6 .L336   2002
519.5'35—dc21   2001057759
                                                 CIP

Printed in the United States of America
10   9   8   7   6   5   4   3   2   1

Contents

II

Preface

This volume is based on material presented at the 22nd biennial conference of the Society for Multivariate Analysis in the Behavioural Sciences (SMABS) held by the Department of Statistics at the London School of Economics and Political Science in July 2000. SMABS is an international research society for advancing research in the area of measurement and psychometrics with emphasis in comparative studies. The SMABS biennial meetings bring together researchers interested in many research disciplines within the social measurement area (e.g., item response theory, test theory, measurement theory, covariance structure analysis, multidimensional scaling, correspondence analysis, multilevel modeling, survey analysis and measurement error, classification, clustering and neural networks).

The theme of the 22nd SMABS conference – theoretical developments and applications in latent variable modeling and structural equation modeling - was realized in the many papers presented during the three days of the meeting. Each paper described original research and developments concerned with the theory and practice of multivariate analysis in the behavioural sciences. At the conclusion of the conference, we asked the authors of specific papers to put together their contributions for publication in a single volume. Chapters presented here represent a particular focused coverage of topics related to latent variable and latent structure models. Although the words in the name of the Society, "Analysis in the Behavioural Sciences", indicate that the contributions are all generally related to methods that provide answers to questions about human behaviour, the methods apply equally well to answers to questions about non-human behaviour.

We have tried to compile a volume that will be of interest to researchers from a wide variety of disciplines including biology, business, economics, education, medicine, psychology, sociology, and other social and health sciences. As such, the chapters are aimed at a broad audience concerned with keeping up on the latest developments and techniques related to latent variable and latent structure models. Each chapter assumes that the reader has already mastered the equivalent of basic multivariate statistics and measurement theory courses that included coverage of issues related to latent variable models.

This volume could not have been completed without the assistance and support provided by many individuals. First, we would like to thank all the contributors and reviewers for their time and effort in getting the various chapters ready for publication. They all worked diligently through the various publication stages. We are particularly indebted to the contributing authors, who gave so generously of their time and expertise to this volume. Their chapters were a genuine pleasure to read and they greatly enhanced our own knowledge of the techniques covered in this volume. Their responsiveness to our editorial suggestions greatly eased our work as editors. We are also grateful to Larry Erlbaum for his continued encouragement and support of our work. Thanks are also due to all the wonderful people on the editorial staff of Lawrence Erlbaum Associates for their assistance and support in putting together this volume. Finally, a special thank you to our colleague and friend Zvi Drezner for his skillful help with handling the various technical issues related to preparing the volume for publication.

George A. Marcoulides

Irini Moustaki

About the Authors

David J. Bartholomew is Emeritus Professor of Statistics at the London School of Economics and Political Science, which he first joined in 1973 having previously been Professor of Statistics at the University of Kent. He is a former ProDirector of the LSE and President of the Royal Statistical Society. His main interest is in the application of statistical ideas in the social sciences especially the development of latent variable methods. Recent publications include *The Statistical Approach to Social Measurement* (Academic Press, 1996) and (with M. Knott) *Latent Variable Models and Factor Analysis* (Arnold, 1999).

William Browne has been a research officer on the Multilevel Models Project at the Institute of Education since 1998. Prior to that he completed a PhD entitled 'Applying MCMC Methods to Multilevel Models' at the University of Bath under the supervision of Professor David Draper. His main research interests are Monte Carlo Markov Chain (MCMC) methodology and the application of these methods to the modelling of complex data structures. He is currently involved in developing new methodology to fit such complex models and programming them in the widely used multilevel modelling software package MLwiN. He is also interested in the dissemination of complex models to applied researchers.

Marcel Croon is an associate professor in the Department of Methodology and Statistics at the Faculty of Social Sciences of Tilburg University (The Netherlands). He teaches courses in research methodology, applied statistics and latent structure models. His research interests are measurement theory in applied statistics for the social and behavioral sciences, and, more specifically, in the general theory of latent structure for continuous and categorical data.

Peter Filzmoser is an assistant professor at the Vienna University of Technology. He received an award for his thesis on 'Principal Planes' from the Vienna University of Technology. He has collaborated extensively with Professor Rousseeuw from the University of Antwerp and with Professor Croux from the Universite Libre de Bruxelles. His research interests are on robust multivariate methods.

Jean-Paul Fox is a post-doctoral researcher in the department of Educational Measurement and Data Analysis at the University of Twente. He received his PhD in 1996 from the University of Twente. Previously, he was employed as a statistician at I\&O Research in Enschede. His research interests include multilevel modeling and item response theory.

Cees A.W. Glas studied psychology with a specialization in mathematical and statistical psychology. From 1981 to 1995 he worked at the National Institute of Educational Measurement (Cito) in the Netherlands. In 1995 he joined the department of Educational Measurement and Data Analysis, at the University of Twente, where he specializes in item response theory and multilevel modeling.

Harvey Goldstein has been Professor of Statistical Methods at the Institute of Education since 1977. Prior to that, from 1971 - 1976 he was chief statistician at the National Children's Bureau and began his professional career as lecturer in statistics at the Institute of Child Health, University of London from 1964-1971. He is currently a member of the Council of the Royal Statistical Society, and has been editor of the Society's Journal, Series A and was awarded the Guy medal in silver in 1998. He was elected a member of the International Statistical Institute in 1987 and a fellow of the British Academy in 1997. He has two main research interests. The first is the use of statistical modelling techniques in the construction and analysis of educational tests. The second is in the methodology of multilevel modelling. He has had continuous funding for this from the Economic and Social research Council (U.K.) since 1986 and has supervised the production (with Jon Rasbash, Min Yang and William Browne) of a widely used software package (*MLwiN*).

Bas T. Hemker is senior research scientist at the National Institute for Educational Measurement (Cito) in Arnhem, The Netherlands. His main research interests are item response theory, computerized adaptive testing and educational measurement.

Sik Yum Lee is a chair professor in the Department of Statistics at The Chinese University of Hong Kong. His research interests are in structural equation modeling, local influence analysis, and nonparametric estimation.

Martin Knott is a senior lecturer in Statistics in the Department of Statistics at the London School of Economics and Political Science. His early interests were in goodness-of-fit and linear modelling, currently working in latent variable modeling and on multivariate distribution theory. Recent publications include (with D. J. Bartholomew) *Latent Variable Models and Factor Analysis* (Arnold 1999).

George A. Marcoulides is Professor of Statistics at California State University, Fullerton. He currently serves as editor of the journal *Structural Equation Modeling* and LEA's *Quantitative Methodology Book Series.*

Irini Moustaki is a lecturer in Social Statistics in the Department of Statistics at the London School of Economics and Political Science. Her research interests include latent variable models, categorical data and missing values in attitudinal surveys.

Colm A. O'Muircheartaigh is a professor in the Irving B. Harris Graduate School of Public Policy Studies and vice president for Statistics and Methodology in the National Opinion Research Center, both at the University of Chicago. His research encompasses measurement errors in surveys, cognitive aspects of question wording, and latent variable models for nonresponse. He joined the University of Chicago from the London School of Economics and Political Science (LSE); he was the first director of The Methodology Institute, the center for research and training in social science methodology at the LSE. He has also taught at a number of other institutions, having served as a visiting professor at the Universities of Padua, Perugia, Florence, and

Bologna, and, since 1975, taught at the Summer Institute of the University of Michigan's Institute for Social Research.

Pilar Rivera is an associate professor in the Business Department at the University of Zaragoza, Spain. She has been involved in applications of structural equation modeling in various areas of marketing research, especially in the area of assessing quality of services and environment policy issues.

Amanda Sacker is a senior research fellow in the Department of Epidemiology and Public Health at University College London. Her research interests have been mainly concerned with the epidemiology of child and adult psychopathology and in social inequalities in health. She has a particular interest in the use of structural equation modelling techniques in longitudinal studies. Current research interests include an ESRC funded project on the childhood origins of adult mental health inequalities. She is also collaborating with Dick Wiggins, amongst others, on an MRC Health of the Public project on geographical, social, economic and cultural inequalities in health.

Albert Satorra is Professor of Statistics in the Department of Economics and Business of the Universitat Pompeu Fabra, in Barcelona. His general area of interest is statistical methodology for economic, business and social science research, especially structural equation modeling, a topic on which he has published numerous articles of methodological content in leading journals.

Klaas Sijtsma is a full professor of methodology and statistics for psychological research in the Department of Methodology and Statistics, Faculty of Social and Behavioral Sciences, at Tilburg University, The Netherlands. He specializes in psychometrics and applied statistics.

Jian Qing Shi is a research assistant in the Department of Computing Science at the University of Glasgow. His research interests include latent variable models, covariance structural analysis, meta-analysis, influence analysis, and nonlinear system controls.

Panagiota Tzamourani is currently working at the Research Department of the Bank of Greece. She has previously worked at the National Centre of Social Research in Britain and the London School of Economics, where she obtained her PhD. Her research interests are in the area of latent trait models.

Andries Van der Ark is assistant professor and postdoctoral researcher in the Department of Methodology and Statistics, at Tilburg University, The Netherlands. His main research interests are item response theory, latent class modeling, and psychological testing.

Richard D. Wiggins is a reader in Social Statistics at the City University in London. Since the early 1990's he has been closely identified with the development of the Graduate Programme in Advanced Social Research Methods and Analysis training at City University. His current research interests span all aspects of the life course. Substantive themes include family diversity and children's well-being, transitions into adulthood and quality of life in early old age. He is also working on geographical, social, economic and cultural inequalities in health under a major Medical Research Council initiative on public health.

Bo-Cheng Wei is Professor of Statistics at Southeast University, Nanjing, People's Republic of China. He is a fellow of the Royal Statistical Society and a member of the American Statistical Association. His research interests focus on nonlinear models and diagnostics methods.

1 Old and New Approaches to Latent Variable Modelling

David J. Bartholomew

London School of Economics and Political Science

1.1 The Old Approach

To find the precursor of contemporary latent variable modeling one must go back to the beginning of the 20th century and Charles Spearman's invention of factor analysis. This was followed, half a century later, by latent class and latent trait analysis and, from the 1960's onwards, by covariance structure analysis. The most recent additions to the family have been in the area of latent time series analysis. This chapter briefly reviews each of these fields in turn as a foundation for the evaluations and comparisons which are made later.

1.1.1 Factor analysis

Spearman's (1904) original paper on factor analysis is remarkable, not so much for what it achieved, which was primitive by today's standards, but for the path-breaking character of its central idea. He was writing when statistical theory was in its infancy. Apart from regression analysis, all of today's multivariate methods lay far in the future. Therefore Spearman had not only to formulate the central idea, but to devise the algebraic and computational methods for delivering the results. At the heart of the analysis was the discovery that one could infer the presence of a latent dimension of variation from the pattern of the pairwise correlations coefficients. However, Spearman was somewhat blinkered in his view by his belief in a single underlying latent variable corresponding to general ability, or intelligence. The data did not support this hypothesis and it was left to others, notably Thurstone in the 1930's, to extend the theory to what became commonly known as multiple factor analysis.

Factor analysis was created by, and almost entirely developed by, psychologists. Hotelling's introduction of principal components analysis in 1933 approached essentially the same problem from a different perspective, but his work seems to have made little impact on practitioners at the time.

It was not until the 1960's and the publication of Lawley and Maxwell's (1971) book *Factor Analysis as a Statistical Method* that any sustained attempt was made to treat the subject statistically. Even then there was little effect on statisticians who, typically, continued to regard factor analysis as an alien and highly subjective activity which could not compete with principal components analysis. Gradually the range of applications widened but without going far beyond the framework provided by the founders.

1.1.2   Latent class analysis

Latent class analysis, along with latent trait analysis (discussed later), have their roots in the work of the sociologist, Paul Lazarsfeld in the 1960's. Under the general umbrella of latent structure analysis these techniques were intended as tools of sociological analysis. Although Lazarsfeld recognized certain affinities with factor analysis he emphasized the differences. Thus in the old approach these families of methods were regarded as quite distinct.

Although statistical theory had made great strides since Spearman's day there was little input from statisticians until Leo Goodman began to develop efficient methods for handling the latent class model around 1970.

1.1.3   Latent trait analysis

Although a latent trait model differs from a latent class model only in the fact that the latent dimension is viewed as continuous rather than categorical, it is considered separately because it owes its development to one particular application. Educational testing is based on the idea that human abilities vary and that individuals can be located on a scale of the ability under investigation by the answers they give to a set of test items. The latent trait model provides the link between the responses and the underlying trait. A seminal contribution to the theory was provided by Birnbaum (1968) but today there is an enormous literature, both applied and theoretical, including books, journals such as *Applied Psychological Measurement* and a multitude of articles.

1.1.4   Covariance structure analysis

This term covers developments stemming from the work of Jöreskog in the 1960's. It is a generalization of factor analysis in which one explores causal relationships (usually linear) among the latent variables. The significance of the word *covariance* is that these models are fitted, as in factor analysis, by comparing the observed covariance matrix of the data with that predicted by the model. Since much of empirical social science is concerned with trying to establish causal relationships between unobservable variables, this form of analysis has found many applications. This work has been greatly facilitated by the availability of good software packages whose sophistication has kept pace with the speed and capacity of desk-top (or lap-top) computers. In some quarters, empirical social research has become almost synonymous with LISREL analysis. The acronym LISREL has virtually become a generic title for linear structure relations modeling.

1.1.5 Latent time series

The earliest use of latent variable ideas in time series appears to have been due to Wiggins (1973) but, as so often happens, it was not followed up. Much later there was rapid growth in work on latent (or "hidden" as they are often called) Markov chains. If individuals move between a set of categories over time it may be that their movement can be modeled by a Markov chain. Sometimes their category cannot be observed directly and the state of the individual must be inferred, indirectly, from other variables related to that state. The true Markov chain is thus latent, or hidden. An introduction to such processes is given in MacDonald and Zucchini (1997). Closely related work has been going on, independently, in the modeling of neural networks. Harvey and Chung (2000) proposed a latent structural time series model to model the local linear trend in unemployment. In this context two observed series are regarded as being imperfect indicators of "true" unemployment.

1.2 The New Approach

The new, or statistical, approach derives from the observation that all of the models behind the foregoing examples are, from a statistical point of view, mixtures. The basis for this remark can be explained by reference to a simple example which, at first sight, appears to have little to do with latent variables. If all members of a population have a very small and equal chance of having an accident on any day, then the distribution of the number of accidents per month, say, will have a Poisson distribution. In practice the observed distribution often has greater dispersion than predicted by the Poisson hypothesis. This can be explained by supposing that the daily risk of accident varies from one individual to another. In other words, there appears to be an unobservable source of variation which may be called "accident proneness". The latter is a latent variable. The actual distribution of number of accidents is thus a (continuous) mixture of Poisson distributions.

The position is essentially the same with the latent variable models previously discussed. The latent variable is a source of unobservable variation in some quantity, which characterizes members of the population. For the latent class model this latent variable is categorical, for the latent trait and factor analysis model it is continuous. The actual distribution of the manifest variables is then a mixture of the simple distributions they would have had in the absence of that heterogeneity. That simpler distribution is deducible from the assumed behaviour of individuals with the same ability - or whatever it is that distinguishes them. This will be made more precise below.

1.2.1 Origins of the new approach

The first attempt to express all latent variable models within a common mathematical framework appears to have been that of Anderson (1959). The title of the paper suggests that it is concerned only with the latent class model and this may have caused his seminal contribution to be overlooked. Fielding (1977) used Anderson's treatment in his exposition of latent structure models but this did not appear to have been taken up until the present author used it as a basis for handling the factor analysis of categorical data (Bartholomew 1980). This work was developed in Bartholomew (1984) by the introduction of exponential family models and the key concept of sufficiency. This approach, set out in Bartholomew and Knott (1999), lies behind the treatment of the present chapter. One of the most general treatments, which embraces a very wide family of models, is also contained in Arminger and Küsters (1988).

1.2.2 Where is the new approach located on the map of statistics?

Statistical inference starts with data and seeks to generalize from it. It does this by setting up a probability model which defines the process by which the data are supposed to have been generated. We have observations on a, possibly multivariate, random variable $\mathbf{x}$ and wish to make inferences about the process which is determined by a set of parameters ξ. The link between the two is expressed by the distribution of $\mathbf{x}$ given ξ. Frequentist inference treats ξ as fixed; Bayesian inference treats ξ as a random variable.

In latent variables analysis one may think of $\mathbf{x}$ as partitioned into two parts $\mathbf{x}$ and $\mathbf{y}$, where $\mathbf{x}$ is observed and $\mathbf{y}$, the latent variable, is not observed. Formally then, this is a standard inference problem in which some of the variables are missing. The model will have to begin with the distribution of $\mathbf{x}$ given ξ and $\mathbf{y}$. A purely frequentist approach would treat ξ and $\mathbf{y}$ as parameters, whereas the Bayesian would need a joint prior distribution for ξ and $\mathbf{y}$. However, there is now an intermediate position, which is more appropriate in many applications, and that is to treat $\mathbf{y}$ as a random variable with ξ fixed. Regarding $\mathbf{y}$ as fixed would enable one to make inferences about the values of $\mathbf{y}$ for these members of the sample. But often one is interested in predicting the values of $\mathbf{y}$ for other members of the population on the basis of their $\mathbf{x}$-values. This is the case, for example, when one is constructing a measuring instrument for some mental ability. That is one wants a means of locating an individual on a scale of ability on the basis of a set of scores, $\mathbf{x}$, obtained in a test. In that case it is more appropriate to treat $\mathbf{y}$ as a random variable also.

This problem can also be expressed in terms of probability distributions as follows. For an observable random variable $\mathbf{x}$, the distribution can be represented in the form

$$f(\mathbf{x} \mid \xi) = \int f(\mathbf{x} \mid \mathbf{y}, \xi) h(\mathbf{y}) \, d\mathbf{y}. \qquad (1.1)$$

Here, for simplicity, the notation is that of continuous random variables, but the point being made is quite general.

1.2.3   Basic relationships

Equation 1.1 reveals an important indeterminacy in the problem defined. One can make any one-to-one transformation of **y** without changing $f(\mathbf{x} \mid \xi)$. In other words the distribution of **y** is indeterminate. There can be no *empirical* justification for choosing one prior distribution for **y** rather than another. This might seem to be a crippling handicap but, as shall now be seen, important deductions can be made which hold for all prior distributions.

The problem is to say something about the missing values, **y**, when one knows **x**. All of the information about **y** given **x** is contained in

$$f(\mathbf{y} \mid \mathbf{x}) = h(\mathbf{y})f(\mathbf{x} \mid \mathbf{y})/f(\mathbf{x}) \tag{1.2}$$

where ξ has been suppressed in the notation because it is not relevant for the point being made.

At first sight one is at an impasse because of the presence of the unknown $h(\mathbf{y})$ on the right hand side. However, suppose that it were the case that $f(\mathbf{x} \mid \mathbf{y})$ could be expressed in the form

$$f(\mathbf{x} \mid \mathbf{y}) = g(\mathbf{X} \mid \mathbf{y})\phi(\mathbf{x}) \tag{1.3}$$

where **X** is a function of **x** of the same dimension as **y**. Then one would find, by substitution into equation 1.2, that

$$f(\mathbf{y} \mid \mathbf{x}) = f(\mathbf{y} \mid \mathbf{X}) \propto h(\mathbf{y})g(\mathbf{X} \mid \mathbf{y}). \tag{1.4}$$

The point of this manoeuvre is that all that one needs to know about **x** in order to determine $f(\mathbf{y} \mid \mathbf{x})$ is the statistic **X**. This provides a statistic which, in a precise sense, contains all the information about **y** which is provided by **x**. In that sense, then, one can use **X** in place of **y**.

The usefulness of this observation depends, of course, on whether or not the representation of (1.3) is possible in a large enough class of problems. One needs to know for what class of models, defined by $f(\mathbf{x} \mid \mathbf{y})$, is this factorization possible. This is a simpler question than it appears to be because other considerations, outlined in Section 3.1 below, mean that one can restrict attention to the case where the x's are conditionally independent (see Equation 1.5). This means that one only has to ask the question of the univariate distributions of the individual x_i's. Roughly speaking this means that one requires that $f(x_i \mid \mathbf{y})$ be a member of an exponential family for all i (for further details see Bartholomew & Knott, 1999). Fortunately this family, which includes the normal, binomial, multinomial and gamma distributions, is large enough for most practical purposes.

The relationship given by Equation 1.3 is referred to as the *sufficiency principle* because it is, essentially, a statement that **X** is sufficient for **y** in the Bayesian sense. It should be noted that, in saying this, all parameters in the model are treated as known.

1.3   The General Linear Latent Variable Model

1.3.1   Theory

The foregoing analysis has been very general, and deliberately so. In order to relate it to the various latent variable models in use the analysis must now be more specific.

In a typical problem $\mathbf{x}$ is a vector of dimension p say, where p is often large. Elements of $\mathbf{x}$ may be scores on test items or responses to questions in a survey, for example. The point of introducing the latent variables $\mathbf{y}$, is to explain the inter-dependencies among the x's. If this can be done with a small number, q, of y's a substantial reduction in dimensionality shall be achieved. One may also hope that the y's can be identified with more fundamental underlying variables like attitudes or abilities.

If the effect of the y's is to induce dependencies among the x's, then one would know that enough y's have been introduced if, when one conditions on them, the x's are independent. That is, one needs to introduce just sufficient y's to make

$$f(\mathbf{x} \mid \mathbf{y}) = \prod_{i=1}^{p} f_i(x_i \mid \mathbf{y}). \tag{1.5}$$

The problem is then to find distributions $\{f_i(x_i \mid \mathbf{y})\}$ such that the sufficiency property holds.

There are many ways in which this can be done but one such way produces a large enough class of models to meet most practical needs. Thus, consider distributions of the following form

$$f_i(x_i \mid \theta_i) = F_i(x_i)G(\theta_i)e^{\theta_i u_i(x_i)} \tag{1.6}$$

where θ_i is some function of $\mathbf{y}$. It is then easily verified that there exists a sufficient statistic

$$\mathbf{X} = \sum_{i=1}^{p} u_i(x_i). \tag{1.7}$$

The particular special case considered, henceforth known as *the general linear latent variable model* (GLLVM), supposes that

$$\theta_i = \alpha_{i0} + \alpha_{i1}y_1 + \alpha_{i2}y_2 + \ldots + \alpha_{iq}y_q \qquad (i = 1, 2, \ldots q). \tag{1.8}$$

This produces most of the standard models - and many more besides.

1.3.2   Examples

Two of the most important examples arise when the x's are (a) all binary or (b) all normal.

The binary case. If x_i is binary then, conditional upon $\mathbf{y}$, it is reasonable to assume that it has a Bernoulli distribution with $\Pr\{x_i = 1 \mid \mathbf{y}\} = \pi_i(\mathbf{y})$. This is a member of the exponential family (1.6) with

$$\theta_i = \text{logit}\,\pi_i(\mathbf{y}) = \alpha_{i0} + \alpha_{i1}y_1 + \alpha_{i2}y_2 + \cdots + \alpha_{iq}y_q \qquad (i = 1, 2, \ldots p) \ (1.9)$$

This is a latent trait model in which q is usually taken to be 1, when it is known as the logit model.

The normal case. If x is normal with $x_i \mid \mathbf{y} \sim N(\mu_i, \sigma_i^2)$ $(i = 1, 2, \ldots p)$ the parameter θ_i in (1.6) is

$$\theta_i = \mu_i/\sigma_i = \alpha_{i0} + \alpha_{i1}y_1 + \ldots + \alpha_{iq}y_q \qquad (i = 1, 2, \ldots p). \qquad (1.10)$$

Since the distribution depends on two parameters, μ_i and σ_i, one of them must be treated as a nuisance parameter. If this is chosen to be σ_i, one may write the model

$$x_i = \lambda_{i0} + \lambda_{i1}y_1 + \lambda_{i2}y_2 + \ldots \lambda_{iq}y_q + e_i \qquad (i = 1, 2, \ldots p) \qquad (1.11)$$

where $\lambda_{ij} = \alpha_{ij}\sigma_i$ $(j = 1, 2, \ldots q)$ and $e_i \sim N(0, \sigma_i^2)$ with $\{e_i\}$ independent of $\mathbf{y}$. This will be recognized as the standard representation of the linear normal factor model.

Other special cases can be found in Bartholomew and Knott (1999) including the latent class model which can be regarded as a special case of the general latent trait model given above.

It is interesting to note that for both of the examples given above

$$X_j = \sum_{i=1}^{p} \alpha_{ij} x_i \qquad (j = 1, 2, \ldots q).$$

Weighted sums of the manifest variables have long been used as indices for underlying latent variables on purely intuitive grounds. The foregoing theory provides a more fundamental rationale for this practice.

1.4   Contrasts Between the Old and New Approaches

1.4.1   Computation

Factor analysis was introduced at a time when computational resources were very limited by today's standards. The inversion of even small matrices was very time consuming on a hand calculator and beset by numerical instabilities. This not only made fitting the models very slow, but it had a distorting effect on the development of the subject. Great efforts were made to devise shortcuts and approximations for parameter estimation. The calculation of standard errors was almost beyond reach. The matter of rotation was as much an art as a science, and this contributed to the perception by some that factor analysis was little better than mumbo jumbo.

Things were little better when latent structure analysis came on the scene in the 1950's. Inefficient methods of fitting based on moments and such like took precedence simply because they were feasible. There was virtually nothing in common between the methods used for fitting the various models beyond their numerical complexity. As computers became more powerful towards the end of the 20th century, a degree of commonality became apparent in the unifying effect of maximum likelihood estimation, but this did not exploit the common structure revealed by the new approach. The possibility of a single algorithm for fitting all models derived from the new approach was pointed out by Bartholomew and Knott (1999, Section 7) and this has now been implemented by Moustaki (1999).

1.4.2   Disciplinary focus

Another distorting feature springs from the diverse disciplinary origins of the various models. Factor analysis was invented by a psychologist and largely developed by psychologists. Latent structure analysis was a product of sociology. This close tie with substantive problems had obvious advantages, principally that the problems tackled were those which are important rather than merely tractable. But it also had disadvantages. Many of the innovators lacked the technical tools necessary and did not always realize that some, at least, were already available in other fields. By focussing on the particular psychological hypothesis of a single general factor, Spearman failed to see the importance of multiple factor analysis. Lazarsfeld emphasized the difference between his own work on latent structure and factor analysis, which were unimportant, and minimized the similarities, which were fundamental. In such ways progress was slowed and professional statisticians, who did have something to offer, were debarred from entering the field. When they eventually did make a tentative entry in the shape of the first edition of Lawley and Maxwell's book in the 1960's, the contribution was not warmly welcomed by either side!

1.4.3   Types of variables

One rather surprising feature which delayed the unification of the subject on the lines set out here runs through the whole of statistics, but is particularly conspicuous in latent variable modelling. This is the distinction between continuous and categorical variables.

The development of statistical theory for continuous variables was much more rapid than for categorical variables. This doubtless owed much to the fact that Karl Pearson and Ronald Fisher were mainly interested in problems involving continuous variables and, once their bandwagon was rolling, that was where the theoreticians wanted to be. There were some points of contact as, for example, on correlation and association but there seems to have been little recognition that much of what could be done for continuous variables could, in principle, also be done for categorical variables or for mixtures of the two types. In part this was a notational matter. A perusal of Goodman's work on latent class analysis (e.g., Goodman, 1974), in which he uses a precise but forbidding notation, obscures rather than reveals the links with latent trait or factor analysis. Formulating the new approach in a sufficiently abstract form to include all types of variables, reveals the essential common structure and so makes matters simpler.

1.4.4 Probability modelling

A probability model is the foundation of statistical analysis. Faced with a new problem the statistician will determine the variables involved and express the relationships between them in probabilistic terms. There are, of course, standard models for common problems, so the work does not always have to be done *ab initio*. However, what is now almost a matter of routine is a relatively recent phenomenon and much of the development of latent variable models lies on the far side of the water-shed, which may be roughly dated to the 1950's. This was common to all branches of statistics but it can easily be illustrated by reference to factor analysis.

In approaching the subject today, one would naturally think in terms of probability distributions and ask what is the distribution of $\mathbf{x}$ given $\mathbf{y}$. Approaching it in this way one might write

$$\mathbf{x} = \mu + \mathbf{\Lambda}\mathbf{y} + \mathbf{e} \tag{1.12}$$

or, equivalently,

$$\mathbf{x} \sim N(\mu + \mathbf{\Lambda}\mathbf{y}, \ \psi) \tag{1.13}$$

with appropriate further assumptions about independence and the distribution of $\mathbf{y}$. Starting from this, one can construct a likelihood function and from that, devise methods of estimation, testing goodness of fit and so on. In earlier times the starting point would have been the structure of the covariance (or correlation) matrix, $\mathbf{\Sigma}$, and the attempt to find a representation of the form

$$\mathbf{\Sigma} = \mathbf{\Lambda}\mathbf{\Lambda}' + \psi. \tag{1.14}$$

In fact, this way of viewing the problem still survives as when (1.14) is referred to as a model.

The distinction between the old and new approaches lies in the fact that, whereas $\mathbf{\Sigma}$ is specific to factor analysis and has no obvious analogue in latent structure analysis, the probabilistic representation of (1.12) and (1.13) immediately generalizes as our formulation of the GLLVM shows.

1.5   Some Benefits of the New Approach

1.5.1   Factor scores

The so-called "factor scores problem" has a long and controversial history, which still has some life in it as Maraun (1996) and the ensuing discussion shows. The problem is how to locate a sample member in the $\mathbf{y}$-space on the basis of its observed value of $\mathbf{x}$. In the old approach to factor analysis, which treated (1.12) as a linear equation in mathematical (as opposed to random) variables, it was clear that there were insufficient equations p to determine the q y's because, altogether, there were $p + q$ unknowns (y's and e's). Hence the y's (factor scores) were said to be indeterminate.

Using the new approach, it is obvious that $\mathbf{y}$ is not uniquely determined by $\mathbf{x}$ but that knowledge of it is contained in the posterior distribution of $\mathbf{y}$ given $\mathbf{x}$. From that distribution one can predict $\mathbf{y}$ using some measure of location of the posterior distribution, such as $E(\mathbf{y} \mid \mathbf{x})$. Oddly enough, this approach has always been used for the latent class model, where individuals are allocated to classes on the basis of the posterior probabilities of belonging to the various classes. The inconsistency of using one method for factor analysis and another for latent class analysis only becomes strikingly obvious when the two techniques are set within a common framework.

1.5.2   Reliability

The posterior distribution also tells something about the uncertainty attached to the factor scores. In practice, the dispersion of the posterior distribution can be disconcertingly large. This means that the factor scores are then poorly determined or, to use the technical term, unreliable. This poor determination of latent variables is a common phenomenon which manifests itself in other ways. For example, it has often been noted that latent class and latent trait models sometimes give equally good fits to the same data. A good example is given by Bartholomew (2000). A latent trait model, with one latent variable, was fitted to one of the classical data sets of educational testing - the Law School Admissions Test - with 5 items. A latent class model with two classes was also fitted to the same data and the results for the two models were hardly distinguishable. It thus appears that it is very difficult to distinguish empirically between a model in which the latent variable is distributed normally and one in which it consists of two probability masses.

A similar result has been demonstrated mathematically by Molenaar and von Eye (1994) for the factor analysis model and the latent profile model. The latter is one where the manifest variables are continuous but the latent variable categorical. They were able to show that, given any factor model, it was possible to find a latent profile model with the same covariance matrix, and conversely. Hence, whenever one model fits the data, the other will fit equally well as judged by the covariances. Once again, therefore, the latent distribution is poorly determined. These conclusions have important implications for linear structural relations models which seek to explore the relationships between latent variables. If very little can be said about the distribution of a latent variable, it is clear that the form of any relationship between them must also be very difficult to determine.

1.5.3 Variability

The calculation of standard errors of parameter estimates and measures of goodness of fit has been relatively neglected. In part this has been due to the heavy computations involved, even for finding asymptotic errors. However, it may also owe something to the strong disciplinary focus which was noted in the previous section. The criterion of "meaningfulness" has often been invoked as a justification for taking the fit of models at face value, even when the sample size is very small. The broad span of professional experience, which is brought to bear in making such judgements, is not to be disregarded, but it cannot replace an objective evaluation of the variability inherent in the method of fitting.

The treatment of latent variable models given in Bartholomew and Knott (1999) lays emphasis on the calculation of standard errors and goodness of fit. In addition to the standard asymptotic theory, which flows from the method of maximum likelihood, it is now feasible to use re-sampling methods like the bootstrap to study sampling variation. This is made the more necessary by the fact that asymptotic sampling theory is sometimes quite inadequate for sample sizes such as one finds in practice (e.g., de Menezes 1999). A further complication arises when a model with more than one latent variable is fitted. This arises because, in the GLLVM, orthogonal linear transformation of the y's leave the joint distribution of the x's unchanged. In factor analysis, this process is familiar as "rotation", but the same point applies to any member of the general family. It means, for example, that there is not one solution to the maximum likelihood equation but infinitely many, linked by linear transformations. Describing the sampling variability of a set of solutions, rather than a point within the set, is not straightforward. Further problems arise in testing goodness of fit. For example, with p binary variables, there are 2^p possible combinations which may occur. The obvious way of judging goodness of fit is to compare the observed and expected frequencies of these response patterns (or cell frequencies). However, if p is large, 2^p may be large compared with the sample size. In these circumstances many expected frequencies will be too small for the usual chi-squared tests to be valid. This sparsity, as it is called, requires new methods on which there is much current research.

1.6   Conclusion

Latent variables analysis is a powerful and useful tool which has languished too long in the shadowy regions on the borders of statistics. It is now taking its place in the main stream, stimulated in part by the recognition that it can be given a sound foundation within a traditional statistical framework. It can justly be claimed that the new approach clarifies, simplifies, and unifies the disparate developments spanning over a century.

References

Anderson, T. W. (1959). Some scaling models and estimation procedures in the latent class model. In U. Grenander (Ed.), *Probability and statistics* (pp. 9-38). New York: Wiley.

Arminger, G. & Küsters, U. (1988). Latent trait models with indicators of mixed measurement level. In R. Langeheine and J. Rost (Eds.), *Latent trait and latent class models*, New York: Plenum.

Bartholomew, D. J. (1980). Factor analysis of categorical data (with discussion). *Journal of the Royal Statistical Society*, 42, 293-321.

Bartholomew, D. J. (1984). The foundations of factor analysis. *Biometrika*, 71, 221-232.

Bartholomew, D. J. (2000). The measurement of standards. In *Educational standards* H. Goldstein and A. Heath (Eds.), for The British Academy, Oxford University Press.

Bartholomew, D. J. & Knott, M. (1999). *Latent variable models and factor analysis* (2nd ed). London, UK: Arnold.

Birnbaum, A. (1968). Some latent trait models and their use in inferring an examinee's ability. In F. M. Lord and M. R. Novick (Eds), *Statistical theories of mental test scores*, Reading, MA: Addison-Wesley.

de Menezes, L. M. (1999). On fitting latent class models for binary data. *British Journal of Mathematical and Statistical Psychology*, 62, 149-168.

Fielding, A. (1977). Latent structure models. In C. A. O'Muircheartaigh and C.Payne (Eds.), *The analysis of survey data: Exploring data structures, Vol 1* (pp. 125-157). Chichester: Wiley.

Goodman, L. A. (1974). The analysis of systems of qualitative variables when some of the variables are unobservable. Part I-A modified latent structure approach. *American Journal of Sociology*, 79, 1179-1259.

Harvey, A. & Chung, C. -H. (2000). Estimating the underlying change in unemployment in the UK (with discussion). *Journal of the Royal Statistical Society*, 163, A, 303-339.

Lawley, D. N. & Maxwell, A. E. (1971). *Factor analysis as a statistical method* (2nd edn), London, UK: Butterworth.

MacDonald, I. L. & Zucchini, W. (1997). *Hidden Markov and other models for discrete-valued time series*. London, UK: Chapman & Hall.

Maraun, M. D. (1996). Metaphor taken as math: indeterminacy in the factor analysis model. *Multivariate Behavioral Research*, 31, 517-538.

Molenaar, P. C. M. & von Eye, A. (1994). On the Arbitrary Nature of Latent Variables. In A. von Eye and C. Clogg (Eds.), *Latent variables analysis* (pp 226-242). Thousand Oaks, CA: Sage Publications.

Moustaki, I. (1999). A latent variable model for ordinal variables. *Applied Psychological Measurement*, 24, 211-223.

Spearman, C. (1904). General intelligence, objectively determined and measured. *American Journal of Psycholgy*, 16, 201-293.

Wiggins, L. M. (1973). *Panel analysis: Latent probability models for attitude and behavior processes*. Amsterdam: Elsevier.

2 Locating 'Don't Know', 'No Answer' and Middle Alternatives on an Attitude Scale: A Latent Variable Approach

Irini Moustaki[1] and Colm O'Muircheartaigh[2]

[1] London School of Economics and Political Science
[2] University of Chicago

2.1 Introduction

A number of latent variable models have recently been proposed for treating missing values in attitude scales (Knott, Albanese, & Galbraith, 1990; O'Muircheartaigh & Moustaki, 1999; Moustaki & O'Muircheartaigh, 2000; Moustaki & Knott, 2000b). This chapter extends that work to allow for different types of non-responses and for identifying the position of middle categories in Likert type scales. The chapter has two aims. The first is to investigate differences between 'Don't Know' responses and refusals in attitudinal surveys. Missing values can occur either when a respondent really does not know the answer to an item (DK) or when a respondent refuses to answer an item (NA). The common practice is to treat all DKs and NAs as missing cases without distinguishing between them. However, it might be that for some questionnaire items respondents choose the DK category when they really have no knowledge of the subject, but in other cases they might use the DK category to avoid expressing an opinion. The same might be true for NA responses. This formulation of missing data allows DKs and NAs to be treated differently and information about attitude to be inferred separately for DKs and NAs. The second aim is to identify the position of the middle category in Likert type scales with respect to the rest of the response categories and derive attitudinal information. Problems arise in the analysis of items with middle categories because they are not strictly ordinal, and it is also inefficient to treat them as nominal polytomous. The methodology proposed is for analyzing scales that consist of any combination of binary, nominal scale polytomous, ordinal scale, and metric items.

The investigation of differences between types of non-response is based on an extension of the model for missing values presented by O'Muircheartaigh and Moustaki (1999), where no distinction was made between types of non-response. That paper discussed a latent variable model for mixed binary and metric normal items. Binary response propensity items were created to measure response propensity. This chapter explores the idea of using polytomous response propensity variables (rather than binary) to distinguish between different types of non-response in a latent variable framework. Using the same methodology but extended to ordinal variables, the issue of middle categories in Likert scales is also discussed.

Both research questions are handled with latent variable models. Table 2.1 gives a list of all the different types of latent variable models that can be used for inferring information about attitude from non-responses or middle categories. All these models are latent trait models and therefore assume that the latent variables are continuous variables. All models, except from 1 and 7, are models that deal with a mixture of item types. A full description of the latent variable models presented in Table 2.1 without missing values can be found in Moustaki (1996), Sammel, Ryan, and Legler (1997), Moustaki and Knott (2000a) and Moustaki (2000b). O'Muircheartaigh and Moustaki (1999) discussed models 1, 4 and 5 in the context of missing values in attitude scales. In this chapter that work is extended to ordinal data (model 3), in order to investigate middle categories in Likert type scales and to models that allow for polytomous response propensity (models 6-10), in order to distinguish between different types of non-response.

Table 2.1. Classification of latent trait models

		Attitudinal items				
		Binary	Nominal	Ordinal	Metric	Mixed
Propensity	Binary	Model 1	Model 2	Model 3	Model 4	Model 5
Items	Nominal	Model 6	Model 7	Model 8	Model 9	Model 10

To make the exposition of the models clearer in this chapter, results for a two factor model ($\mathbf{z} = (z_a, z_r)$) in which factor z_a represents an attitudinal dimension and z_r represents response propensity are presented. The subscripts a and r correspond to attitude and response propensity respectively. The results are easily extended to more than one attitudinal dimension.

The chapter is organized as follows. The next section discusses a number of latent trait models for analyzing different types of attitudinal items with missing values. Posterior plots are used to infer information about attitude from non-response and for distinguishing between DKs and NAs. Finally, a latent trait model for ordinal responses to identify the position of middle categories with respect to the other response alternatives in Likert scales is presented and illustrated with artificial and real examples.

2.2   'Don't Know' and Refusals

Suppose that one has p observed items (of any type) to analyze $x_1, \ldots, x_p$ and there is a proportion of DKs and NAs in each item. p polytomous response propensity variables denoted by v_i are created as follows: when an individual gives a response, then the response variable for this individual will take the value one ($v_i = 1$); when an individual responds DK, then the response variable will take the value 2 ($v_i = 2$); and when an individual does not respond to the item (NA), the response variable will take the value 3 ($v_i = 3$). Therefore, the response variables ($v_1, \ldots, v_p$) are nominal scale items, where the manifest items ($x_1, \ldots, x_p$) can be of any type (models 6-10). For the analysis use $2p$ items; the first p items (attitudinal items) provide information about attitude and the next p items (response propensity variables) provide information about propensity to express an opinion. A two factor model is then fitted to the $2p$ items. Since the manifest items are allowed to be of any type and the response variables to be nominal polytomous variables, at least where the manifest attitudinal items are not polytomous, a mixed model has to be fitted. Details on estimation of the latent trait model for any type of responses and scoring of response patterns on the identified latent dimensions can be found in Moustaki and Knott (2000a)- the emphasis in this chapter is given to the use of those generalized latent trait models in order to distinguish between different types of nonresponse.

Latent variable models for dealing with missing values have been discussed elsewhere in the literature. Knott et al (1990) discuss a non-ignorable nonresponse model for binary items and O'Muircheartaigh and Moustaki (1999) extended the model to mixed binary and metric items. However, both papers deal with binary response propensity variables where no distinction is made between different types of nonresponse. This chapter extends that model to deal with nominal and ordinal manifest attitudinal items (models 2 and 3) and extends it to the case where the response propensity variables are nominal to allow for DK and NA missing values. Using the flexibility of the latent trait model, several different types of nonresponses with respect to the attitude dimension can be identified.

Suppose that there are p attitudinal items of which p_1 are binary, p_2 are nominal polytomous, p_3 are ordinal and p_4 are metric.

a. Binary. Let x_i take on binary values 0 and 1. Suppose that the manifest binary attitudinal item x_i has a Bernoulli distribution with expected value $\pi_{ai}(z_a, z_r)$. The model fitted is the logit, i.e.:

$$\text{logit}\pi_{ai}(\mathbf{z}) = \ln\left(\frac{\pi_{ai}(\mathbf{z})}{1 - \pi_{ai}(\mathbf{z})}\right) = \alpha_{i0} + \alpha_{i1}z_a + \alpha_{i2}z_r, \quad i = 1, \ldots, p_1$$

where

$$\pi_{ai}(\mathbf{z}) = P(x_i = 1 \mid \mathbf{z}) = \frac{e^{\alpha_{i0} + \alpha_{i1}z_a + \alpha_{i2}z_r}}{1 + e^{\alpha_{i0} + \alpha_{i1}z_a + \alpha_{i2}z_r}}.$$

The parameter α_{i0} is an intercept parameter, where the parameters α_{i1} and α_{i2} are factor loadings.

b. Polytomous nominal. In the polytomous case the indicator variable x_i is replaced by a vector-valued indicator function with its s'th element defined as:

$$x_{i(s)} = \begin{cases} 1, \text{ if the response falls in category } s, \text{ for } s = 1, \ldots, c_i \\ 0, \text{ otherwise} \end{cases}$$

where c_i denotes the number of categories of variable i and $\sum_{s=1}^{c_i} x_{i(s)} = 1$. The response pattern of an individual is written as $\mathbf{x}' = (\mathbf{x}'_1, \mathbf{x}'_2, \ldots, \mathbf{x}'_p)$ of dimension $\sum_i c_i$.

The single response function of the binary case is now replaced by a set of functions $\pi_{ai(s)}(\mathbf{z})$ $(s = 1, \ldots, c_i)$ where $\sum_{s=1}^{c_i} \pi_{ai(s)}(\mathbf{z}) = 1$.

The model fitted is again the logit:

$$\log \frac{\pi_{ai(s)}(\mathbf{z})}{\pi_{ai(1)}(\mathbf{z})} = \alpha_{i0(s)} + \alpha_{i1(s)} z_a + \alpha_{i2(s)} z_r, \qquad i = 1, \ldots, p_2; s = 1, \ldots, c_i.$$

As $\pi_{ai(s)}(\mathbf{z})$ is over-parameterized, the parameters of the first category are fixed to zero, $\alpha_{i0(1)} = \alpha_{i1(1)} = 0$.

The above formulation will be used both for the attitudinal polytomous items (models 2 and 7) and the response propensity variables (models 6 to 10). The model for the response propensity variables is written as:

$$\log \frac{\pi_{ri(s)}(\mathbf{z})}{\pi_{ri(1)}(\mathbf{z})} = r_{i0(s)} + r_{i1(s)} z_a + r_{i2(s)} z_r, \qquad i = 1, \ldots, p; s = 1, 2, 3.$$

c. Ordinal. Let $x_1, x_2, \ldots, x_{p_3}$ be the ordinal categorical observed variables. Let m_i denote the number of categories for the ith variable. The m_i ordered categories have probabilities $\pi_{ai(1)}(\mathbf{z}), \pi_{ai(2)}(\mathbf{z}), \cdots, \pi_{ai(m_i)}(\mathbf{z})$, which are functions of the latent variables $\mathbf{z} = (z_a, z_r)$.

The model fitted is the logistic:

$$\text{logit}[\gamma_{i(s)}(\mathbf{z})] = \alpha_{i(s)} - \alpha_{i1} z_a - \alpha_{i2} z_r$$
$$i = 1, \ldots, p_3; \qquad s = 1, \ldots, m_i \qquad (2.1)$$

where $\gamma_{i(s)}(\mathbf{z})$ is the cumulative probability of a response in category s or lower of item x_i, written as:

$$\gamma_{i(s)}(\mathbf{z}) = \pi_{ai(1)}(\mathbf{z}) + \cdots + \pi_{ai,(s)}(\mathbf{z})$$

The parameters $\alpha_{i(s)}$ are referred as 'cut-points' on the logistic scale where $\alpha_{i(1)} \le \alpha_{i(2)} \le \cdots \le \alpha_{i,(m_i)} = +\infty$. The α_{i1} and α_{i2} parameters can be considered as factor loadings since they measure the effect of the latent variables z_a and z_r on some function of the cumulative probability of responding up to a category of the ith item.

d. Metric. The well known linear factor analysis model is assumed for the case where the observed items are metric. Let x_i have a normal distribution with marginal mean α_{i0} and variance Ψ_{ii}.

$$x_i = \alpha_{i0} + \alpha_{i1} z_a + \alpha_{i2} z_r + \epsilon_i, \quad i = 1, \ldots, p_4$$

For all the above models the assumption of conditional independence is made. This means that the responses/nonresponses to the observed items are independent conditional on the latent variables. The latent variables z_a and z_r are taken to be independent with standard normal distributions.

2.3 Model Specification in the Case of Non-Response

The response function can be written in two layers. For each attitude binary item given than an individual has responded ($v_i = 1$):

$$Pr(x_i = 1 \mid z_a, z_r, v_i = 1) = \pi_{ai}(z_a), \quad i = 1, \ldots, p_1. \quad (2.2)$$

For each attitude polytomous nominal item

$$Pr(x_i = s \mid z_a, z_r, v_i = 1) = \pi_{ai(s)}(z_a), \quad i = 1, \ldots, p_2; \quad s = 1, \ldots, c_i. \quad (2.3)$$

For each attitude polytomous ordinal item

$$Pr(x_i = s \mid z_a, z_r, v_i = 1) = \gamma_{ai(s)}(z_a) - \gamma_{ai(s-1)}(z_a),$$
$$i = 1, \ldots, p_3; \quad s = 1, \ldots, m_i. \quad (2.4)$$

For each attitude metric item:

$$(x_i \mid z_a, z_r, v_i = 1) \sim N(\alpha_{i0} + \alpha_{i1} z_a, \Psi_{ii}), \quad i = 1, \ldots, p_4 \quad (2.5)$$

where the assumptions about Ψ_{ii} are the same as the ones made for the complete responses model. For each response propensity variable v_i the probability of responding to an item x_i is equal to the probability of belonging to the first category of the response propensity variable for that item:

$$Pr(v_i = 1 \mid z_a, z_r) = \pi_{ri(1)}(z_a, z_r) \quad i = 1, \ldots, (p_1 + p_2 + p_3 + p_4). \quad (2.6)$$

The models for the different types of variables are given as follows:
For binary attitudinal items (model 6):

$$\text{logit} \pi_{ai}(z_a) = \alpha_{i0} + \alpha_{i1} z_a \quad i = 1, \ldots, p_1. \quad (2.7)$$

For polytomous nominal attitudinal items (model 7):

$$\ln \frac{\pi_{ai(s)}(z_a)}{\pi_{ai(1)}(z_a)} = \alpha_{i0(s)} + \alpha_{i1(s)} z_a; \quad s = 1, \ldots, c_i; \quad i = 1, \ldots, p_2. \quad (2.8)$$

For ordinal attitudinal items (model 8):

$$\text{logit} \gamma_{ai(s)}(z_a) = \alpha_{i0(s)} + \alpha_{i1} z_a; \; s = 1, \ldots, m_i; \; i = 1, \ldots, p_3. \qquad (2.9)$$

For metric attitudinal items (model 9):

$$E(x_i \mid z_a) = \alpha_{i0} + \alpha_{i1} z_a. \qquad (2.10)$$

For the polytomous (nominal) response propensity variables:

$$\ln \frac{\pi_{ai(s)}(z_a, z_r)}{\pi_{ai(1)}(z_a, z_r)} = r_{i0(s)} + r_{i1(s)} z_a + r_{i2(s)} z_r; s = 1, 2, 3; i = 1, \ldots, p\,(2.11)$$

The model (Eq. 2.11) allows attitude and response propensity to affect the probability of responding or not responding to an item leading to a non-ignorable model. It follows that for binary items:

$$Pr(x_i = 1 \mid z_a, z_r) = \pi_{ai}(z_a)\pi_{ri(1)}(z_a, z_r), \quad i = 1, \ldots, p_1.$$

For polytomous nominal items:

$$Pr(x_i = s \mid z_a, z_r) = \pi_{ai(s)}(z_a)\pi_{ri(1)}(z_a, z_r), \quad i = 1, \ldots, p_2.$$

For ordinal items:

$$Pr(x_i = s \mid z_a, z_r) = [\gamma_{ai(s)}(z_a) - \gamma_{ai(s-1)}(z_a)]\pi_{ri(1)}(z_a, z_r), \quad i = 1, \ldots, p_3.$$

For metric items:

$$f(x_i \mid z_a, z_r) = f(x_i \mid z_a, z_r, v_i = (1))\pi_{ri(1)}(z_a, z_r), \quad i = 1, \ldots, p_4.$$

and for response propensity variables:

$$Pr(v_i = (2) \mid z_a, z_r) = \pi_{ri(2)}(z_a, z_r), \quad i = 1, \ldots, p$$

$$Pr(v_i = (3) \mid z_a, z_r) = \pi_{ri(3)}(z_a, z_r), \quad i = 1, \ldots, p.$$

The above formulation of the response function indicates that if an individual responds (Eqs. 2.2, 2.3, and 2.4 and 2.5) then the expressed attitude is not dependent on z_r but the probability that an individual does respond (Eq. 2.6) depends on both z_a and z_r, where z_r is the individual's inherent responsiveness for all questions. In other words, individuals with high z_a may have a different probability of not responding than individuals with low z_a. The coefficients $r_{i1(s)}$ (Eq. 2.11) shows how the probability of expressing an opinion increases or decreases with respect to the attitude dimension.

All the above models can be fitted with the program LATENT Moustaki (2000a) in the following steps: first generate the p polytomous response propensity variables from the original manifest variables; second fit the two factor model to the $2p$ items while constraining the loadings of the second factor for the manifest attitudinal variables, binary, polytomous and metric, to zero. The principal interest in fitting a model to both the attitudinal and the response/nonresponse items is to investigate how attitude affects the probability of obtaining a response, which would enable the estimation of attitude from a failure to respond. This information is contained in the coefficients $r_{i1(2)}$ and $r_{i1(3)}$, which measure the effect of the attitude on the probability of responding DK and NA respectively.

2.4   Posterior Analysis

O'Muircheartaigh and Moustaki (1999) looked at the posterior distribution of the attitude latent variable given one attitudinal item at a time. Plots were used to interpret a nonresponse for a particular item in terms of the implied information about the attitude scale. This chapter also looks at the posterior plots.

From the model parameters information on how attitude is related to propensity to respond is obtained and also information on how likely or unlikely one would get a response for an item. The posterior distribution of the attitude latent variable z_a is examined, given the possible responses for each item. So for binary and polytomous items interest is in observing the relative position of the $h(z_a \mid v_i = (2))$ and $h(z_a \mid v_i = (3))$ with respect to the attitudinal responses e.g. $h(z_a \mid x_i = 0)$ and $h(z_a \mid x_i = 1)$ or $h(z_a \mid x_i = 1)$, $h(z_a \mid x_i = 2), \ldots, h(z_a \mid x_i = c_i)$ and for metric variables at the relative position of $h(z_a \mid v_i = (2))$ and $h(z_a \mid v_i = (3))$ with respect to the three quartiles, minimum and maximum values of x_i. Once the model has been estimated, these posterior probabilities can be computed for all types of items.

To locate an individual on the attitude scale based on their response/ nonresponse pattern the mean of the posterior distribution of the attitude latent variable z_a conditional on the whole response/nonresponse pattern, $E(z_a \mid \mathbf{x}, \mathbf{v})$ is computed. Similarly, to locate an individual on the response propensity scale based on their response/nonresponse pattern, the mean of the posterior distribution of the response propensity latent variable z_r conditional on the whole response/nonresponse pattern, $E(z_r \mid \mathbf{x}, \mathbf{v})$ is computed.

2.5   Goodness of Fit

For testing the goodness-of-fit of the latent variable model for binary data and polytomous data either the Pearson X^2 or the likelihood ratio statistic is used. Problems arising from the sparseness of the multi-way contingency tables in the binary case are discussed in Reiser and Vandenberg (1994). Bartholomew and Tzamourani (1999) proposed alternative ways for assessing the goodness-of-fit of the latent trait model for binary responses based on

Monte Carlo methods and residual analysis. Jöreskog and Moustaki (2001) also explore those goodness of fit measures for the latent trait model with ordinal responses. Significant information concerning the goodness-of-fit of the model can be found in the margins. That is, the two- and three-way margins are investigated for any large discrepancies between the observed and expected frequencies under the model. A chi-squared residual $((O - E)^2/E)$ is computed for different responses for pair and triplets of items. As a rule of thumb, values greater than four suggest that the model does not fit well for these combinations of items. These statistics are used in the applications section to assess goodness-of-fit for the models.

2.6   Middle Categories in Likert Scales

This section discusses the model used to infer information about the middle categories in Likert scale items. For each item x_i a pseudo binary item w_i is created. When there is a definite response, the pseudo item takes the value 1 $(w_i = 1)$ and when an individual expresses uncertainty by choosing the middle category, then the pseudo item takes the value 0 $(w_i = 0)$. It is assumed that an individual either gives a definite response that can be any of the ordered responses (excluding the middle category) or s/he does not give a definite response (middle category). Everything works the same as in the model with binary response propensity (see O'Muircheartaigh & Moustaki, 1999). The only difference now is that the attitudinal items are ordinal rather than binary or metric.

Let $x_1, x_2, \ldots, x_p$ be the categorical observed variables. Let m_i denote the number of categories for the ith variable excluding the middle category. When the middle category is excluded the observed categorical item becomes ordinal. The m_i ordered categories have probabilities

$$\pi_{ai(1)}(z_a, z_r), \pi_{ai(2)}(z_a, z_r), \ldots, \pi_{ai(m_i)}(z_a, z_r)$$

which are functions of the latent variable z_a and z_r. The model fitted is the logistic as described in Equation 2.1. For the binary propensity/pseudo items the logit model for binary responses is also used.

Suppose that the binary response propensity item has a Bernoulli distribution with expected value $\pi_{ri}(z_a, z_r)$. The model fitted is the logit, i.e.:

$$\text{logit}\pi_{ri}(\mathbf{z}) = \ln\left(\frac{\pi_{ri}(\mathbf{z})}{1 - \pi_{ri}(\mathbf{z})}\right) = r_{i0} + r_{i1}z_a + r_{i2}z_r,$$

where

$$\pi_{ri}(\mathbf{z}) = P(w_i = 1 \mid \mathbf{z}) = \frac{\exp^{r_{i0}+r_{i1}z_a+r_{i2}z_r}}{1 + \exp^{r_{i0}+r_{i1}z_a+r_{i2}z_r}}.$$

Under the assumption of conditional independence the vector of latent variables accounts for the interrelationships among the observed ordinal variables and the binary response propensity variables.

For each attitude ordinal item:

$$Pr(x_i = (s) \mid z_a, z_r, w_i = 1) = \pi_{ai(s)}(z_a), \quad i = 1, \cdots, p; s = 1, \ldots, m_i \quad (2.12)$$

For each response (pseudo) item:

$$Pr(w_i = 1 \mid z_a, z_r) = \pi_{ri}(z_a, z_r) \quad i = 1, \cdots, p \quad (2.13)$$

It follows that

$$Pr(x_i = (s) \mid z_a, z_r) = \pi_{ai(s)}(z_a)\pi_{ri}(z_a, z_r)$$

From Equation 2.12, it can be seen that the the probability of giving a definite response depends only on the attitude latent variable (z_a). From Equation 2.13, the probability of expressing a definite response depends both on an attitude (z_a) and a response propensity dimension (z_r). The above model is a latent trait model with mixed ordinal and binary responses.

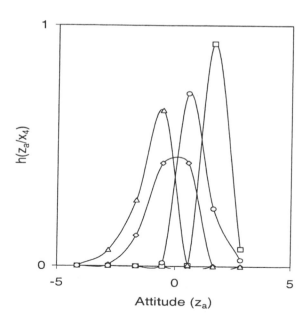

Fig. 2.1. Guttman scale I: Posterior probabilities ($\diamond$, $h(z_a \mid x_4 = 0)$; $\square$, $h(z_a \mid x_4 = 1)$; $\triangle$, $h(z_a \mid x_4 = 8)$; $\circ$, $h(z_a \mid x_4 = 9)$)

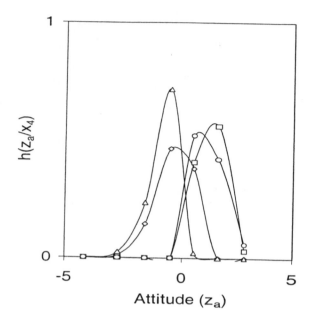

Fig. 2.2. Guttman scale II: Posterior probabilities $(\Diamond, h(z_a \mid x_4 = 0); \Box, h(z_a \mid x_4 = 1); \triangle, h(z_a \mid x_4 = 8); \circ, h(z_a \mid x_4 = 9)$

2.7   Example Applications

The proposed methodology for inferring information about attitude from DK and NA is illustrated through a set of simulated data and data from the British National Survey on Sexual Attitudes and Lifestyles. To illustrate the model proposed for Likert scales with middle categories a data set from the 1992 Eurobarometer survey is used.

2.7.1   Perfect and imperfect Guttman scales

Three different artificial data sets were constructed. The data sets are all Guttman scales. Each data set consists of four binary items. The first data set is given in Table 2.2. Suppose that there is a DK on the fourth item of the response pattern [1 0 0 8], and a NA on the fourth item of the response pattern [1 1 0 9] - DK responses are denoted by '8' and NA by '9'.From the analysis of this data set no ambiguity in the meaning of a DK response is expected since the response pattern [1 0 0 8] can only come from [1 0 0 0]. The same would be expected for the meaning of a NA answer. From Figure 2.1 it can be seen that DK responses are placed slightly below 0 and that NA

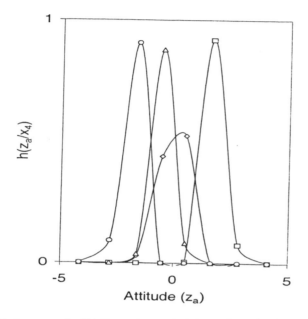

Fig. 2.3. Guttman scale III: Posterior probabilities ($\Diamond$, $h(z_a \mid x_4 = 0)$; $\Box$, $h(z_a \mid x_4 = 1)$; $\triangle$, $h(z_a \mid x_4 = 8)$; $\circ$, $h(z_a \mid x_4 = 9)$

responses lie somewhere between 0 and 1. The discrepancy measure shows a very good fit to all the items but item 4. For positive responses (1,1) the discrepancy measure is smaller than 2.0 for all the combinations of items except for the pairs which include item 4. For these pairs the discrepancies are in the range 10.0-11.0. For responses (1,0), (0,1) and (0,0) the discrepancy measure is smaller than 1 for all pairs of items.

In the second data set given in Table 2.3, the response pattern [1 0 0 8] remained unchanged but the response pattern [1 1 0 9] was replaced with [1 1 1 9]. From Figure 2.2 it can be seen that the effect of that replacement the DK response to be identified is even more below 0 and the NA response moves closer to response 1. The discrepancy measures for this model are all smaller than 1.0 expect for one pair which is equal to 4.0.

Finally, in the last data set given in Table 2.4, missing values occur with the response pattern [1 0 0 8] and [0 0 0 9]. As expected, one can see from Figure 2.3 that a DK response is identified as 0 but the NA response is now identified quite below 0 since the pattern [0 0 0 9] does not even have one positive response. The fit is very good judging from the very small chi-squared residuals on the two-way margins.

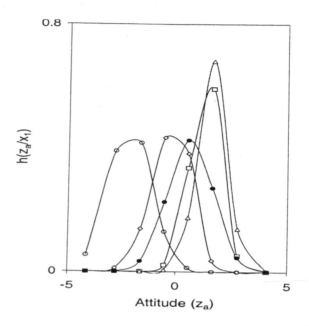

Fig. 2.4. Sexual attitudes: Item 1, Posterior probabilities ($\diamond$, $h(z_a \mid x_1 = 1$); $\square$, $h(z_a \mid x_1 = 2$); $\triangle$, $h(z_a \mid x_1 = 3$); $\bullet$, $h(z_a \mid x_1 = 8$); $\circ$, $h(z_a \mid x_1 = 9$))

Based on the artificial examples discussed above, one can see that the model with the polytomous response propensity variables can distinguish between different types of non-response. Information is used from the whole response pattern and the way the attitudinal and response propensity variables are inter-related. When a non-response has a pattern with no positive responses, individuals are expected to be on the far left side of the attitude dimension. When there is only one positive response in the pattern then individuals will still be on the left side of the attitude dimension. As the number of positive responses increases in the pattern, individuals will start moving to the right side of the attitude dimension.

Table 2.2. Guttman scale I

Response pattern	frequency
1 1 1 1	50
1 1 1 0	50
1 1 0 0	50
1 0 0 0	50
0 0 0 0	50
1 1 0 9	25
1 0 0 8	25

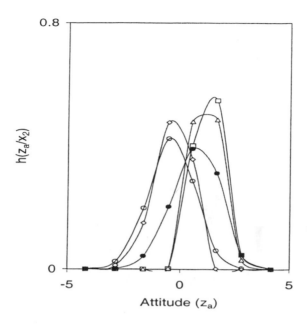

Fig. 2.5. Sexual attitudes: Item 2, Posterior probabilities ($\Diamond$, $h(z_a$ | $x_2 =$ 1); $\Box$, $h(z_a$ | $x_2 = 2)$; $\triangle$, $h(z_a$ | $x_2 = 3)$; $\bullet$, $h(z_a$ | $x_2 = 8)$; $\circ$, $h(z_a$ | $x_2 = 9)$

Table 2.3. Guttman scale II

Response pattern	frequency
1 1 1 1	50
1 1 1 0	50
1 1 0 0	50
1 0 0 0	50
0 0 0 0	50
1 1 1 9	25
1 0 0 8	25

Latent scores based on the posterior mean ($E(z_a \mid \mathbf{x}, \mathbf{v})$) for the three artificial examples are given in Tables 2.5, 2.6 and 2.7. From Table 2.5 it can be seen that response pattern [0 0 0 0] scores distinctively low on the latent dimension and response pattern [1 1 1 1] higher than all the rest. Individuals with response pattern [1 0 0 8] score the same as those with response pattern [1 0 0 0] and also individuals with response pattern [1 1 0 9] have scores similar to those with response pattern [1 1 0 0] and [1 1 1 0]. From Table 2.6 it can be seen that response pattern [1 0 0 8] scores the same as [1 0 0 0], where response pattern [1 1 1 9] scores well above [1 1 1 0] and close to [1 1 1 1]. However, taking into account the variability of those estimates (given

Table 2.4. Guttman scale III

Response pattern	frequency
1 1 1 1	50
1 1 1 0	50
1 1 0 0	50
1 0 0 0	50
0 0 0 0	50
0 0 0 9	25
1 0 0 8	25

Table 2.5. Posterior means for Guttman Scale I

$E(z_a \mid \mathbf{x}, \mathbf{v})$	Response pattern
-1.26 (0.59)	0 0 0 0
-0.55 (0.13)	1 0 0 8
-0.55 (0.11)	1 0 0 0
0.41 (0.35)	1 1 0 0
0.54 (0.05)	1 1 0 9
0.54 (0.07)	1 1 1 0
1.72 (0.32)	1 1 1 1

Table 2.6. Posterior means for Guttman scale II

$E(z_a \mid \mathbf{x}, \mathbf{v})$	Response pattern
-1.71 (0.33)	0 0 0 0
-0.54 (0.07)	1 0 0 8
-0.54 (0.07)	1 0 0 0
-0.33 (0.43)	1 1 0 0
0.54 (0.01)	1 1 1 0
1.01 (0.58)	1 1 1 9
1.29 (0.68)	1 1 1 1

Table 2.7. Posterior means for Guttman scale III

$E(z_a \mid \mathbf{x}, \mathbf{v})$	Response pattern
-1.75 (0.34)	0 0 0 9
-0.73 (0.41)	0 0 0 0
-0.54 (0.01)	1 0 0 8
-0.54 (0.04)	1 0 0 0
0.53 (0.09)	1 1 0 0
0.54 (0.06)	1 1 1 0
1.72 (0.33)	1 1 1 1

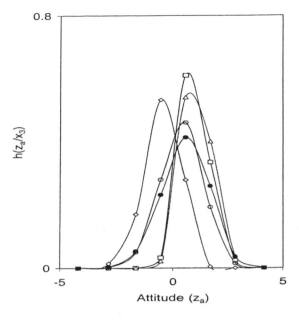

Fig. 2.6. Sexual attitudes: Item 3, Posterior probabilities ($\Diamond$, $h(z_a \mid x_3 = 1)$; $\square$, $h(z_a \mid x_3 = 2)$; $\triangle$, $h(z_a \mid x_3 = 3)$; $\bullet$, $h(z_a \mid x_3 = 8)$; $\circ$, $h(z_a \mid x_3 = 9)$)

in brackets) one could safely say that those response patterns with at least three positive responses score quite high on the latent dimension compared with the rest of the patterns. Finally, from Table 2.7 it can be seen that the response pattern [0 0 0 9] scores below [0 0 0 0] and pattern [1 0 0 8] scores the same as [1 0 0 0].

Table 2.8. Descriptive statistics: percentages

Categories	Item 1	Item 2	Item 3	Item 4	Item 5
Wrong	83.9	75.9	66.7	71.2	32.4
Sometimes wrong	12.5	14.6	18.6	13.0	37.7
Not wrong	2.2	7.2	12.3	13.3	21.2
Don't Know	1.4	2.1	2.3	2.3	8.4
Refusals	0.02	0.07	0.15	0.22	0.15

2.7.2   British Sexual Attitudes survey

The items analyzed in this example were extracted from the 1990–1991 British National Survey of Sexual Attitudes and Lifestyles (NATSSAL). Details on

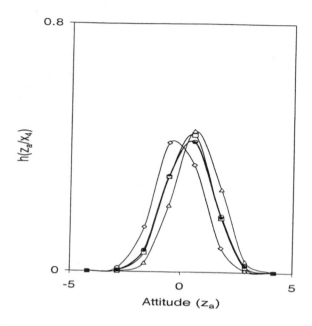

Fig. 2.7. Sexual attitudes: Item 4, Posterior probabilities ($\Diamond$, $h(z_a \mid x_4 = 1)$; $\square$, $h(z_a \mid x_4 = 2)$; $\triangle$, $h(z_a \mid x_4 = 3)$; $\bullet$, $h(z_a \mid x_4 = 8)$; $\circ$, $h(z_a \mid x_4 = 9)$

the sample design and methodology of the survey are published in Wadsworth, Field, Johnson, Bradshaw, and Wellings (1993).

The following five questions concerning the opinions of a sample of 4538 individuals about sexual relationships were analyzed:

1. What about a married person having sexual relations with someone other than his or her partner?
2. What about a person who is living with a partner, not married, having sexual relations with someone other than his or her partner?
3. And a person who has a regular partner they don't live with, having sexual relations with someone else?
4. What about a person having one night stands?
5. What is your general opinion about abortion?

All the above items were originally measured on a 6 point scale with response alternatives 'always wrong', 'mostly wrong', 'sometimes wrong', 'rarely wrong', 'not wrong at all', and 'depends/don't know'. The five items were treated as nominal polytomous. For each item there is a small proportion of refusals as well. For the analysis, categories 'always wrong' and 'mostly wrong' were grouped together, 'sometimes wrong' remained as is and categories 'rarely wrong' and 'not wrong at all' were grouped together. Finally, categories 'depends/don't know' and refusals were treated separately. The

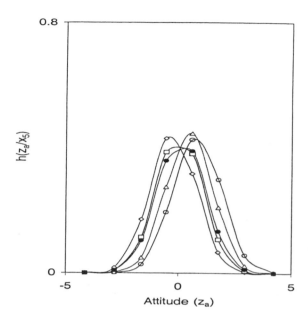

Fig. 2.8. Sexual attitudes: Item 5, Posterior probabilities ($\Diamond$, $h(z_a \mid x_5 = 1)$; $\square$, $h(z_a \mid x_5 = 2)$; $\triangle$, $h(z_a \mid x_5 = 3)$; $\bullet$, $h(z_a \mid x_5 = 8)$; $\circ$, $h(z_a \mid x_5 = 9)$

grouping was done for the purpose of clarity when presenting plots. Items were also analyzed based on their original 6-point scale, and no differences were found in the interpretation of the 'depends/don't know' and refusals.

Table 2.8 gives the frequency distribution of items 1-5. The total number of response patterns with at least one refusal is 25 (21 out of the 25 appear only once). It is a very small proportion relative to the total number of patterns. However, it is worth investigating whether the model proposed in this chapter can infer information about attitude from the refusals and whether refusals are different from the DK's for the individual items.

Table 2.9 gives the patterns with at least one refusal. From Figures 2.4-2.8 it can be seen that for item 1 refusals are identified below category 1, for item 2 they are identified as category 1, for items 3 and 4 they are identified in the middle of the attitude scale, and for item 5 they are identified as category 3. The plots reveal results consistent with those observed in Table 2.9. For example, for items 1 and 2 refusals appear in patterns with low scores on the other attitudinal items. Refusals on item 5 have high scores on the other attitudinal items, and therefore a refusal on that item is identified as category 3 (see Table 2.9). 'Depends/don't know' responses are identified between categories 1 and 2 for the first item, close to response categories 2 and 3 for items 2 and 3 and in the middle of the attitude scale for items 4 and 5.

Table 2.9. Response patterns with at least one refusal

Response Pattern	Response pattern	Response pattern
2 2 3 3 9	1 1 9 1 3	1 1 1 1 9 (2)
9 1 1 1 2	1 9 1 1 2	1 1 1 9 2 (2)
1 1 1 9 1	1 1 3 9 8	1 3 9 9 8
1 1 1 3 9	1 1 9 1 8	1 9 1 1 1
1 2 9 1 1	3 3 3 3 9	1 8 9 1 2
1 1 8 9 9	1 1 2 9 1	1 1 9 1 2
1 1 1 9 3	1 8 3 3 9	1 9 3 1 2
2 1 9 9 3	2 2 3 9 3	

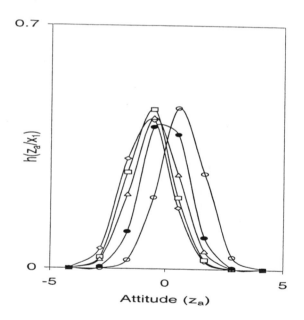

Fig. 2.9. Science and Technology: Item 1, Posterior probabilities ($\diamond$, $h(z_a \mid x_1 = 1)$; $\square$, $h(z_a \mid x_1 = 2)$; $\triangle, h(z_a \mid x_1 = 3)$; $\bullet, h(z_a \mid x_1 = 4)$; $\circ, h(z_a \mid x_1 = 5)$)

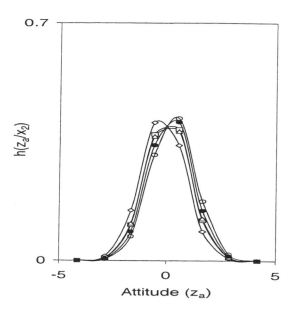

Fig. 2.10. Science and Technology: Item 2, Posterior probabilities ($\Diamond$, $h(z_a \mid x_2 = 1$); $\Box$, $h(z_a \mid x_2 = 2)$; $\triangle$, $h(z_a \mid x_2 = 3)$; $\bullet$, $h(z_a \mid x_2 = 4)$; $\circ$, $h(z_a \mid x_2 = 5)$

Table 2.10 gives the parameter estimates of the model fitted to the five items. Parameter estimates are obtained for all categories of an item, except for the first category that serves as the reference category. All the $\alpha_{i1(s)}$ coefficients are positive, indicating that the five items are all indicators of the same unobserved attitude construct. Parameter estimates $r_{i1(s)}$ show how the log of the odds of being in a certain response category changes as the individual's position on the attitude dimension increases. For the first response propensity item, the value of $r_{i1(2)} = 1.09$ and $r_{i1(3)} = -2.13$. These results indicate that as individuals becomes more liberal they are more likely to answer "don't know" than respond where it is less likely to refuse than respond. As a result, DK responses are identified as close to the upper categories of the scale where refusals are identified on the low categories of the scale. The interpretation of these factor loadings is consistent with the interpretation of the posterior plots.

The fit of the two-factor model on the one-way margins is very good. All chi-square values are in the range 0 to 2.5. The two-way margins for the five attitudinal items show some bad fit for some pairs of items and categories. More specifically, Table 2.11 provides the pairs of attitudinal items and the categories for which the discrepancies were greater than four. The discrepancy

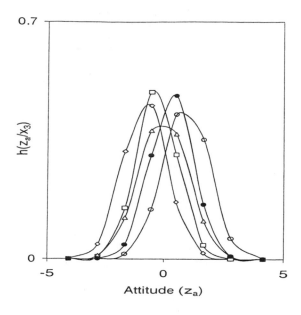

Fig. 2.11. Science and Technology: Item 3, Posterior probabilities ($\diamond$, $h(z_a \mid x_3 = 1)$; $\square$, $h(z_a \mid x_3 = 2)$; $\triangle$, $h(z_a \mid x_3 = 3)$; $\bullet$, $h(z_a \mid x_3 = 4)$; $\circ$, $h(z_a \mid x_3 = 5)$)

measures on the two-way margins for the five response propensity variables were all smaller than 2.0, except for two pairs of items, namely (3,4) categories (3,3), and items (4,5) categories (3,3).

2.7.3   Eurobarometer survey on science and technology

This data set was extracted from the 1992 Eurobarometer survey and is based on a sample of 531 respondents from Great Britain. The following seven questions were chosen from the Science and Technology section of the questionnaires:

1. Science and technology are making our lives healthier, easier and more comfortable.
2. Scientists should be allowed to do research that causes pain and injury to animals like dogs and chimpanzees if it can produce new information about serious human health problems.
3. Technological problems will make possible higher levels of consumption and, at the same time, an unpolluted environment.
4. Because of their knowledge, scientific researchers have a power that makes them dangerous.
5. The application of science and new technology will make work more interesting.

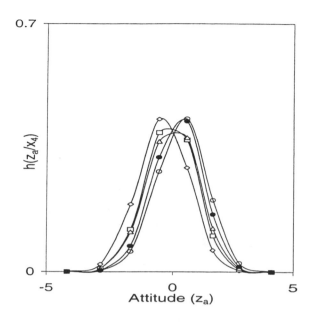

Fig. 2.12. Science and Technology: Item 4, Posterior probabilities ($\Diamond$, $h(z_a \mid x_4 = 1)$; $\square$, $h(z_a \mid x_4 = 2)$; $\triangle$, $h(z_a \mid x_4 = 3)$; $\bullet$, $h(z_a \mid x_4 = 4)$; $\circ$, $h(z_a \mid x_4 = 5)$)

6. Most scientists want to work on things that will make life better for the average person.
7. Thanks to science and technology, there will be more opportunities for the future generations.

Half the respondents (chosen randomly) were asked to select an answer from the following response alternatives: 'strongly agree', 'agree to some extent', 'neither agree nor disagree', 'disagree to some extent', and 'strongly agree'. The remaining half were asked the same set of questions but without the availability of the middle category. In the analysis that follows, only the part of the sample (sample size equal to 531) that had the middle alternative as a response option was used. Items 1, 2, 3, 5, 6 and 7 were recoded so that a high score indicates a positive attitude towards science and technology. To those seven ordinal items the model discussed in section 2.6 was fitted. For the ordinal attitudinal items, only the factor loadings parameters α_{i1} are reported and not the thresholds.

Table 2.12 gives the parameter estimates for the model that combines the ordinal attitudinal items with middle categories with the binary response propensity variables. The parameter estimates given under column r_{i1} show how attitude is related to the log of the odds of giving a definite response against a non definite response. For items 2, 3 and 4 those estimates are close

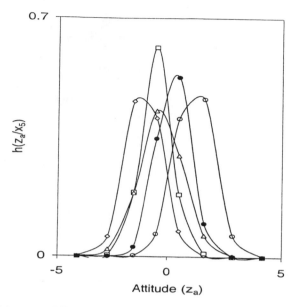

Fig. 2.13. Science and Technology: Item 5, Posterior probabilities ($\diamond$, $h(z_a \mid x_5 = 1)$; $\square$, $h(z_a \mid x_5 = 2)$; $\triangle$, $h(z_a \mid x_5 = 3)$; $\bullet$, $h(z_a \mid x_5 = 4)$; $\circ$, $h(z_a \mid x_5 = 5)$)

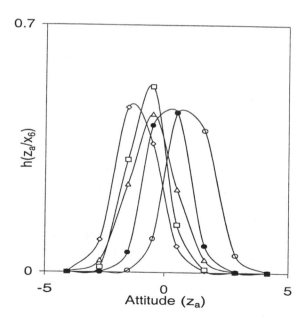

Fig. 2.14. Science and Technology: Item 6, Posterior probabilities ($\diamond$, $h(z_a \mid x_6 = 1)$; $\square$, $h(z_a \mid x_6 = 2)$; $\triangle$, $h(z_a \mid x_6 = 3)$; $\bullet$, $h(z_a \mid x_6 = 4)$; $\circ$, $h(z_a \mid x_6 = 5)$)

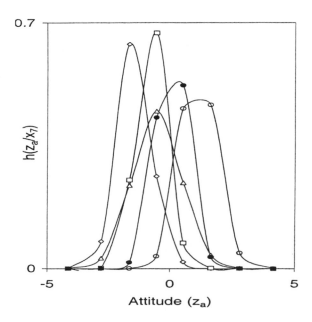

Fig. 2.15. Science and Technology: Item 7, Posterior probabilities ($\Diamond$, $h(z_a \mid x_7 = 1)$; $\square$, $h(z_a \mid x_7 = 2)$; $\triangle$, $h(z_a \mid x_7 = 3)$; $\bullet$, $h(z_a \mid x_7 = 4)$; $\circ$, $h(z_a \mid x_7 = 5)$)

to zero, indicating that increasing or decreasing ones position on the attitude dimension does not make it more likely to give a definite response to those items. For the rest of the items, the parameter estimates are positive indicating that the more positive one is towards science and technology the more likely one is to give a definite response. Figures 9-15 give the posterior distribution of the attitude latent dimension given the different possible responses on each ordinal item. The ordinal items are on a five point scale including the middle category. In the posterior plots the response category 3 indicates the middle category. Middle categories are situated in the middle for all the items. These results are in accordance with the findings of O'Muircheartaigh, Krosnick, and Helic (2000).

2.8 Conclusion

This chapter discussed the application of latent trait models for distinguishing between different types of missing values in attitudinal scales and for inferring information about the middle categories in Likert scales. The main idea was to use the interrelationships among a set of unidimensional observed attitudinal items together with their corresponding set of response propensity variables to extract information about attitude and response propensity. The models were presented for the case where the attitudinal items are unidimensional.

Table 2.10. Sexual attitudes: parameter estimates for the two-factor latent trait model with missing values

Variable x_i	Category	$\alpha_{i0(s)}$	$\alpha_{i1(s)}$	$\alpha_{i2(s)}$
Item 1	2	-3.55	2.67	0.00
	3	-6.36	3.40	0.00
Item 2	2	-4.41	5.22	0.00
	3	-4.79	4.95	0.00
Item 3	2	-2.33	3.31	0.00
	3	-3.02	3.58	0.00
Item 4	2	-1.74	0.51	0.00
	3	-1.90	0.87	0.00
Item 5	2	-0.19	0.27	0.00
	3	-0.49	0.73	0.00
Variable v_i	category	$r_{i0(s)}$	$r_{i1(s)}$	$r_{i2(s)}$
Item 1	2	-9.22	1.09	3.66
	3	-11.5	-2.13	-1.38
Item 2	2	-12.2	1.55	5.68
	3	-11.6	-0.41	-3.04
Item 3	2	-18.8	1.17	10.0
	3	-13.0	0.57	5.40
Item 4	2	-5.07	0.32	1.73
	3	-6.76	0.32	1.21
Item 5	2	-2.73	0.09	0.97
	3	-7.08	0.75	1.05

Table 2.11. Large discrepancies from the two-way margins

	Item 2	Item 3	Item 4	Item 5
Item 1	(2,2) (2,3) (3,2)	(2,2) (2,3) (3,2) (3,3)	(3,3)	
Item 2		(2,2) (2,3) (3,2) (3,3)		
Item 3			(3,3)	
Item 4				(2,1) (1,3) (3,2) (2,3) (4,3)

Although the models can be extended to allow for more attitude dimensions, it will increase the computational time of estimating those models.

The unit of analysis is the whole response pattern of the individuals. In fact, the response patterns are expanded through the pseudo variables to incorporate the response propensity dimension. It was proposed that polytomous pseudo-variables be used when investigating differences between 'don't know' and refusals and binary pseudo variables when investigating the position of middle categories in Likert scales. Finally, through the posterior distribution of the attitude latent variable the relative position of 'don't know'

Table 2.12. Science and Technology-parameter estimates for attitudinal and response propensity items

Ordinal Items		α_{i1}	α_{i1}
1		0.889	0.0
2		0.308	0.0
3		1.049	0.0
4		0.444	0.0
5		1.744	0.0
6		1.571	0.0
7		2.553	0.0
Binary Items	r_{i0}	r_{i1}	r_{i2}
1	3.0240	0.5380	1.1872
2	2.4027	-0.0410	0.5383
3	1.6845	0.0393	1.2095
4	2.7138	-0.0382	1.5823
5	1.6642	0.4538	0.7990
6	2.6088	0.7408	1.0590
7	1.9426	0.6804	0.6198

responses, refusals and middle categories with respect to the observed responses can be identified. Latent trait models allow the computation of the posterior probabilities of the attitude latent variable conditional on the whole response pattern (responses/nonresponses) and conditional on single items.

References

Bartholomew, D. J. & Tzamourani, P. (1999). The goodness-of-fit of latent trait models in attitude measurement. *Sociological Methods and Research*, 27, 525-546.

Jöreskog, K. G. & Moustaki, I. (2001). Factor analysis of ordinal variables: a comparison of three approaches. *To appear Multivariate Behavioural Research.*

Knott, M., Albanese, M. T., & Galbraith, J. (1990). Scoring attitudes to abortion. *The Statistician*, 40, 217-223.

Moustaki, I. (1996). A latent trait and a latent class model for mixed observed variables. *British Journal of Mathematical and Statistical Psychology*, 49, 313-334.

Moustaki, I. (2000a). LATENT: A computer program for fitting a one- or two- factor latent variable model to categorical, metric and mixed observed items with missing values. Technical report, Statistics Department, London School of Economics and Political Science.

Moustaki, I. (2000b). A latent variable model for ordinal variables. *Applied Psychological Measurement*, 24, 211-223.

Moustaki, I. & Knott, M. (2000a). Generalized latent trait models. *Psychometrika*, 65, 391-411.

Moustaki, I. & Knott, M. (2000b). Weighting for item non-response in attitude scales by using latent variable models with covariates. *Journal of the Royal Statistical Society, Series A*, 163, 445-459.

Moustaki, I. & O'Muircheartaigh, C. (2000). Inferring attitude from nonresponse using a latent trait model for nominal scale variables. *STATISTICA*, 259-276.

O'Muircheartaigh, C., Krosnick, J., & Helic, A. (2000). Middle alternatives, and the quality of questionnaire data. Working paper, Harris School, University of Chicago.

O'Muircheartaigh, C. & Moustaki, I. (1999). Symmetric pattern models: a latent variable approach to item non-response in attitude scales. *Journal of the Royal Statistical Society, Series A*,162, 177-194.

Reiser, M. & VandenBerg, M. (1994). Validity of the chi-square test in dichotomous variable factor analysis when expected frequencies are small. *British Journal of Mathematical and Statistical Psychology*, 47, 85-107.

Sammel, R. D., Ryan, L. M., & Legler, J. M. (1997). Latent variable models for mixed discrete and continuous outcomes. *Journal of the Royal Statistical Society, B*, 59, 667-678.

Wadsworth, J., Field, J., Johnson, A. M., Bradshaw, S., & Wellings, K. (1993). Methodology of the national survey of sexual attitudes and lifestyles. *Journal of the Royal Statistical Society, Series A*, 156, 407-421.

3 Hierarchically Related Nonparametric IRT Models, and Practical Data Analysis Methods*

L. Andries van der Ark[1], Bas T. Hemker[2], and Klaas Sijtsma[1]

[1] Tilburg University, The Netherlands
[2] CITO National Institute, The Netherlands

3.1 Introduction

Many researchers in the various sciences use questionnaires to measure properties that are of interest to them. Examples of properties include personality traits such as introversion and anxiety (psychology), political efficacy and motivational aspects of voter behavior (political science), attitude toward religion or euthanasia (sociology), aspects of quality of life (medicine), and preferences towards particular brands of products (marketing). Often, questionnaires consist of a number (k) of statements, each followed by a rating scale with $m + 1$ ordered answer categories, and the respondent is asked to mark the category that (s)he thinks applies most to his/her personality, opinion, or preference. The rating scales are scored in such a way that the ordering of the scores reflects the hypothesized ordering of the answer categories on the measured properties (called latent traits).

Items are indexed $i = 1, \ldots, k$, and item score random variables are denoted by X_i, with realizations $x = 0 \ldots, m$. Such items are known as polytomous items. Because individual items capture only one aspect of the latent trait, researchers are more interested in the total performance on a set of k items capturing various aspects than in individual items. A summary based on the k items more adequately reflects the latent trait, and the best known summary is probably the unweighted total score, denoted by X_+, and defined as

$$X_+ = \sum_{i=1}^{k} X_i. \tag{3.1}$$

This total score is well known from classical test theory (Lord & Novick, 1968) and Likert (1932) scaling, and is the test performance summary most frequently used in practice. Data analysis of the scores obtained from a sample of N respondents, traditionally using methods from classical test theory, may reveal whether X_+ is reliable, and factor analysis may be used to investigate whether X_+ is based on a set of k items measuring various aspects of predominantly the same property or maybe of a conglomerate of properties.

---

* Parts of this chapter are based on the unpublished doctoral dissertation of the second author.

Item response theory (IRT) uses the pattern of scores on the k items to estimate the latent trait value for each respondent (θ), in an effort to obtain a more accurate estimate of test performance than the simple X_+. For some IRT models, known as Rasch models (e.g., Fischer & Molenaar, 1995), their mathematical structure is simple enough to allow all statistical information to be obtained from the total score X_+, thus making the pattern of scores on the k items from the questionnaire superfluous for the estimation of θ. Some advanced applications of Rasch models (and other IRT models not relevant to this chapter), such as equating and adaptive testing, may still be better off with measurement on the θ scale than on the X_+ scale. Most questionnaires could either use X_+ or θ, as long as the ordering of respondents is the only concern of the researcher, and provided that X_+ and θ yield the same respondent ordering.

This chapter concentrates on *nonparametric* IRT (NIRT) models for the analysis of polytomous item scores. A typical aspect of NIRT models is that they are based on weaker assumptions than most *parametric* IRT models and, as a result, often fit empirical data better. Because their assumptions are weaker, θ cannot be estimated from the likelihood of the data, and the issue of which summary score to use, X_+ or θ, cannot come up here. Since a simple count as in Equation 3.1 is always possible, the following question is useful: When a NIRT model fits the data, does X_+ order respondents on the latent trait θ that could be estimated from a parametric IRT model?

The purposes of this chapter are twofold. First, three NIRT models for the analysis of polytomous item scores are discussed, and several well known IRT models, each being a special case of one of the NIRT models, are mentioned. The NIRT models are the *nonparametric partial credit model* (np-PCM), the *nonparametric sequential model* (np-SM), and the *nonparametric graded response model* (np-GRM). Then, the hierarchical relationships between these three NIRT models is proved. The issue of whether the ordering of respondents on the observable total score X_+ reflects in a stochastic way the ordering of the respondents on the unobservable θ is also discussed. The relevant ordering properties are monotone likelihood ratio of θ in X_+, stochastic ordering of θ by X_+, and the ordering of the means of the conditional distributions of θ given X_+, in X_+. Second, an overview of statistical methods available and accompanying software for the analysis of polytomous item scores from questionnaires is provided. Also, the kind of information provided by each of the statistical methods, and how this information might be used for drawing conclusions about the quality of measurement on the basis of questionnaires is explained.

3.2   Three Polytomous NIRT Models

Each of the three polytomous NIRT models belongs to a different class of IRT models (Molenaar, 1983; Agresti, 1990; Hemker, Van der Ark, & Sijtsma, in press; Mellenbergh, 1995). These classes, called *cumulative probability models*, *continuation ratio models*, and *adjacent category models*, have two assumptions in common and differ in a third assumption. The first common assumption, called *unidimensionality* (UD), is that the set of k items measures one scalar θ in common; that is, the questionnaire is unidimensional. The second common assumption, called *local independence* (LI), is that the k item scores are independent given a fixed value of θ; that is, for a k-dimensional vector of item scores $\mathbf{X} = \mathbf{x}$,

$$P(\mathbf{X} = \mathbf{x}|\theta) = \prod_{i=1}^{k} P(X_i = x|\theta). \tag{3.2}$$

LI implies, for example, that during test taking no learning or development takes place on the first s items ($s < k$), that would obviously influence the performance on the next $k - s$ items. More general, the measurement procedure itself must not influence the outcome of measurement. The third assumption deals with the relationship between the item score X_i and the latent trait θ. The probability of obtaining an item score x given θ, $P(X_i = x|\theta)$, is often called the *category characteristic curve* (CCC) and denoted by $\pi_{ix}(\theta)$. If an item has $m + 1$ ordered answer categories, then there are m so-called *item steps* (Molenaar, 1983) to be passed in going from category 0 to category m. It is assumed that, for each item step the probability of passing the item step conditional on θ, called the *item step response function* (ISRF) is monotone (nondecreasing) in θ. The three classes of IRT models and, therefore, the np-PCM, the np-SM, and the np-GRM differ in their definition of the ISRF.

3.2.1 Cumulative probability models and the np-GRM

In the class of cumulative probability models an ISRF is defined by

$$C_{ix}(\theta) = P(X_i \geq x|\theta) = \sum_{y=x}^{m} \pi_{iy}(\theta). \tag{3.3}$$

By definition, $C_{i0}(\theta) = 1$ and $C_{i,m+1}(\theta) = 0$. Equation 3.3 implies that passing the x-th item step yields an item score of at least x and failing the x-th item step yields an item score less than x. Thus, if a subject has an item score x, (s)he passed the first x item steps and failed the next $m - x$ item steps. The np-GRM assumes UD, LI, and ISRFs (Equation 3.3) that are nondecreasing in θ, for all i and all $x = 1, \ldots, m$, without any restrictions on their shape (Hemker, Sijtsma, Molenaar, & Junker, 1996, 1997).

The CCC of the np-GRM, and also of the parametric cumulative probability models, equals

$$\pi_{ix}(\theta) = C_{ix}(\theta) - C_{i,x+1}(\theta).$$

The np-GRM is also known as the monotone homogeneity model for polytomous items (Molenaar, 1997; Hemker, Sijtsma, & Molenaar, 1995).

A well known parametric cumulative probability model is the graded response model (Samejima, 1969), where the ISRF in Equation 3.3 is defined as a logistic function,

$$C_{ix}(\theta) = \frac{\exp[\alpha_i(\theta - \lambda_{ix})]}{1 + \exp[\alpha_i(\theta - \lambda_{ix})]}, \tag{3.4}$$

for all $x = 1, \ldots, m$. In Equation 3.4, λ_{ix} is the location parameter, with $\lambda_{i1} \leq \lambda_{i2} \leq \ldots \leq \lambda_{im}$, and α_i ($\alpha_i > 0$, for all i) is the slope or discrimination parameter. It may be noted that the slope parameters can only vary over items but not over item steps, to assure that $\pi_{ix}(\theta)$ is nonnegative (Samejima, 1972).

3.2.2   Continuation ratio models and the np-SM

In the class of continuation ratio models an ISRF is defined by

$$M_{ix}(\theta) = \frac{P(X_i \geq x|\theta)}{P(X_i \geq x - 1|\theta)}. \tag{3.5}$$

By definition, $M_{i0}(\theta) = 1$ and $M_{i,m+1}(\theta) = 0$. Equation 3.5 implies that subjects that have passed the x-th item step have an item score of at least x. Subjects that failed the x-th item step have an item score of $x - 1$. Subjects with an item score less than $x - 1$ did not try the x-th item step and thus did not fail it. The probability of obtaining a score x on item i in terms of Equation 3.5 is

$$\pi_{ix}(\theta) = [1 - M_{i,x+1}(\theta)] \prod_{y=0}^{x} M_{iy}(\theta). \tag{3.6}$$

The np-SM assumes UD, LI, and ISRFs (Eq. 3.5) that are nondecreasing in θ for all i and all x. Parametric continuation ratio models assume parametric functions for the ISRFs in Equation 3.5. An example is the sequential model (Tutz, 1990), where

$$M_{ix}(\theta) = \frac{\exp(\theta - \beta_{ix})}{1 + \exp(\theta - \beta_{ix})}. \tag{3.7}$$

In Equation 3.7, β_{ix} is the location parameter. Tutz (1990) also presented a rating scale version of this model, in which the location parameter is linearly restricted. The sequential model can be generalized by adding a discrimination parameter α_{ix} (Mellenbergh, 1995); $\alpha_{ix} > 0$ for all i and x, such that

$$M_{ix}(\theta) = \frac{\exp[\alpha_{ix}(\theta - \beta_{ix})]}{1 + \exp[\alpha_{ix}(\theta - \beta_{ix})]}. \tag{3.8}$$

This model may be denoted the *two-parameter sequential model* (2p-SM).

3.2.3 Adjacent-category models and the np-PCM

In the class of adjacent category models an ISRF is defined by

$$A_{ix}(\theta) = \frac{\pi_{ix}(\theta)}{\pi_{i,x-1}(\theta) + \pi_{ix}(\theta)}. \tag{3.9}$$

By definition, $A_{i0}(\theta) = 1$ and $A_{i,m+1}(\theta) = 0$. Equation 3.9 implies that the x-th item step is passed by subjects that have an item score equal to x, but failed by subjects that have an item score equal to $x - 1$. None of the other categories contains information about item step x. The probability of obtaining a score x on item i in terms of Equation 3.9 is

$$\pi_{ix}(\theta) = \frac{\displaystyle\prod_{j=0}^{x} A_{ij}(\theta) \prod_{k=x+1}^{m} [1 - A_{ik}(\theta)]}{\displaystyle\sum_{y=0}^{m} \prod_{j=0}^{y} A_{ij}(\theta) \prod_{k=y+1}^{m} [1 - A_{ik}(\theta)]}. \tag{3.10}$$

The np-PCM assumes UD, LI, and ISRFs (Eq. 3.9) that are nondecreasing in θ for all i and all x (see also Hemker et al., 1996, 1997).

A well known parametric adjacent category model is the partial credit model (Masters, 1982), where the ISRF in Equation 3.9 is defined as a logistic function,

$$A_{ix}(\theta) = \frac{\exp(\theta - \delta_{ix})}{1 + \exp(\theta - \delta_{ix})}, \tag{3.11}$$

for all $x = 1, \ldots, m$, where δ_{ix} is the location parameter. The generalized partial credit model (Muraki, 1992) is a more flexible parametric model, which is obtained by adding a slope or discrimination parameter (cf. Eq. 3.4) denoted α_i that may vary across items.

3.3 Relationships Between Polytomous NIRT Models

The three NIRT models have been introduced as three separate models, but it can be shown that they are hierarchically related. Because the three models have UD and LI in common, the investigation of the relationship between the models is equivalent to the investigation of the relationships between the three definitions of the ISRFs (Eqs. 3.3, 3.5, and 3.9).

First, it may be noted that the ISRFs of the first item step in the np-SM and the np-GRM are equivalent; that is, $M_{i1} = C_{i1}$, and that the ISRFs of the last item step in the np-SM and the np-PCM are equivalent; that is, $M_{im} = A_{im}$. For dichotomous items there is only one item step and the first ISRF is also the last ISRF; therefore, $C_{i1}(\theta) = A_{i1}(\theta) = M_{i1}(\theta) = \pi_{i1}(\theta)$. This case is referred to as the *dichotomous NIRT model*.

Next, it is shown that the np-PCM implies the np-SM and that the np-SM implies the np-GRM, but that the reverse relationships are not true. As a consequence, the np-PCM implies the np-GRM, which was already proved by Hemker et al. (1997).

THEOREM 1: *The np-PCM is a special case of the np-SM.*
PROOF: If the np-PCM holds, $A_{ix}(\theta)$ (Eq. 3.9) is nondecreasing in θ for all i and all x. This implies a monotone likelihood ratio of X_i in θ for all items (Hemker et al., 1997; Proposition); that is, for all items and all item scores c and k, with $0 \leq c < k \leq m$,

$$\frac{\pi_{ik}(\theta)}{\pi_{ic}(\theta)} \text{ is nondecreasing in } \theta. \tag{3.12}$$

Let $x \geq 1$, $c = x - 1$, and $k \geq x$, then Equation 3.12 implies that the ratio $\pi_{ik}(\theta)/\pi_{i,x-1}(\theta)$ is nondecreasing in θ, and also that $\sum_{k=x}^{m}[\pi_{ik}(\theta)/\pi_{i,x-1}(\theta)]$ is nondecreasing in θ. This is identical to

$$\frac{P(X_i \geq x|\theta)}{\pi_{i,x-1}(\theta)} \text{ nondecreasing in } \theta,$$

for all i and all x, and this implies that

$$\frac{\pi_{i,x-1}(\theta)}{P(X_i \geq x|\theta)} + \frac{P(X_i \geq x|\theta)}{P(X_i \geq x|\theta)} = \frac{P(X_i \geq x - 1|\theta)}{P(X_i \geq x|\theta)} \tag{3.13}$$

is non*in*creasing in θ. The reverse of the right-hand side of Equation 3.13, $P(X_i \geq x - 1|\theta)/P(X_i \geq x|\theta)$, which is identical to $M_{ix}(\theta)$ (Eq. 3.5), thus is non*de*creasing for all i and all x. This implies that all ISRFs of the np-SM $[M_{ix}(\theta)]$ are nondecreasing. Thus, it is shown that if the np-PCM holds, the np-SM also holds. The np-SM does not imply the np-PCM, however, because nondecreasingness of $\sum_{k=x}^{m}[\pi_{ik}(\theta)/\pi_{i,x-1}(\theta)]$ does not imply nondecreasingness of each of the ratios in this sum; thus, it does not imply Equation 3.12. Thus, the np-SM only restricts this sum, whereas the np-PCM also restricts the individual ratios.

THEOREM 2: *The np-SM is a special case of the np-GRM.*
PROOF: From the definition of the ISRF in the np-GRM, $C_{ix}(\theta)$ (Eq. 3.3), and the definition of the ISRF in the np-SM, $M_{ix}(\theta)$ (Eq. 3.5), it follows, by successive cancellation, that for all x

$$C_{ix}(\theta) = \prod_{j=1}^{x} M_{ij}(\theta). \tag{3.14}$$

From Equation 3.14 it follows that if all $M_{ij}(\theta)$ are nondecreasing, $C_{ix}(\theta)$ is nondecreasing in θ for all x. This implies that if the np-SM holds, the np-GRM also holds. The np-GRM does not imply the np-SM, however, because nondecreasingness of the product on the right-hand side of Equation 3.14 does not imply that each individual ratio $M_{ij}(\theta)$ is nondecreasing for all x.

To summarize, the np-PCM, the np-SM, and the np-GRM can be united into one hierarchical nonparametric framework, in which each model is defined by a subset of five assumptions:

1. UD;
2. LI;
3. $C_{ix}(\theta)$ nondecreasing in θ, for all i and all x;
4. $M_{ix}(\theta)$ nondecreasing in θ, for all i and all x;
5. $A_{ix}(\theta)$ nondecreasing in θ, for all i and all x.

Note that Theorem 1 and Theorem 2 imply that Assumption 3 follows from Assumption 4, and that Assumption 4 follows from Assumption 5. Assumptions 1, 2, and 3 define the np-GRM; Assumptions 1, 2, and 4 define the np-SM; and Assumptions 1, 2, and 5 define the np-PCM. This means that

$$\text{np-PCM} \Rightarrow \text{np-SM} \Rightarrow \text{np-GRM}.$$

Finally, parametric models can also be placed in this framework. A Venn-diagram depicting the relationships graphically is given in Hemker et al. (in press). Most important is that all well known parametric cumulative probability models and parametric adjacent category models are a special case of the np-PCM and, therefore, also of the np-SM and the np-GRM. All parametric continuation ratio models are a special case of the np-SM and, therefore, of the np-GRM, but not necessarily of the np-PCM. The proof that parametric continuation ratio models need not be a special case of the np-PCM had not been published thus far and is given here.

THEOREM 3: *The 2p-SM is a special case of the np-PCM only if $\alpha_{ix} \geq \alpha_{i,x+1}$, for all i, x, and θ.*
PROOF: Both the 2p-SM (Eq. 3.8) and the np-PCM (Eq. 3.9) assume UD and LI, thus it has to be shown that the ISRFs of the 2p-SM imply that $A_{ix}(\theta)$ (Eq. 3.9) is nondecreasing in θ only if $\alpha_{ix} \geq \alpha_{i,x+1}$, but not vice versa. First, $A_{ix}(\theta)$ is defined in terms of $M_{ix}(\theta)$. It can be shown, by applying Equation 3.6 to the right-hand side of Equation 3.9 and then doing some algebra, that

$$A_{ix}(\theta) = \frac{M_{ix}(\theta) - M_{ix}(\theta)M_{i,x+1}(\theta)}{1 - M_{ix}(\theta)M_{i,x+1}(\theta)}. \tag{3.15}$$

Next, applying Equation 3.8, the parametric definition of the ISRF of the 2p-SM, to Equation 3.15 and again doing some algebra, gives

$$A_{ix}(\theta) = \frac{\exp[\alpha_{ix}(\theta - \beta_{ix})]}{1 + \exp[\alpha_{ix}(\theta - \beta_{ix})] + \exp[\alpha_{i,x+1}(\theta - \beta_{i,x+1})]}. \tag{3.16}$$

If the np-PCM holds, the first derivative of $A_{ix}(\theta)$ with respect to θ is nonnegative for all i, x and θ. Let for notational convenience $\exp[\alpha_{ix}(\theta - \beta_{ix})]$ be denoted $e_{ix}(\theta)$, and let $\exp[\alpha_{i,x+1}(\theta - \beta_{i,x+1})]$ be denoted $e_{i,x+1}(\theta)$. Let the first derivative with respect to θ be denoted by a prime. Then for Equation 3.16 the np-PCM holds if

$$A_{ix}(\theta)' = \frac{e_{ix}(\theta)'[1 + e_{ix}(\theta) + e_{i,x+1}(\theta)] - [e_{ix}(\theta)' + e_{i,x+1}(\theta)']e_{ix}(\theta)}{[1 + e_{ix}(\theta) + e_{i,x+1}(\theta)]^2} \geq 0$$

(3.17)

The denominator of the ratio in Equation 3.17 is positive. Note that $e_{ix}(\theta)' = \alpha_{ix}e_{ix}(\theta)$; and $e_{i,x+1}(\theta)' = \alpha_{i,x+1}e_{i,x+1}$. Thus, from Equation 3.17 it follows that the np-PCM holds if, for all θ,

$$\alpha_{ix} + (\alpha_{ix} - \alpha_{i,x+1})e_{i,x+1}(\theta) \geq 0. \qquad (3.18)$$

Equation 3.18 holds if $\alpha_{ix} \geq \alpha_{i,x+1}$ because in that case α_{ix}, $(\alpha_{ix} - \alpha_{i,x+1})$, and $e_{i,x+1}$ are all nonnegative. However, if $\alpha_{ix} < \alpha_{i,x+1}$, it follows from Equation 3.18 that $A_{ix}(\theta)$ *decreases* in θ if

$$e_{i,x+1}(\theta) > \frac{\alpha_{ix}}{\alpha_{i,x+1} - \alpha_{ix}}.$$

Thus, if $\alpha_{ix} < \alpha_{i,x+1}$, $A_{ix}(\theta)$ *decreases* for

$$\theta > \beta_{i,x+1} + \left(\frac{\ln \alpha_{i,x+1} - \ln \alpha_{ix}}{\ln \alpha_{i,x+1}}\right).$$

This means that for $\alpha_{ix} < \alpha_{i,x+1}$, Equation 3.18 does not hold for all θ. Thus, the np-PCM need not hold if $\alpha_{ix} < \alpha_{i,x+1}$. Note that the reverse implication is not true because nondecreasingness of A_{ix} does not imply the 2p-SM (Eq. 3.8). For example, in the partial credit model (Eq. 3.11) A_{ix} is nondecreasing but the 2p-SM can not hold (Molenaar, 1983).

3.4   Ordering Properties of the Three NIRT models

The main objective of IRT models is to measure θ. NIRT models are solely defined by order restrictions, and only ordinal estimates of θ are available. Summary scores, such as X_+, may provide an ordering of the latent trait, and it is important to know whether the ordering of the summary score gives a stochastically correct ordering of the latent trait. Various ordering properties relate the ordering of the summary score to the latent trait. First, the ordering properties are introduced and, second, these properties for the NIRT models both on the theoretical and the practical level are discussed.

3.4.1   Ordering properties

Stochastic ordering properties in an IRT context relate the ordering of the examinees on a manifest variable, say Y, to the ordering of the examinees on the latent trait θ. Two manifest variables are considered, the item score,

X_i, and the unweighted total score, X_+. The ordering property of *monotone likelihood ratio* (MLR; see Hemker et al., 1996),

$$\frac{P(Y = K|\theta)}{P(Y = C|\theta)} \text{ nondecreasing in } \theta; \text{ for all } C, K; \ C < K, \qquad (3.19)$$

is a technical property which is only interesting here because it implies other stochastic ordering properties (see Lehmann, 1986, p. 84). Two versions of MLR are distinguished: First, MLR of the item score (MLR-X_i) means that Equation 3.19 holds when $Y \equiv X_i$. Second, MLR of the total score (MLR-X_+) means that Equation 3.19 holds when $Y \equiv X_+$.

The first ordering property implied by MLR is *stochastic ordering of the manifest variable* (SOM; see Hemker et al., 1997). SOM means that the order of the examinees on the latent trait gives a stochastically correct ordering of the examinees on the manifest variable; that is,

$$P(Y \geq x|\theta_A) \leq P(Y \geq x|\theta_B), \text{ for all } x; \text{ for all } \theta_A < \theta_B. \qquad (3.20)$$

Here, also two versions of SOM are distinguished: SOM of the item score (SOM-X_i) means that Equation 3.20 holds for $Y \equiv X_i$, and SOM of the total score (SOM-X_+) means that Equation 3.20 holds for $Y \equiv X_+$. It may be noted that SOM-X_i is equivalent to $P(X_i \geq x|\theta)$ (Eq. 3.3) nondecreasing in θ.

The second ordering property implied by MLR is *stochastic ordering of the latent trait* (SOL; see, e.g., Hemker et al., 1997). SOL means that the order of the examinees on the manifest variable gives a stochastically correct ordering of the examinees on the latent trait; that is,

$$P(\theta \geq s|Y = C) \leq P(\theta \geq s|Y = K), \text{ for all } s; \text{ for all } C, K; \ C < K. \qquad (3.21)$$

SOL is more interesting than SOM because SOL allows to draw conclusions about the unknown latent trait. SOL of the item score (SOL-X_i) means that Equation 3.21 holds for $Y \equiv X_i$, and SOL of the total score (SOL-X_+) means that Equation 3.21 holds for $Y \equiv X_+$.

A less restrictive form of SOL, called *ordering of the expected latent trait* (OEL) was investigated by Sijtsma and Van der Ark (2001). OEL means that

$$E(\theta|Y = C) \leq E(\theta|Y = K), \text{ for all } C, K; \ C < K. \qquad (3.22)$$

OEL has only been considered for $Y \equiv X_+$.

3.4.2   Ordering properties in theory

Table 3.1 gives an overview of the ordering properties implied by the np-GRM, the np-SM, the np-PCM, and the dichotomous NIRT model. A "+" indicates that the ordering property is implied by the model, and a "−" indicates that the ordering property is not implied by the model.

Table 3.1. Overview of Ordering Properties Implied by NIRT Models.

Model	MLR-X_+	MLR-X_i	SOL-X_+	SOL-X_i	SOM-X_+	SOM-X_i	OEL
	\multicolumn{7}{c}{Ordering properties}						
np-GRM	−	−	−	−	+	+	−
np-SM	−	−	−	−	+	+	−
np-PCM	−	+	−	+	+	+	−
Dich-NIRT	+	+	+	+	+	+	+

Note: The symbol "+" means "model implies property", and "−" means "model does not imply property". Dich-NIRT means dichotomous NIRT model.

Grayson (1988; see also Huynh, 1994) showed that the dichotomous NIRT model implies MLR-X_+, which implies that all other stochastic ordering properties also hold, both for the total score and the item score. For the np-GRM and the np-PCM the proofs with respect to MLR, SOL, and SOM are given by Hemker et al. (1996, 1997); and for the np-SM such proofs are given by Hemker et al. (in press). The proofs regarding OEL can be found in Sijtsma and Van der Ark (2001) and Van der Ark (2000). Overviews of relationships between polytomous IRT models and ordering properties are given in Sijtsma & Hemker (2000) and Van der Ark (2001).

3.4.3   Ordering properties in practice

In many practical testing situations X_+ is used to estimate θ. It would have been helpful if the NIRT models had implied the stochastic ordering properties, for then under the relatively mild conditions of UD, LI, and nondecreasing ISRFs, X_+ would give a correct stochastic ordering of the latent trait. The absence of MLR-X_+, SOL-X_+, and OEL for most polytomous IRT models, including all NIRT models, may reduce the usefulness of these models considerably. A legitimate question is whether or not the polytomous NIRT models give a correct stochastic ordering in the vast majority of cases, so that in practice under the polytomous NIRT models X_+ can safely be used to order respondents on θ.

After a pilot study by Sijtsma and Van der Ark (2001), Van der Ark (2000) conducted a large simulation study in which for six NIRT models (including the np-GRM, the np-SM, and the np-PCM) and six parametric IRT models the following two probabilities were investigated under various settings. First, the probability that a model violates a stochastic ordering property was investigated and, second, the probability that two randomly drawn respondents have an incorrect stochastic ordering was investigated. By investigating these probabilities under different circumstances (varying shapes of the ISRFs, test lengths, numbers of ordered answer categories, and distributions of θ) it was also possible to investigate which factors increased and decreased the probabilities.

The first result was that under many conditions the probability that MLR-X_+, SOL-X_+, and OEL are violated is typically large for all three NIRT models. Therefore, it not safe to assume that a particular fitted NIRT model will imply stochastic ordering given the estimated model parameters. Secondly, however, the probability that two respondents are incorrectly ordered, due to violations of OEL and SOL, is typically small. When tests of at least five items were used for ordering respondents, less than 2% of the sample was affected by violations of SOL or OEL. This means that, although the stochastic ordering properties are often violated, only a very small proportion of the sample is affected by this violation and, in general, this simulation study thus indicated that X_+ can be used safely to order respondents on θ.

Factors that increased the probability of a correct stochastic ordering were an increase of the number of items, a decrease of the number of answer categories, and a normal or uniform distribution of θ rather than a skewed distribution. Moreover, the np-PCM had a noticeable lower probability of an incorrect stochastic ordering than the np-SM and the np-GRM. The effect of the shape of the ISRFs was different for the three NIRT models. For the np-PCM and the np-SM similarly shaped ISRFs having lower asymptotes that were greater than 0 and upper asymptotes that were less than 1 yielded the best results. For the np-GRM the best results were obtained for ISRFs that differed in shape and had lower asymptotes equal to 0 and upper asymptotes equal to 1.

3.5   Three Approaches for Estimating Polytomous NIRT Models

Generally three approaches for the analysis of data with NIRT models have been proposed. The approaches are referred to as investigation of observable consequences, ordered latent class analysis, and kernel smoothing. The difference between the approaches lies in the assumptions about θ and the estimation of the ISRF. Each approach has its own software and uses its own diagnostics for the goodness of fit investigation. Not every model can be readily estimated with the available software. The software is discussed using two simulated data sets that consist of the responses of 500 simulees to 10 polytomous items with 4 ordered answer categories (these are reasonable numbers in practical psychological research).

Data Set 1 was simulated using an adjacent category model (Eq. 3.9) with ISRF

$$\frac{P(X_i = x|\theta)}{P(X_i = x|\theta) + P(X_i = x - 1|\theta)} = \frac{\exp[\alpha_{ix}(\theta - \beta_{ix})]}{1 + \exp[\alpha_{ix}(\theta - \beta_{ix})]}. \qquad (3.23)$$

In Equation 3.23 the parameters α_{ix} were the exponent of random draws from a normal distribution with mean 0.7 and variance 0.5; hence, $\alpha_{ix} > 0$. The θ values of the 500 simulees and the parameters β_{ix} both were random draws from a standard normal distribution. Equation 3.23 is a special case of the np-PCM and, therefore, it is expected that all NIRT models will fit Data Set 1. An adjacent category model was chosen because continuation ratio models (Eq. 3.5) do not necessarily imply an np-PCM (see Theorem 3) and cumulative probability models (Eq. 3.3) are not very flexible because the ISRFs of the same item cannot intersect.

Data Set 2 was simulated using a two-dimensional adjacent category model with ISRF

$$\frac{P(X_i = x|\theta_1, \theta_2)}{P(X_i = x|\theta_1, \theta_2) + P(X_i = x - 1|\theta_1, \theta_2)} = \frac{\exp[\sum_{d=1}^{2} \alpha_{ixd}(\theta_d - \beta_{ixd})]}{1 + \exp[\sum_{d=1}^{2} \alpha_{ixd}(\theta_d - \beta_{ixd})]}$$

(3.24)

In Equation 3.24, $\alpha_{ix2} = -0.1$ for $i = 1, \ldots, 5$, and $\alpha_{ix1} = -0.1$ for $i = 6, \ldots, 10$. The remaining α_{ix} parameters are the exponent of random draws from a normal distribution with mean 0.7 and variance 0.5 and, therefore, they are nonnegative. This means that the first five items have a small negative correlation with θ_2 and the last five items have a small negative correlation with θ_1. Equation 3.24 is not unidimensional and, due to the negative α_{ix}s, the ISRFs are decreasing in either θ_1 or θ_2. Therefore, it is expected that none of the models will fit Data Set 2. The θ values of the 500 simulees and the parameters β_{ix} both were random draws from a standard normal distribution, and θ_1 and θ_2 were uncorrelated.

3.5.1   Investigation of observable consequences

This approach was proposed by Mokken (1971) for nonparametric scaling of dichotomous items. The approach is primarily focused on model fitting by means of the investigation of observable consequences of a NIRT model. For polytomous items this approach was discussed by Molenaar (1997). The rationale of the method is as follows:

1. Define the model assumptions;
2. Derive properties of the manifest variables that are implied by the model assumptions (observable consequences);
3. Investigate whether or not these observable consequences hold in the data; and
4. Reject the model if the observable consequences do not hold; otherwise, accept the model.

Software. The computer program MSP (Molenaar, Van Schuur, Sijtsma, & Mokken, 2000; Molenaar & Sijtsma, 2000) is the only software encountered that tests observable consequences for polytomous items. MSP has two main purposes: The program can be used to test the observable consequences for

a fixed set of items (dichotomous or polytomous) and to select sets of corre-
lating items from a multidimensional item pool. In the latter case, for each
clustered item set the observable consequences are investigated separately.
MSP can be used to investigate the following observable consequences:

- *Scalability coefficient H_{ij}.* Molenaar (1991) introduced a weighted polytomous version of the scalability coefficient H_{ij}, originally introduced by
Mokken (1971) for dichotomous items. Coefficient H_{ij} is the ratio of the
covariance of items i and j, and the maximum covariance given the mar-
ginals of the bivariate cross-classification table of the scores on items i
and j; that is,

$$H_{ij} = \frac{Cov(X_i, X_j)}{Cov(X_i, X_j)_{\max}}.$$

If the np-GRM holds, then $Cov(X_i, X_j) \geq 0$ and, as a result, $0 \leq H_{ij} \leq 1$
(see Hemker et al., 1995). MSP computes all H_{ij} s and tests whether
values of H_{ij} are significantly greater than zero. The idea is that items
with significant positive H_{ij} s measure the same θ, and MSP deletes
items that have a non-positive or non-significant positive relationship
with other items in the set.
- *Manifest monotonicity.* Junker (1993) showed that if dichotomous items
are conditioned on a summary score that does not contain X_i, for example, the rest score

$$R_{(-i)} = X_+ - X_i, \tag{3.25}$$

then the dichotomous NIRT model implies manifest monotonicity; that
is,

$$P(X_i = 1|R_{(-i)}) \text{ nondecreasing in } R_{(-i)}. \tag{3.26}$$

However, Hemker (cited by Junker & Sijtsma, 2000) showed that a similar manifest monotonicity property is not implied by polytomous NIRT
models; that is, $P(X \geq x|R_{(-i)})$ need not be nondecreasing in $R_{(-i)}$. It is
not yet known whether this is a real problem for data analysis. MSP com-
putes $P(X \geq x|R_{(-i)})$ and reports violations of manifest monotonicity,
although it is only an observable consequence of dichotomous items.

In search for sets of related items from a multidimensional item pool,
MSP uses H_{ij} and the scalability coefficients H_i (a scalability coefficient for
item i with respect to the other items) and H (a scalability coefficient for
the entire test) as criteria. In general, for each scale found, $H_{ij} > 0$, for all
$i \neq j$, and $H_i \geq c$ (which implies that $H \geq c$; see Hemker et al., 1995). The
constant c is a user-specified criterion, that manipulates the strength of the
relationship of an item with θ.

Example. It may be noted that the np-GRM implies $0 \leq H_{ij} \leq 1$, which
can be checked by MSP. Because the np-GRM is implied by the np-SM and
the np-PCM, MSP cannot distinguish these three models by only checking

the property that $H_{ij} > 0$, for all $i \neq j$. So, either all three NIRT models are rejected when at least one $H_{ij} < 0$, or none of the three NIRT models is rejected, when all $H_{ij} > 0$.

MSP can handle up to 255 items. Thus analyzing Data Set 1 and Data Set 2 was not a problem. For Data Set 1, which was simulated using a unidimensional adjacent category model (Eq. 3.23), the ten items had a scalability coefficient $H = .54$, which can be interpreted as a strong scale (see Hemker et al., 1995). None of the H_{ij} values were negative. Therefore, MSP correctly did not reject the np-GRM for Data Set 1. Although manifest monotonicity is not decisive for rejecting the np-GRM, violations may heuristically indicate non-increasing ISRFs. To investigate possible violations of manifest monotonicity in Data Set 1, MSP checked 113 sample inequalities of the type $P(X \geq x | R_{(-i)} = r) < P(X \geq x | R_{(-i)} = r - 1)$; four significant violations were found, which seems a small number given 113 possible violations.

For Data Set 2, which was simulated using a two-dimensional adjacent category model (Eq. 3.24), the ten items had a scalability coefficient of $H = .13$, and many negative H_{ij} values, so that the np-GRM was correctly rejected. If a model is rejected, MSP's search option may yield subsets of items for which the np-GRM is not rejected. For Data Set 2, the default search option yielded two scales: Scale 1 ($H = .53$) consisted of items 3, 4, and 5, and Scale 2 ($H = .64$) consisted of items 6, 7, 8, and 9. Thus, MSP correctly divided seven items of Data Set 2 into two subscales, and three items were excluded. For item 1 and item 2, the H_{ij} values with the remaining items of Scale 1 were positive but non-significant. Item 10 was not included because the scalability coefficient $H_{6,10} = -0.03$. It may be argued that a more conventional criterion for rejecting the np-GRM might be to test whether $H_{ij} < 0$, for all $i \neq j$. This is not possible in MSP, but if the minimum acceptable H is set to 0 and the significance level is set to 0.9999, then testing for $H_{ij} > 0$ becomes trivial. In this case, items 1 and 2 were also included in Scale 1.

3.5.2   Ordered latent class analysis

Croon (1990, 1991) proposed to use latent class analysis (Lazarsfeld & Henry, 1968) as a method for the nonparametric scaling of dichotomous items. The rationale is that the continuous latent trait θ is replaced by a discrete latent variable T with q ordered categories. It is assumed that the item score pattern is locally independent given the latent class, such that

$$P(X_1, \ldots, X_k) = \sum_{s=1}^{q} P(T = s) \times \prod_{i=1}^{k} P(X_i = x_i | T = s), \qquad (3.27)$$

with inequality restrictions

$$P(X_i = 1 | T = s) \geq P(X_i = 1 | T = s - 1), \text{ for } s = 2, \ldots, q, \qquad (3.28)$$

to satisfy the monotonicity assumptions. If $q = 1$, the independence model is obtained.

It may be noted that the monotonicity assumption of the dichotomous NIRT model [i.e., $P(X_i = 1|\theta)$ is nondecreasing in θ] implies Equation 3.28 for all discrete combinations of successive θ values collected in ordinal latent classes. As concerns LI, it can be shown that LI in the dichotomous NIRT model and LI in the ordinal latent class model (Eq. 3.28) are unrelated. This means that mathematically, the ordinal latent class model and the dichotomous NIRT model are unrelated. However, for a good fit to data an ordinal latent class model should detect as many latent classes as there are distinct θ values, and only θs that yield similar response patterns are combined into one latent class. Therefore, if LI holds in the dichotomous NIRT model, it holds by approximation in the ordinal latent class model with the appropriate number of latent classes.

Equation 3.28 was extended to the polytomous ordinal latent class model by Van Onna (2000), who used the Gibbs-sampler, and Vermunt (2001), who used maximum likelihood, to estimate the ordinal latent class probabilities. Vermunt (2001) estimated Equation 3.28 with inequality restrictions

$$P(X_i \geq x|T = s) \geq P(X_i \geq x|T = s - 1), \text{ for } s = 2, \ldots, q, \qquad (3.29)$$

and

$$P(X_i \geq x|T = s) \geq P(X_i \geq x - 1|T = s), \text{ for } x = 2, \ldots, m. \qquad (3.30)$$

Due to the restrictions in Equation 3.29, $P(X_i \geq x|T)$ is nondecreasing in T [cf. Eq. 3.5, where for the np-GRM probability $P(X_i \geq x|\theta)$ is nondecreasing in θ]. Due to the restrictions in Equation 3.30, $P(X_i \geq x|T)$ and $P(X_i \geq x - 1|T)$ are nonintersecting, which avoids negative response probabilities. The latent class model subject to Equation 3.29 and Equation 3.30, can be interpreted as an np-GRM with combined latent trait values. However, as for the dichotomous NIRT model, LI in the np-GRM with a continuous latent trait and LI in the np-GRM with combined latent trait values are mathematically unrelated.

Vermunt (2001) also extended the ordered latent class approach to the np-SM and the np-PCM, and estimated these models by means of maximum likelihood. For ordinal latent class versions of the np-PCM and the np-SM the restrictions in Equation 3.29 are changed into

$$\frac{P(X_i = x|T = s)}{P(X_i = x - 1 \vee x|T = s)} \geq \frac{P(X_i = x|T = s - 1)}{P(X_i = x - 1 \vee x|T = s - 1)}, \text{ for } s = 2, \ldots, q \qquad (3.31)$$

and

$$\frac{P(X_i \geq x|T = s)}{P(X_i \geq x - 1|T = s)} \geq \frac{P(X_i \geq x|T = s - 1)}{P(X_i \geq x - 1|T = s - 1)}, \text{ for } d = 2, \ldots, q \qquad (3.32)$$

respectively. For the np-PCM and the np-SM the ISRFs may intersect and, therefore, restrictions such as Equation 3.30 are no longer necessary.

Software. The computer program ℓEM (Vermunt, 1997) is available free of charge from the world wide web. The program was not especially designed to estimate ordered latent class models, but more generally to estimate various types of models for categorical data via maximum likelihood. The program syntax allows many different models to be specified rather compactly, which makes it a very flexible program, but considerable time must be spent studying the manual and the various examples provided along with the program. ℓEM can estimate the ordinal latent class versions of the np-PCM, the np-GRM, and the np-SM, although these options are not documented in the manual. Vermunt (personal communication) indicated that the command "or1" to specify ordinal latent classes should be changed into "or1(b)" for the np-PCM, and "or1(c)" for the np-SM. For the np-GRM the command "or1(a)" equals the original "or1", and "or1(d)" estimates the np-SM with a reversed scale (Agresti, 1990; Hemker, 2001; Vermunt, 2001). In addition to the NIRT models, ℓEM can also estimate various parametric IRT models. The program provides the estimates of $P(T = s)$ and $P(X_i = x|T = s)$ for all i, x, and s, global likelihood based fit statistics such as L^2, X^2, AIC, and BIC (for an overview, see Agresti, 1990), and for each item five pseudo R^2 measures, showing the percentage explained qualitative variance due to class membership.

Example. For Data Set 1 and Data Set 2, the np-GRM, the np-SM and the np-PCM with $q = 2$, 3, and 4 ordered latent classes we estimated. The independence model ($q = 1$) as a baseline model to compare the improvement of fit was also estimated. Latent class analysis of Data Set 1 and Data Set 2 means analyzing a contingency table with $4^{10} = 1,048,576$ cells, of which 99.96% are empty. It is well known that in such sparse tables likelihood-based fit statistics, such as X^2 and L^2, need not have a chi-squared distribution. It was found that the numerical values of X^2 and L^2 were not only very large (exceeding 10^6) but also highly different (sometimes $X^2 > 1000L^2$). Therefore, X^2 and L^2 could not be interpreted meaningfully, and instead the following fit statistics are given in Table 3.2: loglikelihood (L), the departure from independence (Dep. $= [L(1)-L(q)]/L(1)$) for the estimated models, and the difference in loglikelihood between the ordinal latent class model and the corresponding latent class model without order constraints (Δ). The latter two statistics are not available in ℓEM but can easily be computed. Often the estimation procedure yielded local optima, especially for the np-GRM (which was also estimated more slowly than the np-SM and the np-PCM). Therefore, each model was estimated ten times and the best solution was reported. For some models more than five different optima occurred; this is indicated by an asterisk in Table 3.2.

For all models the loglikelihood of Data Set 1 was greater than the loglikelihood of Data Set 2. Also the departure from independence was greater

Table 3.2. Goodness of Fit of the Estimated np-GRM, np-SM, and np-PCM With ℓEM.

		np-GRM			np-PCM			np-SM		
Data	q	L	Dep.	Δ	L	Dep.	Δ	L	Dep.	Δ
Data Set 1	1	-3576	.000	0	-3576	.000	0	-3576	.000	0
	2	-2949	.175	14	-2980	.167	45	-2950	.175	15
	3	-2853*	.202	34	-2872	.197	53	-2833	.208	24
	4	-2791*	.220	34	-2818	.212	61	-2778	.223	21
Data Set 2	1	-4110	.000	0	-4110	.000	0	-4110	.000	0
	2	-3868*	.058	1	-3917	.047	54	-3869	.059	6
	3	-3761*	.085	108	-3791	.078	138	-3767	.083	114
	4	-3745*	.089	51	-3775*	.092	181	-3763	.084	169

Note: L is the loglikelihood; Dep. is the departure of independence $\frac{L(q)-L(1)}{L(q)}$; Δ is the difference between the loglikelihood of the unconstrained latent class model with q classes and the ordinal latent class model with q classes.

for the models of Data Set 1 than for the models of Data Set 2, which suggests that modeling Data Set 1 by means of ordered latent class analysis was superior to modeling Data Set 2. The difference between the loglikelihood of the ordered latent class models and the unordered latent class models was greater for Data Set 2, which may indicate that the ordering of the latent classes was more natural for Data Set 1 than for Data Set 2. All these finding were expected beforehand. However, without any reference to the real model, it is hard to determine whether the NIRT models should be rejected for Data Set 1, for Data Set 2, or for both. It is even harder to distinguish the np-GRM, the np-SM, and the np-PCM. The fit statistics which are normally used to reject a model, L^2 or X^2, were not useful here. Based on the L^2 and X^2 statistics, only the independence model for Data Set 1 could have been rejected.

3.5.3 Kernel smoothing

Smoothing of item response functions of dichotomous items was proposed by Ramsay (1991) as an alternative to the Birnbaum (1968) three-parameter logistic model,

$$\pi_{i1}(\theta) = \gamma_i + (1 - \gamma_i)\frac{\exp[\alpha_i(\theta - \beta_i)]}{1 + \exp[\alpha_i(\theta - \beta_i)]}, \tag{3.33}$$

where γ_i is a guessing parameter, α_i a slope parameter, and β_i a location parameter. Ramsay (1991) argued that the three-parameter logistic model does not take nonmonotonic item response functions into account, that the sampling covariances of the parameters are usually large, and that estimation algorithms are slow and complex. Alternatively, in the monotone smoothing approach, continuous nonparametric item response functions are estimated using kernel smoothing. The procedure is described as follows (see Ramsay, 2000, for more details):

1. *Estimation of θ.* A summary score (e.g., X_+) is computed for all respondents, and all respondents are ranked on the basis of this summary score; ranks within tied values are assigned randomly. The estimated θ value ($\hat{\theta}$) of the n-th respondent in rank is the n-th quantile of the standard normal distribution, such that the area under the standard normal density function to the left of this value is equal to $n/(N+1)$.

2. *Estimation of the CCC.* The CCC, $\pi_{ix}(\theta)$, is estimated by (kernel) smoothing the relationship between the item category responses and the $\hat{\theta}$s. If desired the estimates of θ can be refined after the smoothing. Douglas (1997) showed that under certain regularity conditions the joint estimates of θ and the CCCs are consistent as the numbers of respondents and items tend to infinity. Stout, Goodwin Froelich, and Gao (2001) argued that in practice the kernel smoothing procedure yields positively biased estimates at the low end of the θ scale and negatively biased estimates at the high end of the θ scale.

Software. The computer program TestGraf98 and a manual are available free of charge from the ftp site of the author (Ramsay, 2000). The program estimates θ as described above and estimates the CCCs for scales with either dichotomous or polytomous items. The estimates of θ may be expressed as standard normal scores or may be transformed monotonely to $E(R_{(-i)}|\hat{\theta})$ (see Equation 3.25) or $E(X_+|\hat{\theta})$. The program provides graphical rather than descriptive information about the estimated curves. For each item the estimated CCCs $[\pi_{ix}(\hat{\theta})]$ and the expected item score given $\hat{\theta}$ $[E(X_i|\hat{\theta})]$ can be depicted. For multiple-choice items with one correct alternative it is also possible to depict the estimated CCCs of the incorrect alternatives. Furthermore, the distribution of $\hat{\theta}$, the standard error of $\hat{\theta}$, the reliability of the unweighted total score, and the test information function are shown. For each respondent the probability of $\hat{\theta}$ given the response pattern, can be depicted.

Testing NIRT models with TestGraf98 is not straightforward because only graphical information is provided. However, if the np-GRM holds, which implies that $P(X_i \geq x|\theta)$ is nondecreasing in θ (Eq. 3.5), then $E(X_i|\theta)$ is also nondecreasing in θ, because

$$E(X_i|\theta) = \sum_{x=1}^{m} P(X_i \geq x|\theta).$$

If a plot in TestGraf98 shows for item i that $E(X_i|\hat{\theta})$ is not nondecreasing in $\hat{\theta}$, this may indicate a violation of the np-GRM and, by implication, a violation of the np-SM, and the np-PCM. Due to the lack of test statistics,

TestGraf98 appears to be a device for an eyeball diagnosis, rather than a method to test whether the NIRT models hold.

Example. For Data Set 1, visual inspection of the plots of $E(X_i|\hat{\theta})$ showed that all expected item scores where nondecreasing in $\hat{\theta}$. This means that no violations of the np-GRM were detected. For Data Set 2, for three items $E(X_i|\hat{\theta})$ was slightly decreasing in $\hat{\theta}$ over a narrow range of $\hat{\theta}$; $E(X_7|\hat{\theta})$ showed a severe decrease in $\hat{\theta}$. Moreover, three expected item score functions were rather flat, and two expected item score functions were extremely flat. This indicates that for Data Set 2, the np-GRM was (correctly) not supported by TestGraf98.

3.6   Discussion

In this chapter three polytomous NIRT models were discussed, the np-PCM, the np-SM, and the np-GRM. It was shown that the models are hierarchically related; that is, the np-PCM implies the np-SM, and the np-SM implies the np-GRM. It was also shown that the 2p-SM only implies the np-PCM if for all items and all item steps the slope parameter of category x is less or equal to the slope parameter of category $x + 1$. This final proof completes the relationships in a hierarchical framework which includes many popular polytomous IRT models (for overviews, see Hemker et al., in press).

NIRT models only assume order restrictions. Therefore, NIRT models impose less stringent demands on the data and usually fit better than parametric IRT models. NIRT models estimate the latent trait at an ordinal level rather than an interval level. Therefore, it is important that summary scores such as X_+ imply a stochastic ordering of θ. Although none of the polytomous NIRT models implies a stochastic ordering of the latent trait by X_+, this stochastic ordering will hold for many choices of ISRFs or CCCs in a specific model, and many distributions of θ. The np-PCM implies stochastic ordering of the latent trait by the item score. In the kernel smoothing approach an interval level score of the latent trait is obtained by mapping an ordinal summary statistic onto percentiles of the standard normal distribution. Alternatively, multidimensional latent variable models can be used if a unidimensional parametric IRT model or a NIRT model do not have an adequate fit. Multidimensional IRT models yield estimated latent trait values at an interval level (e.g., Moustaki, 2000). Multidimensional IRT models are, however, not very popular because parameter estimation is more complicated and persons cannot be assigned a single latent trait score (for a discussion of these arguments, see Van Abswoude, Van der Ark, & Sijtsma, 2001).

Three approaches for fitting and estimating NIRT models were discussed. The first approach, investigation of observable consequences, is the most formal approach in terms of fitting the NIRT models. For fitting a model based on UD, LI, and M, the latent trait is not estimated but the total score is used as an ordinal proxy. The associated program MSP correctly found the structure of the simulated data sets.

In the ordinal latent class approach the NIRT model is approximated by an ordinal latent class model. The monotonicity assumption of the NIRT models is transferred to the ordinal latent class models, but the LI assumption is not. It is not known how this affects the relationship between NIRT models and ordinal latent class models. The latent trait is estimated by latent classes, and the modal class membership probability $P(T = t|X_1, \ldots, X_k)$ can be used to assign a latent trait score to persons. The associated software ℓEM is the only program that could estimate all NIRT models. ℓEM found differences between the two simulated data sets indicating that the NIRT models fitted Data Set 1 but not Data Set 2. It was difficult to make a formal decision.

The kernel smoothing approach estimates a continuous CCC and a latent trait score at the interval level. In this approach there are no formal tests for accepting or rejecting NIRT models. The associated software TestGraf98 gives graphical information. It is believed that the program is suited for a quick diagnosis of the items, but the lack of test statistics prevents the use for model fitting. Moreover, only a derivative of the np-GRM, $E(X_+|\hat{\theta})$, can be examined. However, the graphs displayed by TestGraf98 supported the correct decision about the fit of NIRT models.

References

Agresti, A. (1990). *Categorical data analysis*. New York: Wiley.

Birnbaum, A. (1968). Some latent trait models. In F. M. Lord & M. R. Novick, *Statistical theories of mental test scores* (pp. 397 – 424). Reading, MA: Addison-Wesley.

Croon, M. A. (1990). Latent class analysis with ordered latent classes. *British Journal of Mathematical and Statistical Psychology, 43*, 171-192.

Croon, M. A. (1991). Investigating Mokken scalability of dichotomous items by means of ordinal latent class analysis. *British Journal of Mathematical and Statistical Psychology, 44*, 315-331.

Douglas, J. (1997). Joint consistency of nonparametric item characteristic curve and ability estimation. *Psychometrika, 62*, 7-28.

Fischer, G. H., & Molenaar, I. W. (Eds.). (1995). *Rasch Models: Foundations, recent developments and applications*. New York: Springer.

Grayson, D. A. (1988). Two group classification in latent trait theory: scores with monotone likelihood ratio. *Psychometrika, 53*, 383–392.

Hemker, B. T, (2001), Reversibility revisited and other comparisons of three types of polytomous IRT models. In A. Boomsma, M. A. J. van Duijn & T. A. B. Snijders (Eds.), *Essays in item response theory* (pp. 275 – 296). New York: Springer.

Hemker, B. T., Sijtsma, K., & Molenaar, I. W. (1995). Selection of unidimensional scales from a multidimensional itembank in the polytomous Mokken IRT model. *Applied Psychological Measurement, 19*, 337-352.

Hemker, B. T., Sijtsma, K., Molenaar, I. W., & Junker, B. W. (1996). Polytomous IRT models and monotone likelihood ratio of the total score. *Psychometrika, 61*, 679-693.

Hemker, B. T., Sijtsma, K., Molenaar, I. W., & Junker, B. W. (1997). Stochastic ordering using the latent trait and the sum score in polytomous IRT models. *Psychometrika, 62*, 331-347.

Hemker, B. T., Van der Ark, L. A., & Sijtsma, K. (in press). On measurement properties of continuation ratio models. *Psychometrika.*

Huynh, H. (1994). A new proof for monotone likelihood ratio for the sum of independent variables. *Psychometrika, 59*, 77–79,

Junker, B. W. (1993). Conditional association, essential independence and monotone unidimensional item response models. *The Annals of Statistics, 21*, 1359-1378.

Junker, B. W., & Sijtsma, K. (2000). Latent and manifest monotonicity in item response models. *Applied Psychological Measurement, 24*, 65-81.

Lazarsfeld, P. F., & Henry, N. W. (1968). *Latent structure analysis.* Boston: Houghton Mifflin.

Lehmann, E. L. (1986). *Testing statistical hypotheses.* (2nd ed.). New York: Wiley.

Likert, R. A. (1932). A technique for the measurement of attitudes. *Archives of Psychology, 140.*

Lord, F. M., & Novick M. R. (1968). *Statistical theories of mental test scores.* Reading MA: Addison-Wesley.

Masters, G. (1982). A Rasch model for partial credit scoring. *Psychometrika, 47*, 149-174.

Mellenbergh, G. J. (1995). Conceptual notes on models for discrete polytomous item responses *Applied Psychological Measurement, 19*, 91-100.

Mokken, R. J. (1971). *A theory and procedure of scale analysis.* The Hague: Mouton/Berlin: De Gruyter.

Molenaar, I. W. (1983). *Item steps* (Heymans Bulletin HB-83-630-EX). Groningen, The Netherlands: University of Groningen.

Molenaar, I. W. (1991). A weighted Loevinger H-coefficient extending Mokken scaling to multicategory items. *Kwantitatieve Methoden, 12(37)*, 97-117.

Molenaar, I. W. (1997). Nonparametric models for polytomous responses. In W. J. van der Linden & R. K. Hambleton (Eds.), *Handbook of modern item response theory* (pp. 369 – 380). New York: Springer.

Molenaar, I. W., & Sijtsma, K. (2000). MSP for Windows [Software manual]. Groningen, The Netherlands: iec ProGAMMA.

Molenaar, I. W., Van Schuur, W. H., Sijtsma, K., & Mokken, R. J. (2000). MSP-WIN5.0; A program for Mokken scale analysis for polytomous items [Computer software]. Groningen, The Netherlands: iec ProGAMMA.

Moustaki, I. (2000). A latent variable model for ordinal variables. *Applied Psychological Measurement, 24*, 211-223.

Muraki, E. (1992). A generalized partial credit model: Application of an EM algorithm. *Applied Psychological Measurement, 16,* 159-177.

Ramsay, J. O. (1991). Kernel smoothing approaches to nonparametric item characteristic curve estimation. *Psychometrika, 56,* 611-630.

Ramsay, J. O. (2000, September). TestGraf98 [Computer software and manual]. Retrieved March 1, 2001 from the World Wide Web: *ftp://ego.psych.mcgill.ca/pub/ramsay/testgraf*

Samejima, F. (1969). Estimation of latent ability using a response pattern of graded scores. *Psychometrika Monograph, 17.*

Samejima, F. (1972). A general model for free response data. *Psychometrika Monograph, 18.*

Sijtsma, K., & Hemker, B. T. (2000). A taxonomy of IRT models for ordering persons and items using simple sum scores. *Journal of Educational and Behavioral Statistics, 25,* 391-415.

Sijtsma, K., & Van der Ark, L. A. (2001). Progress in NIRT analysis of polytomous item scores: Dilemmas and practical solutions. In A. Boomsma, M. A. J. van Duijn, & T. A. B. Snijders, (Eds.), *Essays on item response theory* (pp. 297–318). New York: Springer.

Stout, W., Goodwin Froelich, A., & Gao, F. (2001). Using resampling methods to produce an improved DIMTEST procedure. In A. Boomsma, M. A. J. van Duijn, & T. A. B. Snijders, (Eds.), *Essays on item response theory* (pp. 357–375). New York: Springer.

Tutz, G. (1990). Sequential item response models with an ordered response. *British Journal of Mathematical and Statistical Psychology, 43,* 39-55.

Van Abswoude, A. A. H., Van der Ark, L. A., & Sijtsma, K. (2001). *A comparative study on test dimensionality assessment procedures under nonparametric IRT models.* Manuscript submitted for publication.

Van der Ark, L. A. (2000). *Practical consequences of stochastic ordering of the latent trait under various polytomous IRT models.* Manuscript submitted for publication.

Van der Ark, L. A. (2001). Relationships and properties of polytomous item response theory models. *Applied Psychological Measurement, 25,* 273-282.

Van Onna, M. J. H. (2000). Gibbs sampling under order restrictions in a nonparametric IRT model. In W. Jansen & J. Bethlehem (Eds.) *Proceedings in Computational Statistics 2000; Short communications and posters* (pp. 117–118). Voorburg, The Netherlands: Statistics Netherlands.

Vermunt, J. K. (1997, September). *ℓEM*: A general program for the analysis of categorical data [Computer software and manual]. Retrieved September 19, 2001 from the World Wide Web: http://www.kub.nl/faculteiten/fsw/organisatie/departementen/mto/software2.html

Vermunt, J. K. (2001). The use of latent class models for defining and testing non-parametric and parameteric item response theory models. *Applied Psychological Measurement, 25,* 283-294.

4 Fully Semiparametric Estimation of the Two-Parameter Latent Trait Model for Binary Data

Panagiota Tzamourani[1] and Martin Knott[2]

[1] Bank of Greece
[2] London School of Economics and Political Science

4.1 Introduction

The two-parameter latent trait model was first formulated by Birnbaum (1968). The two-parameter latent trait model can be applied to responses of a set of binary items, with the aim of estimating the item parameters and also scoring the individuals on the latent variable scale. The probability of a positive response to an item is given by

$$\pi_i(z) = \frac{\exp(\alpha_{0i} + \alpha_{1i}z)}{1 + \exp(\alpha_{0i} + \alpha_{1i}z)}$$

where α_{0i} is the difficulty parameter and α_{1i} the discrimination parameter for item i.

Estimation of the model is based on an assumed distribution for the latent variable called the prior (usually N(0,1)). Researchers (e.g., Bartholomew, 1988; Bock & Aitkin, 1981) have shown that the shape of the distribution does not greatly affect the parameter estimates, apart from a location and scale effect. However, since the assumption of a parametric form is an arbitrary one, it would be good to be able to estimate the model without this assumption. For example, Bock and Aitkin (1981) suggested estimating the prior together with the item parameters. In particular, they used a discrete prior on a fixed pre-specified grid of points and estimated the probabilities on those points from the data (semiparametric estimation). More recently, Heinen (1996) defined semiparametric estimation as estimating the weights of a fixed number of points, and fully semiparametric estimation as estimating the weights and the position of a fixed number of points for various latent trait models.

The purpose of this chapter is to present an EM algorithm, which carries out fully semiparametric estimation for the two-parameter latent trait model. The approach is based on the theory of nonparametric estimation of mixtures. The original research in this area was initiated by Kiefer and Wolfowitz (1956), who proved that the maximum likelihood (ML) estimator of a structural parameter is strongly consistent, when the incidental parameters (parameters that represent the effects of omitted variables) are independently distributed random variables with a common unknown distribution

F. F is also consistently estimated, although it is not assumed to belong to a parametric class. Laird (1978) showed that the nonparametric ML estimate of mixing distribution F is self-consistent and, under certain general conditions, the estimated distribution must be a step function with finite number of steps. Lindsay (1983) studied the geometry of the likelihood of the estimator of a mixture density and gave conditions on the existence, discreteness, support size characterisation and uniqueness of the estimator. His results are based on the directional derivative of the loglikelihood towards a support point, and this is used in this chapter to discover the optimal number of points needed to approximate the prior for the latent trait model. The theory of nonparametric estimation of the mixing distribution has been applied in the estimation of Generalised Linear Models (e.g., Aitkin, 1996). Examples in several areas of application and methodological developments have been reviewed in Lindsay and Lesperance (1995), whereas Boehning (1995, 1999) reviewed algorithms.

The nonparametric estimation of the 1-parameter latent trait model, better known as the Rasch model, was examined by Cressie and Holland (1983), De Leeuw and Verhelst (1986), Follmann (1988), Lindsay, Clogg, and Grego (1991). De Leeuw and Verhelst (1986) showed that the maximum number of points is $(p + 1)/2$ if p, the number of items, is odd, and $(p + 2)/2$ if p is even, with the first point being equal to $-\infty$ in the latter case. Lindsay et al (1991) made a distinction between concordant cases, when the marginal frequencies of the total scores can be fitted exactly by the model, and discordant cases, when this doesn't happen. In discordant cases, the latent distribution is unique and the number of support points is $p/2$.

Latent trait models for polytomous items can be estimated semiparametrically if they are formulated as Row-Column (RC) association models and the scores of the column variable are not given. This can be done by LEM [1], a computer program written by Vermunt (1997) [2].

4.2   Parametric ML Estimation

Assume that there are p observed variables $X_1, ..., X_p$, taking on values of 0 and 1. Let x_i be the value of the ith item X_i for an individual. The row vector $\mathbf{x}' = (x_1, ..., x_p)$ is called the **response pattern** for that individual. Given the latent variable Z, the responses $X_1, ..., X_p$ are independent and so

---

[1] Because of run-time errors, it was difficult to get LEM to work for the selected examples. In addition, we were not been able to try Latent Gold, the successor to LEM.

[2] It is hard to give a precise estimate of how long the programs take to run. As a general guide, the programs for semiparametric and fully semiparametric estimation may be up to 100 times slower than those for parametric estimation.

the conditional probability for a given z is

$$g(\mathbf{x} \mid z) = \prod_{i=1}^{p} g_i(x_i \mid z)$$

where $g_i(x_i \mid z)$ is the conditional probability of response x_i for the ith item. Since the X_i s are binary,

$$g(\mathbf{x} \mid z) = \prod_{i=1}^{p} \pi_i(z)^{x_i} (1 - \pi_i(z))^{1-x_i}$$

where $\pi_i(z) = P[X_i = 1 \mid z]$. The likelihood of a response pattern is given by

$$f(\mathbf{x}) = \int g(\mathbf{x}|z) h(z) dz$$

The latent variable z is assumed to have standard normal density function $h(z) = 1/\sqrt{2\pi} \exp(-z^2/2)$, which is approximated by Gauss-Hermite quadrature points z_t and their corresponding normalised weights $h(z_t)$, so $f(\mathbf{x})$ can be approximated with

$$f(x) = \sum_{t=1}^{k} g(x|z_t) h(z_t)$$

where k is the number of quadrature points (Straud & Sechrest, 1966). The function to be maximised is:

$$L = \sum_{l=1}^{n} \log f(\mathbf{x}_l),$$

where n is the number of individuals in the sample. The ML estimates are given by setting

$$\partial L / \partial a_{ji} = 0. \tag{4.1}$$

Since the response function is taken to be the logit, Equation(4.1) can be formulated as (Bartholomew & Knott, 1999, pages 81-83):

$$\frac{\partial L}{\partial \alpha_{ji}} = \sum_{t=1}^{k} z_t^j \{r_{it} - N_t \pi_i(z_t)\}, \qquad j = 0, 1. \tag{4.2}$$

where,

$$r_{it} = \sum_{l=1}^{n} x_{li} h(z_t \mid \mathbf{x}_l) \tag{4.3}$$

and

$$N_t = \sum_{l=1}^{n} h(z_t \mid \mathbf{x}_l) \qquad (4.4)$$

The **LATV** program (Bartholomew & Knott, 1999) fits the above model using a modified E-M algorithm proposed by Bock and Aitkin (1981) and modified by Bartholomew (1987) for the logit model. The steps of an E-M algorithm are defined as follows:

- **Step 1.** Choose starting values for α_{0i} and α_{1i}.
- **Step 2.** Compute the values of r_{it} and N_t from Equations (4.3) and (4.4).
- **Step 3.** Obtain improved estimates of the parameters by solving $\frac{\partial L}{\partial \alpha_{ji}} = 0$ for $j = 0, 1$ and $i = 1, 2, ..., p$ treating r_{it} and N_{it} as given numbers.
- **Step 4.** Return to step 2 and continue until convergence is attained.

4.3 Semiparametric ML Estimation

If the latent trait model is estimated semiparametrically, then the prior is estimated together with the item parameters. It is *semiparametric*, rather than *nonparametric*, because a parametric form is still assumed for the response function, though one could say that the prior is estimated nonparametrically. Bock and Aitkin's (1981) method in which the nodes are defined on a grid where the bulk of the distribution is expected to lie and only the weights are estimated from the data is described first. This method is later extended to the *fully* semiparametric method where both the nodes and the weights are estimated from the data.

Estimating the weights involves a small modification on the EM algorithm given previously. At the end of each Maximisation step, the posterior weights $h^*(z_t)$ are computed as follows:

$$h^*(z_t) = \sum_{l=1}^{n} h(z_t \mid \mathbf{x}_l)/n \qquad (4.5)$$

Then Equations (4.3) and (4.4) are calculated with $h^*(z_t)$ in place of $h(z_t)$. The nodes z and the posterior weights $h^*(z_t)$ obtained at the last iteration are taken as the estimates of the approximation - or support - points of the empirical prior distribution. Since the parameters are confounded with the location and scale of the prior distribution, the nodes of the prior at each iteration are standardized so that the mean of the prior is 0 and its variance 1. The mean and the variance are computed from the estimated nodes and weights with $\mu = \sum_{t=1}^{k} z_t h^*(z_t)$ and $\sigma^2 = \sum_{t=1}^{k} (z_t - \mu)^2 h^*(z_t)$.

4.3.1   Results from semiparametric estimation

The data used to illustrate the results are the NFER test 1 for primary school boys (Gorman, White, Orchard, & Tate, 1981), the intercultural scale 9, both for the American and the German samples (Krebs & Schuessler, 1987), and some artificial data generated from the mixture 0.5 N(0,1) + 0.5 N(3,1). NFER test 1 is comprised of 21 items and the sample size of the boys data is 566. Scale 9 consists of 12 items that have to do with 'Future Outlook'. The sample sizes are 1416 and 1490 for the American and German samples respectively. The artificial data (referred to as 'n30') also have 12 items and a sample size of 1490.

Different sets of starting points were tried varying in number from 2 to 16, equally and differently spaced, and with equal and unequal probabilities. In all cases, the points were standardised so that their mean was 0 and their variance 1. The set of 16 points resulted in 9 points with weight greater than 0.005, and the sets of 10 and 8 points resulted in 7 points with weight greater than 0.005 (see Figure 4.1), so it seems that not so many points - far fewer than the number of items - are needed for the estimated prior. It should also be noted that all sets of equidistant points, whatever the initial weights on the points, gave the same final points and weights. However, when the points were not equidistant, different results were obtained. For example, Figure 4.2 shows the resulting distributions of two sets of four starting points, -3, -1, 1, 3 and -3, 0, 1, 3 and two sets of three starting points, -1, 0, 1 and -1, 1, 2, fitted to American scale 9. It can be seen that these are quite different. For the four point priors, we see that the prior from the second set -3, 0, 1, 3 is a two modal distribution, because the two middle points are too close together and one had to carry a low probability. Of course it is hard to compare one set of points with another and judge how much the distributions really differ.

The parameter estimates obtained from priors with different number of support points do not differ a lot. The difficulty parameter estimates are almost indistinguishable and only a small effect is noticeable on the discrimination parameter estimates, namely that they generally get smaller as the number of support point decreases (see Figure 4.3) (This is intuitive, in the sense that if it is assumed that the prior is defined by a small number of points, say three, then the model will be discriminating individuals between the three points/groups only and so the discrimination parameters will be adjusted/estimated accordingly.)

4.4   Fully Semiparametric ML Estimation

Section 4.2 gave the E-M algorithm used to estimate the unknown parameters when the prior has a known parametric form. Now, in order to estimate the zs, the estimation is broken into two parts, that is there are two E- and M-steps: the first E- and M-steps relate to the estimation of the item parameters, whereas the second E- and M-steps relate to the estimation of the latent

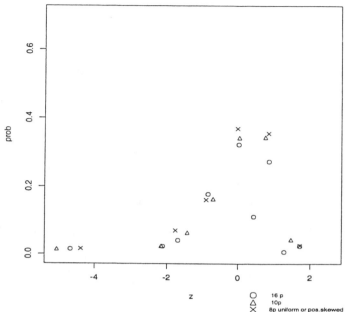

Fig. 4.1. Boys, test 1, support points and weights for empirical priors obtained from different sets of starting points.

nodes. To update the nodes each node is moved by a proportion of the one-dimensional derivatives of the loglikelihood w.r.t. the relevant node. As in Section 4.3, the prior is standardised after each M-step, and then adjust the parameters accordingly, so that the indeterminacy of the location and scale of the prior is avoided.

In order to avoid maximisation under restrictions, the loglikelihood calculated with the standardised $\tilde{z}$s w.r.t. the unstandardised zs is differentiated and update the $\tilde{z}$s with these quantities. Then the loglikelihood will again be calculated with the standardised $\tilde{z}$s and standardised αs, since the likelihoods under standardised prior and parameters and unstandardised prior and parameters are equivalent. In the following, the weight of node z_t is denoted by $h(z_t)$, and the mean and standard deviation of the prior by $\bar{z}$ and σ_z. By differentiating the log-likelihood with respect to the unknown zs gives:

$$\frac{\partial L}{\partial z_t} = \sum_{h=1}^{n} \frac{\partial \ln f(\mathbf{x}_h)}{\partial z_t}$$

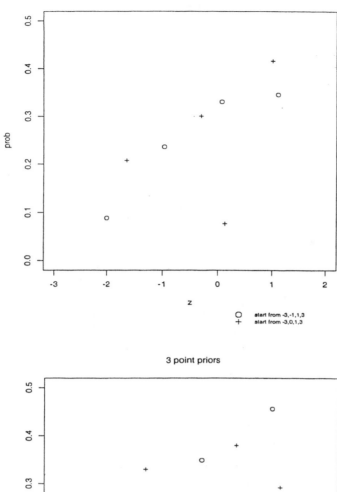

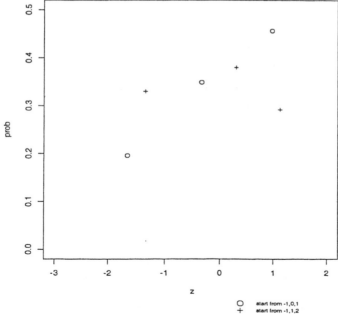

Fig. 4.2. American scale 9, support points and weights for empirical priors obtained from different sets of starting points (equidistant and not-equidistant points).

$$= \sum_{h=1}^{n} \sum_{v=1}^{k} \sum_{j=1}^{k} \frac{\partial g(\mathbf{x}_h | \tilde{z}_j) h(\tilde{z}_j)}{\partial \tilde{z}_v} \frac{1}{f(\mathbf{x}_h)} \frac{\partial \tilde{z}_v}{\partial z_t}$$

which becomes (see Appendix)

$$\frac{\partial L}{\partial z_t} = \sum_{v=1}^{k} \sum_{i=1}^{p} \alpha_{1i}(r_{iv} - \pi_i(\tilde{z}_v)N_v)(-h(z_t) + z_v d_t)$$

$$+ \sum_{i=1}^{p} \alpha_{1i}(r_{it} - \pi_i(z_t)N_t)$$

where

$$r_{iv} = \sum_{h=1}^{n} x_{ih} h(\tilde{z}_v \mid \mathbf{x}_h) \qquad (4.6)$$

$$N_v = \sum_{h=1}^{n} h(\tilde{z}_v \mid \mathbf{x}_h) \qquad (4.7)$$

and $d_t = \partial \tilde{z}_v / \partial z_t$. The weights are calculated by

$$h(z_t) = \sum_{h=1}^{n} h(z_t | \mathbf{x}_h)/n \qquad (4.8)$$

The steps of an EM algorithm are defined as follows:

- **step1:** Choose starting values for α_{i0} and α_{i1}, the initial points $\tilde{z}_t$ and the probabilities $h(\tilde{z}_t)$ of the standardised prior
- **step 2: E-step 1.** Compute the values of r_{it} and N_t from Equations (4.6) and (4.7)
- **step 3: M-step 1.** Obtain improved estimates of the parameters by solving Equation (4.2), where z_t is replaced by $\tilde{z}_t$.
- **step 4: E-step 2.** Compute the values of r_{iv} and N_v from Equations (4.6) and (4.7)
- **step 5: M-step 2** Obtain improved estimates of the points z_t by solving Equation (4.6), and calculate probabilities from Equation (4.8). Standardise the points so that the mean of the prior equals 0 and its standard deviation equals 1 to get new $\tilde{z}_t$. Ascribe $h(z_t)$ to be $h(\tilde{z}_t)$. Calculate the likelihood and check convergence. Return to step 2 and continue until convergence is attained.

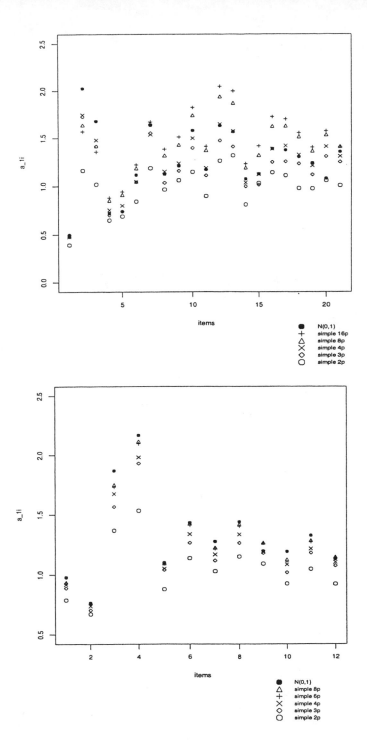

Fig. 4.3. Discrimination parameter estimates (a_{1i}) obtained from different sets of starting points for the Boys, test 1 data (top) and the American scale 9 (bottom)

4.4.1   Results

Table 4.1 shows the estimated approximation points and weights for the American scale 9. The scale consists of 12 items. It is interesting to see how many nodes are needed or can be estimated from this number of items. Starting with 10, 8, 6 and 5 points, all sets gave 5 points with non-zero weight. The 5 point solution from the 5 starting points was the same as the 5 point solution from 6 points, which indicates that there is a unique 5 point approximation for the latent distribution.

Table 4.1. American scale 9: Estimated prior

z_t	-2.287	-0.937	0.042	0.842	2.184
$h(z_t)$	0.063	0.273	0.264	0.364	0.037

Table 4.2. German scale 9: Estimated prior

z_t	-2.149	-0.698	0.287	1.171	2.300
$h(z_t)$	0.094	0.277	0.424	0.175	0.030

Table 4.3. Boys test 1: Estimated prior

z_t	-5.194	-1.779	-0.770	0.056	0.737	1.447
$h(z_t)$	0.015	0.062	0.186	0.359	0.329	0.049

A 4 point prior was also fitted, starting from two different sets of points, one with equidistant and one with non-equidistant points (as in Section 4.4). Both sets gave the same final solution, indicating again that there is a unique 4 point solution. The semiparametric estimation had produced different results for the two different starting values, which is anticipated since the points were fixed and their number too small for the weights to adjust between them.

The same procedure was repeated for German scale 9 and the Boys, test 1 data. The German scale 9 also gave 5 distinct points for the prior (see Table 4.2) and the Boys, test 1, which consists of 21 items, gave 6 distinct points for the prior, a lot fewer than the number of items (see Table 4.3).

So how do the points obtained from fully semiparametric estimation compare with the ones obtained from simple semiparametric estimation? In Figure 4.4 the points and weights obtained from a simple 6 point semiparametric solution and a 5 point fully semiparametric solution for the American and German scale 9 can be seen (no comparision is made with the 5 point simple semiparametric solution because one of the points came out with zero weight. Starting with five points symmetric to zero, the resulting points were: -2.01,-0.97,-0.45,-0.10 and 1.11, with -0.45 carrying zero weight). Since the fully semiparametric prior is more flexible to adjust, it is more economical with the points.

4.4.2 Relationship between number of items to number of approximation points

The previous section illustrated results that established the maximum number of points needed for the prior of the Rasch model. Sets of items were constructed by reducing the number of items sequentially for three datasets, and estimated the prior with different number of points, until all distinct points had non-zero weight. The results for the German scale 9, the mixture of normals and the Boys test 1 data appear in Tables 4.4, 4.5 and 4.6 respectively. Both German scale 9 and the mixture 'n30' have 12 items and 1490 responses. Boys test 1 has 21 items and 566 responses. For the first two datasets the results are the same except for the 6 item solution. The number of points with non-zero weight are in most cases fewer than the maximum number of points suggested for the Rasch model. The only case that exceeds the number of points expected is the case of the first 3 items of German scale 9, where 3 points came out with non-zero weight. For the Boys test 1 data fewer points are being estimated for the prior, which is probably due to the small number of responses. It seems that the number of support points depends both on the number of items and the sample size, though more theoretical work is needed in order to define an exact mathematical relationship, if such exists, as it does for the Rasch model.

Table 4.4. Sets of items of German scale 9: Number of points of prior

no of items	12	11	10	9	8	7	6	5	4	3
no of points needed	5	5	4	5	4	4	3	3	3	3
$p/2$ for p even, $(p+1)/2$ for p odd	6	6	5	5	4	4	3	3	2	2

Table 4.5. Sets of items of 'Mixture of Normals': Number of points of prior

no of items	12	11	10	9	8	7	6	5	4
no of points needed	5	5	4	5	4	4	4	3	3
$p/2$ for p even, $(p+1)/2$ for p odd	6	6	5	5	4	4	3	3	2

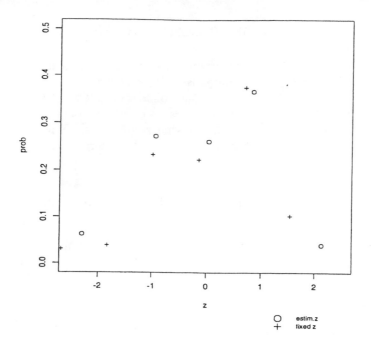

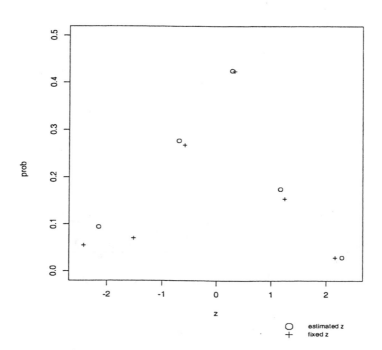

Fig. 4.4. Points and weights of 5 point fully semiparametric prior and 6 point semiparametric prior, American scale 9, left, and German scale 9, right.

Table 4.6. Sets of items of Boys test 1: Number of points of prior

no of items	21	15	12	8
no of points needed	6	5	4	3
$p/2$ for p even, $(p+1)/2$ for p odd	11	8	6	4

4.5   Optimality Criteria

Lindsay, (1983) gave the conditions for the estimated mixing distribution to be optimal, which are based on the directional derivative of the loglikelihood towards a support point of the mixing distribution. This is defined for the proposed model as follows:

$$D(z, f, g) = \sum_{l}^{N} \frac{g(x_l|z)}{f(x_l)} - 1$$

where x_l is a response pattern and N the number of observed response patterns. For fixed item parameter estimates, $D(z, \hat{f}, \hat{g})$ should be equal to zero at each estimated support point z. Moreover $\sup_z D(z, \hat{f}, \hat{g}) = 0$, if $\hat{f}$, $\hat{g}$ are from an optimal prior.

4.5.1   Results

Boys, test 1. After successively fitting the model with different numbers of points, 6 distinct points were obtained with non-zero weight for the prior. (The solutions with more than 6 support points either had two or more points coinciding or one or more points had zero weight). Figure 4.5 shows a plot of Lindsay's D against a possible range of the latent variable. It can be seen that the estimated points fall on the peaks of the D curve, these are at 0, and the D curve does not cross the zero line. This shows that the solution for the prior is optimal.

German scale 9, 12 items. The estimated prior has five support points. Figure 4.6, left, shows Lindsay's D curve and the support points. All five points fall exactly on the peaks of the curve, which are at zero, and again the D curve does not go above the zero line. So this solution seems to be the optimal one.

Now to see what happens if a 4 point prior is fit. The D curve, Figure 4.6 right, shows clearly that this is not optimal. There are peaks around the support points going above zero, indicating that an extra point is needed to bring them down. For the sets consisting of 4 to 11 items the prior came out with 3 to 5 approximation points, the number being equal or smaller than

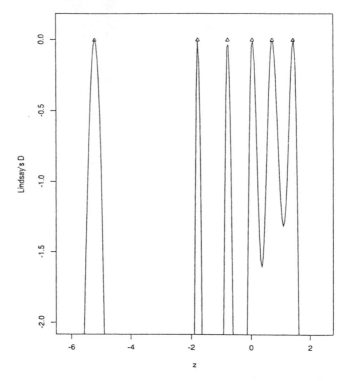

Fig. 4.5. Boys, test 1, Lindsay's D for the 6 point prior.

the maximum number of approximation points needed for the Rasch model. For the 3 item set though, 3 distinct points were obtained. Function D is plotted in Figure 4.7 for the 3 and 2 point priors. In the 3 point solution, the line is flat and goes along 0 after about $z=-0.2$, so both the second and third points have $D=0$. With the 2 point prior D also remains at zero (above -0.2 approximately) so also this solution is optimal. In this case the number of points cannot be determined uniquely.

4.6   Scoring of the Latent Variable

The primary aim of fitting a latent trait model is often to score individuals along the latent variable scale. Knott and Albanese (1993) suggested the use of the posterior means for this purpose. The posterior mean for the individual l with response pattern x_l is defined as follows:

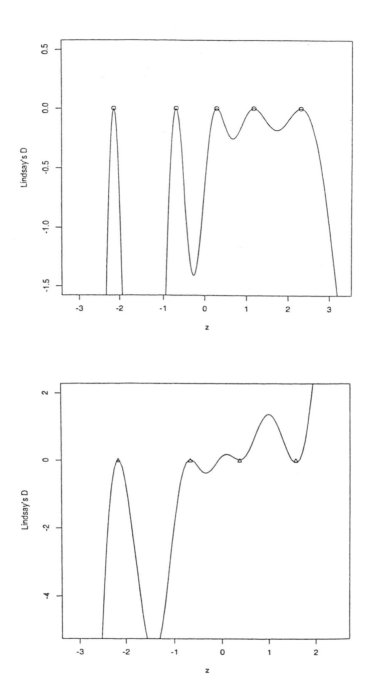

Fig. 4.6. German scale 9, Lindsay's D for the 5 and 4 point fully-semiparametric prior.

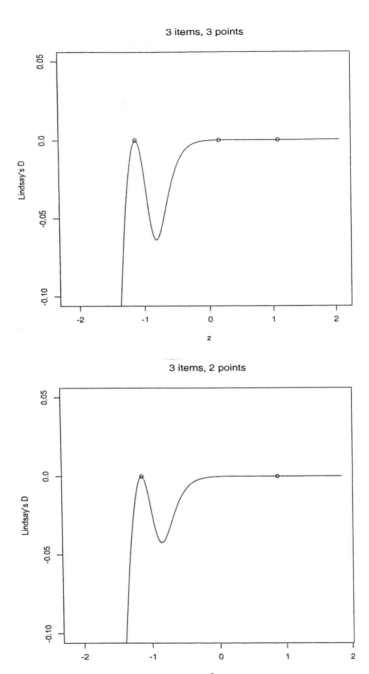

Fig. 4.7. German scale 9, first 3 items, Lindsay's D for the 3 and 2 point fully-semiparametric prior.

$$E(z|x_l) = \sum_{t=1}^{k} z_t h(z_t|x_l) = \sum_{t=1}^{k} z_t g(x_l|z_t)h(z_t)/f(x_l).$$

From the formula it can be seen that the posterior means depend on the prior distribution. The following compares the posterior means obtained with parametric and semiparametric estimation.

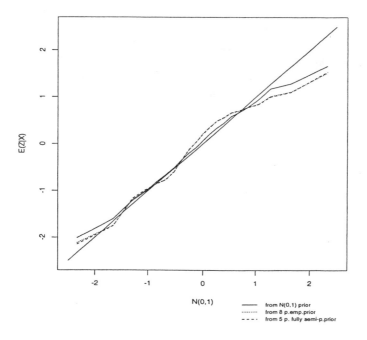

Fig. 4.8. American scale 9, QQ plots of E(Z|X) from N(0,1), semiparametric and fully semiparametric estimation.

Figure 4.8 shows a Quantile - Quantile (QQ) plot of the posterior means obtained from a N(0,1) prior, from an 8 point empirical (simple semiparametric) prior and from the 5 point optimal fully-semiparametric prior against the N(0,1), for the American scale 9. Posterior means obtained from the 5 point fully semiparametric estimation are identical to the posterior means obtained from the 8 point simple semiparametric estimation (the two lines coincide). So, simple and fully semiparametric estimation methods can provide the same results, but with the simple semiparametric estimation more points are needed so that the weights can adjust optimally along these points.

The distribution of the posterior means obtained with a N(0,1) is closer to the N(0,1) than the distribution of the posterior means when the model is fitted semiparametrically, so it seems that the shape of the prior influences the shape of the distribution of the posterior means. Using a semiparametric prior may allow the shape of the 'true' data generating distribution to come through the distribution of the posterior means and thus allow comparisons between the shapes of distributions of different populations that have taken the same tests. Figure 4.9 gives the ogives of the posterior means for American and German scale 9, obtained with the N(0,1) prior (left panel) and the 5 point fully semiparametric prior (right panel), both plotted against the N(0,1) percentiles. Since, the ogives coming from a N(0,1) prior are closer to the N(0,1) and thus 'artificially' closer together, using a fully semiparametric prior is perhaps much more informative.

Appendix

$$\frac{\partial L}{\partial z_t} = \sum_{h=1}^{n} \frac{\partial \ln f(\mathbf{x}_h)}{\partial z_t}$$

$$= \sum_{h=1}^{n} \sum_{v=1}^{k} \sum_{j=1}^{k} \frac{\partial g(\mathbf{x}_h|\tilde{z}_j)h(\tilde{z}_j)}{\partial \tilde{z}_v} \frac{1}{f(\mathbf{x}_h)} \frac{\partial \tilde{z}_v}{\partial z_t}$$

Now,

$$\frac{\partial \pi_i(\tilde{z}_v)}{\partial \tilde{z}_v} = \alpha_{1i}\pi_i(\tilde{z}_v)(1 - \pi_i(\tilde{z}_v))$$

so

$$\sum_{j=1}^{k} \frac{\partial g(\mathbf{x}_h|\tilde{z}_j)}{\partial \tilde{z}_v} = \frac{\partial \ln g(\mathbf{x}_h|\tilde{z}_v)}{\partial \tilde{z}_v} g(\mathbf{x}_h|\tilde{z}_v)$$

$$= \sum_{i=1}^{p} (x_{ih} - \pi_i(\tilde{z}_v))\alpha_{1i}g(\mathbf{x}_h|\tilde{z}_v).$$

Also

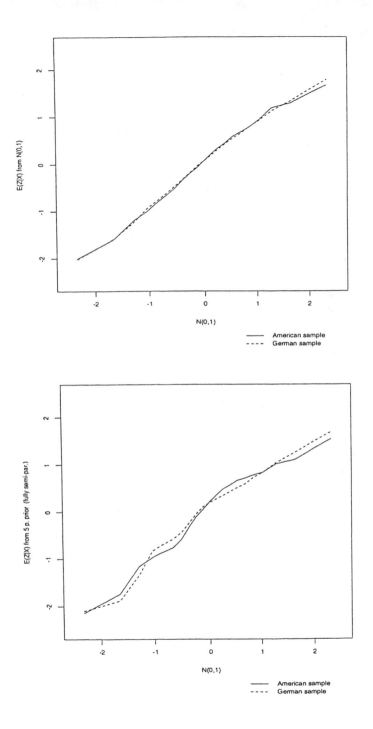

Fig. 4.9. American and German scale 9, QQ plots of posterior means with N(0,1) prior and 5 point nonparametric prior.

$$\frac{\partial \tilde{z}_v}{\partial z_t} = \frac{\partial((z_v - \bar{z})/\sigma_z)}{\partial z_t}$$

$$= \frac{(\partial(z_v - \bar{z})/\partial z_t)\sigma_z - (z_v - \bar{z})(\partial \sigma_z/\partial z_t)}{\sigma_z^2}.$$

Using

$$d_t = \partial \sigma_z/\partial z_t$$

$$= -\sum_{j=1}^{k} h(\tilde{z}_j)h(\tilde{z}_t)z_j + h(\tilde{z}_t)z_t$$

and evaluating the derivative at $\bar{z} = 0$ and $\sigma_z = 1$ if $v \neq t$ gives

$$\frac{\partial \tilde{z}_v}{\partial z_t} = -\partial \bar{z}/\partial z_t - z_v \partial \sigma_z/\partial z_t$$

$$= -h(z_t) - z_v d_t$$

and if $v = t$

$$\frac{\partial \tilde{z}_v}{\partial z_t} = 1 - \partial \bar{z}/\partial z_t - z_t \partial \sigma_z/\partial z_t$$

$$= 1 - h(z_t) - z_t d_t$$

So, the above becomes

$$\frac{\partial L}{\partial z_t} = \sum_{h=1}^{n}\sum_{v=1}^{k}\sum_{i=1}^{p}(x_{ih} - \pi_i(\tilde{z}_v))\alpha_{1i}g(\mathbf{x}_h|\tilde{z}_v)h(\tilde{z}_v)\frac{1}{f(\mathbf{x}_h)}\frac{\partial \tilde{z}_v}{\partial z_t}$$

$$= \sum_{v=1}^{k}\sum_{i=1}^{p}\alpha_{1i}(r_{iv} - \pi_i(\tilde{z}_v)N_v)(-h(\tilde{z}_t) + z_v d_t)$$

$$+ \sum_{i=1}^{p}\alpha_{1i}(r_{it} - \pi_i(z_t)N_t)$$

where

$$r_{iv} = \sum_{h=1}^{n} x_{ih}h(\tilde{z}_v \mid \mathbf{x}_h)$$

$$N_v = \sum_{h=1}^{n} h(\tilde{z}_v \mid \mathbf{x}_h)$$

and $d_t = \partial \sigma_z/\partial z_t$.

References

Aitkin, M. (1996). A general maximum likelihood analysis of overdispersion in generalized linear models. *Statistics and Computing*, 6, 251-262.

Bartholomew, D. J. (1987). *Latent variable models and factor analysis*. London, England: Charles Griffin & Company Ltd.

Bartholomew, D. J. (1988). The sensitivity of latent trait analysis to choice of prioir distribution. *British Journal of Mathematical and Statistical Psychology*, 41, 101-107.

Bartholomew, D.J. & Knott, M. (1999). *Latent variable models and factor analysis* (2nd ed.). London: Arnold.

Brinbaum, A. (1968). *Some latent trait models and their use in inferring an examinee's ability*. Reading, MA: Addison-Wesley.

Bock, R. & Aitkin, M. (1981). Marginal maximum likelihood estimation of item parameters: Application of an EM algorithm. *Psychometrika*, 46, 443-459.

Boehning, D. (1995). A review of reliable maximum likelihood algorithms for semiparametric mixture models. *Journal of Statistical Planning and Inference*, 47, 5-28.

Boehning, D. (1999). *Computer-assisted analysis of mixture and applications, meta-analysis, disease mapping and others*. Vol. 81 of *Monographs on Statistics and Applied Probability*. London: Chapman & Hall.

Cressie, N. & Holland, P. W. (1983). Characterizing the manifest probabilities of latent trait models. *Psychometrika*, 48, 129-141.

De Leuuw, J. & Verhelst, N. (1996). Maximum likelihood estimation in generalized Rasch models. *Journal of Educational Statistics*, 11, 183-196.

Follmann, D. (1988). Consistent estimation in the Rasch model based on nonparametric margins. *Psychometrika*, 53, 553-562.

Gorman, T., White, J., Orchard, L. & Tate, A. (1981). *Language proficience in schools, primary survey report no. 1*. Technical Report, Assessment of Permance Unit, Department of Education and Science.

Heinen, T. 91996). *Latent class and discrete latent trait models: Similarities and differences*. London: Sage Publications.

Kiefer, J. & Wolfowitz, J. (1956). Consistency of the maximum likelihood estimator in the presence of infinitely many incidental parameters. *Annals of Mathematical Statistics*, 27, 887-906.

Knott, M. & Albanese, M. T. (1993). Conditional distributions of a latent variable and scoring for binary data. *Revista Brasileira de Probabilidade e Estatistica*, 6, 171-188.

Krebs, D. & Schuessler, K. F. (1987). *Soziale empfindungen: Ein interkultureller skalenvergleich bei Deutschen und Amerikanern*. Monographien: Sozialwissenschaftliche Methoden. Franfurt/Main, New York: Campus Verlag.

Laird, N. (1978). Nonparametric maximum likelihood estimation of a mixing distribution. *Journal of the American Statistical Association*, 73, 805-811.

Lindsay, B. G. (1983). The geometry of mixture likelihoods: A general theory. *The Annals of Statistics*, 11, 86-94.

Lindsay, B. G., Clogg, C. C, & Grego, J. (1991). Semiparametric estimation in the Rasch model and related exponetial response models, including a simple latent class model for item analysis. *Journal of the American Statistical Association*, 86, 96-107.

Lindsay, B. G. & Lesperance, M. (1995). A review of semiparametric mixture models. *Journal of Statistical Planning and Inference*, 47, 29-39.

Straud, A. & Sechrest, D. (1966). *Gaussian quadrature formulas.* New York: Prentice-Hall.

Vermunt, J. K. (1997). *LEM: A general program for the analysis of categorical data.* Computer Manual. Tilburg University.

5 Analysing Group Differences: A Comparison of SEM Approaches [*]

Pilar Rivera[1] and Albert Satorra[2]

[1] Universidad de Zaragoza, Spain
[2] Universitat Pompeu Fabra. Barcelona, Spain

5.1 Introduction

Structural equation models (SEM) are widely used in empirical research to investigate interrelationships among variables, some of which may be latent (e.g., Bollen, 1989; Bollen & Long, 1993; von Eye & Clogg (1994); Schumacker & Marcoulides, 1998; Steiger, 2001). Generally, the methods are used to study structural relations among latent variables that are related to observable variables through a measurement error model. One example of such SEM use is in behavioral research, when studying the relationship between "attitude" and "behavior" concerning specific issues (e.g., Fishbein & Ajzen, 1975; Ajzen & Fishbein, 1982; Pieters, 1988). Such a relationship is of particular relevance to social environmental studies, where a change in "attitude" (e.g., via education) may produce a change in "behavior", and thus induce a change on individual participation in environmental protection issues.

This chapter involves the use of empirical data from various countries on variables of "attitude" and "behavior" toward environment issues. The focus is on the between-country variation of the relationships among the attitude and behavior variables. The peculiarities of the data permit the use of alternative approaches to SEM analysis with large number of groups, a large sample size in each group and non-normality in manifest variables. The data are extracted from the *International Social Survey Programme -1993* (ISSP-1993 data), involving 22 countries. Thus, a major aim of this chapter is to see how alternative approaches to SEM analysis compare in the presence of non-normality across a reasonable number of countries, each of which has a large sample size. Given the particular type of data and model, a comparison between the multiple-group and the single-group MIMIC approach

[*] This work was carried out at the ZA-EUROLAB at the Zentralarchive für Empirische Sozialforschung (ZA), Cologne. The ZA is a Large Scale Facility (LSF) funded by the Training and Mobility of Researchers (TMR) program of the European Union. The data utilized in this publication were documented and made available by ZA. The data for "ISSP" were collected by independent institutions in each country. Neither the original collectors nor ZA bear any responsibility for the analysis or interpretation presented here. We thank Nick Longford for his detail comments on an earlier version of the paper, the editors and reviewers for very helpful suggestions. Support from Spanish grants DGES PB96-0300, PB97-1009 and BEC2000-0983 is also acknowledged.

is also possible. Finally, a substantive aim of the chapter is to explore the variation across countries in terms of attitude and behavior variables toward Environment[1].

The chapter is organized in several sections. The next section describes alternative approaches and estimation methods available. In addition, the section includes a review of asymptotic robustness of normal theory methods that might be relevant to the questions posed. Section 3 presents the data analyzed. Section 4 reviews the family of models considered. Section 5 describes the main results of the empirical analysis, and Section 6 provides the concluding discussion.

5.2   Statistical Issues with Non-Normal Data

The most standard approach for SEM analysis with continuous variables - and possibly multiple group data - is normal theory maximum likelihood (ML), or the equivalent generalized least-squares (GLS) method based on normal theory. Normal theory (NT) methods have been available for many years in standard computer software for SEM analysis (e.g., LISREL - Jöreskog & Sörbom, 1996; EQS - Bentler, 1995). For early work on SEM analysis with multiple group data and normal theory, see Jöreskog (1971) and Sörbom (1974). For non-normally distributed data, however, an asymptotic distribution-free (ADF) approach has been proposed (Browne, 1984). Nowadays, the ADF approach is available in LISREL and EQS, even for the case of multiple group data. Even though the ADF approach ensures asymptotic efficiency, regardless of the distribution of the data, it has been reported to lack robustness in small data sets. Furthermore, in the case of large models and a sample that is not very large, computational burden and non-convergence and/or improper solutions can occur when using ADF. For small samples, the ADF estimators are biased, as are the estimators of their standard errors (for recent studies that evaluate alternative methods of estimating and testing in SEM under various distribution conditions - except from continuous data - see Kaplan, 1991; Finch, West & MacKinnon, 1997; Green, Akey, Fleming, Hershberger & Marquis, 1997).

An alternative to the ADF approach is pseudo-maximum likelihood (PML) analysis, which is based on the use of the NT maximum likelihood (or GLS) estimation in conjunction with robust standard errors (se) and robust and scaled chi-square test statistics (e.g., Satorra, 1992). In contrast to the ADF approach in which fourth order sample moments are used in computing both parameter estimates, standard errors, and test statistics, in the PML approach the fourth order sample moments are used only for computing standard errors and test statistics (parameter estimates are the same as in ML

---

[1] For full reference on this data, see *Machine Readable Codebook* , *ZA Study 2450, ISSP 1993, Environment*(2nd. Edit.), ZA, Cologne, ZA, 1995.

or GLS). For small samples, PML can be more adequate than the ADF approach, without incurring substantial loss of efficiency. In combination with PML analysis, an alternative to the robust chi-square goodness-of-fit test is the scaled chi-square goodness test (Satorra & Bentler, 1994, 1999).

An additional argument in support of the use of ML or GLS, rather than ADF, is provided by recent results regarding the asymptotic robustness (AR) of normal theory methods. Results for AR guarantee that, under certain conditions, normal theory produces correct inferences even when the normality assumption does not hold (e.g., Satorra, 1993). The conditions for asymptotic robustness are: (i) a model condition (MC), by which no restrictions are imposed on the variances and covariances of the non-normal constituents of the model, and (ii) a distribution condition (DC), of mutual independence among random constituents of the model, such as common and unique factors (condition that replaces the usual assumption of no correlation).

The key result of asymptotic robustness is when both (i) and (ii) hold. In such a case, the NT standard errors (i.e., those of the standard ML or GLS analyses) of estimates of the parameters that are neither variances nor covariances of non-normal constituents of the model (e.g., loadings and regression coefficients) are correct, asymptotically. In addition, under conditions (i) and (ii), the NT chi-square goodness-of-fit tests (i.e., the standard log-likelihood-ratio test statistic) are also appropriate. When AR holds, the robust statistics associated with PML are not required, as they coincide (asymptotically) with those based on normal theory. The asymptotic robustness theory is particular relevant here, since most of the models considered below satisfy the mentioned MC, while DC is plausible (on theoretical grounds) for many of the models.

To this point, the discussion of SEM analysis has been entirely concerned with continuous (CO) variables. SEM analysis, however, is often conducted with categorical variables, defined as ordinal scales (e.g., the Likert scale). Methods that take into account the ordinal (OR) nature of the variables are also nowadays available in standard software for SEM (e.g., LISREL - Jöreskog & Sörbom, 1996; EQS - Bentler, 1995; Mplus - Muthén & Muthén, 1998). Seminal studies for the analysis of SEM with categorical variables include those by Muthén (1984), Christoffersson (1975) and Olsson (1979). This chapter also compares continuous (CO) versus ordinal (OR) methods of analysis, in the context of the ISSP-1993 data set. A basic issue is whether 4- or 5-point Likert-scale variables can be treated as CO variables without substantial distortion of the SEM analysis (for a Monte Carlo evaluation of alternative approaches to SEM with ordinal data, see Coenders, Saris & Satorra, 1997).

When the method recognizes the ordinal nature of the variables, the Pearson correlation matrix can be replaced by the polychoric correlation matrix. Associated with this polychoric correlation matrix, there is a specific matrix of asymptotic covariances. The approach whereby the ML fitting function is used with the polychoric correlation matrix replacing the covariance matrix is examined. The standard errors and test statistics can then be computed by the robust analysis associated with the consistent estimate of the variance matrix of the polychoric covariances. This analysis is carried out by combining PRELIS (to compute the polychoric matrix and asymptotic covariances) and LISREL (to obtain estimates and test statistics), and is called the OR-PML, since it parallels the approach of PML analysis in the case of continuous data. In fact, it uses the same formulae, with appropriate substitution of the covariance matrix and the matrix of asymptotic covariances of the continuous case to those corresponding to the ordinal case[2].

A special feature of the empirical analysis discussed in Section 5 is the large sample size. In large samples, models are usually rejected by the chi-square goodness-of-fit test. The classic argument is that since the chi-square goodness of fit uses the sample size as a multiplying factor, any small (or substantively irrelevant) specification errors will be magnified by the large value of sample size, with the result of a significant chi-square goodness-of-fit test. It has even been argued that for a very large sample size, the chi-square goodness-of-fit test should be abandoned in favor of goodness-of-fit indices. However, it was found that, despite a large sample size, and the fact that in practice models are only approximate, the classic chi-square goodness-of-fit test statistic plays a crucial role in model assessment, especially where typical indexes for goodness of fit were generally found to be insensitive to substantial misfits in the model (for a discussion of this issue and its relation to the power of the chi-square goodness-of-fit test, see Saris, den Ronden & Satorra, 1987).

5.3   Data Used in the Empirical Analysis

The data used in the empirical analysis were extracted from the ISSP-1993 Environment file[3]. It includes variables V1 (environmental conservation), V2 (willingness to sacrifice time) and V3 (prices and resources), which are all indicators of attitude toward environmental issues, and V4 (actual participation in recycling), which is the sole indicator of behavior. Variables V1 - V3 are measured using a 5-point Likert scale, and V4 a 4-point Likert scale. Appendix 1 provides the wording used in the ISSP-1993 survey for these variables, as well as the names of the countries involved, with the sample size of each country in brackets.

The data analyzed resulted from listwise deletion in variables V1-V4. The extent of missing data varies from 61% in Russia to 3% in the Philippines. Overall, 25% of the data items were missing, most of them for variable V4,

---

[2] For comparison, Table 3 shows the chi-square goodness-of-fit test provided by the WLS of LISREL with categorical data.

[3] The data are available from the Zentral Archive at the University of Cologne, Bachemer Str. 40, D-50931 Köln, Germany.

especially in countries where no recycling is available. The five highest values - Russia (61%), Poland (54%), Bulgaria (52%), Czech Republic (51 %) and Slovenia (43 %) – were recorded in countries with a lot of missing data on variable V4 as a result of the response category "recycling not available" (see Q. 19a in Appendix 1). In fact, if all 22 countries are considered, 75% of missing data were due to V4. The approach used in this empirical analysis was to ignore the missingness mechanism and to treat the available data as if they were complete[4].

Inspection of the marginal distributions of variables V1 to V4, overall and across countries, showed that, even though there was a clear non-normality (the variables are on Likert scale), no extreme skewness or ceiling effects were encountered. The variables V1-V4 are ordinal, with four or five categories, so it is tempting to treat them as continuous variables. Thus, the question of the comparison of continuous versus ordinal types of analysis arises. In the case of continuous variable methods, the asymptotic robust theory raises the additional question of whether NT methods give correct results despite the clear non-normality of the data.

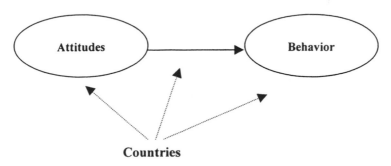

Fig. 5.1. Chapter aims

5.4   Models

The aim of this chapter was to assess country effect to both (a) (mean) level of "attitude" and "behavior", and (b) effect of "attitude" on "behavior". This is depicted in Figure 5.1, where ellipses are used for the theoretical variables, and the effects that "country" has on the levels of the two theoretical variables, as well as on the magnitude of the effect of attitude on behavior are represented by arrows.

---

[4] The robustness of results to this specific missing data problem await further study.

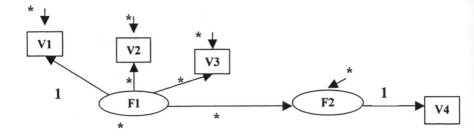

Fig. 5.2. Basic model

The basic structure underlying all the models considered is displayed in Figure 5.2. It comprises a regression in which factors F1 (Attitudes) and F2 (Behavior) are respectively the explanatory and dependent variables. There are also measurement equations, where variables V1-V3 are indicators of F1, while V4 is a single indicator for F2. Table 5.1 and Table 5.2 show the measurement and structural equations in a format that is more suitable for interaction with typical software for SEM analysis. It is important to note that the asterisks in these tables parallel those in Figure 5.2 and represent the model's free parameters. When covariances alone were analyzed, zeros were put in the columns of the variable intercept (INT).

Table 5.1. Measurement equations

Variable	INT	$F1 : Attitude$	$F2 : Behaviour$	Ei
V1 Pay higher Price	0	1	0	*
V2 Pay higher Taxes	0	*	0	*
V3 Cut living standards	0	*	0	*
V4 Behavior	0	0	1	0

Note. Asterisks denote free parameters to be estimated.

The above two-factor model is actually a single-factor model with four indicators, where the loading of variable V4 corresponds to the regression coefficient in Figure 5.2. The single-factor model is depicted in Figure 5.3 and is used for model formulation, with the understanding that loadings include the regression coefficient. To ensure identification of the factor scale, the loading of variable V1 is set equal to 1[5]. In order to characterize the

---

[5] This single-factor model is equivalent to a regression with errors in variables, where V1-V3 are indicators of the regressor and V4 is the response variable.

Table 5.2. Structural equations

Variable	INT	$F1 : Attitude$	D_i
F1: Attitude	0	*	0
F2: Behavior	0	*	*

Note. Asterisks denote free parameters to be estimated.

variation across countries of the mean of factor and/or manifest variables, the means of manifest variables in the analysis must be included. The models considered are listed in Table 5.3 and discussed next.

Table 5.3. Models considered in the study

Across group constraints	Group Design			
	Multiple Group		Single Group	
	Cov.	Mean-Cov	MIMIC	1-Factor model
Loadings & Variances	MG0	MMG0	MIMIC-A	SG-A
			MIMIC-B	
			MIMIC-C	SG-C
Loadings	MG1	MMG1		
Selected set of Loadings	MG12	MMG12		
		MMG12-Cb		
		MMG12-C		
No constraints	MG2			
	MG2-Cb			
	MG2-C			

5.4.1   Multiple group models

Various multiple group models are defined by imposing or releasing restrictions on the means of manifest and latent variables, and on the degree of invariance across groups of all model parameters. First, consider models with no restrictions on the means (i.e., the case of covariance structures -means excluded from the analysis). This leads to multiple group (MG) single-factor models with the following varying degrees of parameter invariance across groups: MG0, all parameters invariant across groups; MG1, invariance of loadings only (i.e. variances of factor and errors are set free across groups); MG2, all parameters free across groups; and MG12, invariance across groups of a selected subset of loadings. A model MG2-C is also considered that allows correlated errors on variables V3 and V4, and MG2-Cb that allows for

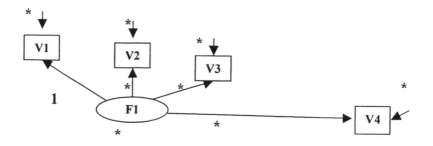

Fig. 5.3. The single-factor model

correlated errors on variables V3 and V4 only on those countries where such correlation's were found to be significant (Germany-West, Germany-East, Great Britain, Italy, Netherlands, New Zealand, Canada, Japan). Note the nested sequence: MG0 < MG1 < MG12 < MG2, where "A < B" denotes model "A" is nested within model "B" (i.e., model "A" is a submodel of "B", with some restrictions on the parameters)

When restrictions are imposed on the means by specifying mean and covariance structures, one obtains the nested sequence of mean restricted multiple group (MMG) models: MMG0 < MMG1 < MMG12. Depending on the level of invariance of the mean intercept parameters across the groups, various models arise. Here, MMG1 denotes the mean restricted multiple group model with loadings invariant across groups and variances of factors and errors free to vary across groups; MMG0 is the model with all the loadings invariant across groups; MMG12 denotes the model with only a subset of loadings invariant across groups. Restrictions on the means imply adding intercept parameters (asterisks) in all the cells of the columns INT of Table 5.1 (except for cell INT-F2, as this cell is redundant with INT-V4). Models MMG0 and MMG1 impose invariance across groups of all the intercept parameters except for INT-F1 (country effect on F1) which is allowed to vary for each country. This parameter is the mean level of factor F1 relative to a baseline group (arbitrarily chosen to be Australia). All the location parameters are set to zero. Model MMG12 allows variation across groups of a selected set of effects of INT to manifest variables, in addition to INT-F1. Note that the large number of groups (22) gives rise to mean structures with a wide range of variation on degrees of freedom (for a discussion of power when testing across group invariance of mean levels of a factor, see Kaplan & George, 1995).

In relation to the asymptotic robustness theory, it is noted that the MC (model condition) holds for models MG1, MG12 and MG2, and the corresponding MMG models, since no restrictions are placed on variances and covariances of factors and errors, not even across groups. Thus, for these models, when DC holds (i.e., factors and errors are mutually independent, not only uncorrelated), the NT analysis gives valid standard errors for loadings and intercept parameters (including the country effects), and valid chi-square goodness-of-fit tests. However, MC does not hold for models MG0 or MMG0, as they restrict variances of factors and errors to be equal across groups. Thus, for models MG0 and MMG0, non-normality of factors and errors may distort the validity of NT standard errors of all parameters and also the chi-square statistics (i.e., robust se and test statistics of PML analysis are required for these models).

5.4.2 The MIMIC approach

Pooling all the samples into a single group, leads to (single group) factor model represented by the path diagram of Figure 5.3, which is denoted by SG-A. SG-C is used to denote the same factor model with a correlated error between variables V3 and V4. Within such a single sample analysis, heterogeneity across groups can be modeled by using the multiple indicator multiple causes (MIMIC) model approach (see Jöreskog & Goldberger, 1975 for a seminal study on the MIMIC model; Muthén, 1989 for the convenience of the MIMIC model approach with large numbers of groups).

Figure 4 depicts the family of MIMIC models considered in the present chapter. There is a single-factor model underlying four manifest variables, and there are group "effects" both on the factor and on the manifest variables. In this graph, the square with double border, labeled "country", represents a set of dummy variables, one less than the number of countries[6]. Table 5.2 also lists the various MIMIC models considered. MIMIC-A, the arrow from country to F1 (arrow in bold); MIMIC-B, arrows from country to F1 and to manifest variables (bold and dashed arrows); MIMIC-C, allows for correlated error between V3 and V4 in addition to the effects from group (bold and dashed arrows and the two-headed arrow – dots and dashes). Note also the nested structure: MIMIC-A < MIMIC-B < MIMIC-C.

Each arrow emanating from "Country" is in fact a set of arrows - one for each country, except for the baseline country. Some of these arrows may not be significant in a specific analysis, and can be set to zero. In fact, in the empirical analysis, the choice of the final set of direct effects from countries on manifest variables has been made on the basis of Lagrange Multiplier test statistics when fitting model MIMIC-A. Such effects point out countries for which the level of some specific observable variable differs from the mean level expected given the common factor F1. This is of interest in practice, since it allows one to "discover" peculiarities of countries relative to some variables.

---

[6] The convention of using a square with double border to represent the set of dummies associated to a categorical variable is adopted. To facilitate implementation of this MIMIC model approach, we feel that SEM software should incorporate simple features to create dummy variables from a categorical variable.

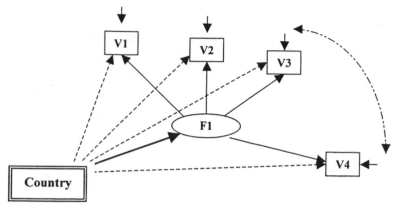

Fig. 5.4. MIMIC models

Note also that the arrows emanating from "Country" affect only the levels of the variables, not their variances or covariances.

It is interesting to compare the (single group) MIMIC modeling approaches with the previously discussed multiple group factor models. A similar structure is imposed by MIMIC-A and MMG0, as in both cases loadings and variances must be equal across groups. There is, however, a fundamental difference between the multiple group models MMG1 or MG1 and the MIMIC model; the former allows for variation across groups of the variance parameters. That is, the MIMIC approach assumes homogeneity across groups of loadings and variance parameters. In fact, Muthén (1989) pointed out that "the MIMIC approach is restricted to modeling under the assumption of a group-invariant covariance matrix for the observed response variables " (p. 564).

The test of the assumption of invariance of variances and loadings can be carried out by comparison of the chi-square goodness-of-fit values of models MG1 and MG0. Note, however, that this test is not robust to the violation of the normality assumption, since it implies testing the equality of variances of non-normal constituents of the model. In such a case, the scaled difference of chi-square statistics, as recently proposed by Satorra and Bentler (in press) could be useful.

The usefulness of the MIMIC model approach is conjectured beyond the restriction of equality across groups of variances of common and unique factors. Indeed, models MIMIC-A and MMG1 differ in that the latter allows for heterogeneous variances across groups. It is expected that with regards to inferences on loadings, the results of MIMIC-A are accurate approximations of those obtained by MMG1. Such robustness of the MIMIC approach to the violation of the homogeneity assumption of variances is of practical relevance, since, in comparison with the multiple group approach, the MIMIC approach is easier to implement and gives results that are easier to comprehend. Note, however, that the assumption of invariance of loadings across groups is not suppressed. The claim is that inferences on loading parameters and effects from independent variables provided by the MIMIC approach are valid, for all practical purposes, assuming a "strongly factorial invariant model" in the sense discussed by Meredith (1993). Finally, it should be pointed out that the above MIMIC models satisfy the MC for AR, thus when common and unique factors are mutually independent (not only un-correlated), the NT analysis provides valid inferences for estimates of loadings and effects from independent variables[7]. The usual NT chi-square should also be valid in this case.

5.5   Empirical Results

This section describes the main results of the empirical analysis when applying the models described in the previous section. For the results corresponding to CO analysis, EQS (Bentler, 1995) was used, and for the OR results PRELIS and LISREL (Jöreskog and Sörbom, 1996) were used. [8] Table 5.3 gives a summary of the chi-square goodness-of-fit values of the models listed in Table 5.2. As interest is in the comparative analysis of alternative methods of estimation, the various alternative chi-square test statistics are listed. Owing to the nested structure by rows, the difference of chi-square values across rows gives test statistics for various restrictions across groups. The hypothesis of equality of variances of common and unique factors is rejected by the data (compare the chi-square values for MG0 – MG1, clearly significant). A correlated error is needed between variables V3 and V4 present in models MG2-C and MG2-Cb. The multiple group model MG2-Cb (that has correlated errors only on a subset of countries) has a non-significant chi-square goodness-of-fit test, despite the large sample size. The hypothesis of invariance across groups of loadings is also rejected (compare models MG2 and MG2-C). This lack of invariance across groups of loadings questions theoretically the validity of the MIMIC model for the data, but the comparison of estimates of the MIMIC and multiple group models leads to the conclusion that the MIMIC model approach is useful, despite the violation of the homogeneity hypothesis. In fact, for the single group analysis, no model that passes the chi-square goodness of fit test (at 5% significance level) both for the MIMIC-C and with the SG-C (irrespective of the method of estimation used) was obtained (possibly due to the loadings heterogeneity across groups, visible in the fit of model MG2-C).

---

[7] Note that non-normality of the common and unique factors could in fact be due to heterogeneity across groups of factor and errors variances.

[8] We were not able to standardize the CO and OR analyses to a single software product, since no package was able (at the time of the analysis) to provide all the statistics desired.

Table 5.4. Overview of chi-square statistics for different models

Across group constraints	Group Design			
	Multiple Group		Single Group	
	Cov.	Mean-Cov.	MIMIC	One Factor Model
Loadings & Variances	MG0 (df=212) 3486.35 ^{a} 3025.62 ^{b} 3439.25 ^{c} 657.21 ^{d} 494.05 ^{e} 574.68 ^{f} - -	MMG0 (df=275) 10466.35 ^{a} - - - - - - -	MIMIC-A (df=65) 7059.30 ^{a} 6887.53 ^{b} - 2318.08 ^{d} 1307.64 ^{e} - MIMIC-B (df=12) 74.16 ^{a} 77.71 ^{b} - 33.64 ^{d} 29.25 ^{e} MIMIC-C (d.f. = 11) 34.72 ^{a} 36.77 ^{b} - 25.04 ^{d} 25.28 ^{e}	SG-A (df=2) 242.21 ^{a} 228.84 ^{b} 223.31 ^{c} 214.84 ^{d} 215.39 ^{e} 214.86 ^{f} - SG-C (df=1) 34.57 ^{a} 33.15 ^{b} 33.19 ^{c} 32.38 ^{d} 32.38 ^{e} 32.38 ^{f}
Loadings	MG1 (df=107) 473.65 ^{a} 442.64 ^{b} 442.59 ^{c} 273.77 ^{d} 303.43 ^{e} 316.69 ^{f}	MMG1 (df=170) 7234.53 ^{a} - - - - -	-	-
Selected set of Loadings	MG12 (df=87) 220.74 ^{a} 205.24 ^{b} 207.92 ^{c} 196.65 ^{d} 216.51 ^{e} 217.71 ^{f}	MMG12 (df=143) 407.36 ^{a} - - - - - MMG12-C b(df=135) 329.01 ^{a} MMG12-C (df=121) 311.90 ^{a}	-	-
No constraints	MG2 (df=44) 149.61 ^{a} 141.34 ^{b} 142.56 ^{c} 125.82 ^{d} 146.69 ^{e} 139.58 ^{f} MG2-C b (df=36) 63.45 ^{a} 59.46 ^{b} 60.95 ^{c} 52.09 ^{d} 54.29 ^{e} 58.14 ^{f} MG2-C (df=22) 50.67 ^{a} 48.30 ^{b} 48.09 ^{c} 39.04 ^{d} 42.86 ^{e} 43.58 ^{f}	-	-	-

^{a} CO – NT chi-square statistics ^{b} CO – Scaled chi-square statistics ^{c} CO – ADF chi-square statistics

^{d} OR – Scaled chi-square statistics ^{e} OR – Robust chi-square statistics ^{f} OR – WLS chi-square statistics

Application of the scaled difference chi-square statistic (Satorra & Bentler, in press) for testing the null hypothesis of invariance across groups of variances of common and unique factors yields a chi-square value of 2449.35 which, in relation to 212–107 = 105 degrees of freedom, clearly rejects the null hypothesis. As argued by Satorra and Bentler (in press), the scaled difference is not necessarily equal to the difference of scaled chi-square statistics (2582.98). Despite the rejection of this hypothesis of homoscedasticity across groups, it can be seen that, with regard to loadings and country effects, the results for model MIMIC-A differ only slightly from those obtained using the multiple group model MMG1. The values of the goodness-of-fit statistics are remarkably similar for the CO and OR approaches. For both approaches, the same model is selected. Both approaches identify the need for a correlated error between variables V3 and V4, reject the hypothesis of homogeneity across groups of variances of common and unique factors, and reject the hypothesis of homogeneity of loadings across groups.

Table 5.5. NT estimates of loading and variance parameters for different models

Models	Loadings				Variances and Covariance					
	F1→V1	F1→V2	F1→V3	F1→V4	F1↔F1	E1↔E1	E2↔E2	E3↔E3	E4↔E4	E3↔E4
MG0	1	1.147	0.938	0.201	0.761	0.482	0.406	0.666	0.908	-
		0.011[a]	0.010	0.008	0.013	0.007	0.009	0.008	0.009	
		0.012[b]	0.011	0.008	0.013	0.010	0.011	0.011	0.007	
MG1	1	1.132	0.945	0.196	-	-	-	-	-	-
		0.010	0.009	0.008						
		0.011	0.010	0.008						
MMG0	1	1.141	0.943	0.224	0.754	0.503	0.428	0.708	1.136	-
		0.011	0.010	0.009	0.012	0.008	0.009	0.009	0.011	
MMG1	1	1.123	0.949	0.236	-	-	-	-	-	-
		0.010	0.009	0.009						
MIMIC-A	1	1.139	0.944	0.225	0.753	0.503	0.430	0.706	1.135	-
		0.011	0.010	0.009	0.012	0.008	0.009	0.009	0.011	
		0.012	0.010	0.009	0.013	0.010	0.012	0.011	0.011	
MIMIC-B	1	1.146	0.936	0.201	0.761	0.481	0.405	0.666	0.907	-
		0.011	0.010	0.008	0.013	0.007	0.009	0.008	0.009	
		0.012	0.011	0.008	0.013	0.010	0.011	0.011	0.007	
MIMIC-C	1	1.150	0.934	0.190	0.760	0.482	0.400	0.670	0.911	0.038
		0.011	0.010	0.008	0.013	0.008	0.009	0.008	0.009	0.006
		0.012	0.010	0.009	0.013	0.010	0.011	0.011	0.007	0.006
SG-A	1	1.146	0.941	0.218	0.806	0.505	0.419	0.712	1.137	-
		0.011	0.010	0.009	0.013	0.008	0.009	0.009	0.011	
		0.012	0.010	0.009	0.014	0.011	0.012	0.011	0.007	
SG-C	1	1.156	0.936	0.192	0.803	0.509	0.406	0.722	1.146	0.100
		0.011	0.010	0.009	0.013	0.008	0.009	0.009	0.011	0.007
		0.012	0.011	0.009	0.014	0.011	0.012	0.011	0.007	0.007

[a] NT se   [b] Robust se

An overview of parameter estimates for the different models and estimation methods is provided in Table 5.4. The small discrepancy in loading estimates when different models are used is evident and also the small discrepancy in NT and robust standard errors, especially for the loading parameters in the models where AR results are applicable. Some differences are observed across groups in the estimated variances of unique and common factors[9], while the estimated common loadings arising from MMG1 and MMG0 are close to each other and to those estimated using the single group approach

---

[9] The estimates of variances are available from the authors upon request. To save space, these results are not given.

of model MIMIC-A. Not only the parameters but also the standard errors are similar. This result is of particular importance in practice, since it shows that when estimating loadings and regression effects, the analysis provided by MIMIC-A is robust to the customary assumption of invariance across groups of all the parameters of the covariance structure.

Table 5.5 shows the standardized values of the loadings for different models and estimation methods. Estimates of loadings (standardized values) when CO is used are generally smaller than estimates when the OR approach is used. The difference is very small in the case of the loading for V4 (regression parameter). In any case, the differences between CO and OR estimates are too small to be substantively relevant.

Table 5.6. CO-OR NT standardized loading parameters for different models

| | Parameter Estimates | | | | | | | | | |
| | Loadings | | | | Variances and Covariance | | | | | |
Models	F1→V1	F1→V2	F1→V3	F1→V4	F1↔F1	E1↔E1	E2↔E2	E3↔E3	E4↔E4	E3↔E4
MG0	0.782 [a]	0.843	0.708	0.181	1.000	0.388	0.288	0.498	0.966	-
	0.835 [b]	0.885	0.752	0.200	1.000	0.303	0.217	0.434	0.960	-
MG1	.	.	.	.	.	.	.	.	.	-
MMG0	0.774	0.834	0.697	0.179	0.968	0.401	0.304	0.514	0.968	-
MMG1	.	.	.	.	.	.	.	.	.	-
MIMIC-A	0.785	0.843	0.710	0.186	0.932	0.384	0.289	0.496	0.966	-
	0.827	0.887	0.748	0.190	0.934	0.316	0.214	0.440	0.964	-
MIMIC-B	0.798	0.860	0.716	0.170	0.913	0.367	0.274	0.467	0.773	-
	0.844	0.901	0.756	0.182	0.914	0.294	0.203	0.407	0.736	-
MIMIC-C	0.797	0.863	0.714	0.160	0.913	0.368	0.270	0.460	0.775	0.029
	0.843	0.903	0.754	0.174	0.914	0.296	0.199	0.409	0.739	0.031
SG-A	0.784	0.847	0.707	0.181	1.000	0.385	0.283	0.499	0.967	-
	0.828	0.887	0.747	0.187	1.000	0.315	0.212	0.442	0.965	-
SG-C	0.782	0.852	0.703	0.159	1.000	0.388	0.274	0.506	0.975	0.077
	0.825	0.893	0.743	0.166	1.000	0.319	0.203	0.448	0.972	0.087

[a] CO - NT
[b] OR - NT

Table 5.6 gives the results for the multiple group models with the lowest number of degrees of freedom (i.e., the MG2 factor model). The table shows parameter estimates for the loading parameters and the values of the NT and scaled chi-square goodness-of-fit tests. AR results for model MG2 show up in the similarity of regular (i.e., NT) and robust standard errors for loading parameters (not so similar for variance parameters) and regular and robust chi-square goodness-of-fit test (including that obtained from the ADF analysis)[10] . Table 5.7 shows the results for model MG2-Cb (which passes the chi-square test at the 5% significance level), though no substantial differences can be reported in the estimates of parameters that are common to both MG2 and MG2-Cb models.

From the analysis of model MG2 in Table 5.6, the generally high values of the loadings for variables V1 to V3 that reflect an adequate measurement model (the standardized values range from .5 to .99) can be reported. V2

---

[10] The robust and non-robust standard errors differ by less than .001, and the correlation across countries among the NT chi-square, the scaled and AO se are above .997, with the mean (across countries) values of these statistics differing by less than .1.

Table 5.7. MG2: CO-NT parameter estimates and chi-square statistics

	Sample	Chi-square (df=2)^a			Loadings				Standardized Loadings			
Countries	Size	ADF	NT	Scaled	F1 → V1	F1 → V2	F1 → V3	F1 → V4	F1 → V1	F1 → V2	F1 → V3	F1 → V4
Australia	1613	0.01	0.01	0.01	1	1.13*	0.92	0.24	0.82	0.85	0.73	0.21
Germany-West	927	29.48	31.30	33.16	1	0.95	0.74	0.15	0.86	0.81	0.68	0.20
Germany-East	949	12.83	12.47	14.09	1	0.91	0.81	0.06	0.84	0.82	0.69	0.07
Great Britain	1091	3.98	3.80	3.90	1	1.19	0.97	0.30	0.82	0.91	0.73	0.25
N. Ireland	600	7.05	6.61	5.82	1	1.11	1.03	0.37	0.79	0.82	0.75	0.32
United States	1364	4.41	4.72	4.50	1	1.16	0.97	0.24	0.81	0.87	0.74	0.20
Hungary	882	5.15	5.41	5.11	1	1.17	0.82	0.23	0.72	0.92	0.68	0.17
Italy	761	10.40	10.99	10.51	1	1.30	0.97	0.26	0.72	0.78	0.66	0.18
Ireland	681	2.28	2.35	2.25	1	0.99	1.08	0.25	0.71	0.71	0.75	0.21
Netherlands	1701	11.31	13.00	11.00	1	1.44	1.14	0.22	0.75	0.86	0.71	0.20
Norway	1110	3.60	3.29	3.21	1	1.01	0.90	0.26	0.84	0.83	0.72	0.24
Czech Rep.	495	4.51	4.67	4.75	1	0.95	0.86	0.13	0.77	0.75	0.66	0.11
Slovenia	587	2.25	2.47	2.34	1	1.05	0.89	0.25	0.89	0.88	0.79	0.24
Poland	754	0.00	0.00	0.00	1	1.06	0.92	0.25	0.81	0.86	0.79	0.24
Bulgaria	564	4.75	5.91	5.11	1	1.05	0.96	0.20	0.90	0.92	0.85	0.30
Russia	760	2.09	2.32	1.81	1	1.22	0.80	0.07	0.78	0.92	0.60	0.08
New Zealand	1137	13.19	14.78	14.08	1	1.21	1.09	0.21	0.77	0.83	0.76	0.17
Canada	1274	9.17	9.14	9.46	1	1.20	0.98	0.21	0.77	0.81	0.71	0.18
Philippines	1165	0.74	0.75	0.75	1	1.23	0.90	0.09	0.67	0.83	0.61	0.08
Israel	761	1.92	2.14	1.94	1	1.35	1.05	0.29	0.73	0.87	0.70	0.23
Japan	1198	6.80	6.76	7.06	1	1.27	0.81	0.06	0.66	0.81	0.53	0.05
Spain	888	6.47	6.59	6.37	1	1.08	1.01	0.12	0.88	0.91	0.87	0.09

*All estimates are significant at 5% level
^{a}These are chi-square for single sample analysis. The overall chi-square for this model is reported in Table 3.

(disposition to pay higher taxes) is the variable with the largest loadings. For V2, the standardized loading ranges across countries from .71 to .92. The loadings associated with V4 are smaller than the other variables, but this loading might be interpreted as a regression coefficient. Its low value does not deteriorate the measurement model for F1. With respect to the goodness of fit of the model, the overall fit is highly significant, in accordance with highly significant chi-square values for the fit in each country. The inclusion of correlation effects in some countries reduces the chi-square test statistic dramatically. For example, in Germany-West, the inclusion of a correlation between V3 (sacrifice standard of living) and V4 (participation in recycling) reduces the χ^2 -value from 31.30 to 2.5^{11} . This is not the case for the Netherlands, where the correlation needed is between V2 (pay higher taxes) and V4 (participation in recycling). For some countries, however, the model has a non-significant chi-square value, despite the large sample size. This is the case for Poland, Australia, Philippines, Russia, Ireland, Israel and Slovenia, where the NT chi-square is smaller than 2.5. Even though all the regression coefficients are significant at the 5% level, for some countries the effect is small enough for it not to be important. The effect between attitude and behavior was estimated to be low for Germany-West, Japan, Russia and Philippines (whose standardized regression coefficient are below .06), as opposed to Northern Ireland, Bulgaria, Great Britain and Norway (with standardized regression coefficients greater than .24). MG2-Cb is selected from among the multiple group models. Its model fit is given in Table

---

[11] In contrast with this marked change in the chi-square statistics, the (LISREL) GFI and AGFI are respectively .98 and .92 for the models without and with the correlation parameter.

7. The results in Table 6 and 7 differ only slightly despite the substantial difference in the corresponding chi-square goodness of fit test statistics.

Table 5.8. MG2-Cb: CO-NT parameter estimates and chi-square statistics

Countries	Chi-square[a] ADF	NT	Scaled	F1 → V1	F1 → V2	F1 → V3	F1 → V4	E3 ↔ E4	F1 → V1	F1 → V2	F1 → V3	F1 → V4	E3 ↔ E4
Australia	0.01	0.01	0.01	1	1.13*	0.92	0.24	0	0.82	0.85	0.73	0.21	0
Germany-West	_[b]	2.50	2.87	1	0.96	0.74	0.13	0.12	0.87	0.82	0.67	0.17	0.19
Germany-East	_	0.22	0.26	1	0.92	0.81	0.04	0.09	0.84	0.82	0.69	0.05	0.12
Great Britain	_	0.11	0.10	1	1.19	0.97	0.29	0.05	0.82	0.91	0.73	0.25	0.06
N. Ireland	7.05	6.61	5.82	1	1.11	1.03	0.37	0	0.79	0.82	0.75	0.32	0
United States	4.41	4.72	4.50	1	1.16	0.97	0.24	0	0.81	0.87	0.74	0.20	0
Hungary	5.15	5.41	5.11	1	1.17	0.82	0.23	0	0.72	0.92	0.68	0.17	0
Italy	3.64	3.64	3.48	1	1.32	0.97	0.21	0.12	0.72	0.78	0.66	0.18	0.11
Ireland	2.28	2.35	2.25	1	0.99	1.08	0.25	0	0.71	0.71	0.75	0.21	0
Netherlands	_	6.41	5.64	1	1.46	1.14	0.21	0.04	0.75	0.86	0.71	0.20	0.07
Norway	3.60	3.29	3.21	1	1.01	0.90	0.26	0	0.84	0.83	0.72	0.24	0
Czech Rep.	4.51	4.67	4.75	1	0.95	0.86	0.13	0	0.77	0.75	0.66	0.11	0
Slovenia	2.25	2.47	2.34	1	1.05	0.89	0.25	0	0.89	0.88	0.79	0.24	0
Poland	0.00	0.00	0.00	1	1.06	0.92	0.25	0	0.81	0.86	0.79	0.24	0
Bulgaria	4.75	5.91	5.11	1	1.05	0.96	0.20	0	0.90	0.92	0.85	0.30	0
Russia	2.09	2.32	1.81	1	1.22	0.80	0.07	0	0.78	0.92	0.60	0.08	0
New Zealand	0.01	0.01	0.01	1	1.22	1.09	0..18	0.09	0.77	0.83	0.76	0.17	0.13
Canada	3.35	3.15	3.37	1	1.21	0.98	0.19	0.06	0.77	0.81	0.71	0.18	0.08
Philippines	0.74	0.75	0.75	1	1.23	0.90	0.09	0	0.67	0.83	0.61	0.08	0
Israel	1.92	2.14	1.94	1	1.35	1.05	0.29	0	0.73	0.87	0.70	0.23	0
Japan	_	0.03	0.04	1	1.28	0.81	0.05	0.07	0.66	0.81	0.53	0.05	0.08
Spain	6.47	6.59	6.37	1	1.08	1.01	0.12	0	0.88	0.91	0.87	0.09	0

*All estimates are significant at 5% level
[a]These are chi-square for single sample analysis.
The d.f. are 1 or 2 depending respectively on whether the correlation is present or not.
The overall chi-square for this model is reported in Table 5.3.
[b]ADF did not converge.

Despite violating the factorial invariance hypothesis, multiple group models and MIMIC approach give comparable results. Table 5.8, shows the results for model MIMIC-C, offers an overview of the variation across countries (in relation to Australia, the baseline country) of the mean levels of latent and manifest variables. For example, the Netherlands have the largest positive country effect on F1 (.405), while the Czech Republic has the largest negative effect on F1 (-.501). With regard to the direct effect of country on variables, there is a large estimated negative value of Russia on V4 (-1.36) and large positive values in both Germany-West (.359) and East (.317). Bulgaria, Israel and Northern Ireland also have a large negative effect on V4.

Table 5.9. MIMIC-C: NT Parameter estimates

Loadings, Variances and Covariance				
	F1	V1	V2	V3	V4
F1	0.760*	1	1.150*	0.934*	0.190*
E		0.482*	0.400*	0.670*	0.911*
E3↔E4				0.038 (0.0048)[a]	

Country Effects					
Countries	F1	V1	V2	V3	V4
Australia [b]	-	-	-	-	-
Germany-West	-0,068	0	0	0.387*	0.359*
Germany-East	-0.580*	0	0.152*	0.513*	0.317*
Great Britain	-0.018	0	0.075*	-0,288*	-0.595*
N. Ireland	-0.123*	0	0	-0.338*	-1.021*
United States	0.031	0	0	-0.208*	-0.181*
Hungary	-0.652	0.206*	0	-0.393*	-0.710*
Italy	0.152	0.152*	-0.346*	0	-0.488*
Ireland	-0.627	0.416*	0	0	-0.713*
Netherlands	0.405*	0	-0.256*	-0.207*	0.124*
Norway	0.010	0	-0.101*	0.264*	-0.667*
Czech Rep.	-0.501*	0	0	-0.178*	-0.390*
Slovenia	0.021	0	0.121*	0	-0.418*
Poland	-0.169*	0	0.106*	-0.210*	-0.766*
Bulgaria	0.014	0	0.171*	0	-1.360*
Russia	-0.059	0.117*	0.372*	0	-1.418*
New Zealand	-0.028	0.081*	0	-0.071*	-0.256*
Canada	0.102*	0	-0.219*	0	-0.070*
Philippines	-0.372*	-0.246*	0	0.091*	-0.446*
Israel	0.125*	0	-0.219*	-0.592*	-1.242*
Japan	-0.049	0	0.099*	0	0.099*
Spain	0.167*	-0.142*	0	0	-0.821*

[a] Estimated covariance between residual errors. The corresponding correlation is in parenthesis
[b] Australia acts as baseline country
*Significant at 5% level

5.6   Discussion and Conclusions

This chapter considered alternative approaches to the analysis of group differences in both the mean levels of manifest and latent variables, and in their mutual relationship. Continuous versus ordinal methods, single group versus multiple group methods, and normal theory versus asymptotic robust methods were applied to the ISSP-1993 environmental survey data. The specific features of the data were the large number of groups, the large sample size in each group, and the marked non-normality of observed variables.

For the ISSP-1993 environmental data, and the given SEM context, it was found that major substantive conclusions are fairly robust to the choice of alternative model strategies and estimation methods. Indeed, alternative approaches to SEM analysis coincide in rejecting: (i) the null hypothesis of homoscedasticity across countries of unique and common factors on attitude and behavior concerning environmental issues, and (ii) the hypothesis of invariance across countries of measurement loadings and the regression effect of attitude on behavior. Furthermore, for some countries, a direct correlation between variable V3 (disposition to cutting standard of living) and V4 (actual recycling behavior), not accounted for by the common factor F, was detected empirically (these findings are supported by the chi-square values shown in Table 5.3).

The differences among the countries in the measurement structure of variables V1-V3 when measuring F1 (positive disposition toward protecting environment), and the variation across countries of the regression effect of F1 to V4, are displayed in Table 5.7 for the multiple group model MG2-Cb. The direct effects of the countries on both the level of the common factor F1 and the manifest variables V1-V4 were isolated and quantified (see Table 5.8).

The MIMIC model was found useful for summarizing the effects of countries on both latent and manifest variables, despite the violation of the assumption of homogeneity across groups of variances of unique and common factors. Minimal differences were found between normal theory and robust standard errors in the case of CO analysis when estimating loading and country effects for those models in which the model condition (MC) of asymptotic robustness applies. Despite the great size of the data set, the chi-square goodness-of-fit test was still found to be useful for model assessment.

References

Ajzen, I., & Fishbein, M. (1982). *Understanding attitudes and predicting social behavior.* Englewood Cliffs, NJ: Prentice-Hall.

Bentler, P.M. (1995). *EQS structural equations program manual.* Encino, CA: Multivariate Software.

Bollen, K.A. (1989). *Structural equations with latent variables.* New York: Wiley.

Bollen, K.A., & Long, S.J. (Eds.) (1993). *Testing structural equation models,* Newbury Park: SAGE Publications.

Browne, M.W. (1984). Asymptotically distribution-free methods for the analysis of covariance structures. *British Journal of Mathematical and Statistical Psychology,* 30, 557-576.

Coenders, G., Saris, W. E., & Satorra, A. (1997). Alternative approach to structural modeling of ordinal data: a Monte Carlo study. *Structural Equation Modeling,* 4, 261-282.

Christoffersson, A. (1975). Factor analysis of dichotomized variables. *Psychometrika,* 40, 5-32.

von Eye, A., & Clogg, C.C. (Eds.) (1994). *Latent variables analysis: Applications for developmental research.* Thousand Oaks: SAGE Publications:

Finch, J. F., West, S. G., & MacKinnon D. P. (1997). Effects of sample size and nonnormality on the estimation of mediated effects in latent variable models, *Structural Equation Modeling,* 4, 87-107.

Fishbein, M., & Ajzen, I. (1975). *Belief, attitude, intention and behavior: an introduction to theory and research.* Reading, Mass: Addison-Wesley.

Green, S. B., Akey T. M., Fleming K. K. Hershberger S. L., & Marquis, J. G. (1997). Effect of the number of scale points on chi-square fit indices in confirmatory factor analysis, *Structural Equation Modeling*, 4, 108-120.

Jöreskog, K. G. (1971). Simultaneous factor analysis in several populations. *Psychometrika*, 36, 409-426.

Jöreskog, K. G., & Goldberger, A. S. (1975). Estimation of a model with multiple indicators and multiple causes of a single latent variable. *Journal of American Statistical Association*, 70, 631-639.

Jöreskog, K. G., & Sörbom D. (1996). *LISREL 8: User's reference guide*. Chicago, Scientific Software International.

Kaplan, D. (1991). The behavior of three weighted least squares estimators for structured means analysis with non-normal Likert variables. *British Journal of Mathematical and Statistical Psychology*, 44, 333-346.

Kaplan, D., & George R. (1995). A study of the power associated with testing factor mean differences under violation of factorial invariance, *Structural Equation Modeling*, 2, 101-118.

Meredith, W. (1993) Measurement invariance, factor analysis and factorial invariance, *Psychometrika*, 58, 525-543.

Muthén, B. O. (1984). A general structural equation model with dichotomous, ordered categorical, and continuous latent variable indicators. *Psychometrika*, 49, 115-132.

Muthén, B. O. (1989). Latent variable modeling in heterogeneous populations. *Psychometrika*, 54, 557-585.

Muthén, L.K., & Muthén B.O. (1998). *Mplus user's guide*. Los Angeles.

Olsson, U. (1979). Maximum likelihood estimation of the polychoric correlation. *Psychometrika*, 44, 443-460.

Pieters, R. G. M. (1988). Attitude-behavior relationships. In W. F. Van Raaij, G. M. Van Veldhoven & K. E. Wärneryd (Eds.), *Handbook of economic psychology* (pp. 144-204). Dordrecht, The Netherlands, Kluwer Academic Publishers.

Saris W.E., den Ronden, J., & Satorra A. (1987). Structural modeling by example: applications in educational. In P.F. Cuttance & J.R. Escob (Eds.), *Sociological, and behavioural research* (pp. 202-220). Cambridge University Press

Satorra A. (1992). Asymptotic robust inferences in the analysis of mean and covariance structures. In P. V. Marsden (Ed.), Sociological methodology 1992 (pp. 249-278). Oxford & Cambridge, MA: Basil Blackwell.

Satorra A. (1993). Asymptotic robust inferences in multi-sample analysis of augmented moment structures. In C. M. Cuadras & C. R. Rao (Eds.), *Multivariate analysis: future directions II* (pp. 211-229). Elsevier: Amsterdam.

Satorra, A. & Bentler, P.M. (1994). Corrections to test statistics and standard errors in covariance structure analysis. In: Alexander von Eye and C.C. Clogg (Eds.). *Latent variables analysis: Applications to developmental research* (pp. 399-419). SAGE Publications, Inc: Thousand Oaks, CA.

Satorra, A. & Bentler, P.M. (in press). A scaled difference chi-square test statistic for moment structure analysis. *Psychometrika*.

Schumacker, R. E., & Marcoulides, G. A. (Eds.) (1998), *Interaction and nonlinear effects in structural equation modeling*. Mahwah, NJ: Lawrence Erlbaum.

Sörbom, D. (1974). A general method for studying difference in factor means and factor structure between groups. *British Journal of Mathematical and Statistical Psychology*, 27, 229-239.

Steiger, J. H. (2001). Driving fast in reverse, The relationship between software development, theory, and education in structural equation modeling, *Journal of the American Statistical Association*, 96, 331-338.

Appendix

Variables used in the study as they appear in the ISSP-1993 questionnaire, and sample size for each country.

Question wordings:

Variable V1. (Q.8a). Protect enviro: pay much higher prices:

"How willing would you be to pay much higher prices in order to protect the environment?"

Variable V2.(Q.8b). Protect enviro: pay much higher taxes:

"And how willing would you be to pay much higher taxes in order to protect the environment?"

Variable V3. (Q.8c). Protect enviro: cut your standard of living.

"And how willing would you be to accept cuts in your standard of living in order to protect the environment?".

The three variables with response options: "Very unwilling" (1), "Fairly unwilling" (2)," Neither willing nor unwilling" (3), "Fairly willing" (4), "Very willing" (5), and (8) and (9) for "Can't choose /don't know" and "NA, refused", respectively.

Variable V4. (Q.19a). Effort: sort glass for recycling.

"How often do you make a special effort to sort glass or tins or plastic or newspapers and so on for recycling?" . This variable with response options: "Always" (1), "Often" (2),"Sometimes" (3), "Never" (4), "Recycling not available where I live" (5), and (8) and (9) for "Can't choose /don't know" and "NA, refused", respectively.

Countries and Sample Sizes:

Australia (1613), Germany-West (927), Germany-East (949), Great Britain (1091), Northern Ireland (600), United States (1364), Hungary (882), Italy (761), Ireland (681), Netherlands (1701), Norway (1110), Czech Republic (495), Slovenia (587), Poland (754), Bulgaria (564), Russia (760), New Zealand (1137), Canada (1274), Philippines (1165), Israel (761), Japan (1198), Spain (888).

6   Strategies for Handling Missing Data in SEM: A User's Perspective *

Richard D. Wiggins[1] and Amanda Sacker[2]

[1] City University, London
[2] University College, London

6.1   Introduction

Missing data has the potential to threaten the analyst's power to detect and interpret substantive relationships in almost every research study. As a consequence, researchers are often faced with a choice of procedures to fill-in data, which vary in their degree of convenience, speed of implementation and depth of underlying theory.

This chapter focuses on the impact of eight alternative strategies for handling item non-response in the context of structural equation modelling (SEM). These strategies are either available within existing SEM packages (e.g., LISREL - Jöreskog & Sörbom, 1996a; AMOS – Arbuckle, 1997) or all-purpose statistical programs (e.g., SPSS for Windows Missing Values Analysis module - SPSS Inc., 1997). Alternatively, there are also available freeware products (e.g., NORM - Schafer, 1997), which require the user to fill-in several plausible versions of the data as a prerequisite to model fitting.

The chapter is organized in several sections. The first section provides a brief overview of the current remedies to handle missing data as applied in this evaluation. The section also includes a synopsis of recent evaluations of missing data handling strategies based on simulation studies. The final section describes a SEM analysis and the context for empirical evaluation.

6.2   Remedies to Handle Missing Data in SEM

All the available strategies in this evaluation assume that missing values are either missing completely at random (MCAR) or missing at random (MAR). Under MCAR the probability of a missing response is independent of both

---

* This work arises from funded activity for training and dissemination under the UK's Economic and Social Research Council's (ESRC) Analysis of Large and Complex Data (ALCD) Programme, Grant No. H519255056. In a substantive context, it represents a collaboration between the authors who are both working on ESRC funded projects under both the Health Variations Programme (Grant No. L128251048) and Youth Programme (Grant No. L134251006). The authors are extremely grateful to an anonymous reviewer who commented on the original paper.

the observed and unobserved data (the unobserved responses are a random sample from the observed data). For MAR the probability that a response is missing depends only on the observed responses and not on the unobserved data itself. Taken together these assumptions describe *ignorable non-response*. Conversely procedures that handle *non-ignorable non-response* or data that are *missing not at random* (MNAR) are based on the premise that respondents and non-respondents with the same values of some observed items differ *systematically* with respect to values of an item missing for the non-respondents. Generally, procedures for MNAR lack generality (Schafer, 1997) and there is limited information on the treatment of systematic missing data in SEM applications (Verleye, Pepermaus & Despontin, 1998) - for further elaboration of these fundamental assumptions also see Little & Rubin (1987).

The procedures to be evaluated in this chapter can be summarised under the following basic three categories: (i) ad hoc based solutions, (ii) simple model based solutions, and (iii) advanced model based solutions. The first category includes three common 'quick-and-easy-to-implement' procedures: listwise deletion, pairwise deletion and mean substitution. Listwise or casewise deletion (LD), where cases with partial responses are deleted to leave a set of *fully observed data*, is simple enough to understand but can lead to a huge loss of information and efficiency (Arbuckle, 1996). Pairwise deletion or the available information method (PD), is often applied when users require covariance or correlation estimates. For any covariance or correlation estimate, the data is used for which there are two recorded observations for each case of the item pair. Of course, this inevitably leads to a different sample size for each computed estimate. Finally, mean substitution (MS) involves substituting the mean for the item based on observed data for the appropriate missing value. Unlike LD and PD, this practice leads to bias under MCAR (Arbuckle, 1996).

Simple model based procedures include the use of the EM algorithm (Dempster, Laird & Rubin, 1977) and such regression methods as those available under SPSS for Windows (SPSS Inc.,1997). The latter is closer to the various hot deck procedures (Ford, 1983), which can be viewed as an extension of more simple ad hoc methodologies, whereas the former is closer to the more advanced model based solutions. Under the regression methods, missing values are estimated using multiple linear regression for a set of predictors (or matching criteria). The user has a number of options to alter the estimates with random components. Under the default (applied here) the procedure adds a residual from a randomly selected complete case. The EM algorithm consists of an E(xpectation)-step and a M(aximisation)-step. Under the default, the data are assumed to be multivariate normal with an arbitrary pattern of missingness. In general, there will be S patterns of missingness. This is essential information for the E-step, which provides the conditional expectation of the missing data, given the observed data and current estimates of parameters that describe the missing data mechanism. In the M-step, maximum likelihood estimates of the parameters are obtained. The rate of convergence will depend on the overall fraction of missing information (for further details see Schafer, 1997; Wiggins, Ely, & Lynch, 2000).

Advanced model procedures provide a range of maximum likelihood procedures. In this category one can consider the imputation procedure (IM) available under PRELIS2 (Jöreskog and Sörbom, 1996b), a data augmentation procedure using NORM, and a full information maximum likelihood (FIML) estimation procedure implemented in AMOS. The imputation procedure available in PRELIS2 was developed as an alternative to LD and PD, which were only likely to be satisfactory under MCAR. In PRELIS2 (p.155-156, Jöreskog and Sörbom, 1996b) values are substituted for missing values from another case that has a similar response pattern across a set of matching variables. Imputations are only made if the ratio of the variances for potential substitutions to that of the variance for the observed values of the item which is missing is less than a prespecified value (the default is 0.5; larger values are not recommended). Allison (1997) and Muthèn, Kaplan and Hollis (1987) developed a modeling approach in LISREL to fill-in data where missing items are defined as latent variables across subsamples of data containing different sets of observed data. The approaches yield estimates that are consistent and asymptotically efficient and asymptotically normally distributed under MCAR or MAR (although the same strategy is available under EQS - Bentler, 1989, 1990 - it is not applied here. A major drawback to the above-mentioned application is that it requires sophisticated SEM programming and is limited to a range of missing data patterns. For a fuller account on the history of the development of various approaches to handle missing data in SEM see Verleye et al (1998). Generally, these treatments are referred to as "full information estimation in SEM" and it is within this context that one can situate Arbuckle's pioneering work (Arbuckle, 1996). Arbuckle (1996) produced a generalization of Maximum Likelihood estimation in confirmatory factor analysis with incomplete data (as developed by Finkbeiner, 1979) which is readily applied in a SEM framework. The procedure is available in AMOS (as applied here) and Mx (Neale, 1994). The method can handle most patterns of missing data.

Alternatively, it is possible to adopt multiple imputation (MI) approaches (Rubin, 1996; Schafer, 1997), to fill-in missing data prior to conducting an SEM analysis. Essentially, MI procedures tackle the problem of overstating the certainty associated with filling in values using a single imputation. In general, under multiple imputation one fills in each missing value a number of times (M). The statistical analysis is then carried out for each of the M distinct filled in data sets. Resulting estimates are then combined using Rubin's Rule (Schafer, 1997). The number of imputations required will depend upon the degree of missingness present. For missingness at around 25%, 5 imputations are sufficient to achieve efficiency approximating 95% (Schafer,

1997), which is surprisingly manageable. Resulting variance-covariance matrices for each of the M filled-in data sets can be presented to a SEM program as a multigroup analysis. The methodology for the filling-in process is described in Schafer (1987) as data augmentation. It bears strong resemblance to the EM method, where stochastic I(mputation)- and P(osterior) - steps (Tanner & Wong, 1987) replace the E- and M-steps. As with the advanced modelling approaches already mentioned above the technique assumes MAR and multivariate normality. For simplicity, the application is abbreviated as NORM (available as freeware via http://www.stat.psu.edu/~jls/), and the methodology is abbreviated as DA.

The above discussion identified eight remedies for handling missing data, which can be subdivided into ad hoc, simple model based and advanced model based solutions. Ad hoc solutions include listwise deletion (LD), pairwise deletion (PD) and mean substitution (MS). Simple model based solutions (as currently available in SPSS for Windows Missing Values Analysis (1997)) include regression modelling (REG) and expectation maximisation (EM). Advanced model based solutions include LISREL's maximum likelihood imputation (IM), data augmentation using NORM (DA) and AMOS' full information maximum likelihood estimation (FIML). Of course, it is recognized that this coverage of software applications is by no means complete. Other packages will also most likely provide similar ad-hoc and simple model based solutions for the data analyst. For advanced model based solutions it was decided to focus on remedies that were routinely available within SEM products and compare these with a filling-in procedure (DA) which was independent of the SEM application. The purpose of the evaluation is to examine empirically how selection of remedies compares for a straightforward SEM model.

Complex simulation studies like the one conducted by Verleye et al (1998) inform our expectation in this evaluation. Their study was based on factorial design identified by five missing data solutions (2 quick methods, LD and PD, and 3 maximum likelihood approaches - EM, Multiple Imputation and FIML), the type of SEM (a measurement model versus a full model), 3 levels of missingness for each variable, (5%,15% and 25%), the process creating the patterns of missingness (MCAR versus MAR) and the distributional assumptions (multivariate normality versus non-normality). Their results suggest that higher efficiency for maximum likelihood solutions should be expected and that these gains will be sharper under MAR than MCAR. The quick to apply ad-hoc solutions will require MCAR data. FIML in AMOS should be the superior maximum likelihood approach. They suggest that departures from normality (using Boomsma, 1983) do not seem to have a considerable impact on the parameter estimates but will undermine the accuracy of these standard errors. Clearly, the level of missingness will fuel differences between the simple and model-based methods. Thus, for this evaluation the FIML estimates are taken as a benchmark for comparing estimates. DA is expected to be close to these estimates whilst ad-hoc solutions will only coincide in so far as the missing data is MCAR.

6.3   The Substantive Context for SEM

The motivation for this evaluation arose from two Economic and Social Research Council Projects under the Health Variations and Youth Programmes. The authors were working in teams with members who were common to both research projects. Each group was making use of data from the 1958 British Cohort Study, often referred to as the National Child Development Study (NCDS). The NCDS is a study of over 17,000 children born in one week in 1958 (Ferri, 1993). There have now been six follow-up sweeps. This chapter illustrates SEM analyses based on circumstances at age 11 years (i.e., in the year 1969). One of the common areas of interest was the relationship between parental socioeconomic status and children's development. The model shown below is a variant on an application by Allison (1987) to Bielby's data on black and non-black males in the United States. Figure 6.1 illustrates the relationship between two latent variables, each drawing upon four manifest variables. SES describes parental socioeconomic status modelled by father's Registrar General's social class, mother's socioeconomic group (SEG), as well as mother and father's age of leaving full-time education (proxies for parental educational attainment). Their achievement in standardized reading and mathematics tests and the verbal and performance intelligence quotient scores from a general ability test model children's educational achievement (EDUC).

It is believed that the data will serve as a good illustration of the dramatic impact that missingness can have when analyzing cohort studies, like the NCDS. Evaluations are carried out by comparing determined parameter estimates and their standard errors to the values obtained with the FIML method. The fitted covariance matrices are also compared to those obtained under the FIML method. Over 30 patterns of missingness can be identified for the eight manifest variables. Altogether only 36% of the original sample have fully observed data. However, a further 44% have two or fewer items missing. So, with the use of an appropriate filling-in strategy one could make much better use of the information available rather than simply abandoning all those cases with one or more item missing. Table 6.1 illustrates the impact of item non-response for these data. Altogether 18% of the original data entries are missing. At the age of 11 few education items are missing (6%). However, parental education was only collected later when the cohort member was 16 years old. Consequently, attrition has a greater impact as does the effect of marriage dissolution. Furthermore, a mother's socio-economic group is only available if she was currently in work when her child was aged 11 years.

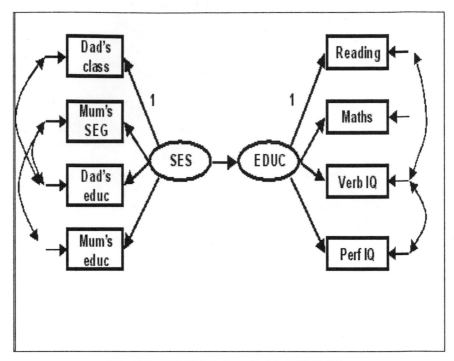

Fig. 6.1. SEM Model applied to NCDS data

Table 6.1. Item non-response for manifest variables

Manifest Variable	Percentage missing
Parental	
Mother's socio-economic group	45%
Father's social class	15%
Age father left full-time education	32%
Age mother left full-time education	30%
Child (cohort member)	
Verbal IQ	6%
Performance IQ	6%
Reading score	6%
Math's Score	6%

Table 6.2. A summary of remedies to handle missingness, their filled-in sample sizes (N) and the applicability of missingness mechanisms

	N	MCAR	MAR	MNAR
LW	5195	√	×	×
PW	10182	√	×	×
MS	15098	√	×	×
REG	15098	√	×	×
EM	15098	√	√	?
IM	8908	√	√	?
DA	5 x 15098	√	√	?
FIML	15098	√	√	?

Table 6.3. Global goodness-of-fit statistics for the 8 remedies to handle missingness

	N	χ^2	df	CFI	RMSEA
FIML	15098	175	14	0.999	0.028
LW	5195	77	14	0.997	0.030
PW	10182	241	14	0.994	0.040
MS	15098	177	14	0.997	0.028
REG	15098	204	14	0.997	0.030
EM	15098	307	14	0.996	0.037
IM	8908	132	14	0.997	0.031
DA (1)	15098	243	14	0.996	0.033
DA (2)	15098	231	14	0.997	0.032
DA (3)	15098	223	14	0.997	0.031
DA (4)	15098	242	14	0.996	0.033
DA (5)	15098	277	14	0.996	0.035

Table 6.4. A summary of model estimates where a √ denotes that the estimate is within 10% of the FIML estimate.

	Measurement				Structural	
	SES		EDUC		SES→EDUC	
	Parm	S.E.	Parm	S.E.	Parm	S.E.
LW	√		√		√	
PW			√			
MS			√	√	√	
REG	√		√	√	√	
EM	√		√	√	√	
IM	√	√	√		√	√
DA	√		√	√	√	

Table 6.5. Estimated values in fitted covariance matrix for FIML together with the deviations from the corresponding values under each of the other remedies.

	V1	V2	V3	V4	V5	V6	V7	V8
FIML								
1. Verbal IQ	87.78							
2. Non-verbal IQ	57.67	58.01						
3. Reading	44.57	31.43	39.68					
4. Maths	76.67	58.27	48.93	107.33				
5. Dad's class	-4.01	-3.05	-2.56	-4.75	1.64			
6. Mum's SEG	-6.49	-4.94	-4.14	-7.68	1.23	5.79		
7. Dad's educ	4.29	3.26	2.73	5.07	-1.00	-1.31	2.60	
8. Mum's educ	3.38	2.57	2.16	4.00	-0.64	-1.31	1.24	1.85
LW								
1. Verbal IQ	-6.01							
2. Non-verbal IQ	-5.42	-4.29						
3. Reading	-2.74	-2.61	-1.35					
4. Maths	-4.78	-4.12	-2.03	-3.12				
5. Dad's class	0.60	0.48	0.34	0.57	-0.18			
6. Mum's SEG	0.79	0.65	0.42	0.69	-0.17	-0.15		
7. Dad's educ	-0.80	-0.63	-0.45	-0.79	0.17	0.22	-0.33	
8. Mum's educ	-0.29	-0.25	-0.15	-0.22	0.07	0.08	-0.08	-0.02
PW								
1. Verbal IQ	-0.11							
2. Non-verbal IQ	-0.09	-0.06						
3. Reading	-0.08	-0.07	-0.05					
4. Maths	-0.17	-0.13	-0.04	-0.14				
5. Dad's class	0.26	0.20	0.16	0.31	0.00			
6. Mum's SEG	1.74	1.33	1.10	2.05	-0.49	-0.09		
7. Dad's educ	-0.39	-0.29	-0.23	-0.44	0.15	0.54	-0.02	
8. Mum's educ	-0.05	-0.04	-0.03	-0.06	0.13	0.55	-0.06	0.00
MS								
1. Verbal IQ	-5.72							
2. Non-verbal IQ	-3.78	-3.76						
3. Reading	-2.93	-2.11	-2.58					
4. Maths	-5.02	-3.81	-3.23	-7.02				
5. Dad's class	0.84	0.64	0.54	1.00	-0.24			
6. Mum's SEG	3.44	2.62	2.19	4.06	-0.67	-2.63		
7. Dad's educ	-1.69	-1.28	-1.07	-1.98	0.40	0.85	-0.83	
8. Mum's educ	-1.24	-0.94	-0.80	-1.47	0.25	0.79	-0.40	-0.55
REG								
1. Verbal IQ	-0.06							
2. Non-verbal IQ	-3.09	0.01						
3. Reading	-2.25	-1.45	-0.01					
4. Maths	-4.36	-3.12	-2.21	-0.05				
5. Dad's class	0.02	0.00	-0.02	0.00	0.00			
6. Mum's SEG	0.31	0.23	0.15	0.34	-0.11	-0.06		
7. Dad's educ	-0.14	-0.09	-0.05	-0.13	0.06	0.15	-0.02	
8. Mum's educ	-0.05	-0.03	-0.01	-0.04	0.04	0.15	-0.24	0.00
EM								
1. Verbal IQ	-4.90							
2. Non-verbal IQ	-3.12	-3.26						
3. Reading	-2.27	-1.49	-2.12					
4. Maths	-4.17	-3.13	-2.37	-5.79				
5. Dad's class	-0.01	-0.01	-0.02	0.00	-0.18			
6. Mum's SEG	0.13	0.10	0.05	0.16	-0.07	-2.02		
7. Dad's educ	-0.06	-0.04	-0.01	-0.06	0.05	0.09	-0.62	
8. Mum's educ	-0.01	-0.01	0.00	-0.02	0.03	0.12	-0.23	-0.45
IM								
1. Verbal IQ	-3.45							
2. Non-verbal IQ	-2.88	-2.42						
3. Reading	-1.62	-1.48	-0.67					
4. Maths	-2.90	-2.24	-1.38	-1.96				
5. Dad's class	0.19	0.15	0.10	0.15	-0.03			
6. Mum's SEG	0.28	0.22	0.13	0.18	-0.03	-0.06		
7. Dad's educ	-0.20	-0.15	-0.09	-0.14	0.03	0.03	-0.04	
8. Mum's educ	-0.15	-0.12	-0.08	-0.11	0.02	0.03	-0.02	0.00
DA								
1. Verbal IQ	0.15							
2. Non-verbal IQ	0.14	0.09						
3. Reading	0.04	0.10	-0.02					
4. Maths	-0.04	-0.01	0.01	-0.12				
5. Dad's class	-0.01	-0.01	-0.01	0.00	0.01			
6. Mum's SEG	-0.01	0.00	-0.01	0.01	0.00	0.02		
7. Dad's educ	-0.09	-0.07	-0.05	-0.12	0.01	0.03	0.03	
8. Mum's educ	-0.01	-0.01	-0.01	-0.02	0.00	-0.01	0.00	0.02

6.3.1   Handling missing data

Table 6.2 lists each of the eight statistical remedies according to their recouped sample size and applicability under three assumptions regarding the missingness mechanism. To recap; MCAR, *missing completely at random,* MAR, *missing at random,* and MNAR, *missing not at random.* The presence of a $\sqrt{}$ confirms the application of the assumption for missingness, whereas a $\times$ confirms the reverse. Strictly, one would expect that none of the remedies would work properly under MNAR. However, there is some evidence in the literature (Little & Rubin, 1980; Muthèn et al., 1987) to suggest that maximum likelihood estimates show less bias under MNAR than simple methods like LD, PD and MS. There is also some evidence to suggest that NORM will produce good results even when data are seriously non-normal (Graham & Hofer, 2000). Consequently, a ? symbol is entered when it is unclear to whether or not the procedure will perform efficiently under such missingness assumptions.

Note that under listwise deletion (LD) by definition just over a third of the original sample with complete data remains. Under pairwise deletion (PD) the filled-in sample base hovers around 10,000. MS, REG, EM, DA and FIML all provide filled in samples of size 15,098. The LISREL imputation (IM), as a result of the restrictions imposed on the imputation procedure, only provides 8908 filled in cases. Under DA 5 filled-in datasets were produced. For the degree of missingness in the original data of 18% this would attain estimates at around 97.0% efficiency. It has been suggested that for both DA and IM it is advisable to use matching variables which are not part of the SEM to enhance the validity of imputed values for missing data (see Schafer 1997 and Appendix B in PRELIS2, Jöreskog and Sörbom 1996a). It was decided that each procedure would be judged in the absence of any additional imputation variables or matching information simply because users will not always be able to draw on the wealth of data available in longitudinal birth cohort studies.

The results are presented in terms of each of the remedies resulting parameter estimates and associated standard error estimates in relation to those obtained for FIML. First, the findings for the educational achievement measurement model are presented (i.e., EDUC in Figure 6.2). These are followed by the findings from the parental socioeconomic status measurement model (i.e., SES in Figure 6.3). Finally, the structural model estimates relating SES and EDUC are presented in Figure 6.4.

6.4   Results

Goodness-of-fit statistics for the model estimated under the different methods for dealing with missingness are provided in Table 6.3. If one assumes that the substantive model is the "correct" approximate model, then given the prior hypotheses about FIML estimation, indices of goodness-of-fit under FIML should provide stronger support for the model than the other remedies for dealing with missingness. The results are consistent with these assumptions. However, it is worth noting that all the methods with the possible exception of PD and EM, yield goodness-of-fit statistics with broadly similar values.

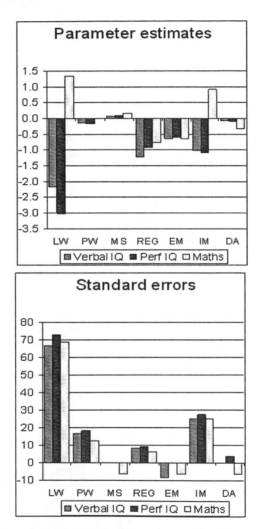

Fig. 6.2. Percentage deviation in measurement model estimates for 'Educational achievement' in comparison with FIML estimates.

Figure 6.2 shows how the estimates and standard errors for the "educational achievement" measurement model using the different remedies for missingness differ from those produced under FIML. Because the metric for 'educational achievement' was set by fixing to unity the path from "EDUC" to "reading", the comparison involves only the other three manifest variables. For the 'educational achievement' variables the LD estimates are not uniformly smaller than the FIML, but there are absolute differences with + and - 3% of the FIML estimates. Interestingly, PD and MS are surprisingly close to the FIML estimates as are the estimates obtained under DA. REG, EM and IM all produce consistently smaller estimates. The relatively large standard errors for LD and IM reflect the relative lack of full information associated with these methods. Otherwise, the standard errors tend to be smaller under EM and DA and, if anything, slightly larger under REG.

The extent of missingness was much greater for the "socioeconomic status" variables than the "educational achievement" variables (Table 6.1). Comparison of parameter estimates for the "socioeconomic status" measurement model with FIML estimates (Figure 6.3) shows that departures are much more pronounced for the ad-hoc solutions, most notably for mean substitution (MS). The relative reduction in the estimate for mother's SEG is quite striking under this procedure and, to a lesser extent under PD. The simple and advanced model based procedures all produce very similar estimates with the exception of regression (REG) which tends to consistently produce smaller estimates. Again, standard errors are uniformly larger under LD but this time not for IM. Standard errors are uniformly smaller for all variables under MS, REG and EM. Unlike the educational achievement measurement model, more noticeable departures for DA in this model are observed.

Next, the structural model for "parental socioeconomic status" to "educational achievement" is examined (see Figure 6.4). For the parameter estimates there is nothing to choose between DA and FIML. With the exception of IM and PD, parameter estimates tend to be within 5% lower than the estimates obtained under DA and FIML. PD estimates are considerably lower. For standard error estimation one sees a steady declining discrepancy in absolute terms across LD to EM estimates. DA estimates are slightly smaller when compared to FIML, but remain closest. So how do these estimates compare overall? Table 6.4 presents the instances where estimates are with 10% of the FIML estimates. Although the 10% limit is non-statistical, it is still quite revealing.

For the example data, none of the remedies is consistently close to FIML across all estimates in the SEM. REG, EM, IM and DA all do consistently well when parameter estimates are considered. Despite its shortfall in sample membership, IM looks quite good across estimates of the standard errors. DA is close, but less so for all standard error estimation. Using this 10% criteria, simple models under regression (REG) and expectation maximisation (EM), which avoid the need for replication, look as robust as DA. An alter-

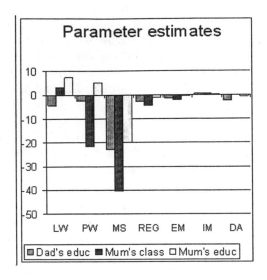

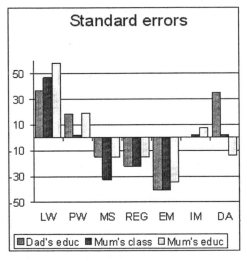

Fig. 6.3. Percentage deviation in measurement model estimates for 'parental socio-economic status' in comparison with FIML estimates.

native comparison of the remedies for missingness can be made by examining the fitted or implied covariance matrix from the eight methods. The results from this comparison are displayed in Table 6.5. Overall, the variances and covariances for the measures of educational achievement are similar for all techniques, but differences between the methods emerge when the degree of missingness increases. For the measures of socioeconomic status, LD and MS performed particularly poorly in comparison with FIML, closely followed by

EM and IM. The implied covariance matrix under FIML was closely repro-
duced under DA.

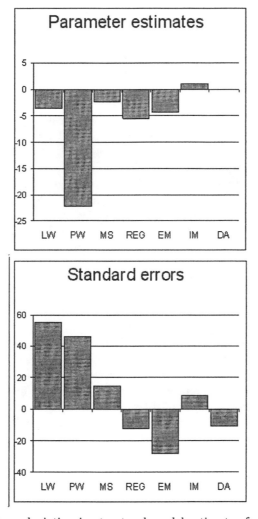

Fig. 6.4. Percentage deviation in structural model estimates for 'Parental socio-
economic status' to 'Educational achievement' in comparison with FIML estimates.

6.5 Conclusions

What can be learned from this fishing trip in the pond of missing data remedies? Ad-hoc solutions are deceptively simple and easy to pull out. Remarkably listwise deletion (LD) produces unbiased parameter estimates for these

data, but its standard errors are larger as a consequence of the reduction in sample size. Pairwise deletion (PD) and mean substitution (MS) are simply not recommended, providing little comfort for quick and easy solutions (see Table 6.4). Simple model-based solutions do reasonably well, but have a number of disadvantages. Apart from the lack of theoretical appeal, regression (REG) provides outliers that are outside of the range of the original data (although it's easy access with SPSS might make it an option when used under multiple imputation). EM, as implemented in SPSS, tends to be rather computer intensive.

In this comparison only eight manifest variables were used and it was only just viable to obtain a solution. And yet, most SEM's for longitudinal analysis are likely to draw upon many more items. Under the advanced model based solutions, IM performs reasonably well but does not appreciably augment the sample. Again, with more items in an SEM study this problem is likely to be more severe. The relative disadvantage with DA under NORM is that it requires the user to produce a number of filled-in data sets (in this instance 5) prior to the application of SEM. However, the resulting estimated variance-covariance matrices from DA under NORM can be presented to SEM programs as routine multi-group analyses (with all estimates constrained to be equal across the groups). Parameter estimates are then averaged properly without further recourse to Rubin's Rule. Standard errors will be downwardly biased but can be adjusted to approximate those required under Rubin's Rule by multiplying them by $\sqrt{g}$, where g is the number of groups used in the analysis. Obviously, FIML is quite attractive, and (with the AMOS package) the user has a theoretically sound methodology which performs very much like DA under NORM. It can be readily applied for larger item sets and appears to handle model complexity quite well. What it does not provide are modification indices for the user who wants to carefully experiment with the inclusion or exclusion of key variables on empirical grounds. To do so, would require the user to develop their SEM using datasets culled under listwise. A remedy that may be questionable! Finally, the performance of DA under NORM is also quite encouraging. As a consequence, users are encouraged to try both FIML and DA under NORM and to routinely compare and contrast the resulting findings both between the methodologies themselves and crude listwise deletion strategies.

References

Allison P.D. (1987). Estimation of linear models with incomplete data. In C.C. Clogg (Ed.) *Sociological Methodology* (pp. 71-103). San Francisco, CA: Jossey-Bass.

Arbuckle, J. L. (1996). Full information estimation in the presence of incomplete data. In G. A. Marcoulides & R. E. Schumacker (Eds.), *Advanced structural equation modeling: Issues and techniques.* Mahwah, NJ: Lawrence Erlbaum Associates.

Arbuckle, J. L. (1997). *Amos User's Guide Version 3.6*, SmallWaters Corporation, USA.

Bentler, P. M. (1989). *EQS structural equations program manual.* Los Angeles, CA: BMDP Statistical Software.

Bentler, P. M. (1990). EQS structural models with missing data. *BMDP Communications*, 22, 9-10.

Boomsma, A. (1983). On robustness of LISREL (maximum likelihood estimation) against small sample size and non-normality. Ph.D thesis. University of Groningen, The Netherlands.

Dempster, A. P., Laird, N. M., & Rubin, D. B. (1977). Maximum likelihood estimation from incomplete data via the EM algorithm. *Journal of the Royal Statistical Society, Series B*, 39, 1-38.

Enders, C. K. (1999). The relative performance of full information maximum likelihood estimation for missing data in structural equation models. Dissertation, University of Nebraska, Lincoln, NE., USA.

Finkbeiner, C. (1979). Estimation for the multiple factor model when data are missing. *Psychometrika*, 44, 409-420.

Ferri, E., (ed) (1993). *Life at 33: the fifth follow-up of the National Child Development Study*, National Children's Bureau, London.

Ford, B.N. (1983). An overview of hot deck procedures. In W.G. Madow, I.Olkin, & D. B.Rubin (Eds.), *Incomplete data in sample surveys, Vol. II: Theory and annotated bibliography.* New York: Academic Press.

Graham, J. W., & Hofer, S. M. (2000). Multiple imputation in multivariate research. In T. Little, K. U. Schnabel, & J. Baumert (Eds.), *Modeling longitudinal and multilevel data.* Mahwah, NJ: Lawrence Erlbaum Associates.

Jöreskog, K. & Sörbom, D. (1996a). *LISREL 8: User's reference guide.* Chcago, IL: Scientific Software International.

Jöreskog, K. and Sörbom, D. (1996b). *PRELIS 2: User's reference guide.* Chicago, IL: Scientific Software International.

Little, R. J. A. and Rubin, D. B. (1987). *Statistical analysis with missing Data.* New York: J. Wiley & Sons.

Muthèn, B., Kaplan, D., & Hollis, M. (1987). On structural equation modeling with data that are not missing completely at random. *Psychometrika*, 52, 431-462.

Neale, M.C. (1994). *Mx: statistical modelling* (2nd edition). Richmond, VA: Department of Psychiatry, Medical College of Virginia.

Rubin, D. S. (1996). Multiple imputation after 18 years. *Journal of the American Statistical Association*, 91, 473-489.

Schafer, J. L. (1997). *Analysis of incomplete multivariate data.* London: Chapman & Hall.

SPSS Inc. (1997) *Missing values analysis 7.5* (valid through version 10.0)

Tanner, M. A. & Wong, W. H. (1987). The calculation of posterior distributions by data augmentation (with discussion). *Journal of the American Statistical Association*, 82, 528-550.

Verleye, G., Pepermaus, R., & Despontin, M. (1998). Missing at random problems and maximum likelihood structural equation modelling. In J. Hox & e. de

Leeuw (Eds.). *Assumptions, robustness, and estimation methods in multivariate modelling*. Amsterdam, The Netherlands: T-T Publikates.

Wiggins, R. D., Ely, M., & Lynch, K. (2000). A comparative evaluation of currently available software remedies to handle missing data in the context of longitudinal design and analysis. In *Social Science Methodology in the New Millennium Proceedings for 5ᵗʰ International Conference on Logic and Methodology*, Cologne.

7 Exploring Structural Equation Model Misspecifications via Latent Individual Residuals [*]

Tenko Raykov[1] and Spirinov Penev[2]

[1] Fordham University
[2] University of New South Wales, Sydney, Australia.

7.1 Introduction

For several decades, structural equation modeling (SEM) has enjoyed a high level of popularity in the behavioral, social, and educational sciences. An important reason is that the methodology permits studying complex multivariate phenomena whereby measurement errors both in the dependent and explanatory variables are accounted for (e.g., Raykov & Marcoulides, 2000). A critical issue in applications of SEM is that of model fit assessment. Over the past 30 years or so an impressive body of literature has accumulated that deals with evaluation of model fit (e.g., Bollen, 1989). With few exceptions however (e.g., Bollen & Arminger, 1991; Neale, 1997; McDonald, 1997; McDonald & Bolt, 1998; Reise & Widaman, 1999; Raykov & Penev, 2001), this literature has been exclusively concerned with indices of overall model goodness of fit.

The present chapter argues in favor of using indices of model fit at the subject level. The concern is with providing further evidence that individual residuals can be particularly beneficial for ascertaining model misspecifications (e.g., Bollen & Arminger, 1991; McDonald, 1997; McDonald & Bolt, 1998). In particular, these residuals are utilized as additional indices of fit in exemplifying that lack of latent relationship in a structural equation model does not imply lack of causal relation between its unobservable variables. The aim is to demonstrate the utility of latent individual residuals as informative adjuncts to routinely used goodness of fit measures, hoping to stimulate thereby further interest, research into, and application of subject level residuals in research employing the popular SEM methodology.

[*] This research was supported by grants from the School of Mathematics, University of New South Wales, and a Fordham University Research Grant. We are greatful to G. A. Marcoulides, G. Arminger, R. P. McDonald, and R. E. Millsap for valuable discussions on individual residual evaluation.

7.2   Background and Definitions

7.2.1   Notation

Using common SEM notation (e.g., Bollen, 1989), $y = (y_1, y_2, ..., y_p)'$ is the vector of observed data on p manifest variables of interest $(p > 1)$ in a linear structural relationships model defined with the following two equations:

$$y = \Lambda\eta + \epsilon, \text{ and} \qquad (7.1)$$

$$\eta = B\eta + \zeta, \qquad (7.2)$$

where η is the $q \times 1$ vector of latent variables, B the $q \times q$ matrix of structural regression coefficients relating the latent variables among themselves (assumed nonzero and such that $I_q B$ is nonsingular, with I_q being the identity matrix of size $q \times q$), Λ is the $p \times q$ factor loadings matrix assumed of full rank, ζ the $q \times 1$ structural regression residual vector with covariance matrix Ψ, and ϵ is the $p \times 1$ normal error terms vector with covariance matrix Θ (e.g., Jöreskog & Sörbom, 1996; as usual in behavioral and social research, we assume positive definite error covariance matrix).

7.2.2   Latent individual residuals

To accomplish the goals of this chapter, interest lies in examining the latent residual ζ in the structural regression equation (7.2). To this end, from Equation (7.2) it follows that

$$\zeta = (I - B)\eta \qquad (7.3)$$

Hence, one can estimate ζ by substituting into the right-hand side of Equation (7.3) estimates for the quantities appearing there:

$$\hat{\zeta} = (I - \hat{B})\hat{\eta} \qquad (7.4)$$

To further use Equation (7.4), note that consistent and asymptotically optimal estimates of its parameters and in particular of the structural regression coefficient matrix, $\hat{B}$, are obtained by fitting the model to data (using appropriate fit function for data distribution; Bollen, 1989; Kaplan, 2000). One can then estimate the remaining element in its right-hand side, η, by utilizing Equation (7.1). Since there is no structural restriction on the error covariance matrix in (7.1), the general linear model theory and principle of weighted least squares yield

$$\hat{\eta} = \left(\hat{\Lambda}'\hat{\Theta}^{-1}\hat{\Lambda}\right)^{-1} \hat{\Lambda}'\hat{\Theta}^{-1}y, \qquad (7.5)$$

where $\hat{\Lambda}$ and $\hat{\Theta}$ are the obtained estimates of the factor loading and error covariance matrices (e.g., Rao, 1973; the inverse $\left(\hat{\Lambda}'\hat{\Theta}^{-1}\hat{\Lambda}\right)^{-1}$ exists with probability 1, due to the earlier made assumptions about Λ and Θ). We note that $\hat{\eta} = \left(\hat{\Lambda}'\hat{\Theta}^{-1}\hat{\Lambda}\right)^{-1}\hat{\Lambda}'\hat{\Theta}^{-1}y$ is the Bartlett estimator of the factors η in the structural equation model defined by (7.1) and (7.2) (e.g., Gorsuch, 1983).

The interest in $\hat{\eta}$ from (7.5) is further justified by a related optimality property seen by a reference to the concept of projection. Accordingly, for an individual raw data point y, its projection upon the column space of Λ (the set of all linear combinations of its columns) using as a weight matrix Θ is defined as $u = \lambda \left(\Lambda'\Theta^{-1}\Lambda\right)^{-1}\Lambda'\Theta^{-1}y$ (e.g., Rao, 1973). As is well-known, u is unique and always exists (Λ is assumed of full-rank), and in fact u represents that point in the column space of Λ that is closest to y in the distance $d_\Theta(.,.)$ defined (induced) by the matrix Θ: $d_\Theta(x, z) = (x - z)'\Theta^{-1}(x - z)$ for a pair of $p \times 1$ vectors x and z (e.g., Raykov & Penev, 2001). The column space of Λ, being the space spanned by the accounted for part of the model, represents the manifold of model-based predictions across all possible choices of its parameters; that is, u is that model-generated point from the raw data space, which is nearest to y in this metric. With this in mind, Equation (7.5) implies that $\hat{u} = \hat{\Lambda}\hat{\eta}$ represents a corresponding set of linear combinations of components of the above estimator $\hat{\eta}$, with weights being appropriate factor loadings. Hence, with this $\hat{\eta}$ Equation (7.5) furnishes the following estimator of the structural residual

$$\hat{\zeta} = (I - \hat{B})\hat{\eta} = (I - \hat{B})\left(\hat{\Lambda}'\hat{\Theta}^{-1}\hat{\Lambda}\right)^{-1}\hat{\Lambda}'\hat{\Theta}^{-1}y \qquad (7.6)$$

It is stressed that $\hat{\zeta}$ is a $q \times 1$ vector that consists of the model-specific residuals for every subject along all studied latent dimensions. (This feature justifies reference to $\hat{\zeta}$ as consisting of "latent individual residuals", abbreviated to LIR.) Thus, the LIR are individual case residuals at the latent variable level, which are: (a) functions of the observed variables; and (b) defined for any structural equation model having a full- rank factor loading matrix (with nonzero B and positive definite error covariance matrix; see discussion and conclusion section for an extension). The next section shows that the LIR can be very informative when evaluating fit of structural equation models, particularly with respect to model misspecifications at the unobservable variable level. Thereby, the LIR will help exemplify that lack of latent relationship in a structural equation model does not imply lack of causation between its latent constructs.

7.3   Lack of Latent Relationship Does Not Imply Lack of Causation: Using Latent Individual Residuals to Refute an "Intuitive" Claim

The study of causality in the behavioral, social, and educational sciences has attracted an enormous amount of interest over the past century. One of the major points raised in favor of considering use of structural equation models when examining causal relations, has been a characteristic feature of these models–the fact that they allow one to evaluate "error-free" relations between latent variables of main interest. At the same time, important concerns have been raised when SEM has been used in this context, specifically with regard to possible misinterpretations of its results (e.g., Freedman, 1987; Rogosa, 1987; Rogosa & Willett, 1985).

Methodological investigations of the nature of causality have identified as an essential component of it the interrelationship between two or more involved variables (e.g., Bollen, 1989). Given this important element and the current frequent utilization of structural equation models in causality related studies, it might appear intuitive to claim that with SEM now allowing "error-free" variable modeling, lack of latent relationship in such a model would imply lack of causality between its unobservable constructs. (For a discussion of a noncausal association in a substantive context, see e.g., Prescott & Kendler, 1999.)

This claim is not justified and in fact misleading. To show it so, the next section exemplifies that it is possible for a structural equation model to possess all of the following properties that are incompatible with the claim: (i) nonsignificant (linear) latent variable relationship; (ii) very good fit, as evaluated with all currently routinely used measures of overall fit; and yet (iii) being based on a strong causal relationship between its latent variables.[1] Unlike these measures of fit that will indicate very good match between model and covariance matrix, the LIR from Equation (7.6) will suggest serious model misspecifications. The following pair of examples will represent theoretically and empirically important instances in which we demonstrate the relevance of the LIR as a very useful (a) adjunct to currently widely used overall fit measures, and (b) warning against making implications of lack of causation from findings of no latent relationship in structural equation models.

7.3.1   Latent curvilinear polynomial relationship

Simulated data were used with $N = 500$ cases and $p = 6$ observed variables representing indicators of two latent constructs that are causally nonlinearly related. The data were generated using the model with the following definition equations:

$$y_1 = \eta_1 + \epsilon_1 \qquad (7.7)$$
$$y_2 = 1.2\eta_1 + \epsilon_2$$

---

[1] The issue of type I error is not pertinent to the remainder of this chapter–the point of the following argument applies regardless whether or not a type I error has been committed when testing for significance a particular parameter in a structural equation model.

$$y_3 = 1.5\eta_1 + \epsilon_3$$
$$y_4 = \eta_2 + \epsilon_4$$
$$y_5 = 1.7\eta_2 + \epsilon_5$$
$$y_6 = 2\eta_2 + \epsilon_6$$
$$\eta_2 = \eta_1^2$$

where η_1 is a standard normal variate while the consecutive error variances are .5, .7, .8, .5, .7, and .9, respectively. Table 7.1 presents the covariance matrix of the simulated data. (Further details on the data generation process can be obtained from the author upon request.) In empirical terms, the last of Equations (7.7) describes a case where the relationship between two studied latent constructs is ("nearly" linearly) decreasing for persons with up to average values on the construct η_1, and increasing similarly for subjects above the mean on it.

Table 7.1. Covariance matrix for data based on Equation (7.7) model ($N = 500$)

Variable	y_1	y_2	y_3	y_4	y_5	y_6
y_1	1.242					
y_2	1.203	1.896				
y_3	1.444	1.740	2.727			
y_4	0.019	0.049	0.132	1.961		
y_5	0.038	0.080	0.176	2.948	5.580	
y_6	0.073	0.123	0.195	3.488	6.117	7.976

Note. N = sample size.

The structural equation model corresponding to the one defined in Equations (7.7) has two constructs measured by the first and second triples of manifest variables, respectively, and is depicted in Figure 7.1. (Note that $\zeta_1 = \eta_1$ by construction and due to the lower-triangular form of the matrix pre-multiplying y in (7.6); e.g., Jöreskog & Sörbom, 1996.) Different versions of this generic simplex (latent auto-regressive) model are often used in behavioral and social research practice.

The model in Figure 7.1 fits the data in Table 7.1 very well, as judged by overall goodness of fit indices widely used in present-day applications of SEM. Indeed, its chi-square value (χ^2) is 5.297, degrees of freedom (df) are 8, associated probability (p) is .725, and root mean square error of approximation (RMSEA) is 0 with a 90% confidence interval (0; .039). In addition, all remaining overall measures provided by LISREL indicate very good fit (e.g., Jöreskog & Sörbom, 1996). The subsequently needed parameter estimates of the model are as follows:

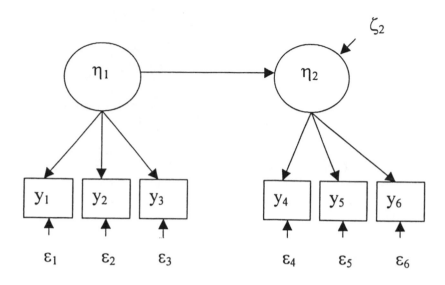

Fig. 7.1. Structural equation model fitted to the data in Table 7.1.

$$\hat{\Lambda} = \begin{bmatrix} 1 & 0 \\ 1.205 & 0 \\ 1.447 & 0 \\ 0 & 1 \\ 0 & 1.754 \\ 0 & 2.705 \end{bmatrix} \tag{7.8}$$

$$\hat{B} = \begin{pmatrix} 0 & 0 \\ 0.045 & 0 \end{pmatrix},$$

$$\hat{\Theta} = \mathrm{diag}(.244, .448, .638, .280, .410, .738),$$

where $\mathrm{diag}(., ., \dots, .)$ denotes diagonal matrix with diagonal entries successively presented in the parentheses.

The critical model parameter–the structural regression coefficient β_{21}–is estimated at .045 with a standard error .062 and pertinent t-value .733, and is thus nonsignificant.[2] The finding suggests no relationship within the fitted structural equation model between its two unobserved variables, η_1 and η_2.

---

[2] The latent correlation is also nonsignificant in the equivalent model obtained from the one in Figure 7.1 by exchanging its one-way arrow and disturbance residual for a covariance parameter (and variance of η_2; e.g., Raykov & Penev, 1999).

It will be incorrect, however, to imply from this finding lack of causality between η_1 and η_2, since in actual fact a causal relationship was built into the data generation mechanism–see last of Equations (7.7).

While the overall fit indices currently routinely used in behavioral and social research present the model in Figure 7.1 as well fitting the data in Table 7.1, its latent individual residuals lead to a different conclusion.[3] To obtain them, use can be made of the short SAS/IML source code in the Appendix (cf. SAS Institute, 1990). Substituting into that code the needed parameter estimates from (7.8), one obtains the LIR as follows (linear combination weight estimates are rounded-off to 3rd digit after decimal point):

$$\hat{\zeta}_1 = .386y_1 + .254y_2 + .214y_3 \tag{7.9}$$
$$\hat{\zeta}_2 = -.017y_1 - .011y_2 - .010y_3 + .211y_4 + .253y_5 + .166y_6.$$

A plot of the dependent variable LIR, $\hat{\zeta}_2$, against the independent latent variable LIR, ζ_1 (i.e., the Bartlett estimator of the independent latent construct) shows now a clear nonlinear relationship, as documented in Figure 7.2.

The parabola-like plot of the LIR against one another in Figure 7.2 resembles the parabolic true relationship between η_1 and η_2 in the used range of variation of the independent construct η_1 (see last of Equations (7.7) and subsequent discussion). Hence, this simple LIR plot suggests that there is a distinct nonlinear component in the relationship between the two latent variables, which is not captured by the fitted model; that is, the LIR indicate a serious misspecification consisting of postulating a linear latent relationship (whereas the true unobservable relationship is nonlinear). Thus, the LIR revealed a (true) nonlinear relationship not accounted for by the finding of a nonsignificant structural regression slope, β_{21}–as indicated before this nonlinear relationship was built into the model as a causal relation but is missed out if the finding of lacking significance of β_{21} is interpreted as indicative of lack of causal relation between η_1 and η_2 (see also Footnote 1).

7.3.2   Latent piece-wise linear relationship

The preceding subsection dealt with a curvilinear polynomial relationship at the latent level, and its findings need not be as informative for a different

---

[3] In addition, the q-plot of covariance matrix residuals indicate some nonlinearity (the curving of the residuals' line is not pronounced). The structural disturbance variance is twice higher than the independent latent variance, and the standard error of the former is some 15 times larger than that of the latter (cf. Raykov, 2000). Whereas the squared multiple correlation coefficient for y4 through y6 are considerably higher than those for y_1 through y_3, all six being at least in the mid .70s, the squared multiple correlation coefficient for the dependent latent variable is rather low, .002. These findings suggest also some possible deviation from linearity but do not indicate its form, unlike the LIR (see Figure 7.2).

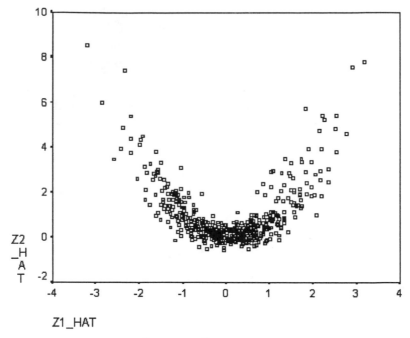

Fig. 7.2. Plot of the LIR $\hat{\zeta}_2$ against $\hat{\zeta}_1$ (see Equations (7.6), (7.7), and (7.9)) for the data set with curvilinear polynomial latent relationship.

construct relationship. The present section is concerned with the LIR potential to sense latent misspecifications, particularly in the context of causality related studies, when the constructs' relationship is other than curvilinear polynomial. To this end, simulated data are used with $N = 500$ subjects on $p = 6$ variables, which were generated using the following model:

$$y_1 = \eta_1 + \epsilon_1 \qquad (7.10)$$
$$y_2 = 1.2\eta_1 + \epsilon_2$$
$$y_3 = 1.5\eta_1 + \epsilon_3$$
$$y_4 = \eta_2 + \epsilon_4$$
$$y_5 = 1.7\eta_2 + \epsilon_5$$
$$y_6 = 2\eta_2 + \epsilon_6$$
$$\eta_2 = \begin{cases} \eta_1 & \text{if } \eta_1 > 0 \\ -\eta_1 & \text{if } \eta_1 < 0 \end{cases}$$

where η_1 is standard normal and the error variances are the same as in the previous example. Note that the structural relationship here is decreasing for negative independent construct values but increasing for positive values of it, i.e., is piece-wise linear. The covariance matrix of the obtained data is given in Table 7.2. Empirically, Equations (7.10) present a case where the relationship between two studied constructs–each assessed by a triple of measures–is linearly decreasing for persons with up to average values on ?1, and increasing so for subjects above the mean on η_1.

Table 7.2. Covariance matrix for data based on model in Equations (7.10) ($N = 500$)

Variable	y_1	y_2	y_3	y_4	y_5	y_6
y_1	1.324					
y_2	1.228	1.934				
y_3	1.548	1.808	2.925			
y_4	0.009	0.059	0.063	0.627		
y_5	0.071	0.198	0.175	0.620	1.515	
y_6	0.034	0.088	0.138	0.747	1.287	2.393

Note. N = sample size.

When fitted to the data in Table 7.2, the model in Figure 7.1 is associated with very good overall fit measures: $\chi^2 = 9.618$, df $= 8$, $p = .293$, RMSEA $= .02$ (0; .058); in addition, all remaining overall measures are quite favorable. The critical model parameter, the structural regression coefficient β_{21}, is estimated at .045 with standard error $= .030$ and t-value $= 1.50$, and is thus nonsignificant.[4] To imply from this finding lack of causality between the unobservable constructs will again be incorrect, however, because a causal relationship was in fact built into to the data generating mechanism–see last pair of Equations (7.10). In the same fashion as before, utilizing the SAS/IML code in the Appendix with this model's parameter estimates one obtains its LIR as follows (see Equation (7.6)):

$$\zeta_1 = .374y_1 + .240y_2 + .234y_3 \tag{7.11}$$
$$\zeta_2 = -.017y_1 - .011y_2 - .010y_3 + .240y_4 + .251y_5 + .157y_6.$$

The plot of the LIR pertaining to the dependent latent variable against the independent construct is shown on Figure 7.3.

This LIR plot similarly suggests that despite very favorable overall fit indices there are serious model misspecifications at the latent level.[5] It is

---

[4] The latent correlation is also nonsignificant in the equivalent model obtained from the one in Figure 7.1 by exchanging its one-way arrow and disturbance residual for a covariance parameter (and variance of η_2; e.g., Raykov & Penev, 1999).

[5] In addition, some 'local' measures of fit suggest that the model is not really fitting well. While the squared multiple correlations for the indicators of the independent

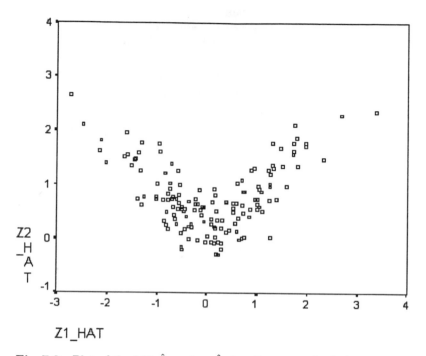

Fig. 7.3. Plot of the LIR $\hat{\zeta}_2$ against $\hat{\zeta}_1$ (see Equations (7.6), (7.10) and (7.11)) for the data set with piece-wise linear latent relationship.

worthwhile noting that as in the last example the LIR plot resembles the particular piece-wise linear true relationship employed in the data generating mechanism within the used range of variation of the independent construct η_1 (see last pair of Equations (7.10)). Thus, in the present case of piece-wise linear, as opposed to curvilinear polynomial, latent relationship the LIR were similarly able to sense important model misspecifications (cf. Raykov, 2000).

The pair of examples presented in this section demonstrate the utility of latent individual residuals and potential that SEM has for sensing important model misspecifications at the unobservable variable level, as well as the hazards of inappropriate and not well-informed SEM applications in causality

---

construct are mostly in the .70s (and the two latent variances are similar), those of y_4 and y_6 are in the mid .50s and .60s, respectively. The q-plot of covariance matrix residuals shows some deviations from linearity but no special pattern is discernible. (This is also an example where deviations from linearity should not be interpreted as indication of curvilinear latent relationship–such one was not built into the data generating mechanism; see Equations (7.10).) Similarly, the squared multiple correlation for the structural equation is rather low: .01. These findings also suggest lack of latent linearity but do not indicate its form, unlike the LIR (see following main text and Figure 7.3).

related studies (see, e.g., also Freedman, 1987). Such applications can occur when found lack of latent relationship is interpreted as implying lack of causal relation between unobservable variables.

7.4 Discussion and Conclusions

The aim of this chapter was to present further evidence that subject level residuals, and in particular latent individual residuals (LIR), can be very useful indicators of misspecifications in structural equation models. A particular LIR application here also demonstrated that a finding of lacking latent relationship in a structural equation model should not be interpreted as implying lack of causality between the involved unobservable constructs. This was exemplified by a pair of instances where the unobserved variables were constructed to be causally and nonlinearly related to one another (Equations (7.7) and (7.10)), yet the structural regression slope was found nonsignificant in the fitted simplex model (Figure 7.1; see also Footnote 1). A misinterpretation in such cases results when attributing lack of causality to the relationship between the two latent variables involved. The LIR contained however useful information about model misspecification in the examples, which was not found in the currently routinely used overall goodness of fit indices (see also Footnotes 3 and 5).

This chapter capitalized on an important analogy in the general context of examination for model misspecifications. The LIR utilization paralleled some applications of observational residuals in conventional regression analysis for the same purpose (e.g., du Toit, Steyn, & Stumpf, 1986). It was stressed however that these frameworks differ in important aspects–latent variables in SEM are unobservable and hence no measurements for them are available, whereas predictor variables are assumed measured (without error) in regression. Nonetheless, as the preceding discussion shows, the underlying general idea of checking for pattern in the relationship between residuals and appropriate independent variables, specifically in this case latent predictors, can be fruitful within the SEM framework as well. (Thereby, as in regression analysis different types of plots may be used; e.g., du Toit et al., 1986.) The examples in this chapter served both as a demonstration of the utility of LIR for purposes of evaluation of structural equation model fit and particularly for examining model misspecifications, and as a reminder that lack of latent (as opposed to observed) covariation found with widely used structural equation models does not exclude the possibility of other than straight-line relationships between their latent variables. Furthermore, the examples demonstrated that informed applications of SEM, including utilization of subject-level residuals, can sense important model misspecifications at the latent relationship level (see also Footnotes 3 and 5; Bollen & Arminger, 1991; McDonald, 1997; McDonald & Bolt, 1998; Raykov, 2000).

The LIR of this chapter represent functions of the Bartlett estimator of factor scores (see Equations (7.5) and (7.6)). A question can therefore be raised about their relationship to the "factor score indeterminacy issue" (e.g., Gorsuch, 1983). It is argued in this regard that the essence of that indeterminacy problem is the lack of unique solution to the factor score estimation problem (due to the lack of sufficient information in the conventional factor analysis model for this purpose). Hence, the problem does not necessarily imply lack of meaningfulness of, or reliable information contained in, a particular set of factor score estimates. In addition, the LIR in Equation (7.6) are linear functions of the Bartlett factor score estimator that results using a statistical optimality principle once the confirmatory factor analysis model is fitted–that of weighted least squares. Moreover, as shown earlier in the chapter the LIR are closely related to the important projection concept that has the optimality property of rendering the closest model-generated point to the raw data. Further, the LIR were exemplified to contain important model misfit information that was not comparably obtainable with other currently available model fit indices (whether of overall or local nature). Thus, the LIR in this chapter do not have to be adversely affected by the factor indeterminacy problem to a degree rendering them uninformative. This statement is also based on the observation that if a structural equation model is correct then the residuals of its latent variables, which result as linear combinations of optimal estimates of scores on its constructs, can be expected to show a random pattern of relationship. It is emphasized, however, that further research is needed before more definitive claims can be made on (a) the specific properties of the LIR as estimators of latent disturbance terms (and/or predictors) in structural equation models, as well as (b) a set of deviation types from random pattern in LIR plots that suffice to suggest model misspecification.

Another related issue that also needs further research is that of the degree to which the LIR can be useful in sensing model misspecifications of a more general nature. In this chapter, two examples were presented that were based on a piece-wise linear and a second-order polynomial latent relationship. Notably, the plot of the LIR against pertinent latent independent variable was found to resemble the pattern of true relationship between the corresponding latent variables (see Figures 7.2 and 7.3). The question that remains to be addressed is whether the LIR will be as informative under other circumstances where the nonlinearity in the true relationship stems from a different class of construct relationships, and/or the number and reliability of employed multiple indicators varies, and/or the type of model misspecification is different. Based on the Weierstrass theorem in mathematical analysis stating that a continuous function can be approximated (sufficiently well) with a set of appropriately chosen polynomials (e.g., Jordan & Smith, 1997), it can be conjectured that the LIR may have potential to sense model misspecifications also in more general cases of (continuous) true construct relationship. In addition, it is worthwhile stressing that if a studied relationship between unobservable variables can be reasonably well approximated by a line, then the LIR should not necessarily be expected to be sensitive to such relatively minor deviations from latent linearity.

In conclusion, the LIR of this chapter may appear to be of relevance only for structural models with linear latent relationships in the form of equations involving their underlying constructs (see Equation (7.6) and assumptions made at the beginning of the chapter). However, for models without such relationships use of the well-known replacement rule can be made (e.g., Lee & Hershberger, 1990). Accordingly, under certain circumstances that are frequently fulfilled in practice (e.g., MacCallum, Wegener, Uchino, & Fabrigar, 1993), such models are equivalent to models differing from them only in the structural equations being exchanged with covariances of pertinent latent residuals (variables). Applying the LIR of this chapter on the former models, one may sense deviations from linearity in the relationship between their latent variables. Such a finding would indicate other than linear relationships between the latent variables of their equivalent models without latent variable equation(s). That is, from the earlier discussion in this chapter follows that a finding of a nonsignificant latent correlation also in a structural model without latent relationship equations does not imply lack of causal relation between its corresponding unobservable variables (see also Footnote 1).

References

Bollen, K. A. (1989). *Structural equations with latent variables.* New York: Wiley.

Bollen, K. A. & Arminger, G. (1991). Observational residuals in factor analysis and structural equation models. In P. V. Marsden (Ed.), *Sociological Methodology* (pp. 235-262). San Francisco, CA: Jossey Bass.

Freedman, D. (1987). As others see us: A case study in path analysis. *Journal of Educational Statistics*, 12, 101-128.

Gorsuch, R. L. (1983). *Factor analysis.* Hillsdale, NJ: Lawrence Erlbaum.

Jordan, D. W. & Smith, P. (1997). *Mathematical techniques.* Oxford: Oxford University.

Jöreskog, K. G., Sörbom, D. (1996). *LISREL 8: User's guide.* Chicago, IL: Scientific Software.

Kaplan, D. (2000). *Structural equation modeling. Foundations and extensions.* Thousand Oaks, CA: Sage.

Lee, S. & Hershberger, S. L. (1990). A simple rule for generating equivalent models in covariance structure modeling. *Multivariate Behavioral Research*, 25, 313-334.

MacCallum, R. C., Wegener, D. T., Uchino, B. N., & Fabrigar, L. R. (1993). The problem of equivalent models in applications of covariance structure analysis. *Psychological Bulletin*, 114, 185-199.

McDonald, R. P. (1997). Haldane's lungs: A case study in path analysis. *Multivariate Behavioral Research*, 32, 1-38.

McDonald, R. P. & Bolt, D. M. (1998). The determinacy of variables in structural equation models. *Multivariate Behavioral Research*, 33, 385-402.

Neale, M. C. (1997). *Mx. Statistical modeling.* Richmond, VA: Department of Psychiatry, Virginia Commonwealth University.

Prescott, C. A. & Kendler, K. S. (1999). Age at first drink and risk for alcoholism: A noncausal association. *Alcoholism: Clinical and Experimental Research,* 23, 101- 107.

Rao, C. R. (1973). *Linear statistical inference and its applications.* New York: Wiley.

Raykov, T. (2000). On sensitivity of structural equation modeling to latent relationship misspecifications. *Structural Equation Modeling,* 7, 596-607.

Raykov, T. & Marcoulides, G. A. (2000). *A first course in structural equation modeling.* Mahwah, NJ: Lawrence Erlbaum.

Raykov, T. & Penev, S. (1999). On structural equation model equivalence. *Multivariate Behavioral Research,* 34, 199-244.

Raykov, T. & Penev, S. (2001). The problem of equivalent structural equation models: An individual residual perspective. In G. A. Marcoulides and R. E. Schumacker (Eds.), *New developments and techniques in structural equation modeling.* Mahwah, NJ: Lawrence Erlbaum.

Reise, S. P. & Widaman, K. F. (1999). Assessing the fit of measurement models at the individual level: A comparison of item response theory and covariance structure approaches. *Psychological Methods,* 4, 3-21.

Rogosa, D. R. (1987). Myths about longitudinal research. In K. W. Schaie, R. T. Campbell, W. M. Meredith, & S. C. Rawlings (Eds.), *Methodological issues in aging research* (pp. 171-209). New York: Springer.

Rogosa, D.R. & Willett, J. (1985). Satisfying a simplex structure is simpler than it should be. *Journal of Educational Statistics,* 10, 99-107.

SAS Institute (1990). *SAS/IML Software.* Cary, NC: SAS Institute.

du Toit, S. H. C., Steyn, A. G. W., & Stumpf, R. H. (1986). *Graphical exploratory data analysis.* New York: Springer.

Appendix

SAS Source Code for Obtaining the Latent Individual Residuals for the Model in Figure 7.1 (see Eqs. (7.6) and (7.9)).

```
DATA LIR;
PROC IML;
THETA={.244 0 0 0 0 0, 0 .448 0 0 0 0, 0 0 .638 0 0 0, 0 0 0 .280 0 0, 0
0 0 0 .410 0, 0 0 0 0 0 .738};
LAMBDA={1 0, 1.205 0, 1.447 0, 0 1, 0 1.754, 0 2.075};
BETA={0 0, .045 0};
ZETA_HAT=(I(2)-BETA)*INV(LAMBDA'*INV(THETA)*LAMBDA)*LAMBDA'*INV(THETA);
PRINT ZETA_HAT;
USE THE ELEMENTS OF THE MATRIX ZETA_HAT TO OBTAIN THE LIR VIA EQUATION (7.6
* AS IN EQUATION (7.9);
QUIT;
```

Note. The numerical entries of the matrices THETA and LAMBDA are the elements of the estimated error covariance and factor loading matrices obtained when the model in Figure 7.1 is fitted to the covariance matrix in Table 7.1 (see Equations (7.9)).

8   On Confidence Regions of SEM Models *

Jian-Qing Shi[1], Sik-Yum Lee[2], and Bo-Cheng Wei[3]

[1] University of Glasgow, Scotland
[2] The Chinese University of Hong Kong
[3] Southeast University, China

8.1   Introduction

Structural equation modeling (Jöreskog, 1978; Bentler, 1983) is an important method for assessing multivariate data. Under certain mild regularity conditions, the basic asymptotic results for statistical inference of the method have been developed. For example, (Browne, 1974, 1984) established the generalized least squares (GLS) theory and showed that the GLS estimator is asymptotically equivalent to the maximum likelihood (ML) estimator. Lee and Bentler (1980) extended the normal GLS theory to models with constraints. It is clear that one of the most important results for practical applications of structural equation modeling (SEM) is that the GLS estimator be asymptotically normal. Based on this result, various null hypotheses about the parameters can be tested. However, it is almost always the case that confidence intervals or regions are "uniformly more informative" than hypothesis tests for making decisions. In fact, confidence intervals (regions) with information on their position and size in the parameter space offer one the opportunity to consider "practical significance" in addition to "statistical significance". Moreover, confidence intervals can be used to test statistical hypothesis, whereas the results of a hypothesis test cannot answer the questions posed in interval or region estimation (for additional arguments preferring confidence intervals or regions to hypothesis tests see Burdick & Graybill, 1992; Wonnacott, 1987).

Confidence regions of parameters in SEM models can be constructed based on the asymptotic normality of the GLS or the ML estimator. However, as seen in the next section, this kind of confidence region is only a linear approximation of the general one. For some situations with nonlinear constraints or nonlinear models, the bias of this linear approximation is significant (see discussion in next section via simulation results). This chapter introduces a geometric approach for constructing more general and accurate confidence regions that improves the linear approximation in the context of GLS estimation.

In the next section, the basic idea for constructing the confidence regions based on the GLS theory is discussed from a geometric point of view. This

---

* Comments from a referee and the editors have led to a greatly improved version of the chapter. One of us (BCW) was partially supported by the NSF of China.

kind of confidence region is called the GLS confidence region. The linear and quadratic approximations of the GLS confidence region are also derived. Section 3 extends the results to parameter subsets. The corresponding confidence regions for models with constraints are discussed in Section 4 and Section 5 provides some illustrative numerical examples.

8.2   Basic Theory of GLS Confidence Region

The following notation is used in this chapter: Assuming A is a p by p symmetric matrix, $\mathrm{vec}(A)$ represents the $p^2 \times 1$ column vector formed by stacking the columns of A, and $\mathrm{vecs}(A)$ represents the column vector obtained from the $p^* = p(p+1)/2$ nonduplicated lower triangular elements of A. Let K_p be the $p^2 \times p^*$ transition matrix such that $\mathrm{vecs}(A) = K_p{'}\mathrm{vec}(A)$ and $\mathrm{vec}(A) = K_p^{-'}\mathrm{vecs}(A)$, where $K_p^- = (K_p{'}K_p)^{-1}K_p{'}$ (Browne, 1974). The right Kronecker product of matrices is denoted by $\otimes$.

8.2.1   Geometric framework of the SEM model

Suppose that the $p \times 1$ random vectors $X_1, \cdots, X_n, X_{n+1}$ are independent and identically distributed as multivariate normal with mean μ_0 and covariance matrix $\Sigma_0 = \Sigma(\theta_0)$, where Σ_0 is a matrix function of a $q \times 1$ vector of unknown parameters θ_0. Let θ be a vector of mathematical variables that are defined in an open subset Θ in the q-dimensional Euclidean space R^q, and can take value θ_0 in Θ. Let S be the sample covariance matrix, $s = \mathrm{vecs}(S)$, and $\sigma(\theta) = \mathrm{vecs}(\Sigma(\theta))$. The first two derivatives of $\sigma(\theta)$ with respect to θ are denoted by Δ and ∇, which are a $p^* \times q$ matrix and $p^* \times q \times q$ array, respectively. The following mild regularity conditions are assumed:

(a) θ is identified; that is $\Sigma(\theta_1) = \Sigma(\theta_2)$ and implies $\theta_1 = \theta_2$.
(b) $\Sigma(\theta)$ is positive definite in a neighborhood Θ_0 of θ_0.
(c)   All first three derivatives of $\sigma(\theta)$ with respect to θ are bounded and continuous in Θ_0 and $\Delta(\theta)$ is of full column rank in Θ_0.

These regularity conditions are satisfied by the most commonly used SEM models. The asymptotic covariance matrix of s is given by

$$\mathrm{Var}(s) = n^{-1}g(\theta) = 2n^{-1}K_p{'}(\Sigma(\theta) \otimes \Sigma(\theta))K_p,$$

where $g^{-1}(\theta)$ is the Fisher information matrix of the X's for $\sigma(\theta)$. Consider the following SEM model:

$$s = \sigma(\theta) + \varepsilon, \tag{8.1}$$

where ε is the residual vector such that $e = \sqrt{n}\varepsilon$ has the appropriate asymptotically normal distribution at θ_0. Equation (8.1) represents one kind of nonlinear regression model, therefore, some geometric approaches (e.g.,

Bates & Watts, 1980; Wei, 1997) can be used. The GLS function (Browne, 1974) is given by

$$G(\theta) = 2^{-1}\text{tr}\{(S - \Sigma(\theta))V\}^2 = [s - \sigma(\theta)]'W[s - \sigma(\theta)], \qquad (8.2)$$

where $W = 2^{-1}K_p^-(V \otimes V)K_p^{-'}$, and V is a positive definite matrix which converges in probability to Σ_0^{-1}. Hence, W will converge in probability to $g^{-1}(\theta_0)$. The GLS estimate, which minimizes $G(\theta)$, is denoted by $\hat{\theta}$. Under the regularity assumptions, it follows from Browne (1974) that

$$\sqrt{n}(\hat{\theta} - \theta_0) \xrightarrow{L} N(0, \ 2[\Delta_0'K_p^-(\Sigma_0^{-1} \otimes \Sigma_0^{-1})K_p^{-'}\Delta_0]^{-1}), \qquad (8.3)$$

where $\xrightarrow{L}$ denotes convergence in a distribution.

Similar to Bates and Watts (1980), Wei (1994), and Wang and Lee (1995), a geometric framework for the nonlinear regression model (8.1) is introduced. Take σ as coordinates in the Euclidean space R^{p^*} (the solution locus π is defined as $\sigma = \sigma(\theta)$, a q-dimensional surface in R^{p^*}). The tangent space T_θ of π at θ is spanned by columns of $\Delta(\theta)$. For any two vectors a and b in R^{p^*}, define the weighted inner product as $< a, b >= a'Wb$, and the corresponding normal space is denoted by T_θ^* (for the geometric concepts such as tangent space and normal space see Millman & Parker, 1977; Seber & Wild, 1989). Suppose that the decomposition of $\Delta(\theta)$ is given by

$$\Delta(\theta) = (Q, N) \begin{pmatrix} R \\ 0 \end{pmatrix} = QR, \qquad (8.4)$$

where R and $L = R^{-1}$ are $q \times q$ nonsingular upper triangular matrices, and the columns of Q and N are orthonormal bases for T_θ and T_θ^*, respectively. The matrices Q and N satisfy

$$Q'WQ = I_q, \quad Q'WN = 0 \quad \text{and} \quad N'WN = I_{p^*-q},$$

where I_q and I_{p^*-q} are identity matrices of order q and $p^* - q$, respectively. Based on reasons given in Bates & Watts (1980), and Wang & Lee (1995), the intrinsic curvature array A^I and the parameter-effects curvature array A^P are given as

$$A^I = [N'W][U], \quad A^P = [Q'W][U]; \quad U = L'\nabla L, \qquad (8.5)$$

where $[\cdot][\cdot]$ indicates the array multiplication as defined in Bates and Watts (1980), and Seber and Wild (1989, p.691). It is well-known that A^I is invariant with respect to parameterization and A^P depends on the parameterizations (Bates & Watts, 1980). Finally, based on the results given in Browne (1974) and Wang and Lee (1995), the first two derivatives $\dot{G}(\theta)$ and $\ddot{G}(\theta)$ of the GLS function $G(\theta)$ can be expressed as

$$\dot{G}(\theta) = -2(\sqrt{n})^{-1}\Delta We, \quad \ddot{G}(\theta) = 2\Delta'W\Delta - 2(\sqrt{n})^{-1}[e'W][\nabla]. \quad (8.6)$$

8.2.2   GLS confidence region

Consider the following test statistic for the null hypothesis $H_0 : \theta = \theta_0$:

$$SD(\theta) = n\{G(\theta) - G(\hat{\theta})\}. \tag{8.7}$$

As shown in Lee and Bentler (1980, Proposition 5), $SD(\theta_0)$ is asymptotically chi-squared with degrees of freedom q. Under the normality assumption, the GLS estimate and the ML estimate are asymptotically equivalent, hence it can be shown that $SD(\theta)$ is asymptotically equivalent to the likelihood ratio statistic. The confidence region is obtained by inverting the corresponding test. Specifically, based on the above $SD(\theta)$, the $100(1 - \alpha)\%$ confidence region for θ is given by

$$C(S) = \{\theta : SD(\theta) \leq \chi^2(q, \alpha)\}, \tag{8.8}$$

where $\chi^2(q, \alpha)$ is the upper α percentage point of chi-square distribution with degrees of freedom q. This is called the GLS confidence region for θ. Since the deviation $SD(\theta)$ strongly depends on the nonlinear functions $\sigma_{ij}(\theta)$, it is usually complicated in the parameter space and is difficult to evaluate. Thus, as pointed out by Hamilton, Watts & Bates (1982), it is valuable to obtain adequate approximate confidence regions.

8.2.3   Linear approximation of the GLS confidence region

With

$$\sigma(\theta) \approx \sigma(\hat{\theta}) + \Delta(\hat{\theta})(\theta - \hat{\theta}) \quad \dot{G}(\hat{\theta}) = 0, and$$

letting $\Delta = \Delta(\hat{\theta})$, gives

$$
\begin{aligned}
G(\theta) \\
&\approx [s - \sigma(\hat{\theta}) - \Delta(\theta - \hat{\theta})]'W[s - \sigma(\hat{\theta}) - \Delta(\theta - \hat{\theta})] \\
&= [s - \sigma(\hat{\theta})]'W[s - \sigma(\hat{\theta})] + (\theta - \hat{\theta})'\Delta'W\Delta(\theta - \hat{\theta}) - 2(\theta - \hat{\theta})'\Delta'W(s - \sigma(\hat{\theta})) \\
&= G(\hat{\theta}) + (\theta - \hat{\theta})'\Delta'W\Delta(\theta - \hat{\theta}).
\end{aligned}
$$

Therefore, the linear approximation of GLS confidence region (8.8) is

$$\{\theta : n(\theta - \hat{\theta})'\Delta'W\Delta(\theta - \hat{\theta}) \leq \chi^2(q, \alpha)\}. \tag{8.9}$$

This approximate region is equivalent to the region based on the large-sample normality of $\hat{\theta}$ in (8.3). In cases with large samples, this is a very efficient approach to calculate confidence region. However, in case of medium or small samples, it should be noted that this linear approximation may be far away from the GLS confidence region if the nonlinearity of the model is strong (further discussion is given in Section 5).

8.2.4   Quadratic approximation of the GLS confidence region

To improve the above linear approximation, a quadratic approximation of the general confidence region can be derived by means of a geometric approach. The idea is to consider a nonlinear transformation τ from Θ to a new parameter space Γ, such that $\tau = \tau(\theta)$. For any subspace $C(S) \subset \Theta$ such that $P_\theta\{\theta : \theta \in C(S)\} \geq 1 - \alpha$, τ transforms $C(S)$ to $K(S) \subset \Gamma$ and that

$$P_\theta\{\theta : \tau(\theta) \in K(S)\} = P_\theta\{\theta : \theta \in C(S)\} \geq 1 - \alpha,$$

where $K(S) = \tau(C(S))$. Based on the reasonings given in Hamilton et al (1982) and Wei (1994), this nonlinear transformation is taken as

$$\tau = \tau(\theta) = \sqrt{n}Q'W\{\sigma(\theta) - \sigma(\hat{\theta})\}. \tag{8.10}$$

The quantities Q, g, R, L, etc. are all evaluated at $\hat{\theta}$. As a new parameter vector, $\tau = \tau(\theta)$ represents an one-to-one mapping from the parameter space Θ to the tangent space $T_{\hat{\theta}}$, and $Q\tau(\theta)$ is just the projection of $\sqrt{n}\{\sigma(\theta) - \sigma(\hat{\theta})\}$ onto the tangent space. The coordinates in τ provide a natural reference system for the solution locus $\sigma = \sigma(\theta)$. Confidence regions for parameters θ in terms of the coordinates $\tau = \tau(\theta)$ can be constructed by using quadratic approximations. Letting the inverse of $\tau = \tau(\theta)$ be $\theta = \theta(\tau)$, gives $\tau(\hat{\theta}) = 0$ and $\theta(0) = \hat{\theta}$.

Lemma 1. The derivatives $\ddot{G}(\theta)$ at $\hat{\theta}$ and the first two derivatives of $\theta(\tau)$ with respect to τ at $\tau = 0$ are given by

$$\ddot{G}(\hat{\theta}) \stackrel{a}{=} 2R'(I_q - B/\sqrt{n})R, \tag{8.11}$$

$$\left(\frac{\partial \theta}{\partial \tau'}\right)_{\tau=0} = L/\sqrt{n}, \quad \text{and} \quad \left(\frac{\partial^2 \theta}{\partial \tau \partial \tau'}\right)_{\tau=0} = -n^{-1}[L][A^P] \tag{8.12}$$

where $\stackrel{a}{=}$ stands for "is asymptotically equivalent to", and $B = [e'WN][A^I]$ evaluated at $\hat{\theta}$. The proof of Lemma 1 is given in the Appendix. The following theorem, which gives the main result for the GLS confidence region, is a consequence of the lemma.

Theorem 1. Under the regularity conditions, the geometric approximation of $100(1 - \alpha)\%$ GLS region of θ is expressed as

$$K(S) = \{\theta : \tau'(I_q - B/\sqrt{n})\tau \leq \chi^2(q, \alpha), \quad \tau = \tau(\theta)\} \tag{8.13}$$

Proof. From Lemma 1, the first two derivatives of $SD(\theta(\tau))$ with respect to τ are given by

$$\left\{\frac{\partial SD(\theta(\tau))}{\partial \tau}\right\}_{\tau=0} = \left\{n(\frac{\partial \theta}{\partial \tau'})'\dot{G}(\theta)\right\}_{\hat{\theta}} = 0;$$

and

$$\left\{ \frac{\partial^2 SD(\theta(\tau))}{\partial \tau \partial \tau'} \right\}_{\tau=0} = \left\{ n(\frac{\partial \theta}{\partial \tau'})'\ddot{G}(\theta)(\frac{\partial \theta}{\partial \tau'}) \right\}_{\hat{\theta}} = 2(I_q - B/\sqrt{n}).$$

Applying the second order Taylor series expansion to (8.8), gives

$$SD(\theta) \approx \tau'(\theta)(I_q - B/\sqrt{n})\tau(\theta), \qquad (8.14)$$

and hence (8.13) is valid.

Under the regularity conditions, $\ddot{G}(\hat{\theta})$ is positive definite, and so is $I_q - B/\sqrt{n}$. Therefore, the approximate GLS region given in (8.13) is an ellipsoid in tangent space $T_{\hat{\theta}}$. Moreover, because B depends only on the intrinsic curvature array A^I, $K(S)$ is invariant to parameterization in the tangent space. Expression (8.13) is similar to the results of Hamilton et al (1982), and Wei (1994) in the context of ML estimation of the exponential family model.

From the above theorem, it is not difficult to construct the confidence region of τ in the tangent plane because it is expressed as an ellipsoid (as given in Eq. (8.13)). However, for statistical inference and interpretation with specific applications, the confidence region of θ is really more valuable. Unfortunately, it is generally quite difficult to calculate the inverse transformation, which maps the tangent plane ellipsoid into the parameter space, and hence difficult to obtain the confidence region of θ in the original parameter space. As a consequence, the following expression, based on the quadratic Taylor series, is commonly used (Bates & Watts, 1981):

$$\theta = \hat{\theta} + L(\tau/\sqrt{n} - \frac{1}{2n}\tau' A^P \tau). \qquad (8.15)$$

Using this approximation of the inverse transformation, the bound of confidence region in terms of τ can be transferred to the bound of confidence region for θ. Since the confidence region in tangent space is an ellipsoid, it is easy to obtain this confidence region. As a result, the confidence region for θ can also be efficiently constructed. As will be seen in the examples given in Section 5, this approximation works quite quickly and well, especially with medium or small samples.

8.3   Regions for Subsets of Parameters

Under some practical situations, the joint confidence region of θ with high dimension may be difficult to construct and interpret. As a consequence, this section considers confidence regions for subsets of the parameters. Let $\theta' = (\theta_1', \theta_2')$ be a partition of θ, where θ_1 is $q_1 \times 1$, while θ_2 is the $q_2 \times 1$ parameter vector of interest, and $q = q_1 + q_2$. Moreover, let $\tau' = (\tau_1', \tau_2')$, $\Delta = (\Delta_1, \Delta_2)$, $R = (R_{ij})$ and $B = (B_{ij})$ for $i, j = 1, 2$ be the corresponding partitions that conform to the partitioning of θ. Let $\tilde{\theta}' = (\tilde{\theta}_1'(\theta_2), \theta_2')$, where

$\tilde{\theta}_1(\theta_2)$ minimized $G(\theta_1, \theta_2)$ for a fixed θ_2. Then the analogous statistic

$$SD(\tilde{\theta}) = n\{G(\tilde{\theta}) - G(\hat{\theta})\} \tag{8.16}$$

is asymptotically chi-squared with degrees of freedom q_2 under the null hypothesis $H_0 : \theta_2 = \theta_{02}$ (Lee & Bentler, 1980). The $100(1 - \alpha)\%$ GLS confidence region of θ_2 is expressed as

$$C_2(S) = \{\theta_2 : SD(\tilde{\theta}) \leq \chi^2(q_2, \alpha)\}. \tag{8.17}$$

Since

$$\frac{\partial \sigma(\tilde{\theta})}{\partial \theta_2} = \Delta_1 \frac{\partial \tilde{\theta}_1}{\partial \theta_2} + \Delta_2, \quad \text{and} \quad \frac{\partial \tilde{\theta}_1}{\partial \theta_2} = -(\Delta_1 W \Delta_1)^{-1} \Delta_1 W \Delta_2,$$

the linear approximating region can be derived through the following Taylor's expansion:

$$\tilde{\sigma}(\theta_2) = \sigma(\tilde{\theta})$$
$$\approx \tilde{\sigma}(\hat{\theta}_2) + \frac{\partial \sigma(\tilde{\theta})}{\partial \theta_2}(\theta_2 - \hat{\theta}_2)$$
$$= \tilde{\sigma}(\hat{\theta}_2) + W^{-1/2}(I - W^{1/2}(\Delta_1 W \Delta_1)^{-1} \Delta_1 W^{1/2})W^{1/2}\Delta_2(\theta_2 - \hat{\theta}_2)$$
$$= \tilde{\sigma}(\hat{\theta}_2) + W^{-1/2}Q_1 W^{1/2}\Delta_2(\theta_2 - \hat{\theta}_2),$$

where $Q_1 = I - W^{1/2}(\Delta_1 W \Delta_1)^{-1} \Delta_1 W^{1/2}$ is a projection matrix. Therefore, using similar derivations as in Equation (8.9), the linear approximation region is expressed as

$$\{\theta_2 : n(\theta_2 - \hat{\theta}_2)' \Delta_2' W^{1/2} Q_1 W^{1/2} \Delta_2(\theta_2 - \hat{\theta}_2) \leq \chi^2(q_2, \alpha)\}. \tag{8.18}$$

To obtain the more general GLS confidence region, one needs to get the approximate tangent space projection of $C_2(S)$. Note that Equations (8.10) and (8.14) are still true at $\theta = \tilde{\theta}$, hence,

$$\tilde{\tau} = \tau(\tilde{\theta}) = \sqrt{n}Q'W\{\sigma(\tilde{\theta}) - \sigma(\hat{\theta})\}, \tag{8.19}$$

$$SD(\tilde{\theta}) \approx \tau'(\tilde{\theta})(I_q - B/\sqrt{n})\tau(\tilde{\theta}). \tag{8.20}$$

From these results, the following theorem is true:

Theorem 2. Under the regularity conditions, the geometric approximation of $100(1 - \alpha)\%$ GLS region for θ_2 is expressed as

$$K_2(S) = \{\theta_2 : \tilde{\tau}_2'(I_2 - T/\sqrt{n})\tilde{\tau}_2 \leq \chi^2(q_2, \alpha), \quad \tilde{\tau}_2 = \tau_2(\theta_2)\}, \tag{8.21}$$

where $T = B_{22} + B_{21}(\sqrt{n}I_1 - B_{11})^{-1}B_{12}$, $I_1 = I_{q_1}$, and $I_2 = I_{q_2}$.

Proof. The approximations to (8.10) and (8.19) give

$$\tau \approx Q'W\Delta(\theta - \hat{\theta}) = \sqrt{n}R(\theta - \hat{\theta})$$

and

$$\tilde{\tau} \approx \sqrt{n}R(\tilde{\theta} - \hat{\theta}),$$

R is upper triangular, $R_{21} = 0$, and

$$\tilde{\tau}_2 = \tau_2 \approx \sqrt{n}R_{22}(\theta_2 - \hat{\theta}_2).$$

On the other hand, it follows from (8.11) that

$$\dot{G}(\tilde{\theta}) \approx \ddot{G}(\hat{\theta})(\tilde{\theta} - \hat{\theta}) = 2R'(I_q - B/\sqrt{n})\tilde{\tau}/\sqrt{n}.$$

Since $(\partial G/\partial\theta_1)_{\tilde{\theta}} = 0$, then $(I_1 - B_{11}/\sqrt{n})\tilde{\tau}_1 - B_{12}\tilde{\tau}_2\sqrt{n} = 0$. Hence,

$$\tilde{\tau}_1 = (\sqrt{n}I_1 - B_{11})^{-1}B_{12}\tilde{\tau}_2, \quad \tilde{\tau}_2 = \tau_2. \tag{8.22}$$

Substituting these results into (8.20) yields (8.21).

It can be seen that $K_2(S)$ is an ellipsoid in the tangent space and invariant under reparameterization. To get the confidence region in the parameter space, the following quadratic Taylor series can be used as a mapping from the tangent plane to the parameter space:

$$\theta_2 = \hat{\theta}_2 + L_{22}(\tau_2/\sqrt{n} - \frac{1}{2n}\tau_2'K\tau_2), \tag{8.23}$$

where $K = [Q_2'W][L_{22}'\nabla_2 L_{22}]$, and ∇_2 is $p^* \times q_2 \times q_2$ portion of ∇ consisting of the second derivatives of $\Sigma(\theta)$ with respect to the parameters of interest.

Both Hamilton (1986) and Wei (1994) obtained confidence regions for subsets of parameters based on score statistics. For completeness, this kind of confidence region for SEM models is given next. Based on (8.6), it can be seen that $G(\theta)$ can be regarded as a quasi-likelihood function, an analogous score test statistic is given as follows.

Lemma 2. The square derivation $SD(\tilde{\theta})$ given in (8.16) can be equivalently expressed as

$$SD(\tilde{\theta}) \stackrel{a}{=} \frac{n}{2}\left\{(\frac{\partial G}{\partial\theta_2})'J^{22}(\frac{\partial G}{\partial\theta_2})\right\}_{\theta=\hat{\theta}}, \tag{8.24}$$

where J^{22} is the lower right corner of J^{-1} and $J = 2\Delta'W\Delta$ is obtained from $E(\ddot{G}(\theta))$.

Theorem 3. Under regularity conditions, the approximate $100(1 - \alpha)\%$ score-based region for θ_2 is expressed as

$$K_2'(S) = \{\theta_2 : \tilde{\tau}_2'(I_2 - T/\sqrt{n})^2\tilde{\tau}_2 \leq \chi^2(q_2, \alpha), \tilde{\tau}_2 = \tau_2(\theta_2)\}. \tag{8.25}$$

The proof of the above lemma and theorem is also given in the Appendix. Expression (8.25) is similar to that of Hamilton (1986) and Wei (1994) in the

ML approach, but the above model assumptions and derivations are quite different from theirs.

8.4   Regions in Constrained Models

Consider the GLS function $G(\boldsymbol{\theta})$ given in (8.2) subject to functional constraints $\boldsymbol{h}(\boldsymbol{\theta}) = \mathbf{0}$, where $\boldsymbol{h}(\boldsymbol{\theta})$ is a $r \times 1$ vector of differentiable functions in $\boldsymbol{\Theta}_0$, a neighborhood of $\boldsymbol{\theta}_0$. The reparameterization approach (Lee & Bentler, 1980) was applied to get the confidence region of $\boldsymbol{\theta}$ under this situation.

Let $s = q - r$, there exists a $s \times 1$ vector $\boldsymbol{\gamma}$ such that $\boldsymbol{\theta} = g(\boldsymbol{\gamma})$ and $\boldsymbol{h}(g(\boldsymbol{\gamma})) = \mathbf{0}$. Let $\partial g(\boldsymbol{\gamma})/\partial \boldsymbol{\gamma}' = \boldsymbol{K}$, and $\hat{\boldsymbol{\gamma}}$ be the unconstrained GLS estimate of $\boldsymbol{\gamma}$ that minimizes

$$G_c(\boldsymbol{\gamma}) = 2^{-1}\mathrm{tr}\{[\boldsymbol{S} - \boldsymbol{\Sigma}(g(\boldsymbol{\gamma}))]\boldsymbol{V}\}^2, \qquad (8.26)$$

and $\hat{\boldsymbol{\theta}}_c = g(\hat{\boldsymbol{\gamma}})$. The solution locus π_c corresponding to the constrained model is $\{\pi_c : \boldsymbol{\sigma} = \boldsymbol{\sigma}(\boldsymbol{\theta}), \quad \boldsymbol{h}(\boldsymbol{\theta}) = \mathbf{0}\}$, which can also be expressed as the following unconstrained form

$$\pi_c : \boldsymbol{\sigma} = \boldsymbol{\sigma}_c(\boldsymbol{\gamma}) = \boldsymbol{\sigma}(g(\boldsymbol{\gamma})), \qquad (8.27)$$

in a s-dimensional surface. Hence, this induces an equivalent unconstrained model, and results of previous sections can be applied.

To introduce similar curvature measures for π_c as in Section 1, let the first two derivatives of $\boldsymbol{\sigma}_c(\boldsymbol{\gamma})$ with respect to $\boldsymbol{\gamma}$ be denoted by $\boldsymbol{\Delta}_c$ and $\boldsymbol{\nabla}_c$, respectively. Moreover, in the sequel, let $\boldsymbol{R}_c, \boldsymbol{L}_c, \boldsymbol{Q}_c, \boldsymbol{N}_c, \boldsymbol{U}_c$ and $\boldsymbol{A}_c^I$ be the corresponding matrices defined in (8.4) and (8.5) in the context of the constrained model. The corresponding intrinsic arrays are

$$\boldsymbol{A}_c^I = [\boldsymbol{N}_c'\boldsymbol{W}][\boldsymbol{U}_c], \qquad \boldsymbol{U}_c = \boldsymbol{L}_c'\boldsymbol{\nabla}_c\boldsymbol{L}_c. \qquad (8.28)$$

To compute $\boldsymbol{A}_c^I$, $p^* \times (p^* - s)$ matrix $\boldsymbol{N}_c$ must be found, whose columns are orthonormal bases of normal space of π_c. It can be seen from (8.27) that $\boldsymbol{\Delta}_c = \boldsymbol{\Delta}\boldsymbol{K} = \boldsymbol{Q}\boldsymbol{R}\boldsymbol{K}$, so the tangent space $\boldsymbol{T}_c$ of π_c is spanned by columns of $\boldsymbol{Q}\boldsymbol{R}\boldsymbol{K}$. Moreover, since $\boldsymbol{H}\boldsymbol{K} = \mathbf{0}$ (Lee & Bentler, 1980), then

$$(\boldsymbol{Q}\boldsymbol{L}'\boldsymbol{H}')'\boldsymbol{W}(\boldsymbol{Q}\boldsymbol{R}\boldsymbol{K}) = \boldsymbol{H}\boldsymbol{K} = \mathbf{0}.$$

Thus, the normal space $\boldsymbol{T}_c^*$ of π_c is spanned by columns of $\boldsymbol{Q}\boldsymbol{L}'\boldsymbol{H}'$ and $\boldsymbol{N}$. These results give $\boldsymbol{N}_c$ and $\boldsymbol{A}_c^I$.

To obtain the confidence regions for constrained models, the transformation (8.10) can be applied to (8.26) and (8.27), which leads to the following one-to-one mapping

$$\boldsymbol{\varphi} = \boldsymbol{\varphi}(\boldsymbol{\gamma}) = \sqrt{n}\boldsymbol{Q}_c'\boldsymbol{W}\{\boldsymbol{\sigma}_c(\boldsymbol{\gamma}) - \boldsymbol{\sigma}_c(\hat{\boldsymbol{\gamma}})\}. \qquad (8.29)$$

Then, applying the results in Theorem 1 to (8.26) and (8.27) yields a GLS confidence region

$$K_c(S) = \{\gamma : \varphi'(I_s - B_c/\sqrt{n})\varphi \leq \chi^2(s, \alpha), \ \varphi = \varphi(\gamma)\}, \tag{8.30}$$

where $B_c = [e_c'WN_c][A_c^I]$ evaluated at $\hat{\theta}_c$, and $e_c = \sqrt{n}[s - \sigma_c(\gamma)]$. On the other hand, it follows from (8.27) that $\sigma_c(\gamma) = \sigma(g(\gamma))$, $g(\hat{\gamma}) = \hat{\theta}_c$ and $g(\gamma) = \theta$, so (8.29) and (8.30) become

$$\varphi_c = \varphi_c(\theta) = \sqrt{n}Q_c'W\{\sigma(\theta) - \sigma(\hat{\theta}_c)\}, \ \text{and}$$
$$K_c(S) = \{\theta : \varphi_c'(I_s - B_c/\sqrt{n})\varphi_c \leq \chi^2(s, \alpha), \ \varphi_c = \varphi_c(\theta)\}.$$

This is a GLS region of θ subject to the constraint $h(\theta) = 0$. Similar results in Theorems 2 and 3 can also be extended to the constrained model.

8.5   Numerical Examples

Two examples are used to demonstrate the accuracy of the linear and quadratic approximation of the GLS confidence region.

8.5.1   Factor analysis model with nonlinear constraints

In the first example, a factor analysis model

$$y = \Lambda f + \varepsilon$$

with the following structure is used:

$$\Lambda' = \begin{bmatrix} 1 & 0 & \lambda & 0 \\ 0 & 1 & 0 & 1/(1-\lambda) \end{bmatrix}, \quad cov(f) = \Phi = \begin{bmatrix} 1 & \phi \\ \phi & 1 \end{bmatrix}, \quad cov(\varepsilon) = \Psi,$$

where Ψ is a diagonal matrix. The elements in Ψ as well as the one's and zero's in Λ and Φ are treated as fixed parameters. The unknown parameters are λ and ϕ are given population values of $\lambda_0 = 1.5$ and $\phi_0 = 0.6$. 55 observations were generated based on the above model from a multivariate normal distribution with the given populations values. From these observations, the GLS estimates, computed via the Newton-Raphson algorithm, are equal to $\hat{\lambda} = 1.51$ and $\hat{\phi} = 0.53$.

The GLS confidence region introduced in Section 2, as well as its quadratic approximation to the geometric confidence region and the linear approximation region were obtained. The GLS confidence region was obtained via the following Monte Carlo method. Values of $\theta = (\lambda, \phi)'$ were uniformly drawn from a selected large enough area, then $SD(\theta)$ were calculated from (8.7). If a $SD(\theta)$ value satisfied the condition in (8.8), the corresponding θ was included as a point in the confidence region. After a sufficiently large number of θ were checked, the skeleton of the confidence region was determined. This confidence region may be regarded as a standard region for comparison. It is important to note that the computation burden is very heavy and accuracy can not be guaranteed by this approach. Even with increasing computer power, it is still quite time consuming with large dimensions of $\boldsymbol{\theta}$.

To obtain the quadratic approximation of the geometric confidence region, the tangent plane ellipsoid given in (8.13) of Theorem 1 was computed and then a map of the quadratic Taylor series (8.15) was used to get the region in the parameter space. The linear approximation confidence region was constructed via (8.9). Figure 8.1 gives the 95% confidence regions. Apparently, the linear approximation is biased; while the quadratic approximation geometric confidence region is close to the GLS confidence region.

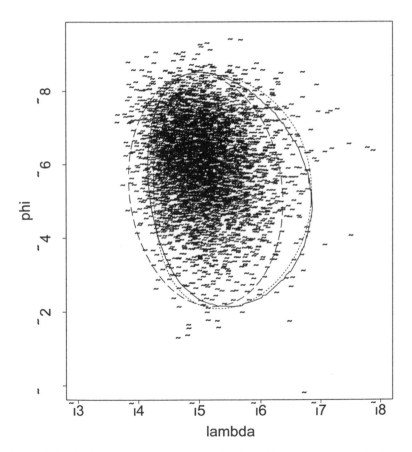

Figure 8.1: Confidence regions of λ and ϕ, where '.' represents 5000 GLS estimates of (λ, ϕ) of simulation, '—' represents the 'standard' GLS region, '· · ·' represents the quadratic approximation of geometric confidence region, and '- · -' represents the linear approximation.

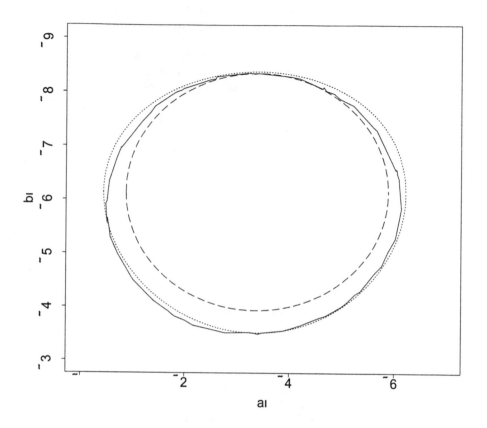

Figure 8.2: Confidence regions of a_1 and b_1 for Personality data, where '—' represents the 'standard' GLS region, '···' represents the quadratic approximation of geometric confidence region, '- · -' represents the linear approximation, and '+' represents the GLS estimate of (a_1, b_1).

The coverage probabilities were also calculated via a standard Monte Carlo simulation with 5000 replications. For the GLS confidence region, its quadratic approximation, and its linear approximation, the coverage probabilities are 0.912, 0.918 and 0.927 respectively, which are all close to $1 - \alpha = 0.95$. All 5000 estimates of simulation are plotted in Figure 8.1. They stand for the empirical distribution of the estimates. Figure 8.1 illustrates that the linear approximation confidence region is skewed to left, while the confidence region by GLS method and the quadratic approximation are more close to the "shape" of the empirical distribution. Since the computational burden of GLS confidence region is heavy, while its quadratic and linear approximations are easy to be achieved, in practice, the quadratic approximation of the GLS is recommended.

8.5.2 Example based on a three-mode model

In this example, an MTMM data set consisting of four personality traits measured by three methods (see Betler & Lee, 1979) was analyzed via the following 3-mode model (see also Lee, 1985; Bentler, Poon & Lee, 1988):

$$\Sigma = (A \otimes B)G\Phi G'(A \otimes B)' + \Psi,$$

with

$$A = \begin{bmatrix} I_A \\ a' \end{bmatrix} \quad \text{and} \quad B = \begin{bmatrix} I_B \\ b' \end{bmatrix},$$

where A and B are 3×2 and 4×3 matrices repectively, $I_A(2 \times 2)$ and $I_B(3 \times 3)$ are fixed identity matrices, $a' = (a_1, a_2)$ and $b' = (b_1, b_2, b_3)$ are parameters, $\Phi(6 \times 6)$ is a fixed identity matrix, the upper triangular elements of $G(6 \times 5)$ are fixed at zero while the remaining elements of G are free parameters, and Ψ is diagonal with $\Psi(1, 1)$ and $\Psi(5, 5)$ fixed at zero. All the parameters in G and Ψ were fixed to the GLS estimates given in Bentler et al (1988).

Based on the theory discussed in this chapter, confidence region for all five parameters in a and b can be obtained. However, in order to display the results clearly, confidence regions in a 2-dimensional plane for a subset of parameters, say $\theta_2 = (a_1, b_1)'$ were constructed via the method developed in the previous section. The GLS confidence region obtained via the Monte Carlo method, the quadratic approximation of the GLS confidence region and the linear approximation of the confidence region are displayed in Figure 8.2. As can be seen in Figure 8.2, the region obtained by linear approximation is an ellipsoid. The region obtained by quadratic approximation, taken into account the nonlinearlity of the model, is more close to the standard GLS confidence region than by linear approximation.

8.6 Discussion

Most existing asymptotic theory in structural equation modeling is derived from the first order of a Taylor's series expansion. Hence, this kind of theory is only a linear approximation of the more general case. As a result, to deal with nonlinear constraints or more complex nonlinear models, better methods that are based on the more general theory are clearly necessary. In this chapter, using a geometric approach in GLS estimation, some better methods for constructing confidence regions were derived. It was shown that the improvement over the linear approximation is significant for nonlinear models and nonlinear constraints. Analogous theory in the context of ML analysis with the normal assumption or the asymptotically distribution-free analysis with arbitrary distribution (e.g. Browne, 1984) can be derived using the proposed geometric approach.

As shown in the example section, the linear approximation is the simplest approach to construct a confidence region. If the sample size is sufficiently large, the region obtained by linear approximation is close to the GLS confidence region. Therefore, this approach can be used in cases with large sample sizes. In cases with medium or small samples, the use of the quadratic approximation is suggested (especially for the model with strong nonlinearlity - see Bates & Watts, 1980). Although Monte Carlo methods can be used to construct an almost exact GLS confidence region, it is quite time consuming if the dimension of θ is large.

Appendix

A.1 Proof of Lemma 1

It follows from (8.4), (8.5) and (8.6) that $\ddot{G}(\theta)$ can be expressed as

$$
\begin{aligned}
\ddot{G}(\theta) &\overset{a}{=} 2\Delta' W \Delta - 2(\sqrt{n})^{-1}[e'W][\nabla] \\
&= 2R' R - 2R'[e'W][U]R/\sqrt{n} \\
&= 2R'(I_q - [e'W][U]/\sqrt{n})R.
\end{aligned}
\tag{A1}
$$

It follows from (8.6) that $\dot{G}(\hat{\theta}) = 0$ implies $(e'WQ)_{\hat{\theta}} \overset{a}{=} 0$, so from (8.5) gives

$$
\begin{aligned}
\{[e'W][U]\}_{\hat{\theta}} &= \{[e'W(QQ'W + NN'W)][U]\}_{\hat{\theta}} \\
&= \{[e'WNN'W][U]\}_{\hat{\theta}} \\
&= \{[e'WN][A^I]\}_{\hat{\theta}} = B.
\end{aligned}
$$

From this and (A1), (8.11) is obtained. To prove (8.12), just note from (8.10), (8.4) and (8.5) that

$$
\left(\frac{\partial \tau}{\partial \theta'}\right)_{\hat{\theta}} = \sqrt{n}R, \quad \left(\frac{\partial^2 \tau}{\partial \theta \partial \theta'}\right)_{\hat{\theta}} = \sqrt{n}R'A^P R.
\tag{A2}
$$

Then

$$
\frac{\partial \tau}{\partial \tau'} = \frac{\partial \tau}{\partial \theta'}\frac{\partial \theta}{\partial \tau'} = I_q,
$$

and hence

$$
\left(\frac{\partial \theta}{\partial \tau'}\right)_{\tau=0} = L/\sqrt{n}.
$$

Moreover,

$$
\frac{\partial^2 \tau}{\partial \tau \partial \tau'} = \left(\frac{\partial \theta}{\partial \tau'}\right)'\left(\frac{\partial^2 \tau}{\partial \theta \partial \theta'}\right)\left(\frac{\partial \theta}{\partial \tau'}\right) + \left[\frac{\partial \tau}{\partial \theta'}\right]\left[\frac{\partial^2 \theta}{\partial \tau \partial \tau'}\right] = 0.
$$

From this and (A2), (8.12) is obtained.

A.2 Proof of Lemma 2

From (8.16), and the second order Taylor series expansion of $SD(\tilde{\theta})$ at $\tilde{\theta}$, gives

$$SD(\tilde{\theta}) = -n\dot{G}'(\tilde{\theta})\delta(\theta) - \frac{1}{2}n\delta'(\theta)\ddot{G}(\tilde{\theta})\delta(\theta) + O_p(n^{-\frac{1}{2}}), \qquad (A3)$$

where $\delta(\theta) = \hat{\theta} - \tilde{\theta}$. To get the partitioned expression of (A3), let $\delta(\theta) = (\delta_1'(\theta), \delta_2'(\theta))'$, where $\delta_1(\theta) = \hat{\theta}_1 - \tilde{\theta}_1$, $\delta_2(\theta) = \hat{\theta}_2 - \theta_2$, and write expansion of $\dot{G}(\hat{\theta}) = 0$ at $\tilde{\theta}$ as

$$\dot{G}(\tilde{\theta}) + \ddot{G}(\tilde{\theta})\delta(\theta) + O_p(n^{-1}) = 0.$$

It yields

$$\dot{G}(\tilde{\theta}) = -\ddot{G}(\tilde{\theta})\delta(\theta) + O_p(n^{-1}), \qquad (A4)$$
$$\delta(\theta) = \{\ddot{G}(\tilde{\theta})\}^{-1}\dot{G}(\tilde{\theta}) + O_p(n^{-1}). \qquad (A5)$$

Now let $\dot{G} = (\dot{G}_1', \dot{G}_2')'$, $\ddot{G} = (G_{ij})$, and $\ddot{G}^{-1} = (G^{ij})$ for $i, j = 1, 2$. Since $\dot{G}_1(\tilde{\theta}) = 0$, from (A4), one gets

$$G_{11}(\tilde{\theta})\delta_1(\theta) + G_{12}(\tilde{\theta})\delta_2(\theta) = O_p(n^{-1}). \qquad (A6)$$

From (A5) and (A6), one gets

$$\delta_2(\theta) = -G^{22}(\tilde{\theta})\dot{G}_2(\tilde{\theta}) + O_p(n^{-1}),$$
$$\delta_1(\theta) = -G_{11}^{-1}(\tilde{\theta})G_{12}(\tilde{\theta})\delta_2(\theta) + O_p(n^{-1}).$$

Since $\dot{G}(\theta) = O_p(n^{-\frac{1}{2}})$ (see (8.6)), $\delta(\theta) = O_p(n^{-\frac{1}{2}})$, substituting the above results into the partitioned expression of (A3) and by a little calculation yield

$$SD(\tilde{\theta}) \stackrel{a}{=} \frac{1}{2}n\dot{G}_2'(\tilde{\theta})G^{22}(\tilde{\theta})\dot{G}_2(\tilde{\theta}). \qquad (A7)$$

On the other hand, it follows from (8.6) that $\ddot{G}(\theta) \stackrel{a}{=} 2\Delta'W\Delta = J$ and $\ddot{G}^{-1} \stackrel{a}{=} J^{-1}$. Hence, $G^{22} \stackrel{a}{=} J^{22}$, and from (A7), (8.24) is obtained.

A.3 Proof of Theorem 3

It follows from (8.6) that

$$\partial G/\partial\theta_2 = -2(\sqrt{n})^{-1}\Delta_2'We \stackrel{a}{=} -2(\sqrt{n})^{-1}\Delta_2'We.$$

Let

$$P = \Delta(\Delta'W\Delta)^{-1}\Delta'W, \quad P_1 = \Delta_1(\Delta_1'W\Delta_1)^{-1}\Delta_1'W$$

and $P_1^* = I_{p*} - P_1$, then $J = 2\Delta'W\Delta$ gives

$$J^{22} = 2^{-1}(\Delta_2'WP_1^*\Delta_2)^{-1}.$$

Substituting the above results into (8.24) yields

$$SD(\tilde\theta) \stackrel{a}{=} \{e'W\Delta_2(\Delta_2'WP_1^*\Delta_2)^{-1}\Delta_2'We\}_{\theta=\tilde\theta}.$$

By similar derivations as shown in Hamilton (1986) and Wei (1994), one gets

$$SD(\tilde\theta) \stackrel{a}{=} \{e'W(P - P_1)e\}_{\theta=\tilde\theta}. \tag{A8}$$

To get (8.25) from this, one needs to compute $(e'W\,Pe)_{\tilde\theta}$ and $(e'WP_1e)_{\tilde\theta}$ in terms of the parameter $\tilde\tau$ defined in (8.16) and (8.19). Expanding $\sigma = \sigma(\theta(\tau))$ at $\tau = 0$, it follows from chain rule and Lemma 1 that

$$\sigma(\theta(\tau)) \approx \sigma(\hat\theta) + (\sqrt{n})^{-1}Q\tau + (2n)^{-1}N(\tau'A^I\tau). \tag{A9}$$

Moreover, since $\tilde e = \sqrt{n}\{s - \sigma(\theta(\tilde\tau))\}$, one gets

$$\tilde e \approx \hat e - Q\tilde\tau - (2\sqrt{n})^{-1}N(\tilde\tau'A^I\tilde\tau).$$

Further, it follows from (A9) that

$$\partial\sigma/\partial\tau' \approx (\sqrt{n})^{-1}Q + (n^{-1})N(A^I\tau),$$

which can be used to obtain the projection matrices P and P_1 because

$$\Delta = \frac{\partial\sigma}{\partial\theta'} = \frac{\partial\sigma}{\partial\tau'}\cdot\frac{\partial\tau}{\partial\theta'}.$$

Using all the above results and some calculations, gives

$$SD(\tilde\theta) \approx \tilde\tau'(I_q - B/\sqrt{n})(I_q - E_1)(I_q - B/\sqrt{n})\tilde\tau,$$

where E_1 is a $q \times q$ matrix with I_{q1} in the upper left corner and zeros elsewhere. Substituting (8.22) into the above expression yields (8.25).

References

Bates, D. M. & Watts, D. G. (1980). Relative curvature measures of nonlinearity (with discussion). *J. Roy. Statist. Soc. Ser. B.*, 40, 1-25.

Bates, D. M. & Watts, D. G. (1981). Parameter transformation for improved approximate confidence regions in nonlinear least squares. *Annals of Statistics*, 9, 1152-1167.

Bentler, P. M. (1983). Some contributions to efficient statistics for structure models: specification and estimation of moment structures. *Psychometrika*, 48, 493-517.

Bentler, P. M. & Lee, S. Y. (1979). A statistical development of three-mode factor analysis. *British Journal of Mathematical and Statistical Psychology*, 32, 87-104.

Bentler, P. M., Poon, W. Y., & Lee, S. Y. (1988). Generalized multimode latent variable models: Implementation by standard programs. *Computational Statistics & Data Analysis*, 6, 107-118.

Browne, M. W. (1974). Generalized least squares estimators in the analysis of covariance structures. *South African Statistical Journal*, 8, 1-24.

Browne, M. W. (1984). Asymptotically distribution-free methods in the analysis of covariance structure. *British Journal of Mathematical and Statistical Psychology*, 37, 62-83.

Burdick, R. K. & Graybill, F. A. (1992). *Confidence intervals on variance components*. New York: Marcel Dekker, Inc.

Hamilton, D. C. (1986). Confidence regions for parameter subsets in nonlinear regression. *Biometrika*, 73, 57-64.

Hamilton, D. C., Watts, D. G., & Bates, D. M. (1982). Accounting for intrinsic nonlinearity in nonlinear regression parameter inference regions. *Annals of Statistics*, 10, 386-393.

Jöreskog, K. G. (1978). Structure analysis of covariance and correlation matrices. *Psychometrika*, 43, 443-477.

Lee, S. Y. (1985). On testing functional constraints in structural equation models. *Biometrika*, 72, 125-131.

Lee, S. Y. & Bentler, P. M. (1980). Some asymptotic properties of constrained generalized least squares estimation in covariance structure models. *South African Statistical Journal*, 14, 121-136.

Millman, R. S. & Parker, G. D. (1977). *Elements of differential geometry*. Englewood Cliffs, NJ: Prentice Hall.

Seber, G. A. F. & Wild, C. J. (1989). *Nonlinear Regression*. New York: Wiley.

Wang, S. J. & Lee, S. Y. (1995). A geometric approach of the generalized least-squares estimation in analysis of covariance structures. *Statistical & Probability Letters*, 24, 39-47.

Wei, B. C. (1994). On confidence regions of embedded models in regular parametric families (A geometric approach). *Australian Journal of Statistics*, 36, 327-328.

Wei, B. C. (1997). *Exponential Family Nonlinear Models*. Singapore: Springer.

Wonnacott, T. (1987). Confidence intervals or hypothesis tests? *Journal of Applied Statistics*, 14, 195-201.

9 Robust Factor Analysis: Methods and Applications

Peter Filzmoser

Vienna University of Technology, Austria

9.1 Introduction

The word *robustness* is frequently used in the literature, and is often stated with completely different meaning. In this contribution robustness means to reduce the influence of "unusual" observations on statistical estimates. Such observations are frequently denoted as *outliers*, and are often thought to be extreme values caused by measurement or transcription errors. However, the notion of outliers also includes observations (or groups of observations) which are inconsistent with the remaining data set. The judgment whether observations are declared as outliers or as "inliers" is sometimes subjective, and robust statistics should serve as a tool for an objective decision. In terms of a statistical model, robust statistics could be defined as follows: *"In a broad informal sense, robust statistics is a body of knowledge, partly formalized into 'theory of robustness', relating to deviations from idealized assumptions in statistics."* (Hampel, Ronchetti, Rousseeuw, & Stahel, 1986). Hence, robust statistics is aimed at yielding reliable results in cases where classical assumptions like normality, independence or linearity are violated.

Real data sets almost always include outliers. Sometimes they are harmless and do not change the results if they are included in the analysis or deleted beforehand. However, they can have a major influence on the results, and completely alter the statistical estimates. Deleting such observations before analyzing the data would be a way out, but this implies that the outliers can indeed be identified, which is not trivial, especially in higher dimensions (see Section 9.2.3).

Another way to reduce the influence of outliers is to fit the majority of the data, which is assumed to be the "good" part of data points. The majority fit is done by introducing a weight function for downweighting outliers, with weights equal to 0 and 1 or taken at the continuous scale. This process where outliers are not excluded beforehand but downweighted in the analysis is called a *robust procedure*. The outliers can be identified afterwards by looking at the values of the weight function or by inspecting the residuals which are large in the robust analysis. In either case, outliers should not simply be deleted or ignored. Rather, an important task is to ask what has caused these outliers. They have to be analyzed and interpreted because they often contain very important information on data quality or unexpected behavior of some observations.

In this chapter different approaches to make factor analysis (FA) resistant against outliers are discussed. There are two strategies to robustify FA: The first way is to identify outliers and to exclude them from further analysis. This approach is discussed in the next section, which also includes some basic tools and techniques from robust statistics essential for understanding the subsequent sections. The second possibility, which will be the main focus of this chapter, is to construct a FA method with the property that outliers will not bias the parameter estimates. The resulting method is called *robust factor analysis*, and accounts for violations from the strict parametric model. The robust method tries to fit the majority of the data by reducing the impact of outlying observations. Results from robust FA are aimed at changing only slightly if the outliers are deleted beforehand from the data set. Section 9.3 is concerned with robustly estimating the covariance or correlation matrix of the data, which is the basis for FA. This approach results in a highly robust FA method with the additional property that influential observations can be identified by inspecting the *empirical influence function*. Section 9.4 presents another robust FA method in which factor loadings and scores are estimated by an interlocking regression algorithm. The estimates are directly derived from the data matrix, rather than the usual covariance or correlation matrix. Section 9.5 introduces a robust method for obtaining the principal component solution to FA, and the final section provides a summary of the chapter.

It should be noted that fitting the bulk of the data, which is typical for robust methods, does not mean ignoring part of the data values. After applying robust methods, it is important to analyze the residuals which are large for outliers. Often, the outliers are not simply "wrong" data values, but observations or groups of observations with different behavior than the majority of data. Classical FA methods, which are in fact based on least squares estimation, try to fit *all* data points with the result that neither the "good" data part nor the "bad" one is well fitted.

9.2   Some Basics of Robust Statistics

9.2.1   The influence function

An important tool for studying the properties of an estimator is the *influence function* (IF) (Hampel et al., 1986). The influence function of T at the distribution G is defined as

$$\text{IF}(x; T, G) = \lim_{\varepsilon \downarrow 0} \frac{T((1-\varepsilon)G + \varepsilon \Delta_x) - T(G)}{\varepsilon} \quad (9.1)$$

where Δ_x is a Dirac measure which puts all its mass in x. The influence function $\text{IF}(x; T, G)$ is a measure for the influence of an infinitesimal amount of contamination at x on the estimator T. In the case of identifying influential observations, (9.1) is formulated in an empirical setting rather than considering the population case. If the theoretical distribution G is replaced in (9.1) by the empirical distribution G_n of a sample $x_1, \ldots, x_n$ ($x_i \in R^p$), one obtains the *empirical influence function* (EIF) of the estimator $T_n = T(F_n)$, which can be evaluated at each data point x_i to determine its influence.

9.2.2 The breakdown value

In robust statistics it is desired to qualify the robustness of an estimator. A rough but useful measure of robustness is the *breakdown value*. As the name indicates, it gives a critical value of contamination at which the statistical estimator "breaks down". The breakdown value was introduced by Hampel (1971) and defined in a finite sample setting by Donoho and Huber (1983). For a data matrix $X \in R^{n \times p}$ ($n > p$) and a statistical estimator T, the (finite sample) breakdown value is defined by

$$\varepsilon_n^*(T, X) = \min \left\{ \frac{m}{n} \; : \; \sup_{X'} \|T(X') - T(X)\| = \infty \right\}, \qquad (9.2)$$

where $\| \cdot \|$ denotes the Euclidean norm. X' is obtained by replacing any m observations of X by arbitrary points. In other words, the breakdown value is the smallest fraction of contamination that can cause an estimator T to run away arbitrarily far from $T(X)$. For many estimators, $\varepsilon_n^*(T, X)$ varies only slightly with X and n, so that its limiting value ($n \to \infty$) is considered.

9.2.3 Outlier identification

Outliers can completely influence the result of a statistical estimation procedure. Hence, it is important to know if the data set includes outliers and which observations are outlying. The detection of outliers is a serious problem in statistics. It is still easy to identify outliers in a 1- or 2-dimensional data set, but for higher dimension visual inspection is not reliable. It is not sufficient to look at all plots of pairs of variables because *multivariate outliers* are not extreme along the coordinates and not necessarily visible in 2-dimensional plots.

Suppose n observations $x_1, \ldots, x_n$ are given with $x_i \in R^p$. A classical approach for identifying outliers is to compute the *Mahalanobis distance*

$$\text{MD}(x_i) = \sqrt{(x_i - \bar{x})^\top S^{-1} (x_i - \bar{x})} \qquad (9.3)$$

for each observation x_i. Here $\bar{x}$ is the p-dimensional arithmetic mean vector and S is the sample covariance matrix. The Mahalanobis distance measures the distance of each observation from the center of the data cloud relative to the size or shape of the cloud. Although the Mahalanobis distance is still frequently used as an outlier measure, it is well known that this approach suffers from the "masking effect" in the case of multiple outliers (Rousseeuw & Leroy, 1987). The outliers attract the arithmetic mean, but they may even inflate S in their direction. Since the inverse of S is taken in (9.3), the outliers may not stick out in relation to non-outliers (i.e., they are masked).

$\bar{x}$ and S, which are both involved in computing the Mahalanobis distance, have the lowest breakdown value 0. So it seems natural to replace these estimates by positive-breakdown estimators $T(X)$ for location and $C(X)$ for covariance, resulting in the *robust distance*

$$\text{RD}(x_i) = \sqrt{(x_i - T(X))^\top C(X)^{-1}(x_i - T(X))} \; . \qquad (9.4)$$

The breakdown value of a multivariate location estimator T is defined by (9.2). A scatter matrix estimator C is said to break down when the largest eigenvalue of $C(X')$ (X' is the contaminated data set) becomes arbitrarily large or the smallest eigenvalue of $C(X')$ comes arbitrarily close to zero. The estimators T and C also need to be equivariant under translations and linear transformations of the data.

Rousseeuw and Van Zomeren (1990) suggested the use of the *minimum volume ellipsoid* (MVE) estimator in (9.4). The MVE estimator was introduced by Rousseeuw (1985), and it looks for the ellipsoid with smallest volume that covers h data points, where $n/2 \leq h < n$. $T(X)$ is defined as the center of this ellipsoid, and $C(X)$ is determined by the same ellipsoid and multiplied by a correction factor to be roughly unbiased at multivariate Gaussian distributions. The breakdown value of the MVE estimator is essentially $(n - h)/n$, which is independent from the dimension p. So for $h \approx n/2$ one attains the maximum possible breakdown value 50%. Large values of the resulting robust distances (9.4) indicate outlying observations. Since the (squared) Mahalanobis distance is, in the case of normally distributed data, distributed according to χ_p^2, a cutoff value of, say, $\chi_{p,0.975}^2$ can be used for declaring observations as outliers.

Many algorithms for computing the MVE estimator have been proposed in the literature (Rousseeuw & Leroy, 1987; Woodruff & Rocke, 1994; Agulló, 1996), but they are computationally demanding, especially in high dimensions. A further drawback of the MVE estimator is its low statistical efficiency. Rousseeuw (1985) also introduced the *minimum covariance determinant* (MCD) estimator for robustly estimating location and covariance. The MCD looks for the $n/2 \leq h < n$ observations of which the empirical covariance matrix has the smallest possible determinant. Then the location estimation $T(X)$ is defined by the average of these h points, and the covariance estimation $C(X)$ is a certain multiple of their covariance matrix. The MCD estimator has breakdown value $\varepsilon_n^* \approx (n - h)/n$ just like the MVE estimator. However, the MCD has a better statistical efficiency than the MVE because it is asymptotically normal (Butler, Davies & Jhun, 1993; Croux & Haesbroeck, 1999). Moreover, Rousseeuw and Van Driessen (1999) developed an algorithm for the computation of the MCD, which is much faster than those for the MVE and which makes even large applications feasible.

9.3 FA Based on a Robust Scatter Matrix Estimator

Factor analysis (FA) is aimed at summarizing the correlation structure of the data by a small number of factors. Traditionally, the FA method takes the covariance or correlation matrix of the original variables as a basis for extracting the factors. The following gives a brief introduction to the FA model.

9.3.1 The FA model

Factor analysis is a standard method in multivariate analysis. At the basis of p random variables $x_1, \ldots, x_p$ one assumes the existence of a smaller number k $(1 \leq k < p)$ of latent variables or factors $f_1, \ldots, f_k$ which are hypothetical quantities and cannot be observed directly. The factors are linked with the original variables through the equation

$$x_j = \lambda_{j1} f_1 + \lambda_{j2} f_2 + \ldots + \lambda_{jk} f_k + \varepsilon_j \tag{9.5}$$

for each $1 \leq j \leq p$. $\varepsilon_1, \ldots, \varepsilon_p$ are called *specific factors* or *error terms*, and they are assumed to be independent of each other and of the factors. The coefficients λ_{jl} are called *loadings*, and they can be collected into the matrix of loadings Λ. Using the vector notations $x = (x_1, \ldots, x_p)^\top$, $f = (f_1, \ldots, f_k)^\top$, and $\varepsilon = (\varepsilon_1, \ldots, \varepsilon_p)^\top$, the model (9.5) can be written as

$$x = \Lambda f + \varepsilon , \tag{9.6}$$

and the usual conditions on factors and error terms can be formulated as $E(f) = E(\varepsilon) = 0$, $\mathrm{Cov}(f) = I_k$, and $\mathrm{Cov}(\varepsilon) = \Psi$, where $\Psi = \mathrm{diag}\,(\psi_1, \ldots, \psi_p)$ is a diagonal matrix. The variances of the error terms $\psi_1, \ldots, \psi_p$ are called specific variances or uniquenesses. ε and f are assumed to be independent.

The essential step in FA is the estimation of the matrix Λ (which is only specified up to an orthogonal transformation) and Ψ. Classical FA methods like principal factor analysis (PFA) and the maximum likelihood method (ML) (e.g., Basilevski, 1994) are based on a decomposition of the covariance matrix Σ of x. It is easy to see that with the above assumptions the FA model (9.5) implies

$$\Sigma = \Lambda \Lambda^\top + \Psi. \tag{9.7}$$

9.3.2 A robust method

Tanaka and Odaka (1989a,b) computed the influence functions (EIFs) for PFA and the ML method based on the sample covariance matrix as estimation of Σ in Equation (9.7). They found that the IFs are unbounded, which means that an outlying observation can have an arbitrary large effect on the parameter estimates. The empirical versions of the IFs (EIF) are no longer reliable in case of multiple outliers because the typical phenomenon of masking can occur. To avoid this, Steinhauser (1998) developed a method for identifying influential observations in FA by drawing random subsamples. The method has some practical limitations, since for reasons of computation time it can only be applied to rather small data sets, and it is able to identify only a group of up to about 10 masked influential observations (Steinhauser, 1998, p. 171).

The sample covariance matrix is very vulnerable to outliers. In order to construct more robust methods, it seems natural to estimate Σ in (9.7) by a robust scatter matrix estimator. Estimations of the unknown parameters Λ and Ψ can then be obtained by a decomposition of the robustly estimated covariance matrix. A first attempt in this direction was made by Kosfeld (1996) who replaced the sample covariance matrix by a multivariate M-estimator (Maronna, 1976). The term *M-estimator* comes from the fact that this estimator is obtained by generalizing the idea of ML estimation (Huber, 1981). Major drawbacks of the M-estimator are the computational complexity (see Marazzi, 1980; Dutter, 1983) and its low breakdown value. For p-dimensional data, the breakdown value of M-estimators is at most $1/p$ (Maronna, 1976), which is far too low especially for higher dimensional data.

A different approach to robustify FA was that by Filzmoser (1999) who used the MVE estimator (see Section 9.2.3) as a robust estimator of the population covariance matrix. Since the MVE attains the largest possible breakdown value 50%, this results in a very robust FA method. However, for a large number of variables the computational complexity increases rapidly, and the method becomes unattractive.

Pison et al. (2001) used the MCD estimator (see Section 9.2.3) as a robust estimator of Σ in Equation (9.7). Good statistical properties and a fast algorithm (Rousseeuw & Van Driessen, 1999) make this a very attractive robust FA method with the following main properties:

- The breakdown value of the method is at most 50% (dependent on the parameter choice for the MCD estimator).
- The usual methods for determining the number of extracted factors and for estimating loadings and scores can be used.
- The method can handle huge data sets. The method does not work for data with more variables than observations.
- The influence function has been derived (Pison et al., 2001), and the empirical influence function can be used to identify influential observations.

Using the MCD estimator, Pison et al. (2001) compared the two factor extraction techniques PFA and ML by means of simulation studies. It turned out that PFA is even preferable to ML, since both loadings and unique variances are estimated with higher precision. Moreover, they derived the IF for PFA based on either the classical scatter matrix or a robust estimate of the covariance matrix like the MCD estimator. Using the sample covariance matrix for PFA yields an unbounded IF, which also confirmed the findings of

Tanaka and Odaka (1989a). However, the MCD estimator as a basis for PFA results in a method with bounded IF.

Pison et al (2001) also computed the IF of PFA based on the correlation matrix ρ. This is important because the variables are often first standardized to mean zero and unit variance (equivalent to replacing the covariance matrix Σ in Eq.(9.7) by the correlation matrix ρ). The correlation matrix is obtained by

$$\rho = \Sigma_D^{-1/2} \Sigma \Sigma_D^{-1/2} \qquad (9.8)$$

where Σ_D consists of the diagonal of Σ and zeroes elsewhere. If the MCD estimator is used to estimate the covariance matrix, a robust correlation matrix is easily obtained by applying (9.8). The IF of PFA based on this robust correlation matrix is again bounded and hence the method is robust with respect to outliers.

An important result of the Pison et al (2001) study is the development of a tool to find influential observations on the parameter estimates of PFA. The IF is computed for the population case with the true underlying distribution G (see Section 9.2.1). However, since G is unknown in an empirical setting, the corresponding mean vector and covariance matrix are replaced by the estimates of the MCD in the formula of the IF. The resulting EIF can then be evaluated at each data point and measures the effect on the parameter estimates of PFA. So the EIF is an important data analytic tool because it identifies those observations in a data set with large influence.

Note that influential observations can also be identified by the robust distance (9.4) by taking the MCD estimates of location and scatter for T and C. The robust distance identifies the outliers (see Section 9.2.3), and some of the outliers (or all) are influential observations. So it can happen that an outlier has only a small influence on the FA. This situation is similar to regression analysis where points which are far away from the data cloud are identified as outliers. However, if they are on the linear trend of the bulk of the data, these outliers do not affect the regression line and hence are not influential. In regression analysis, these are called "good leverage points" (Rousseeuw & Van Zomeren, 1990).

9.3.3 Example

From 1992-1998 the Geological Surveys of Finland (GTK) and Norway (NGU) and the Central Kola Expedition (CKE) in Russia carried out a large multi-media, multi-element geochemical mapping project (see http://www.ngu.no/Kola) across a 188000 km^2 area north of the Arctic Circle (Figure 9.1). In the summer and autumn of 1995, the entire area between 24° and 35.5°E up to the Barents Sea coast was sampled. More than 600 samples were taken, and at each sample site 5 different layers were considered: terrestrial moss, humus (the O-horizon), topsoil (0-5 cm), and the B- and C-horizon of Podzdol profiles. All samples were subsequently analyzed for more than 50 chemical elements. [1]

Fig. 9.1. General location map of the Kola Project area, reprinted from Reimann and Melezhik (2001) with permission from Elsevier Science.

One of the aims of the project was to investigate how deep the atmospherically transported pollutants have penetrated the soil cover. Since industrial pollution should be visible in the upper layers, the humus layer was chosen to find an answer. Typical elements for pollution are Cobalt (Co), Copper (Cu), Iron (Fe), Nickel (Ni) and Vanadium (V), and to some extent also Silver (Ag) and Arsenic (As). Since the measurements are element concentrations, the data were log-transformed (quite common in geochemistry–Rock, 1988).

First of all, it is interesting to identify the outliers. This is important for underlining the necessity of a robust analysis, and also for mapping the extreme values. To identify the outliers, the robust distances (9.4) are computed by taking the MCD estimator for obtaining robust estimates of location

---

[1] The whole data set is available in the form of a geochemical atlas (Reimann et al., 1998) and as a downloadable data set at http://www.pangaea.de/Projects/Kola-Atlas/.

and scatter (see Section 9.2.3). The outliers are then visualized by drawing the robust distances against the Mahalanobis distances (9.3). This so-
called *distance-distance plot* was introduced by Rousseeuw and Van Driessen
(1999), and is presented in Figure 9.2. If the data were not contaminated then

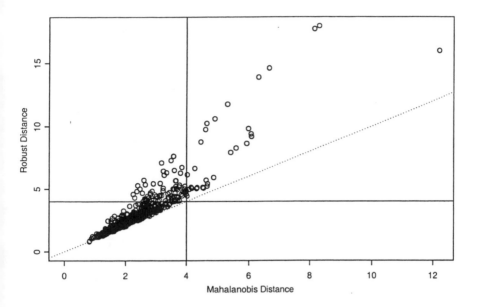

Fig. 9.2. Identification of outliers by the distance-distance plot.

both distance measures would yield the same result and all points would lie
near the dotted line. A horizontal and a vertical line trough the cutoff value
$\sqrt{\chi^2_{7;0.975}} \approx 4$ (see Section 9.2.3) divides Figure 9.2 into 4 parts.

- Part 1 ($\mathrm{MD}(x_i) \leq 4$ and $\mathrm{RD}(x_i) \leq 4$) includes regular observations which
  are not declared as outliers, neither by the classical Mahalanobis distance
  nor by the robust distance.
- Part 2 ($\mathrm{MD}(x_i) > 4$ and $\mathrm{RD}(x_i) \leq 4$) is empty and indicates observations
  which are wrongly identified as outliers by the classical method.
- Part 3 ($\mathrm{MD}(x_i) > 4$ and $\mathrm{RD}(x_i) > 4$) includes observations which are
  identified as outliers by both methods.
- Part 4 ($\mathrm{MD}(x_i) \leq 4$ and $\mathrm{RD}(x_i) > 4$) is probably the most interesting part. It includes masked outliers (i.e., observations which are not
  identified as outliers by the Mahalanobis distance but which are outliers
  according to the robust distance).

It is interesting to see the location of the outliers on the map. Figure 9.3
(left) uses the Mahalanobis distance from above as a criterion of outlyingness.

Regular observations (i.e., parts 1 and 4 from above) are presented by the symbol ○ and outliers (i.e., parts 2 and 3 from above) by ● and ∗. Figure 9.3 (right) uses the same symbols, but the outlier criterion is the robust distance from above. Now, outliers would immediately be assigned to values with high pollution. One has to be careful here, since an outlier could also be a value which is extremely small. Therefore, the symbol ∗ is used to indicate outliers where *each* component is smaller than the average. So, values with ∗ are extremely less polluted regions. The outliers found by the robust method reveal much better the real emitters. Figure 9.3b, which uses the robust distance clearly identifies two regions with serious pollution. These are the regions around Nikel, Zapolyarnij and Monchegorsk in Russia (see Figure 9.1) with large smelters. In fact, these three point sources belong to the world-wide largest sources of SO_2- and heavy metal pollution. On the other hand, there is a large region in the north-west which is not affected by industrial emission (some outliers might be caused by the effect of sea spray).

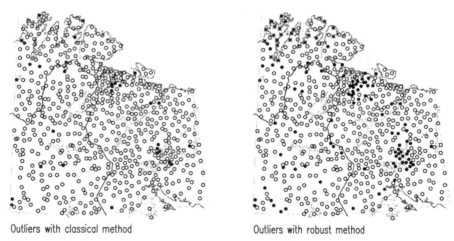

Outliers with classical method   Outliers with robust method

Fig. 9.3. Outliers in the considered area: identification by the classical (left) and robust (right) method. The plots show regular observations (○), outliers (●), and low outliers (∗).

Now to compare classical FA (PFA) with robust FA based on the MCD estimator. For both methods, 2 factors are extracted and rotated according to the varimax criterion (Kaiser, 1958). The loadings are displayed in Figure 9.4. The given percentages on top of the plots of Figure 9.4 indicate the percentage of total variation explained by the factor model. The first factor explains a major part of the variability, and the first two factors explain 78% for the classical method (a) and 72% for the robust method (b). The vertical line, which separates the two factors, is drawn according to the sum of squared loadings of each factor, and represents the variability explained by

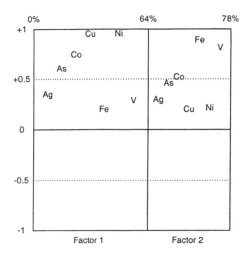

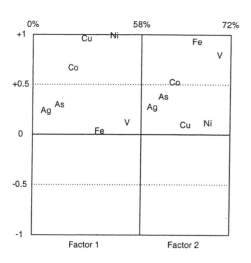

Fig. 9.4. Loadings for the classical FA method (top) and for MCD-based FA (bottom).

each factor. The loadings are presented by the abbreviations of the elements in the plots. The factors of the robust analysis can be interpreted as soluble (Factor 1) versus particulared (Factor 2) pollution. The loadings of the classical and robust analysis are quite similar, especially the second factor is almost identical. However, the contribution of some elements (e.g., As) to the first factor is much stronger for the classical method, and this allows no meaningful interpretation of the factor.

The corresponding factor scores are shown in Figure 9.5. In order to compare classical and robust FA, the values in the maps have the same scaling (according to the robust scores), which is due to the boxplot representation in the legends. The first factor shows the effect of soluble pollution. The regions around the large smelters (see above) are strongly affected. The robust analysis reveals much better the distribution of the dust in the air than the classical analysis. The values are decreasing to the west and to the north. Factor 2 represents the effect of particulared pollution, and it is interesting to see that this kind of pollution is much more locally restricted than the previous one. There is no big difference between the classical and the robust analysis since the loadings are very similar (Figure 9.4). Large values in the west might be due to the dust emission of smaller cities. An interesting detail which can be seen clearly in the robust analysis (bottom right) is a band of large values from the industrial center around Monchegorsk to the seaport Murmansk (see also Figure 9.1). This band corresponds exactly with the traffic connection.

A last picture of this analysis is diplayed in Figure 9.6. The top plot shows the factor scores from robust FA. In the direction of Factor 1 the scores allow a visual separation into smaller (∘) and larger (•) values. The bottom plot shows the points in the map, and the effect of dust by soluble pollution (large values of Factor 1) is again clearly visible.[2]

9.4   Factor Analysis by Interlocking Regression

9.4.1   Overview

This section describes an alternative method to robustify FA. The procedure is quite different to that presented above, because the unknown parameters are estimated by directly taking the data matrix without passing via an estimate of the covariance matrix. The method was introduced by Croux et al. (2001) and uses the technique of interlocking regression (or alternating regression–Wold, 1966). Using the sample version of model (9.5) given by

$$x_{ij} = \sum_{l=1}^{k} \lambda_{jl} f_{il} + \varepsilon_{ij} \tag{9.9}$$

for $i = 1, \ldots, n$ and $j = 1, \ldots, p$, and considering the factor scores f_{il} for a moment as constants with unknown preliminary estimates, provides a regression problem in which the loadings λ_{jl} (regression coefficients) can be estimated by linear regressions of the x_{ij} on the scores. On the other hand, if preliminary estimates of the loadings are available, the scores f_{il} can be

---

[2] The above analysis was done with the software packages Splus (MathSoft, Inc., Seattle, WA USA – http://www.mathsoft.com/splus) and DAS (Dutter et al., 1992).

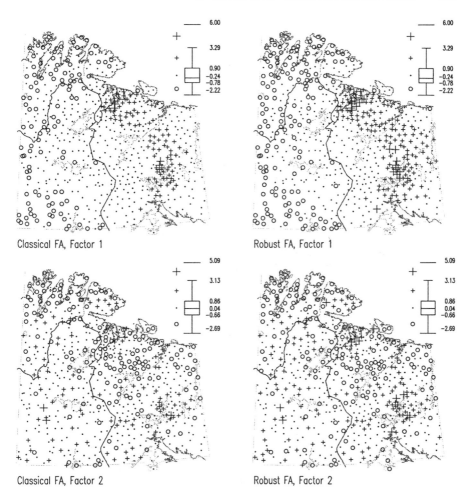

Fig. 9.5. Factor scores for the classical FA method (left) and for MCD-based FA (right).

estimated by linear regressions of the x_{ij} on the loadings. These two steps are repeated until convergence of the algorithm. Moreover, estimates $\hat{\psi}_j$ for the uniquenesses ψ_j can easily be obtained from the residuals. In view of possible outliers, all estimations will be done robust by taking a weighted L^1 regression estimator, which is robust in this setting and can be computed fast.

This approach is called FAIR, from *factor analysis by interlocking regression*. The method is "fair" in the sense that it treats the rows and columns of the data matrix in the same way, which is useful for dealing with missing values and outliers.

The main features of the FAIR estimator are:

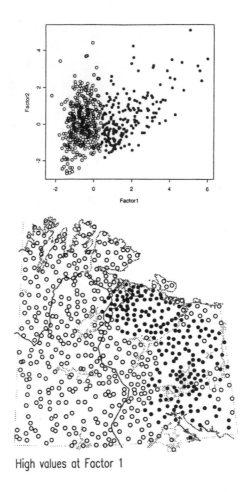

High values at Factor 1

Fig. 9.6. Scatterplot of the factor scores for MCD-based FA (top). The scores are visually clustered into two groups which are shown in the map (bottom).

- FAIR yields robust parameter estimates of the FA model.
- The factor scores are estimated together with the factor loadings.
- The number of variables can exceed the number of observations.
- The procedure can handle missing data.
- Negative values as estimations of the specific variances cannot occur.
- Like other FA methods, FAIR is not designed to extract factors which allow the best interpretation. Hence, if this is desired, the estimation procedure should be followed by a factor rotation (Harman, 1976).

9.4.2   The Principle

The FAIR approach starts with the $n \times p$ data matrix X containing the individuals (cases, objects) in the rows and the observed variables (characteristics) in the columns. To obtain invariance with respect to a change of measurement units, assume that the variables are already standardized to have zero location and unit spread. Since the intention is to construct a robust procedure, the standardization has to be done in a robust way. A traditional choice for this purpose is to use the median for the estimation of the location and the median absolute deviation (MAD) for spread estimation (both estimators attain the maximum breakdown value 50%), resulting in

$$x_{ij} \leftarrow \frac{x_{ij} - \mathrm{med}_i(x_{ij})}{\mathrm{MAD}_i(x_{ij})}. \tag{9.10}$$

The MAD is defined by

$$\mathrm{MAD}_i(x_{ij}) = 1.4826 \cdot \underset{i}{\mathrm{med}} \, |x_{ij} - \underset{k}{\mathrm{med}}(x_{kj})|$$

with the constant 1.4826 for obtaining consistency at univariate normal distributions. This initial standardization corresponds to a FA approach based on the correlation matrix rather than on the covariance matrix. However, a main difference with the usual FA estimation procedures is that FAIR does not use the correlation matrix for the parameter estimation, but takes directly the data matrix for estimating loadings and scores.

Denote the number of extracted factors by k. The ith score vector is given by $\boldsymbol{f}_i = (f_{i1}, \ldots, f_{ik})^\top$, while the jth loading vector is $\boldsymbol{\lambda}_j = (\lambda_{j1}, \ldots, \lambda_{jk})^\top$. Both the loading vectors and the score vectors are unknown. Denote by $\boldsymbol{\theta} = (\boldsymbol{f}_1^\top, \ldots, \boldsymbol{f}_n^\top, \boldsymbol{\lambda}_1^\top, \ldots, \boldsymbol{\lambda}_p^\top)$ the vector of all scores and loadings, and let

$$\hat{x}_{ij}(\boldsymbol{\theta}) = \sum_{l=1}^{k} f_{il}\lambda_{lj} = \boldsymbol{f}_i^\top \boldsymbol{\lambda}_j = \boldsymbol{\lambda}_j^\top \boldsymbol{f}_i$$

be the fitted value of x_{ij} according to the model (9.9). By choosing $\boldsymbol{\theta}$ such that the fitted and the actual values of the data matrix are close together, estimates $\hat{\boldsymbol{f}}_i$ are defined for the score vectors and $\hat{\boldsymbol{\lambda}}_j$ for the loading vectors. The fitted data matrix $\hat{X}$ can then be decomposed as

$$\hat{X} = \hat{F}\hat{\Lambda}^\top \tag{9.11}$$

where the rows of $\hat{F}$ are the estimated scores and the rows of $\hat{\Lambda}$ are the estimated loadings. This results in an objective function for estimating the unknown parameters $\boldsymbol{\theta}$ of the form

$$\hat{\boldsymbol{\theta}} = \underset{\boldsymbol{\theta}}{\mathrm{argmin}} \sum_{i=1}^{n} \sum_{j=1}^{p} g(x_{ij} - \hat{x}_{ij}(\boldsymbol{\theta})) \tag{9.12}$$

where g is a function applied to the residuals $x_{ij} - \hat{x}_{ij}(\boldsymbol{\theta})$. The choice of the function g depends on both robustness properties of the estimation procedure and computational issues (see subsequent sections). For optimal estimates $\hat{\boldsymbol{F}}$ and $\hat{\boldsymbol{\Lambda}}$, it must hold that $\hat{\boldsymbol{f}}_i$ minimizes $\sum_{j=1}^{p} g(x_{ij} - \boldsymbol{f}_i^\top \hat{\boldsymbol{\lambda}}_j)$ and $\hat{\boldsymbol{\lambda}}_j$ minimizes $\sum_{i=1}^{n} g(x_{ij} - \hat{\boldsymbol{f}}_i^\top \boldsymbol{\lambda}_j)$. Therefore, instead of minimizing both sums in Equation (9.12) at the same time, one fixes an index j and scores $\boldsymbol{f}_i$ and selects the $\boldsymbol{\lambda}_j$ to minimize

$$\sum_{i=1}^{n} g(x_{ij} - \boldsymbol{f}_i^\top \boldsymbol{\lambda}_j). \tag{9.13}$$

The above problem is now linear instead of bilinear and can (in general) be solved much easier. Assuming that the outcome of the function g is non-negative, one sees immediately that minimizing Equation (9.13) consecutively for $j = 1, \ldots, p$ corresponds to minimizing Equation (9.12) for fixed scores. Analogously, for fixed loadings $\boldsymbol{\lambda}_j$, finding the $\boldsymbol{f}_i$ by minimizing

$$\sum_{j=1}^{p} g(x_{ij} - \boldsymbol{f}_i^\top \boldsymbol{\lambda}_j) \tag{9.14}$$

(for each $i = 1, \ldots, n$ in turn) corresponds to minimizing (9.12) when the loadings are given. Alternating Equations (9.13) and (9.14) leads to an iterative scheme.

After the estimation of loadings and scores one can estimate the residuals by

$$\hat{\varepsilon}_{ij} = x_{ij} - \hat{x}_{ij} = x_{ij} - \hat{\boldsymbol{f}}_i^\top \hat{\boldsymbol{\lambda}}_j,$$

and subsequently also the specific variances using $\hat{\psi}_j = (\text{MAD}_i(\hat{\varepsilon}_{ij}))^2$. Note that the estimates $\hat{\psi}_j$ are positive by construction, so there are never problems with negatively estimated specific variances (Heywood case). Classical FA procedures with the additional assumption of positive uniquenesses are computationally intensive (Ten Berge & Kiers, 1991; Kano, 1998).

It is important to note that the estimates $\hat{\boldsymbol{F}}$ and $\hat{\boldsymbol{\Lambda}}$ are only specified up to an orthogonal transformation. Since $\hat{\boldsymbol{X}} = (\hat{\boldsymbol{F}}\boldsymbol{\Gamma})(\hat{\boldsymbol{\Lambda}}\boldsymbol{\Gamma})^\top$ for any orthogonal k by k matrix $\boldsymbol{\Gamma}$, it follows that $\hat{\boldsymbol{F}}\boldsymbol{\Gamma}$ and $\hat{\boldsymbol{\Lambda}}\boldsymbol{\Gamma}$ attain the same value for the objective function (Eq. 9.12). However, the fitted values $\hat{\boldsymbol{X}}$ and the matrix $\hat{\boldsymbol{\Lambda}}\hat{\boldsymbol{\Lambda}}^\top$ are well defined and all estimators considered share these properties.

9.4.3   The LS criterion

The above decrease in the value of the objective function (9.12) at each step is fulfilled by taking g as the square function, which results in the least squares (LS) criterion

$$\hat{\boldsymbol{\theta}}_{LS} = \operatorname*{argmin}_{\boldsymbol{\theta}} \sum_{i=1}^{n} \sum_{j=1}^{p} (x_{ij} - \hat{x}_{ij}(\boldsymbol{\theta}))^2. \tag{9.15}$$

The estimation of the loadings and scores is done according to Equations (9.13) and (9.14) by applying the LS regression algorithm. The resulting $\hat{X}$ can be seen as the "best" approximation (in the least squares sense) of the data matrix X by a rank k matrix.

The LS solution can also be obtained in another way. Assume that the rank of $\hat{X}$ is at most $k < p$, while the rank of X is typically p. The Eckart-Young theorem (Gower & Hand, 1996, p. 241) says that this best fit can be obtained by performing a singular value decomposition $X = UDV^{\top}$ of the data matrix. By replacing all singular values in D by zero except for the k largest ones, one obtains D_k and finally $\hat{X} = UD_kV^{\top}$. By taking $\hat{F} = \sqrt{n}U$ and $\hat{\Lambda} = VD_k/\sqrt{n}$ one obtains the so-called *principal component solution* to the FA problem (see also Section 9.5). Moreover, the sample covariance matrix of the estimated score vectors equals $\hat{F}^{\top}\hat{F}/n = I_k$ which is consistent with the assumption $\mathrm{Cov}(f) = I_k$.

A major drawback of the LS criterion is its non-robustness against outlying observations (Rousseeuw & Leroy, 1987). The breakdown value of LS regression is 0%, which means that even one "bad" observation can completely tilt the regression line. This results in biased estimations which will have a severe influence in the iterative regression scheme of FAIR because the estimations are also used as predictors. Taking LS regression yields the same result as the classical approach of Gabriel (1978) for the singular value decomposition.

9.4.4 The L^1 criterion

The L^1 criterion (or *least absolute deviations* criterion) is known to give a very robust additive fit to two-way tables (Hubert, 1997; Terbeck & Davies, 1998). The objective function (9.12) yields the estimator

$$\hat{\theta}_{L1} = \operatorname*{argmin}_{\theta} \sum_{i=1}^{n} \sum_{j=1}^{p} |x_{ij} - \hat{x}_{ij}(\theta)|. \tag{9.16}$$

The estimations for loadings and scores are found by performing L^1 regressions in the iterative scheme given by Equations (9.13) and (9.14), and this leads to a decreasing value of the criterion (9.16) in each step. Moreover, L^1 regressions are computationally fast to solve (Bloomfield & Steiger, 1983) and hence also attractive from this point of view. Unfortunately, L^1 regression is sensitive to outliers in the x-direction (space of the predictors) (Rousseeuw & Leroy, 1987), and hence its breakdown value is 0%.

9.4.5 The weighted L^1 criterion (FAIR)

Outliers in the x-space are called *leverage points*. The term "leverage" comes from mechanics, because such a point pulls LS and L^1 solutions towards it.

If outlying score or loading vectors are present, the LS and L^1 regressions can be heavily influenced by them. By downweighting these leverage points, their influence can be reduced. The resulting criterion is called weighted L^1 regression, defined by

$$\hat{\theta}_{FAIR} = \underset{\theta}{\operatorname{argmin}} \sum_{i=1}^{n} \sum_{j=1}^{p} w_i(\theta) v_j(\theta) |x_{ij} - \hat{x}_{ij}(\theta)|. \qquad (9.17)$$

The row weights w_i are downweighting outlying scores. The outliers in the k-dimensional space given by the collection of score vectors $F = \{f_i | 1 \leq i \leq n\}$ are identified with the help of the robust distance (Section 9.2.3), which is given by

$$\mathrm{RD}(f_i) = \sqrt{(f_i - T(F))^{\top} C(F)^{-1} (f_i - T(F))} \quad \text{for } i = 1, \dots, n \quad (9.18)$$

(Rousseeuw & van Zomeren, 1990). T and C are MVE or MCD estimates of location and scatter, respectively. The robust distances can be compared with the critical value $\chi^2_{k,0.95}$ which is the upper 5% critical value of a chi-squared distribution with k degrees of freedom. Hence, the weight for the scores is defined by

$$w_i(\theta) = \min(1, \chi^2_{k,0.95} / \mathrm{RD}(f_i)^2) \quad \text{for } i = 1, \dots, n. \qquad (9.19)$$

Regular observations receive weight 1, and the weights for outliers depends on the "outlyingness" of the score vectors. The weight function (9.19) was used by Simpson et al (1992) and yielded stable results. Becker and Gather (2001) suggested the use of the MVE estimator for estimating location and scatter in (9.18) since it performs well as an outlier identifier.

The set of column weights v_j ($j = 1, \dots, p$) for downweighting outlying loading vectors is defined analogously:

$$v_j(\theta) = \min(1, \chi^2_{k,0.95} / \mathrm{RD}(\lambda_j)^2) \quad \text{for } j = 1, \dots, p, \qquad (9.20)$$

where

$$\mathrm{RD}(\lambda_j) = \sqrt{(\lambda_j - T(\Lambda))^{\top} C(\Lambda)^{-1} (\lambda_j - T(\Lambda))}. \qquad (9.21)$$

Note that, since the true loadings and scores are unobserved, w_i and v_j depend on the unknown parameter vector θ. Hence, row and column weights have to be re-computed in each iteration step. Finding proper weights w_i and v_j means essentially to identify outliers in a k-dimensional space. Since k is usually low, the computational effort is reasonable. The result of (9.17) is named the FAIR estimator. The estimator is also "fair" in the sense that it will not be misled by outlying observations.

9.4.6 Other criteria

There are still other possibilities for defining g in the objective function (9.12), or equivalently, in the iterative scheme given by (9.13) and (9.14). The following discusses the use of some important robust regression techniques.

Consider the first equation (9.13) of the iteration scheme in more detail. Fixing the index j and assuming that the scores $\boldsymbol{f}_i$ are already known, estimate the unknown loadings, one has to minimize

$$\hat{\boldsymbol{\lambda}}_j = \operatorname*{argmin}_{\boldsymbol{\lambda} \in R^k} \sum_{i=1}^{n} g(x_{ij} - \boldsymbol{\lambda}^\top \hat{\boldsymbol{f}}_i) \ . \tag{9.22}$$

Considering M-estimators for regression (Huber, 1981), (9.22) is rewritten as

$$\hat{\boldsymbol{\lambda}}_j = \operatorname*{argmin}_{\boldsymbol{\lambda} \in R^k} \sum_{i=1}^{n} \rho(x_{ij} - \boldsymbol{\lambda}^\top \hat{\boldsymbol{f}}_i) \ , \tag{9.23}$$

where ρ is a symmetric function with a unique minimum at zero. It is common to differentiate this expression with respect to the regression coefficients which yields

$$\sum_{i=1}^{n} \psi(x_{ij} - \boldsymbol{\lambda}^\top \hat{\boldsymbol{f}}_i) \hat{\boldsymbol{f}}_i = \boldsymbol{0} \ . \tag{9.24}$$

ψ is the derivative of ρ, and its choice depends on the desired properties of downweighting large residuals. The use of the Huber function

$$\psi_c(t) = \min(c, \max(t, -c))$$

with an appropriate constant c results in a statistically more efficient regression method than L^1 regression (Hampel et al., 1986). However, the breakdown value is again 0% because of the sensitivity with respect to leverage points. Moreover, the computational complexity is much higher than for L^1 regression.

A highly robust regression method is *least median of squares* (LMS) regression (Rousseeuw, 1984). Rather than minimizing the sum of a function of the residuals like in (9.22), the LMS estimator is given by

$$\hat{\boldsymbol{\lambda}}_j = \operatorname*{argmin}_{\boldsymbol{\lambda} \in R^k} \operatorname*{med}_{i}(x_{ij} - \boldsymbol{\lambda}^\top \hat{\boldsymbol{f}}_i) \tag{9.25}$$

which has a 50% breakdown value.

Another method is the *least trimmed squares* (LTS) method (Rousseeuw, 1984). The residuals in (9.22) are given by $r_i = x_{ij} - \boldsymbol{\lambda}^\top \hat{\boldsymbol{f}}_i$ for $i = 1, \ldots, n$ (j is fixed). If the squared residuals $(r^2)_{1:n} \le \cdots \le (r^2)_{n:n}$ are ordered, the LTS estimator is defined by

$$\hat{\boldsymbol{\lambda}}_j = \operatorname*{argmin}_{\boldsymbol{\lambda} \in R^k} \sum_{i=1}^{h} (r^2)_{i:n} \ . \tag{9.26}$$

This definition is very similar to LS with the difference that the largest $n - h$ residuals are not used in the summation. The choice of $h = n/2$ yields a breakdown value of 50%.

Both LMS and LTS can result in a non-decreasing objective function (9.12), in which case the iterative algorithm is not converging (Croux et al., 1999). The reason for this phenomenon is that the weighting of the outliers is not done in a smooth way like in the weight functions (9.19) and (9.20) of the FAIR approach (e.g., by definition of the LTS method only weight 1 for non-outliers and weight 0 for outliers is used). Moreover, both LMS and LTS are very time consuming algorithms, although a LTS regression algorithm has recently been developed (Rousseeuw & Van Driessen, 2000), which is much faster than all available algorithms for LMS. Interlocking regression using the LMS algorithm was considered in the context of singular value decomposition by Ukkelberg and Borgen (1993).

Experience and simulations have shown that the FAIR approach is preferable to all considered methods with respect to computation time, robustness, and stable convergence of the algorithm (Croux et al., 1999).

9.4.7   The FAIR algorithm

The FAIR estimator given by (9.17) can be approximated by the iterative scheme (9.13) and (9.14). The following outlines the complete algorithm in detail.

- **Scaling.** The data are first scaled in a robust way:

$$x_{ij} \leftarrow \frac{x_{ij} - \mathrm{med}_i(x_{ij})}{\mathrm{MAD}_i(x_{ij})} \ . \tag{9.27}$$

  Standardizations using other robust estimators of location and scale could be considered, but this traditional choice is very robust and easy to compute.
- **Starting values.** It is important to initialize the algorithm with robust starting values because otherwise the global minimum of the objective function (9.17) may not be well approximated, or the convergence of the algorithm could slow down. Starting values $\hat{f}_i^{(0)}$ for the factor scores can be obtained by performing robust PCA, since PCA can be seen as a special case of FA (see Section 9.5). The procedure of Croux and Ruiz-Gazen (1996) is suitable for this purpose because it can deal with $p > n$, is highly robust and fast to compute. Moreover, it computes just the first k principal components (the only ones needed here), which reduces the computation time even further. Experiments have shown that the choice of the starting values is not too crucial for finding a good approximation (Croux et al., 1999).
- **Iteration process.** Suppose that the iteration process has reached step t $(t \geq 1)$ of the algorithm, and the $\hat{f}_i^{(t-1)}$ are available.

* *Regression of the columns.* First compute weights $w_i^{(t)}$ as defined in (9.19), which downweight outliers in the set of estimated score vectors $\{\hat{f}_i^{(t-1)} | 1 \le i \le n\}$ in R^k. Then compute

$$\hat{\lambda}_j^{(t)} = \underset{\lambda \in R^k}{\text{argmin}} \sum_{i=1}^{n} w_i^{(t)} |x_{ij} - \lambda^\top \hat{f}_i^{(t-1)}| \qquad (9.28)$$

for each column $j = 1, \dots, p$. This corresponds to applying p times (weighted) L^1 regression (each column of the data matrix is regressed on the k-dimensional scores). Note that the weights $w_i^{(t)}$ will not change during the p regressions, since the scores $\hat{f}_i^{(t-1)}$ do not alter. So, the weights only need to be computed once every iteration step. They require computation of a robust scatter estimator in the factor space, which is usually of a low dimension k.

* *Regression of the rows.* The weights $v_j^{(t)}$ for downweighting outliers in the set of estimated loading vectors $\{\hat{\lambda}_j^{(t)} | 1 \le j \le p\}$ in R^k are computed according to (9.20). The scores are updated by

$$\hat{f}_i^{(t)} = \underset{f \in R^k}{\text{argmin}} \sum_{j=1}^{p} v_j^{(t)} |x_{ij} - f^\top \hat{\lambda}_j^{(t)}| \qquad (9.29)$$

for $i = 1, \dots, n$. This means that each row of the data matrix is regressed on the k-dimensional loadings (n regressions).

* *Convergence.* The values of the objective function (9.17) computed for the estimates obtained in step $t-1$ and step t are compared. If there is no essential difference in the objective function, the iterative process is stopped and we set $\hat{f}_i = \hat{f}_i^{(t)}$ for $1 \le i \le n$ and $\hat{\lambda}_j = \hat{\lambda}_j^{(t)}$ for $1 \le j \le p$. If not, another iteration (step $t+1$) is run. Although no proof of convergence exists, many simulations and examples have shown its good numerical and statistical performance (Croux et al., 1999).

− **Orthogonalization.** This part of the algorithm for orthogonalizing the factors is optional. Suppose that the estimated scores and loadings are transformed by

$$\hat{F} \leftarrow \hat{F} \hat{\Sigma}_f^{-1/2} \quad \text{and} \quad \hat{\Lambda} \leftarrow \hat{\Lambda} \hat{\Sigma}_f^{1/2}$$

where $\hat{\Sigma}_f$ is the estimated covariance matrix of the estimated scores $\{\hat{f}_i | 1 \le i \le n\}$. Then the fitted values will not change since $\hat{X} = \hat{F}\hat{\Lambda}^\top = \hat{F}\hat{\Sigma}_f^{-1/2}(\hat{\Lambda}\hat{\Sigma}_f^{1/2})^\top$. Moreover, the model condition $\text{Cov}(f) = I_k$ is fulfilled now. To keep the robustness properties of the whole algorithm, $\hat{\Sigma}_f$ has to be computed in a robust way, for example by the MCD estimator (in k dimensions, where k is small).

– **Factor rotation.** This part is also optional, and is used for obtaining a better interpretation of the factors (a goal of FA). Rotation can be formulated mathematically by $\tilde{\Lambda} = \hat{\Lambda}T$, where T is a $k \times k$ transformation matrix and $\tilde{\Lambda}$ are the rotated estimated loadings. Since the fitted values should not change, the rotated scores are computed by $\tilde{F} = \hat{F}(T^{\top})^{-1}$. This formula can be simplified in case of orthogonal rotation (T is an orthogonal matrix) to $\tilde{F} = \hat{F}T$. The transformation matrix T is obtained by applying the usual orthogonal or oblique rotation methods (Harman, 1976).

– **Residuals, outliers, biplot.** The residuals are obtained as $\hat{\varepsilon}_{ij} = x_{ij} - \hat{x}_{ij} = x_{ij} - \hat{f}_i^{\top}\hat{\lambda}_j$. When applying a robust method, outliers can be visualized by inspecting the residuals which are large in that case. Hence, a plot of the residuals versus (i, j) in the horizontal plane is very useful for detecting outliers. In the case that $k = 2$, one can represent the observations by $(\hat{f}_{i1}, \hat{f}_{i2})$ and the variables by $(\hat{\lambda}_{j1}, \hat{\lambda}_{j2})$ in the same 2D plot, called the biplot (Gower & Hand, 1996).

– **Uniquenesses.** The uniquenesses or specific variances are estimated by $\hat{\psi}_j = (\text{MAD}_i(\hat{\varepsilon}_{ij}))^2$ for $j = 1, \ldots, p$ (see Section 9.4.2). This is in contrast with most other FA procedures which estimate the uniquenesses beforehand or simultaneously to the loadings. An alternative way of estimating the uniquenesses is to use appropriate weights in Equation (9.29) which account for the heteroscedasticity given by the FA model. However, experiments indicate that additional weighting in the interlocking regression scheme can affect the stability of the algorithm (Croux et al., 1999).[3]

9.4.8   Remarks

– **The case $p > n$.** A principle of the FAIR method is to treat columns and rows of the data matrix in the same way (see (9.28) and (9.29)). This implies that the method can be used for both cases $n > p$ and $p > n$ (and, of course, also for $n = p$). This is an important feature since many social science applications typically have more variables than observations.

– **Robustness of FAIR.** The influence function of the FAIR estimator has not been computed up to now. However, the robustness of the method has been investigated by simulation studies (Croux et al., 1999). It turns out that FAIR is comparable to the MCD-based FA approach (Section 9.3) concerning the estimation of the loadings and uniquenesses. The mean (median) squared errors for the overal fit, for the reduced correlation

---

[3] An Splus function for FAIR is available at the website http://www.statistik.tuwien.ac.at/public/filz/. The function allows one to apply all previously mentioned regression methods for interlocking regression: LS, L^1, weighted L^1 (FAIR), M-estimators, LTS and LMS.

matrix, and for the uniquenesses are (in the presence of contamination) smallest for the FAIR method in comparison to PFA, the MCD-based FA method, and the alternating regression based method using LS and L^1 regressions.

FAIR can withstand a higher number of outlying cells than the MCD based method. If an observation contains an outlying cell, MCD (and also other robust scatter matrix estimators) will declare the whole observation as outlying, while FAIR still uses the information of the other cells of that observation for parameter estimation. The worst case situation for FAIR is when many cells of one row or one column of a data matrix are corrupted. Then the robust distances used for weighting rows or columns may be incorrectly estimated and the resulting estimates from weighted L^1 regression can be biased.

- **Missing data.** The procedure can handle missing data. This is due to the same argument stated previously. A missing cell can be replaced by an arbitrary value (outlier) and FAIR takes the information of the outlying cells to estimate the parameters.

- **Number of factors.** Croux et al. (1999) introduced a robust R^2 measure for the FAIR method. It resembles the definition of the R^2 measure in classical regression and is defined by

$$R_{FAIR}^2(k) = 1 - \left(\frac{\sum_{i=1}^n \sum_{j=1}^p w_i v_j |x_{ij} - \hat{x}_{ij}|}{\sum_{i=1}^n \sum_{j=1}^p w_i v_j |x_{ij}|} \right)^2 \tag{9.30}$$

for measuring the variability explained by k factors. The weights are given by (9.19) and (9.20), respectively. The measure can be plotted against the number k of factors, and this robust R^2 plot can be used for the selection of an appropriate number of factors. The analogous measure for the LS fit (9.15) is

$$R_{LS}^2(k) = 1 - \frac{\sum_{i=1}^n \sum_{j=1}^p (x_{ij} - \hat{x}_{ij})^2}{\sum_{i=1}^n \sum_{j=1}^p x_{ij}^2}. \tag{9.31}$$

- **FANOVA model.** The FAIR method can be extended to the FANOVA model introduced by Gollub (1968), which combines aspects of *analysis of variance* (ANOVA) with factor analysis. The ANOVA model is given by

$$x_{ij} = \mu + a_i + b_j + \delta_{ij} \tag{9.32}$$

where μ is the overall mean, a_i represents the row effect, b_j the column effect, and δ_{ij} are residuals. The terms δ_{ij} can also be seen as interactions between rows and columns, and in case they contain further structure they can be described by a factor model $\delta_{ij} = \sum_{l=1}^k \lambda_{jl} f_{il} + \varepsilon_{ij}$. This gives the FANOVA model

$$x_{ij} = \mu + a_i + b_j + \boldsymbol{f}_i^\top \boldsymbol{\lambda}_j + \varepsilon_{ij} \tag{9.33}$$

with the residuals ε_{ij} containing white noise. The unknown parameters in (9.33) can be estimated simultaneously by an extension of the FAIR algorithm (Croux et al., 1999).

9.4.9   Example

Consider a data set from the 1991 Austrian census. The data are presented in Table 9.1, with the values rounded to the first decimal.[4]

Table 9.1. Styrian districts data, rounded to the first decimal. The abbreviations of the districts and variables are explained in the text.

	chi	old	ind	tra	tou	ser	agr	mou	une	uni	pri	cnd	cdi
G	13.7	22.6	23.1	19.8	3.1	51.6	0.6	0.0	6.9	15.9	69.9	3.8	11.3
BM	15.9	22.4	46.0	13.0	5.6	29.5	4.8	1.1	8.7	5.5	86.0	9.3	46.8
DL	18.8	19.4	42.3	11.9	4.7	22.9	17.5	2.3	4.6	4.7	89.0	12.6	63.3
FB	20.3	18.6	33.0	11.5	4.3	21.9	28.8	0.0	3.3	3.2	92.0	13.0	60.5
FF	18.5	21.2	38.4	16.1	4.6	25.4	15.1	0.0	4.9	5.4	88.2	10.2	56.7
GU	18.9	18.1	41.5	12.9	5.6	25.0	13.7	1.4	3.9	5.6	86.3	6.0	72.5
HB	21.1	17.6	33.6	11.9	6.9	23.2	23.6	3.7	3.7	3.7	91.0	20.5	60.3
JU	17.5	20.9	47.1	11.3	4.1	26.7	8.4	1.9	6.0	5.1	87.8	12.7	51.6
KN	18.1	21.4	44.1	10.9	3.3	31.3	9.9	1.7	5.7	5.3	87.9	8.7	54.0
LB	19.5	18.2	35.8	13.6	5.1	26.3	18.0	0.3	5.3	3.6	90.5	12.0	64.8
LE	14.5	24.4	38.2	11.6	4.9	37.0	4.7	0.8	9.9	6.1	86.1	10.5	46.4
LI	18.8	20.2	33.2	13.0	9.5	32.6	10.5	3.0	6.9	5.3	88.1	13.7	47.8
MZ	16.8	23.4	50.4	9.7	6.0	25.3	7.4	1.9	6.4	4.5	87.7	9.0	48.5
MU	20.5	19.2	30.1	9.5	6.8	31.0	21.3	5.0	4.4	5.4	88.0	24.8	59.2
RA	18.1	21.5	24.5	10.7	4.5	28.5	31.0	0.0	3.9	4.1	90.9	13.3	54.2
VO	17.3	21.1	40.0	10.6	4.9	25.1	12.0	3.2	7.9	4.2	88.3	10.9	62.4
WZ	20.5	18.6	42.1	11.5	4.9	20.2	19.7	2.9	4.2	4.1	89.8	11.4	61.3

13 variables were measured for all 17 political districts of Styria, which is part of Austria. One district is the capital Graz (G). The typical rural districts are Feldbach (FB), Hartberg (HB), Liezen (LI), Murau (MU), Radkersburg (RA), and Weiz (WZ), while typical industrial regions are Bruck/Mur (BM), Judenburg (JU), Knittelfeld (KN), and Mürzzuschlag (MZ). Graz-Umgebung (GU) is the surroundings of Graz. The remaining districts are Deutschlandsberg (DL), Fürstenfeld (FF), Leibnitz (LB), Leoben (LE), and Voitsberg (VO). The variables are the percentage of children (< 15 years) (chi) and old people (> 60 years) (old), the percentages of employed people in the industry (ind), trade (tra), tourism (tou), service (ser), and agriculture (agr),

---

[4] The original data can be obtained from the author and are used for the computations presented.

and the percentage of unemployed people (une). Other variables are the percentage of mountain farms (mou), of people with university education (uni), of people which just attended primary school (pri), of employed people not commuting daily (cnd), and the percentage of employed people commuting to another district (cdi).

The following compares the FAIR approach (which uses weighted L^1 regressions) with the non-robust counterpart using LS regressions. Note that MCD-based FA (Section 9.3) cannot be applied to this data set since current computer programs for the MCD require $n > 2p$ (Rousseeuw & Van Driessen, 1999). First an appropriate number of factors must be selected. For this one can use the R^2 measures given by (9.31) for the LS-based method and (9.30) for FAIR. Since the number of variables is $p = 13$ one can at most compute 6 factors for the FAIR method $(p > 2k)$. Figure 9.7 presents the R^2 plots for both methods. $k = 3$ factors were selected explaining 83.7% of the total variation for the LS procedure and 77.7% for FAIR. The factors were extracted by the two methods and rotated according to the varimax criterion. Before inspecting loadings and scores, the residuals (Figure 9.8) are inspected for information about the quality of the fit. The residuals $x_{ij} - \hat{x}_{ij}$ are drawn in the vertical direction, and the axes labeled by "Variables" and "Districts" represent the columns and rows of the residual matrix, respectively. The top plot shows the residuals of the non-robust LS procedure, and the bottom plot shows the residuals of FAIR. Note the different scale of the vertical axes: -1.5 to 1.5 for the LS method and -6 to 8 for the robust FAIR method. The residual plot of FAIR reveals a few large outliers in the first row, which is district Graz (G). This indicates that Graz is clearly distinct from most other districts. There is another large residual with value 2.4 for FF (row 5) at the variable tra (column 4) which is also visible in the data matrix. The touristy district of Liezen (LI, row 12) shows large residuals for the variables indicating the percentages of employed people in trade and tourism (tra, tou, columns 4 and 5). The LS procedure typically masks the outliers. LS tries to fit *all* data values, and *all* resulting residuals are quite small. However, because the outliers have affected the fit, the parameter estimates are biased. As a consequence, subsequent factor or loading plots cannot be realistic.

Figure 9.9 shows the biplot representations of the first two factors for the LS-based method (top) and for FAIR (bottom). The biplot has the advantage that both loadings and scores can be presented in one plot, and it allows interpretation of the relations between observations and variables (Gower & Hand, 1996). The plot of the classical method is clearly dominated by the outlier Graz (G). The configuration of objects and variables in the plot is quite different to the robust counterpart, which was already expected from the residual plot above. Graz appears in the plot for the FAIR method as an outlier again. Fortunately the biplot is robust, implying that Graz will not influence too much the estimates of loadings and scores. Factor 1 separates the industrial (low values) and rural (high values) regions, and to a smaller extend

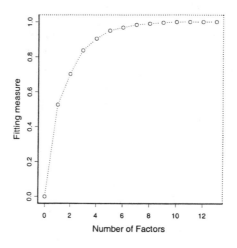

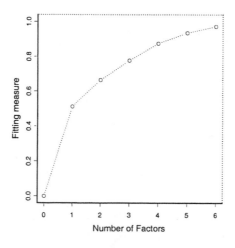

Fig. 9.7. R^2 plot for the LS-based FA method (top) and for FAIR (bottom).

Factor 2 allows the same separation. Two typical agricultural districts, MU and HB, are characterized by less places of work (except in agriculture), and hence there are many persons 'commuting not daily' (cnd) (they work outside the whole week). On the other hand, GU has a high value for commuting to another district (cdi), namely to Graz. LE which has its own university and is a typical industrial region with a large percentage of highly educated individuals (uni), many people employed in service (ser), many old people (old), and a large percentage of unemployed people (une).

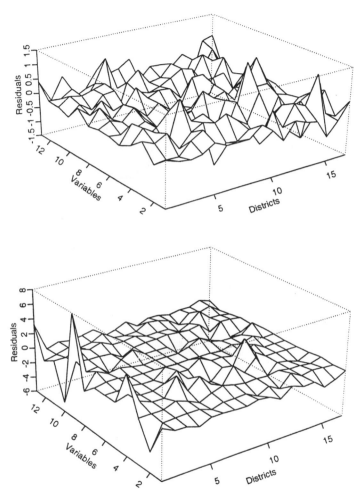

Fig. 9.8. Residuals of the LS-based method (top) and of FAIR (bottom).

Finally, uniquenesses can be estimated by the residual variances. Figure 9.10 presents the residual matrix by means of parallel boxplots for each column (variable). The left plot shows the results of the LS-based method and the right plot presents the results of the FAIR method. The different scale of the two plots in Figure 9.8 were already noted. This effect is also visible here, and is caused by the non-robustness of the LS-based method. The lengths of the boxes represent a robust measure of the residual variances, which are estimates of the uniquenesses. The plot for the FAIR method shows a relatively

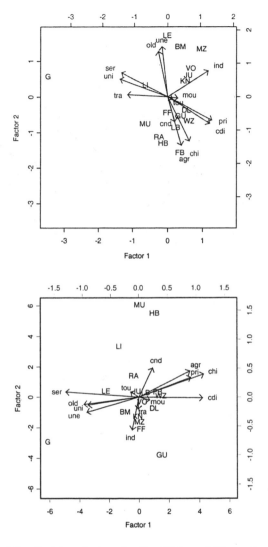

Fig. 9.9. Biplot of the first two factors for the LS-based FA method (top) and for FAIR (bottom).

high specific variance for the fourth variable (percentage of employed people in trade). This means that the 3-factor model explains less of the variation of this variable.

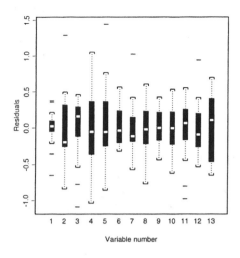

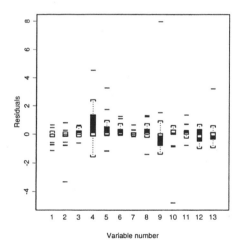

Fig. 9.10. Parallel boxplots of the columns (variables) of the residual matrix for the LS-based FA method (top) and for FAIR (bottom). The lengths of the boxes are robust estimates of the uniquenesses.

9.5 Robust Principal Component Solution to FA

9.5.1 Introduction

Principal component analysis (PCA) goes back to Pearson (1901) but was originally developed by Hotelling (1933). The aim of PCA is to reduce the dimensionality of observed data in order to simplify the data representation.

The dimension reduction is done by introducing a new (orthogonal) coordinate system where the first few coordinates or components are constructed to include as much information as possible. Hence, the dimensionality is reduced to these few components. PCA is one of the most important tools in multivariate analysis, and it is also a basic module for many other multivariate methods (e.g., Jackson, 1991).

Let $x = (x_1, \ldots, x_p)^\top$ be a p-dimensional random vector with $E(x) = \mu$ and $\text{Cov}(x) = \Sigma$. Consider the linear transformation

$$z = \Gamma^\top(x - \mu) \tag{9.34}$$

with $\Gamma = (\gamma_1, \ldots, \gamma_p)$ being an orthogonal $(p \times p)$ matrix with unit vectors γ_j, i.e. $\gamma_j^\top \gamma_j = 1$, for $j = 1, \ldots, p$. With the choice of γ_j being the eigenvectors of Σ to the corresponding eigenvalues a_i ($a_1 \geq a_2 \geq \ldots \geq a_p \geq 0$), Equation (9.34) is known as the principal component (PC) transformation. It is easy to see that $\text{Cov}(z) = \text{diag}(a_1, \ldots, a_p)$. So, the variance of the jth PC

$$z_j = \gamma_j^\top(x - \mu) \tag{9.35}$$

corresponds to the jth eigenvalue, the PCs are arranged in decreasing order of their variances, and the PCs are orthogonal to each other.

Defining the jth column of the loadings matrix Λ as $\lambda_j = \sqrt{a_j}\gamma_j$ for $j = 1, \ldots, p$, one can rewrite the model (9.7) as

$$\Sigma = \Lambda\Lambda^\top + 0 \tag{9.36}$$

with 0 being a $(p \times p)$ matrix of zeroes. Hence, the factor loadings of the jth factor are, apart from the scaling factor $\sqrt{a_j}$, the coefficients of the jth PC. The specific variances Ψ in (9.7) are reduced to the matrix 0, which means that the model does not include specific factors like the FA model (Eq. 9.5). Note that the FA representation in Equation (9.36) is exact, but it allows no simplification of Σ since there are as many factors as variables. A better way is to approximate Σ by a smaller number k of common factors,

$$\Sigma \approx \Lambda\Lambda^\top \tag{9.37}$$

with Λ being a $(p \times k)$ matrix. This assumes that the error terms ε in the FA model (9.6) are of minor importance and that they can be ignored in the decomposition of the covariance matrix Σ. Hence, if one allows for specific factors ε, one may take the same assumption as for the FA model, namely to consider their covariance matrix Ψ as a diagonal matrix. The diagonal elements ψ_i are thus the diagonal elements of $\Sigma - \Lambda\Lambda^\top$.

The sample PCs are defined according to (9.35) by using the corresponding sample counterparts. For a given $(n \times p)$ data matrix X with observations $x_1, \ldots, x_n$, the population mean μ is traditionally estimated by the arithmetic mean vector

$$\bar{x} = \hat{\mu} = \frac{1}{n}\sum_{i=1}^{n} x_i ,$$

and the population covariance matrix Σ by the sample covariance matrix

$$S = \widehat{\Sigma} = \frac{1}{n-1} \sum_{i=1}^{n} (x_i - \bar{x})(x_i - \bar{x})^\top .$$

The eigenvectors and eigenvalues are computed from S, and one obtains the pairs $(\hat{a}_1, \hat{\gamma}_1), \ldots, (\hat{a}_p, \hat{\gamma}_p)$ with $\hat{a}_1 \geq \hat{a}_2 \geq \ldots \geq \hat{a}_p$. The sample PCs are then given by

$$z_j = (X - 1\bar{x}^\top)\hat{\gamma}_j \qquad \text{for} \qquad j = 1, \ldots, p \qquad (9.38)$$

where 1 is a vector of length n with elements 1.

Like in the population case, the estimated factor loadings are defined by $\hat{\lambda}_j = \sqrt{\hat{a}_j}\hat{\gamma}_j$ $(j = 1, \ldots, p)$. By taking only k factors $(k < p)$, the k loading vectors are collected, which correspond to the k largest eigenvalues $\hat{a}_j$ as columns in the matrix $\hat{\Lambda}$ to obtain $\hat{\Lambda}\hat{\Lambda}^\top$ as an approximation of S. The estimated specific variances $\hat{\psi}_j$ are taken as the diagonal elements of the residual matrix $S - \hat{\Lambda}\hat{\Lambda}^\top$. This procedure is known as the principal component solution to FA (e.g., Johnson & Wichern, 1998, p. 522). As the basic tool of this approach is PCA, the robustification of PCA is described next.

9.5.2   Robust PCA

Classical PCA as described above is very sensitive to outlying observations because arithmetic mean and sample covariance are involved (both have breakdown value 0). The PCs are determined by the eigenvectors computed from the sample covariance matrix S. Classical PCs may thus be strongly "attracted" by outliers with the consequence that these PCs will not describe the main structure of the data.

An obvious way to robustify PCA is to robustly estimate mean and scatter. The eigenvectors computed from the robustly estimated covariance matrix will also be robust, and the robust PCs can be defined due to Equation (9.35). As in Section 9.3, the MCD estimator can be used for this purpose. Of course, this is not the only choice, and the question of which robust covariance matrix estimator to use has been addressed by Croux and Haesbroeck (2000).

The following describes a different approach to robustify PCA. This method is based on the idea of projection pursuit and was first developed by Li and Chen (1985). It is characterized by the following properties:

- The resulting PCs are highly robust.
- The number of variables in the data set can exceed the number of observations.
- The procedure can handle missing data.

- The PCs are directly estimated, without passing by a robust estimate of the covariance matrix.
- The user can choose the number of PCs to be computed.
- A fast algorithm exists (Croux & Ruiz-Gazen, 1996).
- The IF has been derived (Croux & Ruiz-Gazen, 2000).
- A robust estimation of the covariance matrix can be computed at the basis of the robust PCs.

9.5.3   The Principle

Projection pursuit (PP) is a method for finding interesting structures in a p-dimensional data set. These interesting structures are contained in subspaces of low dimension (usually 1- or 2-dimensional), and they are found by maximizing a projection index. For example, the index can be a measure of deviation of the projected data from normality (Friedman & Tukey, 1974).

PCA can be seen as a special case of PP (Huber, 1985) by defining the projection index as a (univariate) measure of dispersion. Hence, one is interested in finding directions with maximal dispersion of the data projected on these directions. This is exactly the aim of PCA, with the additional assumption of orthogonality of the directions or components. For PCA the dispersion measure is the classical variance, which is not robust. Replacing the sample variance by a robust measure of dispersion results in a robust PCA method.

For given observations $x_1, \ldots, x_n \in \mathbb{R}^p$, collected as rows in a data matrix X we define the 1-dimensional projection of X by Xb or, equivalently by $(x_1^\top b, \ldots, x_n^\top b)$ for a coefficient vector $b \in \mathbb{R}^p$. For a (univariate) scale estimator S one can measure the dispersion of the projected data by $S(x_1^\top b, \ldots, x_n^\top b)$. S is the projection index, and one can either take the classical sample standard deviation (for obtaining classical PCs) or a robust estimator of scale. The first "eigenvector" $\hat{\gamma}_1$ is then defined as the maximum of $S(Xb)$ with respect to the (normed) vector b,

$$\hat{\gamma}_1 = \underset{\|b\|=1}{\operatorname{argmax}} \, S(x_1^\top b, \ldots, x_n^\top b) \ . \tag{9.39}$$

The associated first "eigenvalue" is given by

$$\hat{a}_1 = S^2(x_1^\top \hat{\gamma}_1, \ldots, x_n^\top \hat{\gamma}_1) \ . \tag{9.40}$$

Suppose that the first $k - 1$ eigenvectors or projection directions ($k > 1$) have already been found. The kth eigenvector is then defined by

$$\hat{\gamma}_k = \underset{\|b\|=1, b \perp \hat{\gamma}_1, \ldots, b \perp \hat{\gamma}_{k-1}}{\operatorname{argmax}} \, S(x_1^\top b, \ldots, x_n^\top b) \ , \tag{9.41}$$

and the associated eigenvalue by

$$\hat{a}_k = S^2(x_1^\top \hat{\gamma}_k, \ldots, x_n^\top \hat{\gamma}_k) \ . \tag{9.42}$$

As a by-product of this approach, one can easily compute the (robust) co-variance matrix by

$$C = \sum_{j=1}^{p} \hat{a}_j \hat{\gamma}_j \hat{\gamma}_j^{\mathsf{T}} \ . \tag{9.43}$$

Li and Chen (1985) showed that this estimator is equivariant at elliptical models and consistent. Moreover, the breakdown value of the eigenvectors and eigenvalues is the same as the breakdown value of the scale estimator Croux and Ruiz-Gazen (2000) additionally derived the influence function of the estimators for the eigenvectors, eigenvalues, and the associated dispersion matrix. They computed Gaussian efficiencies for different choices of the scale estimator S, namely for the classical standard deviation, the median absolute deviation (MAD), the M-estimator of scale, and the Q_n estimator of Rousseeuw and Croux (1993) defined for a sample $\{y_1, \ldots, y_n\} \subset \mathbf{R}$ as

$$Q_n(y_1, \ldots, y_n) = 2.2219\{|y_i - y_j|; 1 \leq i < j \leq n\}_{([n/2]+1)\binom{n}{2}} \ .$$

So, Q_n is defined as the first quartile of the pairwise differences between the data, and because it attains the maximal breakdown point and has good efficiency properties, the Q_n is a good choice as a projection index (Croux & Ruiz-Gazen, 2000).

9.5.4   Algorithm

The maximization problem (Eq. 9.41) was solved by Li and Chen (1985) using a complicated computer intensive algorithm. Thus, for practical purposes, this method is rather unattractive. Croux and Ruiz-Gazen (1996) introduced a new fast algorithm which is described next.

Suppose that the first $k - 1$ eigenvalues are already known ($k > 1$). For finding the kth projection direction, a projection matrix is defined as

$$\boldsymbol{P}_k = \boldsymbol{I}_p - \sum_{j=1}^{k-1} \hat{\gamma}_j \hat{\gamma}_j^{\mathsf{T}} \tag{9.44}$$

for projection on the orthogonal complement of the space spanned by the first $k - 1$ eigenvectors (for $k = 1$ one can take $\boldsymbol{P}_k = \boldsymbol{I}_p$). The kth "eigenvector" is then defined by maximizing the function

$$b \ \longrightarrow \ \hat{s}(\boldsymbol{X}\boldsymbol{P}_k b) \tag{9.45}$$

under the conditions $b^{\mathsf{T}} b = 1$ and $\boldsymbol{P}_k b = b$. The latter condition ensures orthogonality to previously found projection directions because

$$b = \boldsymbol{P}_k b = \boldsymbol{I}_p b - \sum_{j=1}^{k-1} \hat{\gamma}_j \hat{\gamma}_j^{\mathsf{T}} b \quad \Longleftrightarrow \quad \hat{\gamma}_j^{\mathsf{T}} b = 0 \text{ for } j = 1, \ldots, k-1 \ .$$

The function (9.41) defines a non-trivial maximization problem, and in principle one has to search the solution in an infinite set of possible directions. For practical reasons the search is restricted to the set

$$B_{n,k} = \left\{ \frac{P_k(x_1 - \hat{\mu}(X))}{\|P_k(x_1 - \hat{\mu}(X))\|}, \ldots, \frac{P_k(x_n - \hat{\mu}(X))}{\|P_k(x_n - \hat{\mu}(X))\|} \right\} . \qquad (9.46)$$

$B_{n,k}$ contains n normed vectors, each passing an observation and the center $\hat{\mu}(X)$, and projected on the orthogonal complement by P_k. As location estimate $\hat{\mu}$ of X, Croux and Ruiz-Gazen (1996) propose the L^1-median which is defined as

$$\hat{\mu}(X) = \underset{\mu \in R^p}{\mathrm{argmin}} \sum_{i=1}^{n} \|x_i - \mu\| , \qquad (9.47)$$

where $\| \cdot \|$ stands for the Euclidean norm. It has maximal breakdown value, is orthogonal equivariant, and a fast algorithm for its computation exists (Hössjer & Croux, 1995). Another possibility is to take the coordinatewise median, which is, however, not orthogonal equivariant.

The algorithm outlined above has successfully been used by Filzmoser (1999) in a geostatistical problem. It was also used by Croux et al. (1999) for obtaining starting values for the FAIR algorithm (see Section 9.4).[5] As the algorithm computes the eigenvalues sequentially, one can stop at a desired number rather than computing all p eigenvalues. This is important in applications with a large number of variables, when only the main structure, expressed by the first few PCs, is of interest. The algorithm also works for $n < p$. However, if n is very small, the approximation given by (9.46) might be inaccurate.

9.5.5   Example

Consider a data set based on the financial accounting information of 80 companies from the United Kingdom for the year 1983. The data were collected in the *Datastream* database, and published by Jobson (1991) and Steinhauser (1998). A total of 13 financial variables are considered:

---

[5] An Splus function of the algorithm is available at the website
http://www.statistik.tuwien.ac.at/public/filz/.

x_1 return on capital

x_2 ratio of working capital flow to current liabilities

x_3 ratio of working capital flow to total debt

x_4 gearing ratio or debt-equity ratio

x_5 $\log_{10}$ of total sales

x_6 $\log_{10}$ of total assets

x_7 ratio of net fixed assets to total assets

x_8 capital intensity or ratio of total sales to total assets

x_9 gross fixed assets to total assets

x_{10} ratio of total inventories to total assets

x_{11} pay-out ratio

x_{12} quick ratio

x_{13} current ratio

Steinhauser (1998) used this data set in the context of factor analysis. He tried to find the most influential observations, and found out (using several methods) that the masked observations 21, 47, 61, 66 influence the estimation of the loadings matrix.

In order to compare classical PCA with the PP approach to robust PCA, two representations of the PCA results are made: (i) a plot of the first two PCs, and (ii) a boxplot of all PCs. Figure 9.11 shows the plots of the first two principal axes for the classical and for the robust method. It was expected that this plot would reveal the main structure of the data set because the PCs are ordered by the magnitude of their explained variance. However, the figures are quite different. The plot for classical PCA is mainly determined by outliers, and the structure of the data can hardly be detected. The plot for the robust PCs also shows some outliers, but relations between the objects are much better visualized.

The above phenomenon can be explained by inspecting Figure 9.12 which shows parallel boxplots of the scores for all p PCs. The boxplots for classical PCA confirm that the PCs are strongly attracted by the outliers. The first PC is defined as the direction maximizing the sample variance. However, the sample variance is strongly increased by the two huge outliers 47 and 66. The robust variance of the first PC expressed by the size of the box is rather small. It is even smaller than the robust variance of the second PC. The bottom plot of Figure 9.12 shows the boxplots of the robust PCs. The variances (size of the boxes) are decreasing with increasing number of component. So it is certain that the first PCs will indeed capture the main structure of the data. Since a robust measure of the variance is maximized (using an M-estimator of scale), outliers which are visible by the boxplot presentations will not determine the direction of the PCs.

It is argued that outliers can easily be identified by classical PCA because they plot far away from the main data cloud. This is true for the example data as some outliers are clearly visible in Figure 9.11 (top). The problem is that it is not clear whether *all* outliers are visible in the plot. Even if the prospective

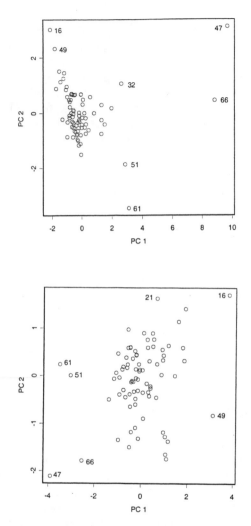

Fig. 9.11. Scores of the first two principal components for classical PCA (top) and robust PCA (bottom) for the financial accounting data.

outliers are deleted, other hidden or masked outliers can still strongly bias the result of classical PCA. If interest lies in identifying the outliers of the data set, one could compute the robust distances for each observation. The robust distance (9.4) is defined by replacing in the formula of the Mahalanobis distance the classical estimates of mean and scatter by robust counterparts (see Section 9.2.3). The MCD estimator can be used for this purpose, as can the estimates resulting from the PP based PCA approach. Since robust

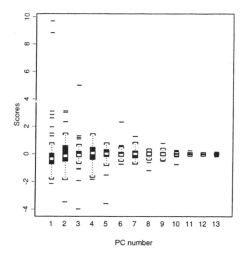

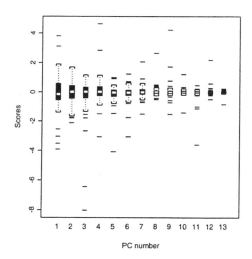

Fig. 9.12. Boxplots of all principal component scores for classical PCA (top) and robust PCA (bottom) for the financial accounting data.

estimates of eigenvectors and eigenvalues were computed, a robust estimation of the covariance matrix is given by (9.43). The L^1 median is also computed as a robust estimation of the mean. Figure 9.13 plots the robust distances of the estimates of robust PCA versus the robust distances using the MCD estimator. The dotted line would indicate equal values for both methods, and the vertical and horizontal line indicate the critical value $\chi^2_{13} = 4.973$. Both methods detect the same outliers which is an important message because this

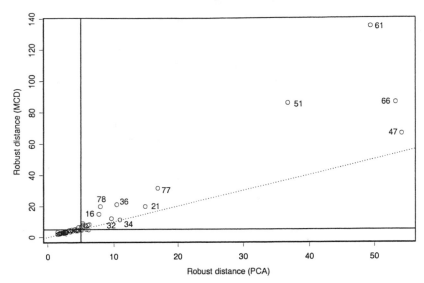

Fig. 9.13. Robust distances computed from robust PCA versus robust distances from the MCD.

implies that the structure of the estimated covariance matrices is about the same. Objects 47, 51, 61 and 66 are huge outliers, which are also visible in Figure 9.11, but there is still a group of smaller outliers not identified by the plot of the first two PCs. The scale of the axes is quite different because the MCD-based distances are systematically larger than the robust distances using the PCA estimates. This could be corrected by computing appropriate consistency factors.

9.6   Summary

Factor analysis is an important tool for analyzing multivariate data. However, if the data include outliers, the parameter estimates can be strongly biased providing meaningless results. The identification of the outliers is not a trivial problem that can be solved by visual inspection of data. This chapter presented methods able to identify outliers for the situations when the number of observations is larger than the number of variables and vice versa.

Several different methods to robustify FA were discussed in this chapter. For example, FA can easily be robustified by taking a robust estimation of the covariance matrix of the data (Pison et al., 2001), with loadings, uniquenesses and factor scores estimated in the usual way. The minimum covariance determinant (MCD) estimator (Rousseeuw, 1985) is a good choice for this purpose because it yields highly robust estimates and a fast algorithm is available to handle huge data sets (Rousseeuw & Van Driessen, 1999).

In contrast to the above method, Croux et al's (1999) method estimates the parameters directly from the (centered and scaled) data matrix, without passing by a covariance matrix, by applying an alternating regression scheme (Wold, 1966). Since rows and columns of the data matrix are treated in the same way, the method can deal with the case of more variables than observations. Another advantage is that the factor scores are estimated together with the factor loadings. The robustness of the method is ensured by taking a robust regression technique in the alternating regression scheme. Since the algorithm is computationally expensive, it is important that the regression method is fast to compute. It turns out that using weighted L^1 regression is a good choice because it is fast to compute, very robust, and results in a converging algorithm (called FAIR–Croux et al., 1999).

The final robust PCA method originates from the principal component solution to FA and is based on the idea of projection pursuit (Li & Chen, 1985). The method is highly robust and can be used for data sets with more variables than observations. A computational advantage, especially for huge data sets, is that one can stop the computation of the principal components at a desired number of components. As a by-product, one obtains a robustly estimated covariance matrix, which can be used for outlier identification. Finally, a fast algorithm (Croux & Ruiz-Gazen, 1996) also makes this method attractive for practical use.

References

Agulló, J. (1996). Exact iterative computation of the minimum volume ellipsoid estimator with a branch and bound algorithm. In A. Prat (Ed.), *Proceedings in computational statistics*, Vol. 1 (pp. 175-180). Heidelberg: Physica-Verlag.

Basilevsky, A. (1994). *Statistical factor analysis and related methods: Theory and applications*. New York: Wiley & Sons.

Becker, C. & Gather, U. (2001, in press). The largest nonidentifiable outlier: A comparison of multivariate simultaneous outlier identification rules. *Computational Statistics and Data Analysis*.

Bloomfield, P. & Steiger, W.L. (1983). *Least absolute deviations: Theory, applications, and algorithms*. Boston, MA: Birkhäuser.

Butler, R.W., Davies, P.L., & Jhun, M. (1993). Asymptotics for the minimum covariance determinant estimator. *The Annals of Statistics*, 21, 1385-1400.

Croux, C., Filzmoser, P., Pison, G., & Rousseeuw, P. J. (1999). Fitting factor models by robust interlocking regression. Technical Report TS-99-5, Department of Statistics, Vienna University of Technology.

Croux, C. & Haesbroeck, G. (1999). Influence function and efficiency of the minimum covariance determinant scatter matrix estimator. *Journal of Multivariate Analysis*, 71, 161-190.

Croux, C. & Haesbroeck, G. (2000). Principal component analysis based on robust estimators of the covariance or correlation matrix: influence functions and efficiencies. *Biometrika*, 87, 603-618.

Croux, C. & Ruiz-Gazen, A. (1996). A fast algorithm for robust principal components based on projection pursuit. In A. Prat (Ed.). *Computational statistics* (pp. 211-216). Heidelberg: Physica-Verlag.

Croux, C. & Ruiz-Gazen, A. (2000). *High breakdown estimators for principal components: the projection-pursuit approach revisited.* Technical report, ECARES, University of Brussels (ULB), 2000.

Donoho, D.L. & Huber, P.J. (1983). The notion of breakdown point. In P. Bickel, K. Doksum, and J.L. Hodges Jr. (Eds.). *A Festschrift for Erich Lehmann.* Belmont, CA: Wadsworth.

Dutter, R. (1983). *COVINTER: A computer program for computing robust covariances and for plotting tolerance ellipses.* Technical Report 10, Institute for Statistics, Technical University, Graz.

Dutter, R., Leitner, T., Reimann, C., & Wurzer, F. (1992). Grafische und geostatistische Analyse am PC. In R. Viertl (Ed.), *Beiträge zur Umweltstatistik,* volume 29, pages 78–88, Vienna, Schriftenreihe der Technischen Universität Wien.

Filzmoser, P. (1999). Robust principal components and factor analysis in the geostatistical treatment of environmental data. *Environmetrics,* 10, 363-375.

Friedman, J.H. & Tukey, J.W. (1974). A projection pursuit algorithm for exploratory data analysis. *IEEE Transactions on Computers,* 23, 881-890.

Gabriel, K.R. (1978). Least squares approximation of matrices by additive and multiplicative models. *Journal of the Royal Statistical Society B,* 40, 186-196.

Gollob, H.F. (1968). A statistical model which combines features of factor analytic and analysis of variance techniques. *Psychometrika,* 33, 73-116.

Gower, J. & Hand, D. (1996). *Biplots.* New York: Chapman & Hall.

Hampel, F.R. (1971). A general qualitative definition of robustness. *Annals of Mathematical Statistics,* 42, 1887-1896.

Hampel, F.R., Ronchetti, E.M., Rousseeuw, P.J., & Stahel, W. (1986). *Robust statistics: The approach based on influence functions.* New York: Wiley & Sons.

Harman, H.H. (1976). *Modern factor analysis.* Chicago, IL: University of Chicago Press.

Hössjer, O. & Croux, C. (1995). Generalizing univariate signed rank statistics for testing and estimating a multivariate location parameter. *Nonparametric Statistics,* 4, 293-308.

Hotelling, H. (1933). Analysis of a complex of statistical variables into principal components. *Journal of Educational Psychology,* 24, 417-441, 498-520.

Huber, P.J. (1981). *Robust statistics.* New York: Wiley & Sons.

Huber, P.J. (1985). Projection pursuit. *The Annals of Statistics,* 13, 435-475.

Hubert, M. (1997). The breakdown value of the l_1 estimator in contingency tables. *Statistics and Probability Letters,* 33, 419-425.

Jackson, J.E. (1991). *A user's guide to principal components.* New York: Wiley & Sons.

Jobson, J.D. (1991). *Applied Multivariate data analysis. Vol. I: Regression and experimental design.* New York: Springer-Verlag.

Johnson, R. & Wichern, D. (1998). *Applied multivariate statistical analysis.* London, England: Prentice-Hall.

Kaiser, H.F. (1958). The varimax criterion for analytic rotation in factor analysis. *Psychometrika,* 23, 187-200.

Kano, Y. (1998). Improper solutions in exploratory factor analysis: Causes and treatments. In A. Rizzi, M. Vichi, and H.-H. Bock (Eds.) (pp. 375-382). *Advances in data science and classification.* Berlin: Springer-Verlag.

Kosfeld, R. (1996). Robust exploratory factor analysis. *Statistical Papers*, 37, 105-122.

Li, G. & Chen, Z. (1985). Projection-pursuit approach to robust dispersion matrices and principal components: Primary theory and Monte Carlo. *Journal of the American Statistical Association*, 80, 759-766.

Marazzi, A. (1980). ROBETH: A subroutine library for robust statistical procedures. In M.M. Barritt and D. Wishart (Eds.) (pp. 577-583). *COMPSTAT 1980: Proceedings in computational statistics.* Wien: Physica-Verlag.

Maronna, R.A. (1976). Robust M-estimators of multivariate location and scatter. *The Annals of Statistics*, 4, 51-67.

Pearson, K. (1901). On lines and planes of closest fit to systems of points in space. *Phil. Mag. (6)*, 2, 559-572.

Pison, G., Rousseeuw, P.J., Filzmoser, P., & Croux, C. (2001, in press). Robust factor analysis. *Journal of Multivariate Analysis.*

Reimann, C., Äyräs, M., Chekushin, V., Bogatyrev, I., Boyd, R., de Caritat, P., Dutter, R., Finne, T.E., Halleraker, J.H., Jæger, Ø., Kashulina, G., Lehto, O., Niskavaara, H., Pavlov, V., Räisänen, M.L., Strand, T., & Volden, T. (1998). *Environmental geochemical atlas of the Central Barents Region.* Geological Survey of Norway (NGU), Geological Survey of Finland (GTK), and Central Kola Expedition (CKE), Special Publication, Trondheim, Espoo, Monchegorsk.

Reimann, C. & Melezhik, V. (2001). Metallogenic provinces, geochemical provinces and regional geology – what causes large-scale patterns in low-density geochemical maps of the C-horizon of podzols in Arctic Europe? *Applied Geochemistry, 16,* 963-983.

Rock, N.M.S. (1988). *Numerical Geology*, volume 18 of *Lecture Notes in Earth Sciences.* Berlin: Springer Verlag.

Rousseeuw, P.J. (1984). Least median of squares regression. *Journal of the American Statistical Association*, 79, 871-880.

Rousseeuw, P.J. (1985). Multivariate estimation with high breakdown point. In W. Grossmann, G. Pflug, I. Vincze, and W. Wertz (Eds.). (pp. 283-297). *Mathematical statistics and applications*, Vol. B. Budapest: Akadémiai Kiadó.

Rousseeuw, P.J. & Croux, C. (1993). Alternatives to the median absolute deviation. *Journal of the American Statistical Association*, 88, 1273-1283.

Rousseeuw, P.J. & Leroy, A.M. (1987). *Robust regression and outlier detection.* New York: Wiley & Sons.

Rousseeuw, P.J. & Van Driessen, K. (1999). A fast algorithm for the minimum covariance determinant estimator. *Technometrics*, 41, 212-223.

Rousseeuw, P.J. & Van Driessen, K. (2000). A fast algorithm for highly robust regression in data mining. In J.G. Bethlehem and P.G.M. van der Heijden (Eds.). (pp 421-426). *COMPSTAT: Proceedings in computational statistics.* Heidelberg: Physica-Verlag.

Rousseeuw, P.J. & Van Zomeren, B.C. (1990). Unmasking multivariate outliers and leverage points. *Journal of the American Statistical Association*, 85, 633-651.

Simpson, D., Ruppert, D., & Carroll, R. (1992). On one-step GM estimates and stability of inferences in linear regression. *Journal of the American Statistical Association*, 87, 439-450.

Steinhauser, U. (1998). Influential observations in exploratory factor analysis: Identification and limitation of influence. In H. Strecker, R. Féron, M.J. Beckmann, and R. Wiegert (Eds.), *Applied statistics and econometrics*. Vol. 44. Vandenhoeck und Ruprecht, Göttingen.

Tanaka, Y. & Odaka, Y. (1989a). Influential observations in principal factor analysis. *Psychometrika*, 54, 475–485.

Tanaka, Y. & Odaka, Y. (1989b). Sensitivity analysis in maximum likelihood factor analysis. *Communications in Statistics–Theory and Methods*, 18, 4067-4084.

Ten Berge, J.M.F. & Kiers, H.A.L. (1991). A numerical approach to the exact and the approximate minimum rank of a covariance matrix. *Psychometrika*, 56, 309-315.

Terbeck, W. & Davies, P. (1998). Interactions and outliers in the two-way analysis of variance. *The Annals of Statistics*, 26, 1279-1305.

Ukkelberg, Å, & Borgen, O. (1993). Outlier detection by robust alternating regression. *Analytica Chimica Acta*, 277, 489-494.

Wold, H. (1966). Nonlinear estimation by iterative least square procedures. In F.N. David, (Ed.). (pp. 411-444). *Research papers in statistics: Festschrift for Jerzy Neyman*. New York: Wiley.

Woodruff, D.L. & Rocke, D.M. (1994). Location and shape in high dimension using compound estimators. *Journal of the American Statistical Association*, 89, 888–896.

10   Using Predicted Latent Scores in General Latent Structure Models

Marcel Croon

Tilburg University, The Netherlands

10.1   General Latent Structure Models

Statistical models with latent variables are very popular in the social and behavioral sciences. Much of this popularity is explained by the contribution these models make to the solution of the severe measurement problems that have plagued these sciences. Although theoretical developments have lead to some improvement in the quality of the measurement procedures used in these sciences, a lot is still "measurement by fiat" (Torgerson, 1958). Researchers in these fields collect responses to sets or scales of indicator variables that are *assumed* to be related to the underlying theoretical construct, and use a subject's scale score as a proxy for the unobservable latent score. Although most measurement scales are used after meticulous item selection and test construction procedures with the aim to enhance the reliability and the validity of the scale, the problem still remains that the link between the unobserved latent score and the observed scale score is an indirect one.

It is in the context of making explicit the relationship between indicators and their underlying theoretical constructs that the popularity of statistical models with latent variables has to be understood. Models with latent variables are generally known as latent structure models, and have a long and well-documented history (Lazarsfeld & Henry, 1968; Haberman, 1979; Bollen, 1989; Hagenaars, 1990; von Eye & Clogg, 1994; Heinen, 1996; Bartholomew & Knott, 1999). Although latent structure models may take on different forms, they all have one important characteristic in common: they all start from specific assumptions about the relationship between the latent variables and their observed manifest indicators. Which assumptions are made in this respect mainly depends on the measurement level of the latent and manifest variables. Bartholomew and Knott (1999) give a rather complete overview of the different types of latent structure models.

Apart from a specification of how the manifest indicators are related to the latent variables, most latent structure models also contain a structural part in which hypothetical causal relationships between exogenous variables and latent variables, and among the latent variables themselves are explicitly formulated. The form of this structural part also depends on the measurement level of the variables involved. For continuous variables, one resorts most often to a linear regression model to describe the effects of "independent" variables on "dependent" ones; for discrete variables, one often uses a log-linear or a logit model to describe these effects.

From a more formal point of view, any latent structure model leads to a decomposition of the joint distribution of observed and latent variables. One simple example, which will also be used as an illustration later in this chapter, should make this point clear. In this example, no specification whether the variables involved are continuous or discrete is made, and the same notation is used to denote discrete probability distributions or continuous density functions. Random variables are denoted by capital letters, and the values they assume by the corresponding lower-case letter. In order to simplify the notation, probability distributions and density functions are only written as functions of random values.

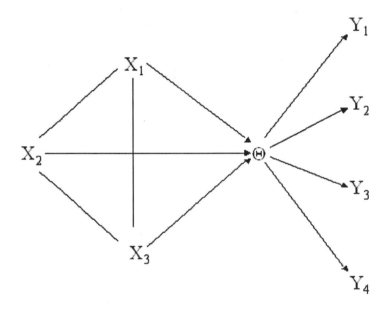

Fig. 10.1. Simple latent structure model

Figure 10.1 is a graphical representation of a simple latent structure model in which three exogenous variables X_1, X_2 and X_3 are assumed to have effects on a latent variable Θ, which is measured by four indicator variables Y_1, Y_2, Y_3, and Y_4. The figure represents relations among observed and unobserved variables as a chain graph (Lauritzen, 1996). The exogenous variables X_1, X_2 and X_3 are connected by undirected line segments, indicating possible association or dependence among them. Since they are exogenous, their mutual association is considered as being caused by factors from outside the model. Furthermore, from each exogenous variable an arrow is pointing to the latent variable Θ. This is the graphical representation of the assumption that the conditional distribution of Θ depends on X_1, X_2 and X_3. Finally, from Θ itself four arrows emanate into the direction of the indicator variables, and since no other arrows arrive in the indicator variables, this implies that the distribution of each of the Y_j is assumed to depend only on Θ.

Defining $X = (X_1, X_2, X_3)$ and $Y = (Y_1, Y_2, Y_3, Y_4)$, one may write the joint distribution of (X, Θ, Y) as $p(x, \theta, y) = p(x; \alpha)p(\theta|x; \beta)p(y|\theta; \gamma)$. Note that all functions in the last expression are denoted by the same symbol p. This simplified notation is used because it will usually be clear from the context which probability distributions or density functions are involved in the discussion. Furthermore, each distribution function is characterized by its own set of unknown parameters, which are denoted by α, β, and γ. Reference to these parameters is also omitted in the algebraic expressions when it is clear from the context which parameters are involved.

10.2   Estimation Methods in Latent Structure Models

Although several different methods have been proposed to obtain consistent and efficient parameter estimates, it is the maximum likelihood (ML) estimation method that has been used most often in this respect. ML estimation maximizes the value of the joint probability or density function for the observed variables with respect to the unknown parameters. For latent structure models, the joint distribution for the observed variables is obtained by integrating the latent variables out of the joint distribution function for observed and latent variables. For the example in Figure 10.1, ML maximizes $p(x, y) = \int p(x, \theta, y)d\theta$, in which the integration is over the scalar variable θ. ML estimation usually requires complex optimization procedures but application of the EM-algorithm (Dempster, Laird & Rubin, 1977) often alleviates the computational burden of the optimization process (for technical details consult McLachlan & Krishnan, 1997).

ML estimation has several attractive statistical properties (Lehmann & Casella, 1998). ML is a full-information method since it is based on the complete likelihood for all observed variables and estimates all parameters simultaneously. Based on an explicit statistical model of the data, ML estimation yields estimates of the standard errors of the parameter estimates. If the estimation is based on the correct model, ML yields asymptotically consistent and efficient estimates of the parameters under quite general conditions. Moreover, for some (but not all) latent structure models, ML produces a single test statistics for assessing the global model fit.

However, full information methods like ML also have their drawbacks. Because they are based on explicit statistical assumptions which in practice are never strictly satisfied, the optimal properties of ML estimates, their standard errors and the global test statistics are not always guaranteed. Every statistical model is at best a good approximation of reality, but any discrepancy between reality and model can adversely affect the properties of the estimates, their standard errors and the test statistics. Moreover, by fitting the complete model in a single simultaneous estimation procedure, misspecification in some part of the model may have negative consequences for the accuracy of the parameter estimates in other parts of the model, even if the latter have been specified correctly. So, for example, misspecifying the structural part of the model may distort the estimates of the parameters in the measurement part. Although the model on which the analysis of the data is based should be dictated by theoretical considerations, in practice researchers are often in doubt or ignorant about its fine details. So, if the correct (or best approximating) model is not known in advance, some model search procedure has to be used, and, taking into account the above considerations, it is doubtful whether a full information method is the best alternative to use in this respect. Maybe one should prefer a search strategy which splits up the global model in different autonomous parts, and fits each part separately to different parts of the data. In such a strategy the appropriateness of each part of the model is assessed independently of the others, and if some faults or deficiencies are found in the original formulation of one of the parts, this would have no consequences for the rest of the model.

Even though the EM-algorithm has reduced the computational burden of ML in fitting latent structure models, it still remains impractical if large numbers of observed variables occur in the model. It is, for example, not uncommon in psychological research to use tests or questionnaires consisting of 50 or more items. If the data encompass several tests of this size, their analysis by a full information method becomes practically impossible. Here too the splitting up of the global model in manageable units seems to be obligatory. Quite recently, interest in the development of limited information methods in latent structure estimation has gained momentum, but hitherto all of these efforts have been limited to the case of linear structural equations models.

Extending Hägglund's (1982) work on instrumental variable techniques in factor analysis, Bollen (1996) proposed the use of instrumental variables in the estimation of linear structural equation models with latent variables. This approach requires that for each of the latent variables one of its indicators be selected as a scaling variable. By substituting this scaling variable for the latent construct, the original system of equations is reformulated in such a way that only observed variables are involved. The ensuing system of equations can then be solved by means of two-stage least squares (TSLS). Bollen (1996) also shows how standard errors of the parameter estimates can be obtained using this TSLS estimators and provides diagnostics for evaluating the instrumental variables.

Lance, Cornwell, and Mulaik (1988) proposed a noniterative estimator which makes use of the principles of extension analysis (Horn, 1973; McDonald, 1978). This approach starts with the estimation of the parameters of the measurement model by means of a factor analysis on the complete set of indicator variables. Subsequently, estimates of the covariances of the latent variables with the perfectly measured exogenous variables are obtained, and this variance-covariance matrix is used to estimate the regression coefficients in the structural part of the model.

This chapter discusses an alternative limited information method, which makes use of predicted latent scores to test the causal hypotheses formulated in the structural submodel. In this approach, one starts with the separate estimation of the parameters of the measurement submodels and then proceeds to the estimation or prediction of the subjects' scores on the latent variables. Once these predicted latent scores are available, they are treated as observed scores, and enter the subsequent analyses based on the structural submodel. This approach is quite general and is, at least in principle, applicable to all types of latent structure models. Furthermore, the structural analyses can be performed by standard statistical methods as linear or logistic regression analysis, and do not require specifically developed software. However, it will be shown that a naive use of these predicted latent scores is very problematic since it leads to inconsistent estimates of the parameters of the joint distributions in which latent variables are involved. The theoretical analysis will not only show where the problems originate, but will also suggest how one can correct for distortions in those joint distributions. This chapter also discusses the use of predicted latent scores from a population point of view and ignores the statistical issues that arise when applying the approach to finite samples[1].

10.3   On Using Predicted Latent Scores

The model in Figure 10.1 represents a very simple causal hypothesis that three exogenous variables have an effect on a latent variable Θ. If the variable Θ was observed, this simple model could easily be tested by some standard statistical technique. If all variables involved were continuous, regression analysis could be used to estimate the effects of each X_i on Θ. If all variables were categorical, log-linear analysis or logistic regression could be used. However, Θ is not observed, nor are any of the observed Y's a perfect indicator for it. However, for most latent structure models, it is possible to predict the scores that subjects have on the latent variable Θ once the parameters of the measurement submodel are known. The next section briefly discusses

---

[1] It is important to note that in this chapter the term "latent score predictor" is used instead of "latent score estimator" since the subjects' factor scores are considered as random variables and not as unknown parameters that have to be estimated.

latent score prediction methods for two specific examples of latent structure models: (i) the latent class model, and (ii) the factor analysis model. In both examples the posterior distribution of Θ given Y plays an essential role, and this approach can easily be extended to all latent structure models.

10.3.1   Latent score prediction in the latent class model.

In the latent class model (Lazarsfeld & Henry, 1968; Hagenaars, 1990; Clogg, 1995) the population of subjects is partitioned in a number of homogeneous subpopulations, the latent classes, and in each subpopulation a simple independence model (with class specific parameters) is assumed to hold for the manifest variables. Interpreted as a measurement model, the latent class model identifies the subpopulations or classes as the values of an underlying latent variable of nominal level. The assumption that the manifest variables are independent when the latent variable is held constant is called local independence. Under local independence, one may derive for the joint distribution of the m indicator variables that

$$p(y_1, ..., y_m) = \sum_\theta [\pi(\theta) \prod_{j=1}^m p(Y_j = y_j|\theta)]. \tag{10.1}$$

In this expression θ represents the label of the discrete latent class number, and $\pi(\theta)$ is the population proportion of subjects belonging to class θ. Hence, the values of $\pi(\theta)$ represent the population distribution of the latent variable Θ. The item response probability $p(Y_j = y_j|\theta)$ is the class specific probability of response y_j to the j-th indicator variable in class θ.

In the latent class model, a subject's latent score is simply the qualitative label of the latent class to which he or she belongs. Predicting a subject's latent score then amounts to assigning him or her to a particular class. In such an assignment rule, the conditional probability distribution of Θ given the responses Y on the indicator variables plays an essential role. Elementary probability theory implies that

$$p(\theta|y) = \frac{p(y|\theta)\pi(\theta)}{p(y)}. \tag{10.2}$$

Once the parameters of the measurement model are known, the expression for the posterior distribution of Θ given Y can be used to assign the subjects to a latent class. In most applications, the *modal assignment rule* is used i.e., each subject is assigned to that latent class θ for which p(θ|y) is maximal. An alternative is the *random assignment rule*, which assigns a subject to a class by drawing randomly a single element from the appropriate posterior distribution. When using the modal assignment rule, all subjects with the same response pattern on Y receive the same predicted latent score; under the random assignment rule, however these subjects could receive different latent scores, but the distribution of predicted latent scores assigned to subjects with the same response pattern should reflect the posterior distribution p(θ|y) appropriate for that response pattern.

10.3.2   Latent score prediction in the factor analytic model

Factor score prediction has a very long tradition in the factor analytic literature, but has not been entirely without controversy because of the issue of factor score indeterminacy. The essence of this issue is that, if the factor scores on the common and unique factors are considered as unknown subject parameters in the factor analytic model, one obtains a system of linear equations with more unknowns than equations. Consequently, this system has no unique solution for the factor scores. Recently, Maraun (1996) reactivated the discussion on the implications of this indeterminacy problem for the validity of the factor analytic model. In this chapter, Bartholomew's (1996) point of view is followed. Bartholomew (1996), following Maraun's paper, pointed out that a subject's factor scores should not be considered as unknown constants but as unobserved realizations of a random variable. From this perspective, it makes more sense to talk about "factor score prediction" than "factor score estimation".

The discussion of factor score prediction begins with the normal factor model (as described by Bartholomew & Knott, 1999). Assume that the conditional distribution of the observed variables Y given the common factors Θ is normal with expected value $A\theta$ and diagonal variance/covariance matrix Δ^2:

$$p(y|\theta) = N(A\theta, \Delta^2). \tag{10.3}$$

If Θ is assumed to be normal with mean equal to 0 and variance/covariance matrix Φ, it follows that the posterior distribution of Θ given Y is normal:

$$p(\theta|y) = N(\Phi A' \Sigma_{yy}^{-1} y, \Phi - \Phi A' \Sigma_{yy}^{-1} A\Phi) \tag{10.4}$$

with

$$\Sigma_{yy} = A\Phi A' + \Delta^2. \tag{10.5}$$

This result on the conditional distribution of the latent variables, given the scores on the indicator variables, can be used to assign latent factor scores to the subjects. If the *modal assignment rule* is used, every subject with response pattern y on the indicator variables will obtain the same predicted latent score $\Phi A' \Sigma^{-1} y$, which is the well-known regression predictor for the factor scores. If the *random assignment rule* is used, subjects with the same response pattern y on the indicator variables will not necessarily obtain the same predicted factor scores, but their scores will be sampled independently from the appropriate normal conditional distribution as given above.

The regression factor score predictor is only one of many different predictors which have been proposed in the factor analytic literature (e.g., the least squares predictor, the Bartlett predictor, and the Anderson-Rubin predictor).

All these predictors, as well as the regression predictor, are linear combinations $W'y$ of the observed indicator variables. The least square predictor, is defined by

$$W = A(A'A)^{-1},\tag{10.6}$$

the Bartlett predictor is defined by

$$W = \Delta^{-2}A(A'\Delta^{-2}A)^{-1},\tag{10.7}$$

and the Anderson-Rubin predictor by

$$W = \Delta^{-2}A(A'\Delta^{-2}\Sigma_{yy}\Delta^{-2}A)^{-1/2}.\tag{10.8}$$

These linear factor predictors are almost always used in a deterministic way so that subjects with the same response pattern on the observed indicator variables receive the same factor score value. In factor analysis random assignment rules are almost never used (for a comparison of different factor score predictors and discussion of their properties, see McDonald & Burr, 1967; Saris, de Pijper & Mulder, 1978; Krijnen, Wansbeek & ten Berge, 1996; ten Berge, Krijnen, Wansbeek & Shapiro, 1999).

10.3.3   Against the naive use of predicted latent scores

Returning to the example in Figure 10.1, suppose one wanted to investigate the relation between the exogenous variables $X = (X_1, X_2, X_3)$ and the latent variable Θ. This requires that one study the properties of the conditional distribution $p(\theta|x)$. Since Θ is unobserved, $p(\theta|x)$ itself is not observable, but one could substitute the predicted latent scores for the latent scores on Θ. Now define the latent variable T (with scores t) as the random variable that represents the predicted latent scores. The question then is whether the observable conditional distribution $p(t|x)$ is a good estimate of the unobservable distribution $p(\theta|x)$. In general, the answer is no: $p(t|x)$ is a biased estimate of $p(\theta|x)$, and conclusions about the relation between X and Θ based on $p(t|x)$ may considerably deviate from the true state of affairs. This point will be illustrated by extending the causal model from Figure 10.1 to incorporate a variable T in it. Since T only depends on the observed indicator variables Y, as shown in Figure 10.2, one may draw an arrow from each indicator variable to T, indicating that the distribution of T depends on Y. Since no other arrows are directed at T, the distribution of T only depends on Y. The form of the conditional distribution of T given Y depends on the kind of assignment rule that has been used to define T. If a random assignment rule has been used, $p(t|y)$ is actually identical to the posterior distribution $p(\theta|y)$. If, on the other hand, a modal assignment rule was used, the conditional distribution $p(t|y)$ is a degenerate distribution with all its probability mass or density concentrated in a single point.

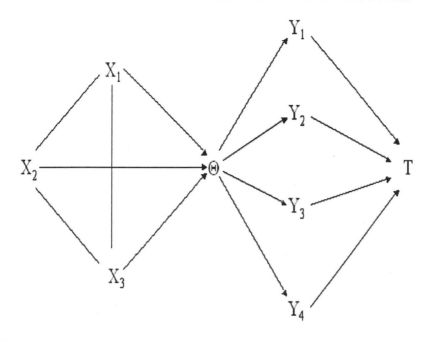

Fig. 10.2. Extended latent structure model

Consider the assumption that all random variables are absolutely continuous [2]. This implies that a random assignment rule has been used, since for a
modal assignment rule the distribution $p(t|y)$ is degenerate, and, hence, cer-
tainly not absolutely continuous. Later the case of modal assignment rules are
discussed to show that basically the same conclusions apply here. Moreover,
it is also shown that for discrete variables replacing integration by summation
yields identical results[3].

---

[2] A random variable X is absolutely continuous if there exists a continuous density
function $f(x)$ such that $Prob(a \leq X \leq b) = \int_a^b f(x)dx$ with respect to Lebesgue
measure. There also exist continuous random variables that are not absolutely
continuous but these continuous singular random variables are rather weird objects that play no significant role in application oriented statistics (Lehmann &
Casella, 1998, p. 15).

[3] Riemann-Stieltjes integration theory could have been used to treat the discrete
and the continuous cases in a more unified way, but it would have made our
discussion much more formal and technical.

For the extended model of Figure 10.2, the joint distribution of the absolutely continuous random variables X, Θ, Y, and T can be written as a product of density functions:

$$p(x, \theta, y, t) = p(x)p(\theta|x)p(y|\theta)p(t|y). \qquad (10.9)$$

Integrating Y and Θ over their respective supports gives

$$p(x, t) = \int \int p(x)p(\theta|x)p(y|\theta)p(t|y)dyd\theta$$

$$= p(x) \int p(\theta|x)(\int p(y|\theta)p(t|y)dy)d\theta.$$

Note that integration over Y is multidimensional whereas integration over Θ is unidimensional. Define

$$K(t|\theta) = \int p(y|\theta)p(t|y)dy \qquad (10.10)$$

then

$$p(t|x) = \int K(t|\theta)p(\theta|x)d\theta. \qquad (10.11)$$

Hence, the densities p(t|x) and p(θ|x) are related by an integral equation with kernel K(t|θ), which is actually the conditional density of T given Θ. It can also be seen that in general p(t|x) and p(θ|x) will be different, unless the kernel K(t|θ) is the identity kernel.

Some adaptation of the argument is needed when a modal assignment rule is used. In this case the conditional distribution p(t|y) is degenerate since for each response pattern y there is only one score t(y) for which p(t|y) is different from zero. In this situation it is better to consider the cumulative conditional distribution of T given X:

$$P(t|x) = Prob(T \leq t|x). \qquad (10.12)$$

Under quite general conditions it may be derived for absolutely continuous random variables that

$$P(t|x) = \int Prob(T \leq t|\theta)p(\theta|x)d\theta \qquad (10.13)$$

with

$$Prob(T \leq t|\theta) = \int_R p(y|\theta)dy.$$

The last integral is over a region R the space of the indicator variables Y:

$$R = \{y : t(y) \leq t\} \qquad (10.14)$$

(i.e., R is the set of response patterns for which the assigned score is smaller than or equal to t). This shows that for modal assignment rules the cumulative conditional distributions of T given X and of Θ given X will not be identical.

Conclusions based on an examination of the relationship between X and T will not necessarily hold for the relationship between X and Θ.

In many applications of latent structure models, there is no interest in estimating the complete conditional distributions $p(\theta|x)$ or $P(\theta|x)$, but only in estimating the regression of Θ on X. Here too, substituting T for Θ and regressing T on X will lead to incorrect results. Restricting ourselves to absolutely continuous random variables and assuming that all expected values exist, the regression of T on X is defined by

$$E(t|x) = \int tp(t|x)dt \quad = \int E(t|\theta)p(\theta|x)d\theta. \tag{10.15}$$

This result shows that the functional forms of the regression of Θ on X and of T on X are not necessarily identical. So, even if the regression of Θ on X is linear, the regression of T on X need not be linear itself: Much depends on the regression of T on Θ. If the regression of T on Θ itself is linear, then for some constants a and b one has

$$E(t|\theta) = a + b\theta \tag{10.16}$$

and,

$$E(t|x) = a + bE(\theta|x). \tag{10.17}$$

In this case both regression equations belong to the same functional class. If the regression of the true latent scores Θ on X is linear, so is regression of the predicted scores T on X. Unless $b = 1$, the regression coefficients in the equations for T and Θ will differ however, and regressing T on X will not yield the values of the coefficients in the regression equation for the true latent scores. When the constants a and b are known, the coefficients in the equation for T on X can be corrected to obtain consistent estimates of the corresponding coefficients in the equation for Θ on X.

The general results obtained so far demonstrate that substituting predicted latent scores for the true latent scores and treating the predicted scores as observed variables in the analyses for the structural part of the model will generally lead to inconsistent estimation of the joint distribution of the latent variable with observed exogenous variables. Treating the predicted latent scores as observed variables not only leads to biased estimates of the joint distribution of a latent variable with exogeneous manifest variables, it also yields an inconsistent estimate of the joint distribution of two or more latent variables, as the following example will show. Figure 10.3 represents a model with two correlated or associated univariate latent variables Θ_1 and Θ_2, which are each measured by specific sets Y_1 and Y_2 of indicator variables.

The number of indicator variables in each set has been left unspecified, and in Figure 10.3 Y_1 and Y_2 should be interpreted as vectors of indicator variables. Assuming that all variables involved are absolutely continuous, the joint density of Θ_1, Θ_2, Y_1 and Y_2 can be factored as

$$p(\theta_1, \theta_2, y_1, y_2) = p(\theta_1, \theta_2)p(y_1|\theta_1)p(y_2|\theta_2). \tag{10.18}$$

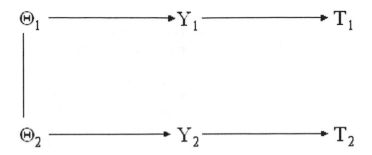

Fig. 10.3. Model with two correlated latent variables

Once the parameters of the measurement parts of the model have been estimated, the predicted latent score can be obtained. In Figure 10.3 they are represented by the random variables T_1 and T_2, with variable T_1 only depending on Y_1, T_2 only on Y_2. Now defining

$$K_1(t_1|\theta_1) = \int p(t_1|y_1)p(y_1|\theta_1)dy_1,$$

and

$$K_2(t_2|\theta_2) = \int p(t_2|y_2)p(y_2|\theta_2)dy_2,$$

it then follows that

$$p(t_1, t_2) = \int \int K_1(t_1|\theta_1)K_2(t_2|\theta_2)p(\theta_1, \theta_2)d\theta_1 d\theta_2. \qquad (10.19)$$

This shows that also the joint distributions of estimated and true latent scores are related by an integral equation that distorts the relations between the latent variables in such a way that estimates of the strength of the association between them is not consistently estimated on the basis of the predicted latent scores, but in this example two different kernels are involved. It is easy to see that, in general, as many kernels are needed as there are different latent variables in the model.

10.3.4   Solving the integral equation

The two previous examples show that the naive strategy of substituting predicted latent scores for the true scores results in inconsistent estimation of the relevant parameters (either those that describe the association or correlation among the latent variables, or the latent and observed exogenous variables). The relationship between a joint distribution in which predicted latent scores T are involved and the joint distribution for the corresponding latent variable Θ can be described by means of an integral equation. In order to answer the question whether this integral equation can be solved, which functions are known and which are unknown must be first considered.

For the model in Figure 10.1, the conditional distribution p(t|x) and the kernel K(t|θ) can be determined once the parameters of the measurement model have been estimated and the predicted latent scores have been obtained for all subjects. The only unknown function in the integral equation is p(θ|x). An integral equation of this type with the unknown function occurring under the integral sign is known as a Fredholm integral equation of the first kind (Cochran, 1972). This type of equation cannot in general be easily solved, but in some particular cases solutions can be derived. This chapter offers a discussion of this equation and its solution for the latent class and factor analysis models.

The solution for the latent class model.   In a latent class model, Θ and T are discrete variables whose values are the labels of the latent classes. If M latent classes are needed to represent the data, both T and Θ take on values in the set {1,2,...,M}. When all the indicator variables Y are discrete, only a finite number of different response patterns can occur in the data. It is also assumed that the exogenous variables X are discrete so that all joint distributions can be represented as contingency tables. Although all variables involved in the latent class model are discrete, the general results, derived earlier under the assumption that all random variables are absolutely continuous, remain valid provided integration is replaced by summation over all possible values of the random variable. So, for the model in Figure 10.2 the kernel becomes

$$K(t|\theta) = \sum_y p(t|y)p(y|\theta) \qquad (10.20)$$

with the summation running over all possible response patterns of Y.

The probabilities p(y|θ) can be calculated once the parameters of the latent class model have been estimated, and the probabilities p(t|y) are known, once the assignment rule has been decided. If a random assignment rule is used, p(t|y) is identical to the posterior distribution p(θ|y). If a modal assignment rule is used, there exists a value $t_0(y)$ for each response pattern y so that p($t_0(y)$|y) $\geq$ p(t|y) for all t. Then the modal assignment rule defines

$$p(t_0(y)|y) = 1$$

$$p(t|y) = 0 \quad for \quad t \neq t_0(y).$$

Now, define the subset W(t) of response patterns y as those response patterns for which the subject is assigned to latent class t:

$$W(t) = \{y : t_0(y) = t\}$$

then

$$K(t|\theta) = \sum\nolimits_{y \in W(t)} p(y|\theta).$$ (10.21)

Hence, irrespective of whether the modal or the random assignment procedure is used, the kernel can be determined on the basis of the data and the parameter estimates in the latent class model.

The integral equation that relates p(t|x) to p(θ|x) can now be written as

$$p(t|x) = \sum\nolimits_{\theta} K(t|\theta)p(\theta|x).$$ (10.22)

This fundamental relationship describes how p(θ|x) is related to p(t|x). Bolck, Croon and Hagenaars (2001) show that the strength of the relationship between X and Θ, as measured by the odds ratios, is underestimated in the conditional distribution of T given X. They prove that, provided all odds ratios are finite, none of the odds ratio in the joint distribution of T and X can become larger than the largest odds ratio in the distribution of Θ and X. When the parameters of the measurement model have been estimated and latent scores have been assigned to the subjects, the conditional distribution p(t|x) is easily determined by counting how many subjects with response pattern x on X have been assigned a score t on T.

Given the conditional distribution p(t|x) and an estimate of the kernel K(t|θ), can a better estimate of the true conditional distribution p(θ|x) be derived? If K is the number of different response patterns on X, the fundamental relation between p(t|x) and p(θ|x) can be written in matrix notation after defining the following matrices: the K × M matrix A with elements a_{xt} = p(t|x), the M × M matrix Q with elements $q_{\theta t}$ = K(t|θ), and the K × M matrix B with elements $b_{x\theta}$ = p(θ|x):

$$A = BQ.$$ (10.23)

If matrix Q is invertible, this equation can be solved for B:

$$B = AQ^{-1},$$

and B is nothing else than an estimate of p(θ|x) in matrix notation. So, the last expression defines a correction procedure which can be applied to an estimate of p(t|x) and which supposes that the kernel K(t|θ) is known. In practical applications, the kernel will not be known in advance, but can be estimated once the parameters of the measurement model are estimated and the score assignment procedures has been applied. This correction procedure only works if the matrix Q that represents the kernel is invertible.

When is Q not invertible? Q is certainly not invertible when there is a value t of T for which under the modal assignment rule the set W(t) is empty. In this case the corresponding row in Q is zero. If the random assignment rule is used, Q will in general be of full rank, but may be ill-conditioned when the indicators have low validity for the latent variable (for a more thorough discussion of the conditions on Q which guarantee the validity of correction procedure described above, see Bolck, Croon, & Hagenaars, 2001).

For a latent class model shown in Figure 10.3, the integral equation that relates $p(t_1,t_2)$ and $p(\theta_1, \theta_2)$ can also be rewritten in matrix notation. Define the matrices A, B, Q_1 and Q_2 as follows:

$$a_{t_1 t_2} = p(t_1, t_2)$$
$$b_{\theta_1 \theta_2} = p(\theta_1, \theta_2)$$
$$q_1(\theta_1 t_1) = K_1(t_1|\theta_1)$$
$$q_2(\theta_2 t_2) = K_2(t_2|\theta_2).$$

Then, the integral equation can be written as

$$A = Q'_1 B Q_2. \tag{10.24}$$

If both matrices Q_1 and Q_2 are invertible, a consistent estimate of the joint distribution of Θ_1 and Θ_2 can be obtained as

$$B = Q'_1{}^{-1} A Q_2^{-1}.$$

10.4   A Large Sample Numerical Illustration

This section illustrates the theoretical results with an example based on a model in which a single exogenous variable X is assumed to have an effect on a latent variable Θ, which is measured by ten equivalent dichotomous items. Both X and Θ are trichotomous. Table 10.1 contains the marginal distribution of X and the conditional distribution of Θ given X in the population.

Table 10.1. Population distributions of X and Θ given X

	$p(x)$	$p(\Theta=1|x)$	$p(\Theta=2|x)$	$p(\Theta=3|x)$
X=1	0.30	0.6	0.3	0.1
X=2	0.45	0.3038	0.3797	0.3165
X=3	0.25	0.0940	0.2938	0.6121

The conditional distribution of Θ given X was chosen so that all four local odds ratios were equal to 2.5, a value which represents a moderately strong association between X and Θ. The response probabilities for the ten equivalent dichotomous indicators were as follows:

$$p(Y = 2|\Theta = 1) = 0.25$$
$$p(Y = 2|\Theta = 2) = 0.50$$
$$p(Y = 2|\Theta = 3) = 0.75.$$

This implies that the two local odds in the table $\Theta \times Y$ are equal to 3, which represents a rather strong association between the latent variable and each of its indicators. A large sample of N=10000 subjects was drawn from the population defined in this way. Such a large sample was drawn in order to show that the discrepancies between the true conditional distribution of Θ given X and the uncorrected sample distribution of T given X is not due to sampling error, but represents a systematic bias that does not disappear as N goes to infinity.

The first stage in the analysis of the simulated data consisted of an unconstrained latent class analysis on the indicator variables using LEM (Vermunt, 1997). Only the results of the solution with the correct number of latent classes are reported here. As expected for such a large sample, all estimates of the response probabilities were very close to their true value and also the latent class distribution was accurately estimated. Once the response probabilities and the latent class distribution were estimated, the subjects were assigned to a latent class on the basis of their posterior distribution $p(t|y)$. Only the results obtained with the modal assignment rule that assigns each subject to the latent class with the highest posterior probability are discussed. By simply counting how many subjects with a particular score on X were assigned to each of the three latent classes, the conditional distribution of T given X can be determined. The estimate of the conditional distribution of T given X is presented in Table 10.2.

Table 10.2. Estimated conditional distribution of T given X

	$p(T=1|x)$	$p(T=2|x)$	$p(T=3|x)$
X=1	0.5601	0.3131	0.1268
X=2	0.3211	0.3584	0.3204
X=3	0.1356	0.3449	0.5195

Compared to the true conditional distribution of Θ given X, the distribution of T given X is somewhat more flattened. This is also evident from the values of the four local odds ratios for this distribution which are equal to 1.9967, 2.2071, 2.2798 and 1.6849, respectively. All four are smaller than the true value of 2.5, and so is their geometric mean of 2.0282. This observation agrees with the expectation that the strength of association between Θ and X is underestimated by the association between T and X.

The sample estimate of the conditional distribution of T given Θ, the kernel of the integral equation, is given in Table 10.3. The probabilities in this table can be interpreted as the probabilities that a subject in a particular class will be correctly or incorrectly classified. It can be seen that the probability of misclassification is rather high in all three classes, and especially so in the second class, and this misclassification is the responsible factor for

Table 10.3. Conditional distribution of T given Θ

	T=1	T=2	T=3
$\Theta = 1$	0.8009	0.1954	0.0037
$\Theta = 2$	0.1815	0.6236	0.1948
$\Theta = 3$	0.0063	0.2111	0.7826

the underestimation of the strength of association of Θ with any extraneous variable when using predicted scores T.

Table 10.4. Corrected conditional distribution of T given X

	T=1	T=2	T=3
X=1	0.6370	0.2715	0.0914
X=2	0.3148	0.3691	0.3161
X=3	0.0904	0.3279	0.5818

Since the 3 × 3 matrix that represents the kernel is not singular, it can be inverted and a corrected estimate of the distribution of Θ given X can be obtained. This corrected distribution is given in Table 10.4. It is clear that the corrected conditional distribution of T given X is closer to the true distribution of Θ given X than the uncorrected one. That the association between Θ and X is now more accurately estimated than beforehand is shown by the values of the four local odds ratios in the corrected table. They are now equal to 2.7501, 2.5439, 3.0952, and 2.0717, respectively. These values are much closer to the true value of 2.5, and so is their geometric mean of 2.5880.

This corrected estimate of $p(\theta|x)$ can also be compared with its estimate obtained under a full information (FI) estimation procedure in which the complete data, including the exogenous variable X as well as all indicator variables Y, were analyzed under the correct model. Table 10.5 contains the FI estimate of the conditional distribution of Θ given X. The four local odds ratios for this tabel are 2.9369, 2.5108, 2.9168, and 2.1168, respectively, and their geometric mean is 2.5976. It can be seen that the full information and the corrected limited information estimates of $p(\theta|x)$ are very similar, and that the strength of the association between Θ and X as measured by the local odds ratios is estimated equally accurate in both tables.

10.4.1 The solution for the factor analysis model

The properties of predicted latent scores in factor analysis are discussed from two different points of view. For the first, the general approach is applied

Table 10.5. Full information estimate of conditional distribution of Θ given X

	$\Theta = 1$	$\Theta = 2$	$\Theta = 3$
X = 1	.6509	.2670	.0821
X = 2	.3190	.3843	.2967
X = 3	.0975	.3426	.5599

to the specific case of the factor model by making some additional distributional assumptions about the latent variables in the model. The results obtained pertain to a random version of a particular well-known factor score predictor, the regression predictor. For the second, the general case of linear factor predictors without making explicit distributional assumptions about the variables is considered (only the assumption of linearity and homoscedasticity of the regression of Θ on X, and of T on Θ is made). The results obtained under these conditions are valid for a broad class of deterministic linear factor predictors and are very relevant for practical applications.

The normal factor model.   Following Bartholomew and Knott's (1999) discussion of the normal factor model, the model represented in Figure 1 is rephrased as a statistical factor model in the following way. For the distribution of Θ given X, it is assumed that

$$p(\theta|x) = N(Bx, \sigma^2_{\theta.x}) \tag{10.25}$$

in which N(.,.) is the general multivariate normal density with its dimensionality clear from the context. Since Θ is a scalar random variable, B is a row vector of regression coefficients.

The distribution of Y given Θ is given by

$$p(y|\theta) = N(A\theta, \Delta^2) \tag{10.26}$$

in which A is a column vector of common factor loadings of the indicator variables, and Δ^2 is the diagonal variance/covariance matrix for the unique factors. It then follows that

$$p(\theta) = N(0, B\Sigma_{xx}B' + \sigma^2_{\theta.x}) \tag{10.27}$$

Without loss of generality one may assume that Θ is scaled to unit variance. Then the conditional distribution of Θ given Y is

$$p(\theta|y) = N(A'\Sigma_{yy}^{-1}y, \omega) \tag{10.28}$$

with

$$\omega = A'\Sigma_{yy}^{-1}A.$$

For the one-factor model it is known that

$$\Sigma_{yy}^{-1} = \Delta^{-2} - \Delta^{-2}A(1 + A'\Delta^{-2}A)^{-1}A'\Delta^{-2},$$

from which it follows that

$$\omega = A'\Sigma_{yy}^{-1}A = \frac{A'\Delta^{-2}A}{1 + A'\Delta^{-2}A}.$$

Consequently, one has $0 \le \omega \le 1$. If factor scores are assigned by sampling a value from each subject's appropriate posterior distribution $p(\theta|y)$, a random version of the well-known regression factor score predictor is actually used. The conditional distribution of T given Θ, the kernel $K(t|\theta)$, for this random assignment rule is then given by

$$K(t|\theta) = N(\omega\theta, 1 - \omega^2). \tag{10.29}$$

For the distribution of T given X, then

$$p(t|x) = N[\omega.Bx, 1 - \omega^2(1 - \sigma_{\theta.x}^2)]. \tag{10.30}$$

A comparison of the conditional distributions $p(\theta|y)$ and $p(t|y)$ shows that the regression of T on X will not yield consistent estimates of the regression vector B for the true latent variable Θ. However, since Θ is a scalar variable in this example, the relation between corresponding coefficients from both equations is a very simple one: coefficients in the equation for T are equal to the corresponding coefficients in the equation for Θ multiplied by ω. Since $\omega \le 1$, it also follows that each coefficient in the equation for Θ is underestimated by the corresponding coefficient in the equation for T. However, the same result suggests a way to correct the coefficients in the equation for T: dividing each coefficient in the equation of T by an estimate of ω should yield a consistent estimate of the corresponding coefficient in the equation for Θ.

For the error variances from both equations, the following relation can be derived:

$$\frac{1 - \sigma_{t.x}^2}{1 - \sigma_{\theta.x}^2} = \omega^2.$$

Since $\omega \le 1$, the true value of the standard regression error is overestimated by regressing T on X. However, here too the relation between the estimated error variance and its true value can be used to derive a consistent estimate of $\sigma_{\theta.x}$:

$$\sigma_{\theta.x}^2 = 1 - \frac{1}{\omega^2}(1 - \sigma_{t.x}^2).$$

Deterministic linear factor predictors. As previously indicated, factor scores are almost always estimated in a deterministic may by computing a linear combination $w'y$ of the scores on the indicator variables. This section discusses the properties of this general class of factor score predictors. It turns out that no specific statistical assumptions about the distribution of the unobserved and observed variables are needed to derive the essential (and practically applicable) properties of these deterministic factor score predictors. It suffices to assume that the regressions involved in the model are linear and homoscedastic. The results described in this section extend those obtained already by Tucker (1971).

Suppose that, as in the model represented by Figure 10.1, there is a structural model in which observed exogenous variables X have an effect on a single latent variable Θ, which is measured by a set of m indicator variables Y. As for the measurement part of this model, Y is assumed to satisfy a factor analytic model with one common factor:

$$y = A\theta + e \tag{10.31}$$

with A an m-dimensional column vector of factor loadings. The mutually uncorrelated unique factors E are also uncorrelated with the common factor Θ and with all exogenous variables. Then

$$\Sigma_{yy} = AA'\sigma_\theta^2 + \Delta^2 \tag{10.32}$$

in which σ_θ^2 is the variance of the common factor and Δ^2 the diagonal variance/covariance matrix of the unique factors. Without loss of generality it could be assumed that the common factor is scaled to unit variance, but here the results for a more general form are reported. A second very important result is:

$$\Sigma_{xy} = \Sigma_{x\theta}A' \tag{10.33}$$

in which $\Sigma_{x\theta}$ is a column vector containing the covariances of the exogenous variables with Θ.

Suppose now that a linear factor score predictor T with scores $t = w'y$ is defined. Since Θ and T are univariate, one may prove:

$$\sigma_t^2 = (w'A)^2\sigma_\theta^2 + w'\Delta^2w \tag{10.34}$$

and

$$\Sigma_{xt} = \Sigma_{x\theta}A'w. \tag{10.35}$$

The first result implies that in general the variance of T will be not be equal to the variance of Θ. The second expression shows that in general the covariance of an exogenous variable X with T will be different from its covariance with Θ. However, both expressions provide means to obtain a consistent estimate of the variance of Θ, and of its covariances with each of the exogenous variables. Noting that since $w'A$ is scalar, one may write

$$est\ \sigma_\theta^2 = \frac{\sigma_t^2 - w'\Delta^2 w}{(w'A)^2},$$

and

$$est\ \Sigma_{x\theta} = \frac{1}{w'A}\Sigma_{xt}.$$

The results can be simplified if a linear factor score predictor is used for which $w'A = 1$ holds. Predictors that satisfy this requirement are called conditionally unbiased predictors since they imply that $E(t|\theta) = \theta$. For conditionally unbiased the previously obtained results imply that $E(t|x) = E(\theta|x)$, meaning that the regressions of T on X and of Θ on X are identical. If the regression of Θ on X is linear, then so is the regression of T on X and the true regression coefficients in the equation for Θ are consistently estimated by the corresponding coefficients in the equation for T.

The least squares predictor and the Bartlett predictor are two examples of a conditionally unbiased predictor. The regression predictor and the Anderson-Rubin predictors, on the other hand, are not conditionally unbiased predictors. For conditionally unbiased predictors the following hold:

$$\sigma_t^2 = \sigma_\theta^2 + w'\Delta^2 w,$$

and

$$\Sigma_{xt} = \Sigma_{x\theta}$$

Since $w'\Delta^2 w \geq 0$, a conditionally unbiased factor score predictor always overestimates the variance of the latent variable, but the covariance of an exogenous variable with the latent factor is consistently estimated by its covariance with a conditionally unbiased predictor of the factor scores.

Now consider the regression of Θ on X. The assumptions of linearity and homoscedasticity are usually stated as

$$E(\theta|x) = \beta_{\theta|x}\ x,$$

and

$$var(\theta|x) = \sigma_{\theta|x}^2.$$

Standard linear regression theory implies that

$$\beta_{\theta|x} = \Sigma_{xx}^{-1}\Sigma_{x\theta}. \tag{10.36}$$

If T (instead of Θ) is regressed on X, the regression coefficients are given by

$$b_{t|x} = \Sigma_{xx}^{-1} \Sigma_{xt} = \Sigma_{xx}^{-1} \Sigma_{x\theta} A' w = \beta_{\theta|x} A' w. \tag{10.37}$$

Hence $b_{t|x}$ is not a consistent predictor of $\beta_{\theta|x}$ unless a conditionally unbiased factor score predictor is used, but for factor score predictors, which are not conditionally unbiased, the latter expression can be used in a correction procedure to derive a consistent estimate of $\beta_{\theta|x}$.

Another important observation is that none of the linear predictors yields a consistent estimate of the standard error. The variance of the prediction errors in the regression of Θ on X is given by

$$\sigma_{\theta|x}^2 = \sigma_\theta^2 - \Sigma_{\theta x} \Sigma_{xx}^{-1} \Sigma_{x\theta}. \tag{10.38}$$

For the regression of the linear factor score predictor T on X, one has

$$\sigma_{t|x}^2 = \sigma_t^2 - \Sigma_{tx} \Sigma_{xx}^{-1} \Sigma_{xt}. \tag{10.39}$$

For a conditionally unbiased predictor T, it follows that

$$\sigma_{t|x}^2 = \sigma_{\theta|x}^2 + w' \Delta^2 w, \tag{10.40}$$

which proves that the regression of T on X overestimates the variance of the prediction errors. However, the last expression can also be used to derive a consistent estimate of this variance:

$$est\ \sigma_{\theta|x}^2 = \sigma_{t|x}^2 - w' \Delta^2 w.$$

The preceding discussion has highlighted the attractive properties of conditionally unbiased factor predictors. If the preceding discussion might suggest that conditionally unbiased factor score predictors always guarantee consistent estimates of the coefficients in a regression equations in which a latent variable is involved, the next example proves the contrary. Figure 4 represents a model in which a first latent variable Θ_1, measured by a first set of indicator variables Y_1, has an effect on a second latent variable Θ_2, measured by second set of indicators Y_2.

This model is similar to the model shown in Figure 10.3, but explicitly assumes that there is a causal ordering among the latent variables. For each latent variable a factor analytic model with one common factor is supposed to hold:

$$y_1 = A_1\theta_1 + e_1,$$
$$y_2 = A_2\theta_2 + e_2.$$

All unique factors are mutually uncorrelated, and each unique factor is uncorrelated with both common factors and with all exogenous variables X. It

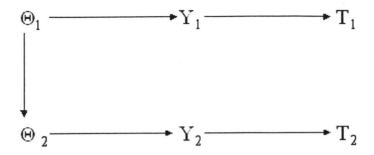

Fig. 10.4. Model with causal ordering among latent variables

is left open how many indicator variables each set Y_1 or Y_2 contains, but it is assumed that each factor analysis model is identified when considered in isolation. In general, this would require at least three indicators per latent variable. Now define linear factor predictors as

$$T_1 = w_{1'}Y_1, \qquad T_2 = w_{2'}Y_2, \tag{10.41}$$

with w_1 and w_2 based on two separate factor analyses of Y_1 and Y_2, respectively. Then

$$\sigma_{t_1 t_2} = w'_1 \Sigma_{y_1 y_2} w_2 = w'_1 A_1 \sigma_{\theta_1 \theta_2} A'_2 w_2. \tag{10.42}$$

Hence, the covariance between the factor score estimates of two different latent variables is not a consistent estimate of the covariance between the factors, unless conditionally unbiased factor score predictors are used.

For the regression of Θ_2 on Θ_1 one has

$$\beta_{\theta_2 . \theta_1} = \frac{\sigma_{\theta_1 \theta_2}}{\sigma_{\theta_1}^2}. \tag{10.43}$$

For the regression of T_2 on T_1 a conditionally unbiased predictor leads to:

$$b_{t_2 . t_1} = \frac{\sigma_{t_1 t_2}}{\sigma_{t_1}^2} = \frac{\sigma_{\theta_1 \theta_2}}{\sigma_{\theta_1}^2 + w'_1 \Delta_1^2 w_1} = \beta_{\theta_2 . \theta_1} \times \frac{\sigma_{\theta_1}^2}{\sigma_{\theta_1}^2 + w'_1 \Delta_1^2 w_1}. \tag{10.44}$$

Even for conditionally unbiased factor predictors, regressing T_2 on T_1 leads to an underestimation of the "true" regression coefficient. Once again, the last result can be used as a correction procedure to obtain a consistent estimate of the regression coefficients.

The previous analyses show where the problems originate. When using a conditionally unbiased factor score predictor, the covariances between two latent variables as well as the covariance of a latent variable with an exogenous variable are consistently estimated by the corresponding statistics computed on the predicted scores. However, the variances of the latent factors are overestimated when T is substituted for Θ. In order to obtain consistent estimates of the coefficients of regression equations with latent variables, one must simply correct the variances of the estimated factor scores by subtracting the quantity $w'\Delta^2 w$ from the observed variance of T.

For factor score predictors that are not conditionally unbiased, the correction procedures are more involved since now all variances and covariances have to be corrected. The following relations must be used to obtain corrected estimates:

$$\sigma_{\theta_1 \theta_2} = \frac{\sigma_{t_1 t_2}}{(w'_1 A_1)(w'_2 A_2)} \tag{10.45}$$

$$\sigma_\theta^2 = \frac{\sigma_t^2 - w'\Delta^2 w}{(w'A)^2} \tag{10.46}$$

$$\sigma_{x\theta} = \frac{\sigma_{xt}}{w'A}. \tag{10.47}$$

Note that the Anderson-Rubin predictor, which produces uncorrelated factor scores with unit variances, directly yields the correct estimate of the variance of the factor scores, but still requires a correction procedure for the covariances of the latent variables with the exogenous variables.

10.5   A Numerical Illustration

This section illustrates the previous theoretical arguments with a numerical illustration. A very large random sample of N = 10000 elements was drawn from a population based on the model shown in Figure 10.5 . Assume that two exogenous variables X_1 and X_2 have effects on two latent variables Θ_1 and Θ_2. Moreover, Θ_1 is assumed to have an effect on Θ_2. Both latent variables are each measured by ten different indicators. All variables are standardized and the correlation between X_1 and X_2 is set equal to 0.40. The population regression equations for Θ_1 and Θ_2 are:

$$\Theta_1 = 0.45X_1 + 0.35X_2 + E_1,$$
$$(\sigma_{E_1} = 0.7409),$$
$$\Theta_2 = 0.40X_1 + 0.20X_2 + 0.30\Theta_1 + E_2,$$
$$(\sigma_{E_2} = 0.6639).$$

For each latent variable the indicator variables has different loadings varying between 0.40 and 0.76 in steps equal to 0.04.

The data analysis consisted of several stages. First, each set of ten indicators was separately factor analysed according to the one-factor model
using ML estimation. The results of the factor analyses are not given in any
detail here, but merely note that all estimates of the factor loadings were
close to their true values. Next, for both latent variables factor scores were
determined using four different prediction methods: the regression (R), the
Bartlett (B), the least-squares (LS), and the Anderson-Rubin (AR) method.
For each of the four sets of factor scores, the scores for Θ_1 were regressed on
X_1 and X_2, the scores for Θ_2 on X_1, X_2, and Θ_1. These different regression
analysis were first performed on the uncorrected variance and covariances,
and subsequently on the corrected values.

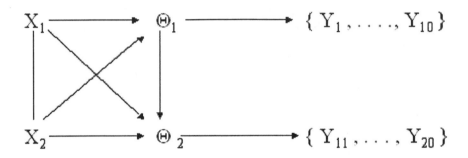

Fig. 10.5. Example model

Table 10.6. Uncorrected regression coefficients and standard errors for Θ_1

	True	R	B	LS	AR
X_1	0.45	0.3940	0.4594	0.4585	0.4255
X_2	0.35	0.2918	0.3402	0.3414	0.3151
σ_E	0.7409	0.7255	0.8457	0.8504	0.7833

Table 10.7. Corrected regression coefficients and standard errors for Θ_1

	True	R	B	LS	AR
X_1	0.45	0.4594	0.4594	0.4585	0.4594
X_2	0.35	0.3402	0.3402	0.3414	0.3402
σ_E	0.7409	0.7412	0.7412	0.7411	0.7412

Table 10.6 contains the estimates of the regression coefficients and the standard error in the uncorrected analyses for Θ_1. Table 10.7 contains the corrected results for Θ_1. Several observations can be made with respect to these results. Since no latent variable occurs as an independent variable in the regression equation for Θ_1, using the factor scores provided by the Bartlett or the least-squares method yields consistent estimates of the regression coefficients; the use of the regression or the Anderson-Rubin method, on the other hand, leads to biased estimates of these parameters. The estimate of the standard error is biased for all four methods. These observations agree with the theoretical developments.

After correction, all four methods yield estimates of the regression coefficients and the standard error which are close to their true values. The most remarkable result in this respect is that upon correction the regression, Bartlett, and Anderson-Rubin method all lead to exactly the same parameter values. This result has not been discussed before and is explained more thoroughly in Croon, Bolck, and Hagenaars (2001). Here it suffices to state that it is a consequence of the fact that for the one-factor model the factor score coefficients for the three methods are proportional to each other. Moreover, the extent to which this phenomenon occurs also depends on which estimation method is used in the factor analyses. If the traditional Principal Axis Factoring method had been used, only the corrected values for the Bartlett and the Anderson-Rubin method would have been identical. The uncorrected results for Θ_2 are given in Table 10.8. The corrected results are given in Table 10.9.

Table 10.8. Uncorrected regression coefficients and standard errors for Θ_2

	True	R	B	LS	AR
X_1	0.40	0.3640	0.4285	0.4306	0.3949
X_2	0.20	0.1835	0.2160	0.2173	0.1991
Θ_1	0.30	0.2337	0.2351	0.2309	0.2344
σ_E	0.6639	0.6737	0.7932	0.7984	0.7311

Table 10.9. Corrected regression coefficients and standard errors for Θ_2

	True	R	B	LS	AR
X_1	0.40	0.3956	0.3956	0.3965	0.3956
X_2	0.20	0.1902	0.1902	0.1907	0.1902
Θ_1	0.30	0.3087	0.3087	0.3069	0.3087
σ_E	0.6639	0.6628	0.6628	0.6630	0.6628

Since the regression equation for Θ_2 contains Θ_1 as an independent variable, all four uncorrected methods lead to biased estimates of the regression parameters, but using the corrected variances and covariances removes the systematic bias. Note here also that after correction the regression, Bartlett, and Anderson-Rubin method give exactly identical results. The corrected results for the least-squares method slightly differ from this common solution but is still very close to it.

10.6   Discussion

The results reported in this chapter are generalizations about the effects of measurement error in observed variables on the estimates of the parameters of their joint distribution (Fuller, 1987). Let X and Y be two error-prone measurements of unobserved variables ξ and η. Then it is well known that the regression coefficient of X in the regression of Y on X is an underestimate of the true regression coefficient of ξ in the regression of η on ξ. If, however, the reliability coefficients of X and Y are known, the estimate of the regression coefficient of X can be corrected in order to obtain a better estimate of the true regression coefficients. The results presented in this chapter generalize these basic observations to more general models.

This chapter showed how the naive use of predicted latent scores in subsequent statistical analyses based on a latent structure model will generally lead to erroneous conclusions. It was proved that, under quite general conditions, the joint distributions of exogenous and latent variables Θ and the joint distribution of the latent variables themselves are inconsistently estimated if predicted latent scores T are substituted for the latent variables. Moreover, assuming that each latent variable is measured by its own set of indicator variables, it was shown that the unobservable distribution $p(X, \Theta)$ and the observed distribution $p(X, T)$ are related by an integral equation with as kernel the conditional distribution $p(T|\Theta)$. It was also shown that, in general, the regression of T on X is not of the same functional type as the regression of Θ on X. If, however, the regression of T on Θ itself is linear, then the regressions of T on X and of Θ on X are of the same form.

Although these results seem to argue strongly against any limited information method that uses predicted latent scores, it was also shown for some very important specific examples of latent structures models the integral equation can be solved for $p(X,\Theta)$ in terms of the observable distributions $p(X,T)$ and $p(T|\Theta)$. In a similar way a consistent estimate of the joint distribution of the latent variables Θ can be derived from the joint distribution of the predicted scores T. For the latent class models this correction procedure requires matrix inversions; for the factor analysis model, corrected values for the variances and covariances for the latent variables are required.

This chapter discussed the use of predicted latent scores from a population point of view. The statistical issues that arise when these correction procedures are used with small samples were deliberately not considered. Similarly, no discussion was offered concerning how efficient these procedures are in terms of standard errors nor how the standard errors can be estimated. Some partial results are known for the factor model (Croon, Bolck, & Hagenaars, 2001) but more research is clearly needed.

References

Bartholomew, D. J. (1996). Comment on: Metaphor taken as math:Indeterminacy in the factor model.*Multivariate Behavioral Research*, 31, 551-554.

Bartholomew, D. J., & Knott, M. (1999). *Latent variable models and factor analysis*. London: Arnold.

Bolck, A., Croon, M. A., & Hagenaars, J. A. (2001). On the use of latent scores in causal models for categorical variables. Submitted.

Bollen, K. A. (1989). *Structural equations with latent variables*. New York: Wiley.

Bollen, K. A. (1996). An alternative two stage least squares (2SLS) estimator for latent variable equations. *Psychometrika*, 61, 109-121.

Clogg, C. C. (1995). Latent class models: Recent developments and prospects for the future. In G. Arminger, & C.C. Clogg (Eds.). (pp. 311-359). *Handbook of statistical modelling for the social and behavioral sciences*. New York: Plenum.

Cochran, J. A. (1972). *The analysis of linear integral equations*. New York: McGraw Hill.

Croon, M. A., Bolck, A., & Hagenaars, J. A. (2001). On the use of factor scores in linear structural equations models. In preparation.

Dempster, A. P., Laird, N. M., & Rubin, D. B. (1977). Maximum likelihood from incomplete data via the EM algorithm, *Journal of the Royal Statistical Society (Series B)*, 39, 1-38.

Fuller, W. A. (1987). *Measurement error models*. New York: Wiley.

Haberman. S. J. (1979). *The analysis of qualitative data. Volume 2: New developments*. New York: Academic Press.

Hagenaars, J. A. (1990). *Categorical longitudinal data: Log-linear panel, trend, and cohort analysis*. Newbury Park, CA: Sage.

Hägglund, G. (1982). Factor analysis by instrumental variables. *Psychometrika*, 47, 209-222.

Heinen, A. (1996). *Latent class and discrete latent trait models: Similarities and differences*. Thousand Oaks, CA: Sage.

Horn, J. L. (1973). On extension analysis and its relation to correlations between variables and factor scores. *Multivariate Behavioral Research*, 8, 477-489.

Krijnen, W. P., Wansbeek, T. , & ten Berge, J. M. F. (1996). Best linear predictors for factor scores. *Communications in Statistics: Theory and Methods*, 25, 3013-3025.

Lance, C. E., Cornwell, J. M., & Mulaik, S. (1988). Limited information parameter estimates for latent or mixed manifest and latent variable models. *Multivariate Behavioral Research*, 23, 155-167.

Lazarsfeld, P. F. , & Henry, N. W. (1968). *Latent structure analysis*. New York: Houghton-Mifflin.

Lauritzen, S. L. (1996). *Graphical models*. London: Clarendon.

Lehmann, E. L., & Casella, G. (1998). *Theory of point estimation*. New York: Springer.

McDonald, R. P. (1978). Some checking procedures for extension analysis. *Multivariate Behavioral Research*, 13, 319-325.

McDonald, R. P., & Burr, E. J. (1967). A comparison of four methods of constructing factor scores. *Psychometrika*, 32, 381-401.

McLachlan, G. J. and Krishnan, J. (1997). *The EM algorithm and extensions*. New York: Wiley.

Maraun, M. D. (1996). Metaphor taken as math: Indeterminacy in the factor analysis model. *Multivariate Behavioral Research*, 31, 517-538.

Torgerson, W. S. (1958). *Theory and methods of scaling*. New York: Wiley.

Saris, W. E., de Pijper M. , & Mulder, J. (1978). Optimal procedures for estimation of factor scores. *Sociological Methods and Research*,7, 85-106.

Ten Berge, J. M. F. , Krijnen, W. P., Wansbeek, T., & Shapiro, A. (1999). Some new results on correlation-preserving factor scores prediction methods. *Linear Algebra and its Applications*, 289, 311-318.

Tucker, L. R. (1971). Relations of factor score estimates to their use. *Psychometrika*, 36, 427-436.

Vermunt, J. K. (1997). *Loglinear models for event history analysis*. Thousand Oaks, CA: Sage.

Von Eye, A., & Clogg, C. C. (1994). *Latent variables analysis: Applications for developmental research*. Thousand Oaks, CA: Sage.

11 Multilevel Factor Analysis Modelling Using Markov Chain Monte Carlo Estimation*

Harvey Goldstein and William Browne

Institute of Education, University of London

11.1 Introduction

Traditional applications of structural equation models have, until recently, ignored complex population data structures. Thus, for example, factor analyses of achievement or ability test scores among students have not adjusted for differences between schools or neighbourhoods. In the case where a substantial part of inter-individual differences can be accounted for by such groupings, inferences which ignore this may be seriously misleading. In the extreme case, if *all* the variation was due to a combination of school and neighbourhood effects, a failure to adjust to these would lead to the detection of apparent individual level factors which would in fact be non-existent.

Recognising this problem, McDonald and Goldstein (1989) presented a multilevel factor analysis and structural equation model where individuals are recognised as belonging to groups and explicit random effects for group effects are incorporated. They presented an algorithm for maximum likelihood estimation (this model was further explored by Longford & Muthèn, 1992; McDonald, 1993). Raudenbush (1995) applied the EM algorithm to estimation for a 2-level structural equation model. Rowe and Hill (in press) show how existing multilevel software can be used to provide approximations to maximum likelihood estimates in general multilevel structural equation models.

In this chapter these models are extended in two ways. First, it is shown how a Markov Chain Monte Carlo (MCMC) algorithm can be used to fit such models. An important feature of the MCMC approach is that it decomposes the computational algorithm into separate steps, for each of which there is a relatively straightforward estimation procedure. This provides a chain sampled from the full posterior distribution of the parameters from which one can calculate uncertainty intervals based upon quantiles etc. The second advantage is that the decomposition into separate steps allows one to easily extend the procedure to the estimation of very general models, and an illustration of how this can be done is provided.

* **Acknowledgements** This work was partly carried out with the support of a research grant from the Economic and Social Research Council for the development of multilevel models in the Social Sciences. We are very grateful to Ian Langford, Ken Rowe and Ian Plewis for helpful comments.

A fairly general 2-level factor model can be written as follows, using standard factor and multilevel model notation:

$$
\begin{aligned}
&Y = \Lambda_2 v_2 + u + \Lambda_1 v_1 + e \\
&Y = \{y_{rij}\}, \\
&r = 1, ..., R \quad i = 1, ..., n_j \quad j = 1, ..., J
\end{aligned}
\tag{11.1}
$$

where the "uniquenesses" u (level 2), e (level 1) are mutually independent with covariance matrix Ψ_1, and there are R response measures. The Λ_1, Λ_2 are the loading matrices for the level 1 and level 2 factors and the v_1, v_2 are the independent factor vectors at level 1 and level 2. Note that there can be different numbers of factors at each level. By adopting the convention of regarding the measurements themselves as constituting the lowest level of the hierarchy, Equation 11.1 is regarded as a 3-level model. Extensions to more levels are straightforward.

Model (11.1) allows for a factor structure to exist at each level and one needs to further specify the factor structure, for example that the factors are orthogonal or patterned with corresponding identifiability constraints. Further restrictions can be imposed. For example, one may wish to model the uniquenesses in terms of further explanatory variables. In addition, one can add measured covariates to the model and extend to the general case of a linear structural or path model (see discussion).

11.2   A Simple Illustration

To illustrate these procedures consider a simple single level model which can be written as

$$
\begin{aligned}
&y_{ri} = \lambda_r \nu_i + e_{ri}, \quad r = 1, ..., R, \quad i = 1, ..., N \\
&\nu_i \sim N(0, 1), \quad e_{ri} \sim N(0, \sigma_{er}^2)
\end{aligned}
\tag{11.2}
$$

This can be viewed as a 2-level model with a single level 2 random effect (ν_i) with variance constrained to 1 and R level 1 units for each level 2 unit, each with their own (unique) variance.

If the values of the "loadings" λ_r were known, then Model (11.2) could be fitted directly as a 2-level model, with the loading vector as the explanatory variable for the level 2 random effects with variance constrained to be equal to 1; if there are any measured covariates in the model their coefficients could also be estimated at the same time. Conversely, if the values of the random effects ν_i were known, one could estimate the loadings; this would now be a single level model with each response variate having its own variance. These considerations suggest that an EM algorithm can be used in the estimation where the random effects are regarded as missing data (see Rubin & Thayer, 1982). In this chapter a stochastic MCMC algorithm is proposed.

MCMC works by simulating new values for each unknown parameter in turn from their respective conditional posterior distributions assuming the other parameters are known. This can be shown to be equivalent (upon convergence) to sampling from the joint posterior distribution. MCMC procedures generally incorporate prior information about parameter values and so are fully Bayesian procedures. In this chapter diffuse prior information is assumed, although algorithms are given that assume generic prior distributions (see below). Inference is based upon the chain values: conventionally the means of the parameter chains are used as point estimates but medians and modes (which will often be close to maximum likelihood estimates) are also available, as illustrated. This procedure has several advantages. In principle it allows one to provide estimates for complex multilevel factor analysis models with exact inferences available. Since the model is an extension of a general multilevel model one can theoretically extend other existing multilevel models in a similar way. Thus, for example, one could consider cross-classified structures and discrete responses as well as conditioning on measured covariates. Another example is the model proposed by Blozis and Cudeck (1999) where second level residuals in a repeated measures model are assumed to have a factor structure. The following section describes the procedure by applying it to the simple example of Equation (11.2) and then applies it to more complex examples.

11.3 A Simple Implementation of the Algorithm

The computations have all been carried out in a development version of the program *MLwiN* (Rasbash et al., 2000). The essentials of the procedure are described next.

Assume that the factor loadings have normal prior distributions, $p(\lambda_r) \sim N(\lambda_r^*, \sigma_{\lambda r}^2)$ and that the level 1 variance parameters have independent inverse Gamma priors, $p(\sigma_{er}^2) \sim \Gamma^{-1}(a_{er}^*, b_{er}^*)$. The * superscript is used to denote the appropriate parameters of the prior distributions.

11.3.1 This model can be updated using a very simple three step Gibbs sampling algorithm

Step 1: Update λ_r $(r=1,\ldots,R)$ from the following distribution: $p(\lambda_r) \sim N(\hat{\lambda}_r, D_r)$ where

$$D_r = \left(\frac{\sum_i \nu_i^2}{\sigma_{er}^2} + \frac{1}{\sigma_{\lambda r}^2}\right)^{-1} \quad and \quad \hat{\lambda}_r = D_r\left(\frac{\sum_i \nu_i y_{ri}}{\sigma_{er}^2} + \frac{\lambda_r^*}{\sigma_{\lambda r}^2}\right)$$

Step 2: Update ν_i $(i=1,\ldots,N)$ from the following distribution: $p(\nu_i) \sim N(\hat{\nu}_i, D_i)$ where

$$D_i = \left(\frac{\sum_r \lambda_r^2}{\sigma_{er}^2} + 1\right)^{-1} \quad and \quad \hat{\nu}_i = D_i\left(\frac{\sum_r \lambda_r^2 y_{ri}}{\sigma_{er}^2}\right)$$

Step 3: Update σ_{er}^2 from the following distribution: $p(\sigma_{er}^2) \sim \Gamma^{-1}(\hat{a}_{er}, \hat{b}_{er})$ where $\hat{a}_{er} = N/2 + a_{er}^*$ and $\hat{b}_{er} = \frac{1}{2}\sum_i e_{ri}^2 + b_{er}^*$.

To study the performance of the procedure, a small data set using the following model and parameters was simulated:

$$
\lambda = \begin{pmatrix} 1 \\ 2 \\ 3 \\ 4 \end{pmatrix}, \quad \Psi_1 = \begin{pmatrix} 0.2 & & & \\ & 0.3 & & \\ & & 0.4 & \\ & & & 0.5 \end{pmatrix}, \quad N = 20, \quad R = 4 \tag{11.3}
$$

$$
y_{ri} = \lambda_r v_i + e_{ri}, \tag{11.4}
$$

The lower triangle of the correlation matrix of the responses is

$$
\begin{bmatrix} 1 & & & \\ 0.93 & 1 & & \\ 0.92 & 0.97 & 1 & \\ 0.89 & 0.97 & 0.99 & 1 \end{bmatrix}
$$

All the variables have positively skewed distributions, and the chain loading estimates also have highly significant positive skewness and kurtosis. The initial starting value for each loading was 2 and for each level 1 variance (uniqueness) was 0.2. Good starting values will speed up the convergence of the MCMC chains.

Table 11.1 shows the maximum likelihood estimates produced by the AMOS factor analysis package (Arbuckle, 1997) together with the MCMC results. The factor analysis program carries out a prior standardisation so that the response variates have zero means. In terms of the MCMC algorithm, this is equivalent to adding covariates as an "intercept" term to Equation 4, one for each response variable; these could be estimated by adding an extra step to the above algorithm. Prior centring of the observed responses can be carried out to improve convergence.

The loading estimates are summarised by taking both the mean and medians of the chain. The mode can also be computed, but in this data set for the variances it is very poorly estimated and is given only for the loadings. In fact, the likelihood surface with respect to the variances is very flat. The MCMC chains can be summarised using a Normal kernel density smoothing method (Silverman 1986).

The estimates and standard errors from the MCMC chain are larger than the maximum likelihood estimates. The standard errors for the latter will generally be underestimates, especially for such a small data set since they use the estimated (plug in) parameter values. The distributions for the variances in particular are skew so that median rather than mean estimates seem preferable. Since sampling is from the likelihood, the maximum likelihood estimate will be located at the joint parameter mode. Although this has not been computed, as can be seen from the loading estimates the univariate modes are closer to the maximum likelihood estimates than the means or

Table 11.1. Maximum likelihood estimates for simulated data set together with MCMC estimates using chain length 50,000 burn in 20.

Parameter	ML estimate (s.e.)	MCMC mean estimates (s.d.)	MCMC median estimates	MCMC modal estimates
λ_1	0.92 (0.17)	1.03 (0.22)	1.00	0.98
λ_2	2.41 (0.41)	2.71 (0.52)	2.65	2.59
λ_3	3.86 (0.57)	3.91 (0.72)	3.82	3.71
λ_4	4.30 (0.71)	4.82 (0.90)	4.71	4.58
σ_{e1}^2	0.15 (0.05)	0.17 (0.07)	0.16	
σ_{e2}^2	0.25 (0.09)	0.31 (0.14)	0.28	
σ_{e3}^2	0.09 (0.10)	0.10 (0.17)	0.06	
σ_{e4}^2	0.43 (0.20)	0.55 (0.31)	0.50	

medians. Table 11.2 shows good agreement between the variable means and the fitted intercept terms.

Table 11.2. Variable means and fitted intercepts

Variable	Mean	Intercept
1	0.54	0.57
2	0.64	0.71
3	1.12	1.21
4	1.28	1.36

The structure described by Equations 11.3 and 11.4 was also fitted with a simulated data set of 200 cases rather than 20. The results are given in Table 11.3 for the maximum likelihood estimates and the means and medians of the MCMC procedure. A closer agreement can be seen in this table. The MCMC estimates are slightly higher (by up to 2%) than the maximum likelihood ones, with the modal estimates being closest. In more complex examples one may need to run the chain longer with a longer burn in and also try more than one chain with different starting values. For example, a conventional single level factor model could be fitted using standard software to obtain approximations to the level 1 loadings and unique variances.

11.4 Other Procedures

Geweke and Zhou (1996) consider the single level factor model with uncorrelated factors. They use Gibbs sampling and consider identifiability constraints. Zhu and Lee (1999) also consider single level structures including non-linear models that involve factor products and powers of factors. They use Gibbs steps for the parameters and a Metropolis Hastings algorithm for simulating from the conditional distribution of the factors. They also provide

Table 11.3. Model (11.3) & (11.4) with 200 simulated individuals. 5000 cycles.

Parameter	ML estimate (s.e.)	MCMC mean estimates (s.d.)	MCMC median estimates	MCMC mode estimates
λ_1	0.95 (0.06)	0.97 (0.06)	0.96	0.96
λ_2	1.86 (0.10)	1.89 (0.10)	1.89	1.88
λ_3	2.92 (0.15)	2.98 (0.16)	2.97	2.97
λ_4	3.86 (0.20)	3.94 (0.20)	3.93	3.92
σ_{e1}^2	0.22 (0.023)	0.23 (0.024)	0.22	0.22
σ_{e2}^2	0.27 (0.033)	0.27 (0.033)	0.27	0.27
σ_{e3}^2	0.38 (0.058)	0.38 (0.060)	0.38	0.38
σ_{e4}^2	0.39 (0.085)	0.39 (0.087)	0.38	0.38

a goodness-of-fit criterion (see discussion). It appears, however, that their algorithm requires individuals to have complete data vectors with no missing responses, whereas the procedure described in this chapter has no such restriction.

Scheines, Hoijtink, and Boomsma, (1999) also use MCMC and take as data the sample covariance matrix, for a single level structure, where covariates are assumed to have been incorporated into the means. They assume a multivariate normal prior with truncation at zero for the variances. Rejection sampling is used to produce the posterior distribution. They discuss the problem of identification, and point out that identification issues may be resolved by specifying an informative prior.

McDonald and Goldstein (1989) show how maximum likelihood estimates can be obtained for a 2-level structural equation model. They derive the covariance structure for such a model and show how an efficient algorithm can be constructed to obtain maximum likelihood estimates for the multivariate normal case. Longford and Muthèn (1992) develop this approach. The latter authors, together with Goldstein (1995, Chapter 11) and Rowe and Hill (1997) also point out that consistent estimators can be obtained from a 2-stage process as follows. A 2-level multivariate response linear model is fitted using an efficient procedure such as maximum likelihood. This can be accomplished, for example as pointed out earlier by defining a 3-level model where the lowest level is that of the response variables (see Goldstein, 1995, Chapter 8 and Model (11.5) below). This analysis will produce estimates for the (residual) covariance matrices at each level and each of these can then be structured according to an underlying latent variable model in the usual way. By considering the two matrices as two "populations" one can also impose constraints on, say, the loadings using an algorithm for simultaneously fitting structural equations across several populations.

Rabe-hesketh, Pickles, and Taylor (2000) consider a general formulation, similar to model 7 below, but allowing general link functions, to specify multilevel structural equation generalised linear models (GLLAMM). They consider maximum likelihood estimation using general maximisation algorithms and a set of macros has been written to implement the model in the program STATA.

In the MCMC formulation presented in this chapter, it is possible to deal with incomplete data vectors and also to use informative prior distributions, as described below. The algorithm can also be extended to the non-linear factor case using a Metropolis Hastings step when sampling the factor values, as in Zhu and Lee (1999).

11.5 General Multilevel Bayesian Factor Models

Extensions to models with further factors, patterned loading matrices and higher levels in the data structure are straightforward. Consider the 2-level factor model

$$y_{rij} = \beta_r + \sum_{f=1}^{F} \lambda_{fr}^{(2)} \nu_{fj}^{(2)} + \sum_{g=1}^{G} \lambda_{gr}^{(1)} \nu_{gij}^{(1)} + u_{rj} + e_{rij}$$

$$u_{rj} \sim N(0, \sigma_{ur}^2), \quad e_{rij} \sim N(0, \sigma_{er}^2),$$

$$\nu_{fj}^{(2)} \sim MVN_F(0, \Omega_2), \quad \nu_{gij}^{(1)} \sim MVN_G(0, \Omega_1)$$

$$r = 1, ..., R, \quad i = 1, ..., n_j, \quad j = 1, ..., J, \quad \sum_{j=1}^{J} n_j = N$$

Here R responses for N individuals are split between J level 2 units. F sets of factors, with $\nu_{fj}^{(2)}$ defined at level 2 and G sets of factors, with $\nu_{gij}^{(1)}$ defined at level 1 are given. For the fixed part of the model, the algorithm is restricted to a single intercept term β_r for each response although it is easy to extend the algorithm to arbitrary fixed terms. The residuals at levels 1 and 2, e_{rij} and u_{rj} are assumed to be independent.

Although this allows a very flexible set of factor models it should be noted that in order for such models to be identifiable suitable constraints must be put on the parameters. See Everitt (1984) for further discussion of identifiability. These will consist of fixing the values of some of the elements of the factor variance matrices, Ω_1 and Ω_2 and/or some of the factor loadings, $\lambda_{fr}^{(2)}$ and $\lambda_{gr}^{(1)}$, or specifying informative priors.

The algorithms presented will give steps for all parameters and so any parameter that is constrained will simply maintain its chosen value and will not be updated. It is initially assumed that the factor variance matrices, Ω_1 and Ω_2 are known (completely constrained) and a discussion is provided about how the algorithm can be extended to encompass partially constrained variance matrices. The parameters in the following steps are those available at the current iteration of the algorithm.

11.6   Prior Distributions

For the algorithm assume the following general priors:

$$p(\beta_r) \sim N(\beta_r^*, \sigma_{br}^2)$$

$$p(\lambda_{fr}^{(2)}) \sim N(\lambda_{fr}^{(2)*}, \sigma_{2fr}^2), p(\lambda_{gr}^{(1)}) \sim N(\lambda_{gr}^{(1)*}, \sigma_{1gr}^2)$$

$$p(\sigma_{ur}^2) \sim \Gamma^{-1}(a_{ur}^*, b_{ur}^*), p(\sigma_{er}^2) \sim \Gamma^{-1}(a_{er}^*, b_{er}^*)$$

With the assumption that the factor variance matrices are known, one can use a Gibbs sampling algorithm which will involve updating parameters in turn by generating new values from the following 8 sets of conditional posterior distributions.

Step 1: Update current value of $\beta_r (r=1,\ldots,R)$ from the following distribution
$$p(\beta_r) \sim N(\hat{\beta}_r, D_{br}) \text{ where}$$

$$D_{br} = \left(\frac{N}{\sigma_{er}^2} + \frac{1}{\sigma_{br}^2} \right)^{-1}$$

and

$$\hat{\beta}_r = D_{br} \left(\frac{\sum_{ij} d_{rij}^\beta}{\sigma_{er}^2} + \frac{\beta_r^*}{\sigma_{br}^2} \right)$$

where

$$d_{rij}^\beta = e_{rij} - \beta_r$$

Step 2: Update $\lambda_{fr}^{(2)}$ $(r=1,\ldots,R, \; f=1,\ldots,F$ where not constrained) from the following distribution: $p(\lambda_{fr}^{(2)}) \sim N(\hat{\lambda}_{fr}^{(2)}, D_{fr}^{(2)})$ where

$$D_{fr}^{(2)} = \left(\frac{\sum_j n_j (\nu_{fj}^{(2)})^2}{\sigma_{er}^2} + \frac{1}{\sigma_{2fr}^2} \right)^{-1}$$

and

$$\hat{\lambda}_{fr}^{(2)} = D_{fr}^{(2)} \left(\frac{\sum_{ij} \nu_{fj}^{(2)} d_{rijf}^{(2)}}{\sigma_{er}^2} + \frac{\lambda_{fr}^{(2)*}}{\sigma_{2fr}^2} \right)$$

where

$$d_{rijf}^{(2)} = e_{rij} - \lambda_{fr}^{(2)} \nu_{fj}^{(2)}$$

Step 3: Update $\lambda_{gr}^{(1)}$ ($r=1,\ldots,R$, $g=1,\ldots,G$ where not constrained) from the following distribution: $p(\lambda_{gr}^{(1)}) \sim N(\hat{\lambda}_{gr}^{(1)}, D_{gr}^{(1)})$ where

$$D_{gr}^{(1)} = \left(\frac{\sum_{ij}(\nu_{gij}^{(1)})^2}{\sigma_{er}^2} + \frac{1}{\sigma_{1gr}^2} \right)^{-1}$$

and

$$\hat{\lambda}_{gr}^{(1)} = D_{gr}^{(1)} \left(\frac{\sum_{ij} \nu_{gij}^{(1)} d_{rijg}^{(1)}}{\sigma_{er}^2} + \frac{\lambda_{gr}^{(1)*}}{\sigma_{1gr}^2} \right)$$

where

$$d_{rijg}^{(1)} = e_{rij} - \lambda_{gr}^{(1)} \nu_{gij}^{(1)}$$

Step 4: Update $\nu_j^{(2)}$ ($j=1,\ldots,J$) from the following distribution: $p(\nu_j^{(2)}) \sim MVN_F(\hat{\nu}_j^{(2)}, D_j^{(2)})$ where

$$D_j^{(2)} = \left(\sum_r \frac{n_j \lambda_r^{(2)} (\lambda_r^{(2)})^T}{\sigma_{er}^2} + \Omega_2^{-1} \right)^{-1}$$

and

$$\hat{\nu}_j^{(2)} = D_j^{(2)} \left(\sum_r \sum_{i=1}^{n_j} \frac{\lambda_r^{(2)} d_{rij}^{(2)}}{\sigma_{er}^2} \right)$$

where

$$d_{rij}^{(2)} = e_{rij} - \sum_{f=1}^{F} \lambda_{fr}^{(2)} \nu_{fj}^{(2)},$$

$$\lambda_r^{(2)} = (\lambda_{1r}^{(2)}, \ldots, \lambda_{Fr}^{(2)})^T,$$

$$\nu_j^{(2)} = (\nu_{1j}^{(2)}, \ldots, \nu_{Fj}^{(2)})^T$$

Step 5: Update $\nu_{ij}^{(1)}$ ($i = 1, \ldots, n_j, j = 1, \ldots, J$) from the following distribution: $p(\nu_{ij}^{(1)}) \sim MVN_G(\hat{\nu}_{ij}^{(1)}, D_{ij}^{(1)})$ where

$$D_{ij}^{(1)} = \left(\sum_r \frac{\lambda_r^{(1)} (\lambda_r^{(1)})^T}{\sigma_{er}^2} + \Omega_1^{-1} \right)^{-1}$$

and

$$\hat{v}_j^{(1)} = D_{ij}^{(1)} \left(\sum_r \frac{\lambda_r^{(1)} d_{rij}^{(1)}}{\sigma_{er}^2} \right)$$

where

$$d_{rij}^{(1)} = e_{rij} - \sum_{g=1}^{G} \lambda_{gr}^{(1)} v_{gj}^{(1)},$$

$$\lambda_r^{(1)} = (\lambda_{1r}^{(1)}, ..., \lambda_{Gr}^{(1)})^T,$$

$$v_{ij}^{(1)} = (v_{1ij}^{(1)}, ..., v_{Gij}^{(1)})^T$$

Step 6: Update $u_{rj}(r=1,...,R,\ j=1,...,J)$ from the following distribution: $p(u_{rj}) \sim N(\hat{u}_{rj}, D_{rj}^{(u)})$

where

$$D_{rj}^{(u)} = \left(\frac{n_j}{\sigma_{er}^2} + \frac{1}{\sigma_{ur}^2} \right)^{-1}$$

and

$$\hat{u}_{rj} = \frac{D_{rj}^{(u)}}{\sigma_{er}^2} \sum_{i=1}^{n_j} d_{rij}^{(u)}$$

where

$$d_{rij}^{(u)} = e_{rij} - u_{rj}$$

Step 7: Update σ_{ur}^2 from the following distribution: $p(\sigma_{ur}^2) \sim \Gamma^{-1}(\hat{a}_{ur}, \hat{b}_{ur})$ where $\hat{a}_{ur} = J/2 + a_{ur}^*$ and $\hat{b}_{ur} = \frac{1}{2} \sum_j u_{rj}^2 + b_{ur}^*$.

Step 8: Update σ_{er}^2 from the following distribution: $p(\sigma_{er}^2) \sim \Gamma^{-1}(\hat{a}_{er}, \hat{b}_{er})$ where $\hat{a}_{er} = N/2 + a_{er}^*$ and $\hat{b}_{er} = \frac{1}{2} \sum_{ij} e_{rij}^2 + b_{er}^*$.

Note that the level 1 residuals, e_{rij} can be calculated by subtraction at every step of the algorithm.

11.7   Unconstrained Factor Variance Matrices

In the general algorithm it was assumed that the factor variances are all constrained. Typically, one would fix the variances to equal 1 and the covariances to equal 0 and have independent factors. This form permits the simplification of steps 4 and 5 of the algorithm to univariate normal updates for each factor separately. One may however wish to consider correlations between the factors. Here one will have to modify the algorithm to allow another special case where the variances are constrained to be 1 but the covariances can be freely estimated. Where the resulting correlations obtained are estimated to be close to 1 or −1 then one may be fitting too many factors at that particular level. As the variances are constrained to equal 1 the covariances between factors equal the correlations between the factors. This means that each covariance is constrained to lie between −1 and 1. Only the factor variance matrix at level 2 is considered here, as the step for the level 1 variance matrix simply involves changing subscripts. The following priors are used:

$$p(\Omega_{2,lm}) \sim Uniform(-1,1) \ \forall \ l \neq m$$

Here $\Omega_{2,lm}$ is the l, m−th element of the level 2 factor variance matrix. These covariance parameters are updated using a Metropolis step and a Normal random walk proposal (see Browne & Rasbash, in preparation) for more details on using Metropolis Hastings methods for constrained variance matrices).

Step 9 : At iteration t generate $\Omega_{2,lm}^* \sim N(\Omega_{2,lm}^{(t-1)}, \sigma_{plm}^2)$ where σ_{plm}^2 is a proposal distribution variance that has to be set for each covariance. Form a proposed new matrix Ω_2^* by replacing the l, m-th element of $\Omega_2^{(t-1)}$ by $\Omega_{2,lm}^*$. If Ω_2^* is positive definite, set $\Omega_{2,lm}^{(t)} = \Omega_{2,lm}^*$ with probability $\min(1, p(\Omega_2^* | \nu_{fj}^{(2)}) / p(\Omega_2^{(t-1)} | \nu_{fj}^{(2)})$, and $\Omega_{2,lm}^{(t)} = \Omega_{2,lm}^{(t-1)}$ otherwise, or if not positive definite.

Here $p(\Omega_2^* | \nu_{fj}^{(2)}) = \prod_j |\Omega_2^*|^{-1/2} \exp((\nu_{fj}^{(2)})^T (\Omega_2^*)^{-1} \nu_{fj}^{(2)})$ and

$$p(\Omega_2^{(t-1)} | \nu_{fj}^{(2)}) = \prod_j |\Omega_2^{(t-1)}|^{-1/2} \exp((\nu_{fj}^{(2)})^T (\Omega_2^{(t-1)})^{-1} \nu_{fj}^{(2)})$$

This procedure is repeated for each covariance that is not constrained.

Missing Data. The example that is discussed in this chapter has the additional difficulty that individuals have different numbers of responses. This is not a problem for the MCMC methods if one is prepared to assume missingness is at random or effectively so by design. This is equivalent to giving the missing data a uniform prior. One then has to simply add an extra Gibbs sampling step to the algorithm to sample the missing values at each iteration. As an illustration, consider an individual who is missing response r. In a factor model the correlation between responses is explained in the factor terms and conditional on these terms the responses for an individual are independent and so the conditional distributions of the missing responses have simple forms.

Step 10: Update y_{rij} $(r=1,\ldots,R,\ i=1,\ldots,n_j,\ j=1,\ldots,J\ \forall\ y_{rij}$ that are missing) from the following distribution, given the current values, $y_{rij} \sim N(\hat{y}_{rij}, \sigma_{er}^2)$ where $\hat{y}_{rij} = \beta_r + \sum_{f=1}^{F} \lambda_{fr}^{(2)} v_{fj}^{(2)} + \sum_{g=1}^{G} \lambda_{gr}^{(1)} v_{gij}^{(1)} + u_{rj}$.

11.8   Example

The example uses a data set discussed by Goldstein (1995, Chapter 4) and consists of a set of responses to a series of 4 test booklets by 2439 pupils in 99 schools. Each student responded to a core booklet containing Earth Science, Biology and Physics items and to a further two booklets randomly chosen from three available. Two of these booklets were in Biology and one in Physics. As a result there are 6 possible scores, one in Earth Science, three in Biology and 2 in Physics, each student having up to five. A full description of the data is given in Goldstein (1995).

A multivariate 2-level model fitted to the data gives the following maximum likelihood estimates for the means and covariance/correlation matrices in Table 11.4. The model can be written as follows

$$y_{ijk} = \sum_{h=1}^{6} \beta_i x_{hjk} + \sum_{h=1}^{6} \gamma_i x_{hjk} z_{jk} + \sum_{h=1}^{6} u_{ijk} x_{hjk} + \sum_{h=1}^{6} v_{ik} x_{hjk}$$

$$\begin{pmatrix} u_1 \\ u_2 \\ u_3 \\ u_4 \\ u_5 \\ u_6 \end{pmatrix} \sim N(0, \Omega_u) \qquad \begin{pmatrix} v_1 \\ v_2 \\ v_3 \\ v_4 \\ v_5 \\ v_6 \end{pmatrix} \sim N(0, \Omega_v) \qquad (11.5)$$

$x_{hjk} = 1$ *if* $h = i$, 0 *otherwise*
$z_{jk} = 1$ *if a girl*, $= 0$ *if a boy*
i indexes response variables,
j indexes students,
k indexes schools

Two 2 level factor models are now fit to these data, as shown in Table 11.5. Improper uniform priors are used for the fixed effects and loadings and $\Gamma^{-1}(\epsilon, \epsilon)$ priors for the variances with $\epsilon = 10^{-3}$. The fixed effects in Table 11.5 are omitted, since they are very close to those in Table 11.4. Model A has two factors at level 1 and a single factor at level 2. For illustration, all the variances are constrained to be 1.0, and covariance (correlation) between the level 1 factors are allowed to be estimated. Inspection of the correlation structure suggests a model where the first factor at level 1 estimates the loadings for Earth Science and Biology, constraining those for Physics to be zero (the physics responses have the highest correlation), and for the second factor at level 1 to allow only the loadings for Physics to be unconstrained. The high correlation of 0.90 between the factors suggests that perhaps a single factor will be an adequate summary. Although the results are not presented in this chapter, a similar structure for two factors at the school level where the correlation is estimated to be 0.97 was also studied, strongly suggesting a single factor at that level.

Table 11.4. Science attainment estimates.

Fixed	Estimate (s.e.)
Earth Science Core	0.838 (0.0076)
Biology Core	0.711 (0.0100)
Biology R3	0.684 (0.0109)
Biology R4	0.591 (0.0167)
Physics Core	0.752 (0.0128)
Physics R2	0.664 (0.0128)
Earth Science Core (girls - boys)	-0.0030 (0.0059)
Biology Core (girls - boys)	-0.0151 (0.0066)
Biology R3 (girls - boys)	0.0040 (0.0125)
Biology R4 (girls - boys)	-0.0492 (0.0137)
Physics Core (girls - boys)	-0.0696 (0.0073)
Physics R2 (girls - boys)	-0.0696 (0.0116)

Level 2 (School)						
	E.Sc. core	Biol. Core	Biol R3	Biol R4	Phys. core	Phys. R2
E.Sc. core	0.0041					
Biol. core	0.68	0.0076				
Biol R3	0.51	0.68	0.0037			
Biol R4	0.46	0.68	0.45	0.0183		
Phys. core	0.57	0.90	0.76	0.63	0.0104	
Phys. R2	0.54	0.78	0.57	0.65	0.78	0.0095
Level 1 (Student)						
	E.Sc. core	Biol. Core	Biol R3	Biol R4	Phys. core	Phys. R2
E.Sc. core	0.0206					
Biol. core	0.27	0.0261				
Biol R3	0.12	0.13	0.0478			
Biol R4	0.14	0.27	0.20	0.0585		
Phys. core	0.26	0.42	0.11	0.27	0.0314	
Phys. R2	0.22	0.33	0.14	0.37	0.41	0.0449

Random: Variances on diagonal; correlations off-diagonal.

For model B the three topics of Earth Science, Biology and Physics were separated in order to separately have non-zero loadings on three corresponding factors at the student level. This time the high inter-correlation is that between the Biology and Physics booklets with only moderate (0.49, 0.55) correlations between Earth Science and Biology and Physics. This suggests that one needs at least two factors to describe the student level data and that the preliminary analysis suggesting just one factor can be improved. Since the analyses are for illustrative purposes no further possibilities were pursued with these data. Note that Model B at level 1 is strictly non-identified, given uniform priors. The constraint of a positive definite factor covariance matrix provides estimates of the factor correlations, and loadings, which are means over the respective feasible regions.

11.9   Discussion

This chapter has shown how factor models can be specified and fitted. The MCMC computations allow point and interval estimation with an advantage over maximum likelihood estimation in that full account is taken of the uncertainty associated with the estimates. In addition, it allows full Bayesian modelling with informative prior distributions which may be especially useful for identification problems. As pointed out in the introduction, the MCMC algorithm is readily extended to handle the general structural equation case, and further work is being carried out along the following lines. For simplicity the single level model case is considered to illustrate the procedure.

One kind of fairly general, single level, structural equation model can be written in the following matrix form (see McDonald, 1985 for some alternative representations)

$$
\begin{aligned}
A_1 v_1 &= A_2 v_2 + W \\
Y_1 &= \Lambda_1 v_1 + U_1 \\
Y_2 &= \Lambda_2 v_2 + U_2
\end{aligned}
\tag{11.6}
$$

Where Y_1, Y_2 are observed multivariate vectors of responses, A_1 is a known transformation matrix, often set to the identity matrix, A_2 is a coefficient matrix which specifies a multivariate linear model between the set of transformed factors, v_1, and v_2, Λ_1, Λ_2 are loadings, U_1, U_2 are uniquenesses, W is a random residual vector and W, U_1, U_2 are mutually independent with zero means. The extension of this model to the multilevel case follows that of the factor model and the discussion is restricted to sketching how the MCMC algorithm can be applied to Equation (11.6). Note, that as before one can add covariates and measured variables multiplying the latent variable terms as shown in Equation (11.6). Note that A_2 can be written as the vector A_2^* by stacking the rows of A_2. For example if

Table 11.5. Science attainment MCMC factor model estimates.

Parameter	A Estimate (s.e.)	B Estimate (s.e.)
Level 1: factor 1 loadings		
E.Sc. core	0.06 (0.004)	0.11 (0.02)
Biol. core	0.11 (0.004)	0*
Biol R3	0.05 (0.008)	0*
Biol R4	0.11 (0.009)	0*
Phys. core	0*	0*
Phys. R2	0*	0*
Level 1: factor 2 loadings		
E.Sc. core	0*	0*
Biol. core	0*	0.10 (0.005)
Biol R3	0*	0.05 (0.008)
Biol R4	0*	0.10 (0.009)
Phys. core	0.12 (0.005)	0*
Phys. R2	0.12 (0.007)	0*
Level 1: factor 3 loadings		
E.Sc. core	-	0*
Biol. core	-	0*
Biol R3	-	0*
Biol R4	-	0*
Phys. core	-	0.12 (0.005)
Phys. R2	-	0.12 (0.007)
Level 2: factor 1 loadings		
E.Sc. core	0.04 (0.007)	0.04 (0.007)
Biol. core	0.09 (0.008)	0.09 (0.008)
Biol R3	0.05 (0.009)	0.05 (0.010)
Biol R4	0.10 (0.016)	0.10 (0.016)
Phys. core	0.10 (0.010)	0.10 (0.010)
Phys. R2	0.09 (0.011)	0.09 (0.011)
Level 1: residual variances		
E.Sc. core	0.017 (0.001)	0.008 (0.004)
Biol. core	0.015 (0.001)	0.015 (0.001)
Biol R3	0.046 (0.002)	0.046 (0.002)
Biol R4	0.048 (0.002)	0.048 (0.002)
Phys. core	0.016 (0.001)	0.016 (0.001)
Phys. R2	0.029 (0.002)	0.030 (0.002)
Level 2: residual variances		
E.Sc. core	0.002 (0.0005)	0.002 (0.0005)
Biol. core	0.0008 (0.0003)	0.0008 (0.0003)
Biol R3	0.002 (0.0008)	0.002 (0.0008)
Biol R4	0.010 (0.002)	0.010 (0.002)
Phys. core	0.002 (0.0005)	0.002 (0.0005)
Phys. R2	0.003 (0.0009)	0.003 (0.0009)
Level 1 correlation factors 1 & 2	0.90 (0.03)	0.55 (0.10)
Level 1 correlation factors 1 & 3	-	0.49 (0.09)
Level 1 correlation factors 2 & 3	-	0.92 (0.04)

* indicates constrained parameter. A chain of length 20,000 with a burn in of 2000 was used. Level 1 is student, level 2 is school.

$$A_2 = \begin{pmatrix} a_0 & a_1 \\ a_2 & a_3 \end{pmatrix}, \quad then \quad A_2^* = \begin{pmatrix} a_0 \\ a_1 \\ a_2 \\ a_3 \end{pmatrix}$$

The distributional form of the model can be written as

$$A_1 v_1 \sim MVN(A_2 v_2, \Sigma_3)$$
$$v_1 \sim MVN(0, \Sigma_{v_1}), v_2 \sim MVN(0, \Sigma_{v_2})$$
$$Y_1 \sim MVN(\Lambda_1 v_1, \Sigma_1), Y_2 \sim MVN(\Lambda_2 v_2, \Sigma_2)$$

with priors

$$A_2^* \sim MVN(\hat{A}_2^*, \Sigma_{A_2^*}), \quad \Lambda_1 \sim MVN(\hat{\Lambda}_1, \Sigma_{\Lambda_1}), \quad \Lambda_2 \sim MVN(\hat{\Lambda}_2, \Sigma_{\Lambda_2})$$

and $\Sigma_1, \Sigma_2, \Sigma_3$ having inverse Wishart priors. The coefficient and loading matrices have conditional normal distributions as do the factor values. The covariance matrices and uniqueness variance matrices involve steps similar to those given in the earlier algorithm. The extension to two levels and more follows the same general procedure as shown earlier.

The model can be generalised further by considering m sets of response variables, $Y_1, Y_2, ...Y_m$ in Equation (11.6) and several, linked, multiple group structural relationships with the k-th relationship having the general form

$$\sum_h V_h^{(k)} A_h^{(k)} = \sum_g V_g^{(k)} A_g^{(k)} + W^{(k)}$$

and the above procedure can be extended for this case. Note that the model for simultaneous factor analysis (or, more generally, structural equation model) in several populations is a special case of this model, with the addition of any required constraints on parameter values across populations.

The model can also be generalised to include fixed effects, responses at level 2 and covariates Z_h for the factors, which may be a subset of the fixed effects covariates X

$$Y^{(1)} = X\beta + \Lambda_2^{(1)} v_2 Z_2^{(1)} + u^{(1)} + \Lambda_1^{(1)} v_1 Z_1 + e^{(1)}$$

$$Y^{(2)} = \Lambda_2^{(2)} v_2 Z_2^{(2)} + u^{(2)}$$

$$Y^{(1)} = \{y_{rij}\}, \quad Y^{(2)} = \{y_{rj}\}$$

$$r = 1, ..., R \quad i = 1, ..., i_j \quad j = 1, ..., J$$

(11.7)

The superscript refers to the level at which the measurement exists, so that, for example, y_{1ij}, y_{2j} refer respectively to the first measurement in the

i-th level 1 unit in the j-th level 2 unit (say students and schools) and the second measurement taken at school level for the j−th school.

Further work is currently being carried out on applying these procedures to non-linear models and specifically to generalised linear models. For simplicity consider the binomial response logistic model as anillustration. Write

$$E(y_{ij}) = \pi_{ij} = [1 + \exp -(a_i + \lambda_i v_j)]^{-1}$$

$$y_{ij} \sim \text{Bin}(\pi_{ij}, n_{ij})$$

(11.8)

The simplest model is the multiple binary response model ($n_{ij} = 1$) that is referred to in the psychometric literature as a unidimensional item response model (Goldstein & Wood, 1989; Bartholomew & Knott, 1999). Estimation for this model is not possible using a simple Gibbs sampling algorithm, but as in the standard binomial multilevel case (see Browne, 1998) any Gibbs steps that do not have standard conditional posterior distributions could be replaced with Metropolis Hastings steps.

The issues that surround the specification and interpretation of single level factor and structural equation models are also present in multilevel versions. Parameter identification has already been discussed; another issue is the boundary "Heywood" case. Such solutions occur where sets of loading parameters tend towards zero or a correlation tends towards 1.0 and have been observed. A final important issue that only affects stochastic procedures is the problem of "flipping states". This means that there is not a unique solution even in a 1-factor problem as the loadings and factor values may all flip their sign to give an equivalent solution. When the number of factors increases there are greater problems as factors may swap over as the chains progress. This means that identifiability is an even greater consideration when using stochastic techniques.

For making inferences about individual parameters or functions of parameters one can use the chain values to provide point and interval estimates. These can also be used to provide large sample Wald tests for sets of parameters. Zhu and Lee (1999) propose a chi-square discrepancy function for evaluating the *posterior predictive* p-value, which is the Bayesian counterpart of the frequentist p-value statistic (Meng, 1994). In the multilevel case the α − level probability becomes

$$\hat{p}_B(Y) = (\sum_{i=1}^{J} i_j)^{-1} \sum_{i=1}^{i_j} \chi_\alpha^2(i_j p) \geq D(Y_i | \theta^{(i)}, \hat{v}^{(i)})$$

$$D(Y_i | \theta^{(i)}, \hat{v}^{(i)}) = Y_i^T \Sigma_i^{-1} Y_i$$

(11.9)

where Y_i is the vector of responses for the i−th level 2 unit and Σ_i is the (non-diagonal) residual covariance matrix.

References

Arbuckle, J.L. (1997). *AMOS: Version 3.6.* Chicago: Small Waters Corporation.

Bartholomew, D. J. and Knott, M. (1999). *Latent variable models and factor analysis.* (2nd ed.). London: Arnold.

Browne, W. (1998). *Applying MCMC methods to multilevel models.* PhD thesis, University of Bath.

Browne, W. & Rasbash, J. (2001). MCMC algorithms for variance matrices with applications in multilevel modeling. (in preparation)

Blozis, S. A. & Cudeck, R. (1999). Conditionally linear mixed-effects models with latent variable covariates. *Journal of Educational and Behavioural Statistics,* 24, 245-270.

Everitt, B. S. (1984). *An introduction to latent variable models.* London: Chapman and Hall.

Geweke, J. & Zhou, G. (1996). Measuring the pricing error of the arbitrage pricing theory. *The Review of International Financial Studies,* 9, 557-587.

Goldstein, H. (1995). *Multilevel statistical models.* London: Edward Arnold.

Goldstein, H., & Wood, R. (1989). Five decades of item response modelling. *British Journal of Mathematical and Statistical Psychology,* 42, 139-167.

Longford, N., & Muthèn, B. O. (1992). Factor analysis for clustered observations. *Psychometrika,* 57, 581-597.

McDonald, R. P. (1985). *Factor analysis and related methods.* Hillsdale, NJ: Lawrence Erlbaum Associates.

McDonald, R. P. (1993). A general model for two-level data with responses missing at random. *Psychometrika,* 58, 575-585.

McDonald, R.P., & Goldstein, H. (1989). Balanced versus unbalanced designs for linear structural relations in two-level data. *British Journal of Mathematical and Statistical Psychology,* 42, 215-232.

Meng, X. L. (1994). Posterior predictive p-values. *Annals of Statistics,* 22, 1142-1160.

Rabe-hesketh, S., Pickles, A. & Taylor, C. (2000). Sg129: Generalized linear latent and mixed models. *Stata Technical Bulletin,* 53, 47-57.

Rasbash, J., Browne, W., Goldstein, H., Plewis, I., Draper, D., Yang, M., Woodhouse, G., Healy, M., & Cameron, B. (2000). *A users guide to MLwiN* (second edition). London, Institute of Education.

Raudenbush, S. W. (1995). Maximum Likelihood estimation for unbalanced multilevel covariance structure models via the EM algorithm. *British Journal of Mathematical and Statistical Psychology,* 48, 359-70.

Rowe, K. J., & Hill, P. W. (1997). *Simultaneous estimation of multilevel structural equations to model students' educational progress.* Paper presented at the Tenth International Congress for School effectiveness and School Improvement, Memphis, Tennessee.

Rowe, K. J., & Hill, P.W. (in press). Modelling educational effectiveness in classrooms: The use of multilevel structural equations to model students' progress. *Educational Research and Evaluation.*

Rubin, D. B., & Thayer, D. T. (1982). EM algorithms for ML factor analysis. *Psychometrika*, 47, 69-76.

Scheines, R., Hoijtink, H. & Boomsma, A. (1999). Bayesian estimation and testing of structural equation models. *Psychometrika*, 64, 37-52.

Silverman, B. W. (1986). *Density Estimation for Statistics and Data analysis*. London: Chapman and Hall.

Zhu, H.-T. & Lee, S.-Y. (1999). Statistical analysis of nonlinear factor analysis models. *British Journal of Mathematical and Statistical Psychology*, 52, 225-242.

12 Modelling Measurement Error in Structural Multilevel Models

Jean-Paul Fox and Cees A.W. Glas

University of Twente, The Netherlands

12.1 Introduction

In a wide variety of research areas, analysts are often confronted with hierarchically structured data. Examples of such data structures include longitudinal data where several observations are nested within individuals, cross-national data where observations are nested in geographical, political or administrative units, data from surveys where respondents are nested under an interviewer, and test data for students within schools (e.g., Longford, 1993). The nested structures give rise to multilevel data and a major problem is to properly analyze the data taking into account the hierarchical structures.

There are two often criticized approaches for analyzing variables from different levels in a single level. The first is to disaggregate all higher order variables to the individual level. That is, data from higher levels are assigned to a much larger number of units at Level 1. In this approach, all disaggregated values are assumed to be independent of each other, which is a misspecification that threatens the validity of the inferences. In the second approach, the data at the individual level are aggregated to the higher level. As a result, all within group information is lost. This is especially serious because relations between the aggregated variables can be much stronger and different from the relations between non-aggregated variables (see Snijders & Bosker, 1999, pp. 14). When the nested structure within multilevel data is ignored, standard errors are estimated with bias.

A class of models that takes the multilevel structure into account and makes it possible to incorporate variables from different aggregation levels is the class of so-called multilevel models. Multilevel models support analyzing variables from different levels simultaneously, taking into account the various dependencies. These models entail a statistically more realistic specification of dependencies and do not waste information. The importance of a multilevel approach is fully described by Burstein (1980). Different methods and algorithms have been developed for fitting a multilevel model, and these have been implemented in standard software. For example, the EM algorithm (Dempster et al., 1978), the iteratively reweighted least squares method of Goldstein (1986), and the Fisher scoring algorithm (Longford, 1993), have become available in specialized software for fitting multilevel models (e.g., HLM, Raudenbush et al., 2000; MLwiN Goldstein et al., 1998; Mplus, Muthén & Muthén, 1998; and VARCL, Longford, 1990).

The field of multilevel research is broad and covers a wide range of problems in different areas. In social and behavioural science research, the basic problem is to relate specific attributes of individuals and characteristics of groups and structures in which the individuals function. For example, in sociology multilevel analysis is a useful strategy for contextual analysis, which focuses on the effects of the social context on individual behavior (Mason et al., 1983). In the same way, relating micro and macro levels is an important problem in economics (Baltagi, 1995). Moreover, with repeated measurements of a variable on a subject, interest is focused on the relationship of the variable to time (Bryk & Raudenbush, 1987; Goldstein, 1989; Longford, 1993). Further, Bryk and Raudenbush (1987) have introduced multilevel models in meta-analysis. The multilevel model has also been used extensively in educational research (e.g., Bock, 1989; Bryk & Raudenbush, 1987; Goldstein, 1987; Hox, 1995). Finally, extensive overviews of multilevel models can be found in Heck and Thomas (2000), Hüttner and van den Eeden (1995), Kreft and de Leeuw (1998), and Longford (1993).

In many research areas, studies may involve variables that cannot be observed directly or are observed subject to error. For example, a person's mathematical ability cannot be measured directly, only the performance on a number of mathematical test items. Also, data collected from respondents contain reponse error (i.e., there is response variation in answers to the same question when repeatedly administered to the same person). Measurement error can occur in both independent explanatory and dependent variables. The reliability of explanatory variables is an important methodological question. When reliability is known, corrections can be made (Fuller, 1987), or, if repeated measurements are available, reliability can be incorporated into the model and estimated directly. The use of unreliable explanatory variables leads to biased estimation of regression coefficients and the resulting statistical inference can be very misleading unless careful adjustments are made (Carroll et al., 1995; Fuller, 1987). To correct for measurement error, data that allow for estimation of the parameters in the measurement error model are collected. Measurement error models have been applied in different research areas to model errors-in-variables problems, incorporating error in the response as well as in the covariates. For example, in epidemiology covariates, such as blood pressure or level of cholesterol, are frequently measured with error (e.g., Buonaccorsi, J., 1991; Müller & Roeder, 1997; Wakefield & Morris, 1999). In educational research, students' pre-test scores, socio-economic status or intelligence are often used as explanatory variables in predicting students' examination results. Further, students' examination results or abilities are measured subject to error or cannot be observed directly. The measurement errors associated with the explanatory variables or variables that cannot be observed directly are often ignored or analyses are carried out using assumptions that may not always be realistic (e.g., Aitkin & Longford, 1986; Goldstein, 1987).

Although the topic of modeling measurement error has received considerable attention in the literature, for the most part, this attention has focused on linear measurement error models; more specifically, the classical additive measurement error model (e.g., Carroll et al., 1995; Fuller, 1987; Goldstein, 1987; Longford, 1993). The classical additive measurement error model is based on the assumption of homoscedasticity, which entails equal variance of measurement errors conditional on different levels of the dependent variable. Furthermore, it is often assumed that measurement error variance can be estimated from replicate measurements or validation data, or that it is a priori known for identification of the model. Often the measurement error models are very complex. For example, certain epidemiology studies involve nonlinear measurement error models to relate observed measurements to their true values (e.g., Buonaccorsi & Tosteson, 1993; Carroll et al., 1995). In educational testing, item response models relate achievements of the students to their response patterns (e.g., Lord, 1980 or van der Linden & Hambleton, 1997).

Measurement error models are often calibrated using external data. To correct for measurement error in structural modeling, the estimates from the measurement error model are imputed in the estimation procedure for the parameters of the structural model. This method has several drawbacks. In case of a single measurement with a linear regression calibration curve for the association of observed and true scores, and a homoscedastic normally distributed error term, the results are exact (Buonaccorsi, 1991). But if a dependent or explanatory variable subject to measurement error in the structural model has a nonconstant conditional variance, the regression calibration approximation suggests a homoscedastic linear model given that the variances are heteroscedastic (Carroll et al., 1995, pp. 63). Also, in case of a nonlinear measurement error model and a nonlinear structural model, the estimates can be biased (Buonaccorsi & Tosteson, 1993; Carroll et al., 1995, pp. 62-69).

Until recently, measurement error received little attention in the Bayesian literature (Zellner, 1971, pp. 114-161). Solutions for measurement error problems in a Bayesian analysis (e.g., Gelfand & Smith, 1990; Geman & Geman, 1984) were mainly developed after the introduction of Markov Chain Monte Carlo (MCMC) sampling (e.g., Bernardinelli et al., 1997; Mallick & Gelfand, 1996; Müller & Roeder, 1997; Richardson, 1996; Wakefield & Morris, 1999). The Bayesian framework provides a natural way of taking into account all sources of uncertainty in the estimation of the parameters. Also, the Bayesian approach is flexible; different sources of information are easily integrated and the computation of the posterior distributions, which usually involves high-dimensional integration, can be carried out straightforwardly by MCMC methods.

This chapter deals with measurement error in both the dependent and independent variables of a structural multilevel model. The observed data consist of responses to questionnaires or tests and contain measurement error. It will be shown that measurement error in both dependent and independent variables leads to attenuated parameter estimates of the structural multilevel model. Therefore, the response error in the observed variables is modeled by an item response model and a classical true score model to correct for attenuation. The Gibbs sampler can be used to estimate all parameters of both the measurement model and the structural multilevel model at once. With the use of a simulation study both models are compared to each other.

The chapter is divided into several sections. The first section describes a substantive example in which the model can be applied. Then, several different measurement error models for response error are discussed. After describing the combination of the structural model with different measurement error models, fitting these models is discussed. Finally, it is shown that the parameter estimates of the structural multilevel model are attenuated when measurement error is ignored. This is illustrated with an artificial example. The chapter concludes with a discussion.

12.2   School Effectiveness Research

Monitoring student outcomes for evaluating teacher and school performance has a long history. A general overview with respect to the methodological aspects and findings in the field of school effectiveness research can be found in Scheerens and Bosker (1997). Methods and statistical modeling issues in school effectiveness studies can be found in Aitkin and Longford (1986) and Goldstein (1997). The applications in this chapter focus on school effectiveness research with a fundamental interest in the development of knowledge and skill of individual students in relation to school characteristics. Data are analyzed at the individual level and it is assumed that classrooms, schools, and experimental interventions have an effect on all students exposed to them. In school or teacher effectiveness research, both levels of the multilevel model are important because the objects of interest are schools and teachers as well as students. Interest may exist in the effect on student learning of the organizational structure of the school, characteristics of a teacher, or the characteristics of the student.

Multilevel models are used to make inferences about the relationships between explanatory variables and response or outcome variables within and between schools. This type of model simultaneously handles student-level relationships and takes into account the way students are grouped in schools. Multilevel models incorporate a unique random effect for each organizational unit. Standard errors are estimated taking into account the variability of the random effects. This variation among the groups in their sets of coefficients can be modeled as multivariate outcomes which may, in turn, be predicted from Level 2 explanatory variables. The most common multilevel model for analyzing continuous outcomes is a two-level model in which Level 1 regression parameters are assumed to be multivariate normally distributed across Level 2 units. Here, students (Level 1), indexed ij $(i = 1, \ldots, n_j, j = 1, \ldots, J)$, are nested within schools (Level 2), indexed j $(j = 1, \ldots, J)$. In its general form, Level 1 of the two level model consists of a regression model, for each of the J Level 2 groups $(j = 1, \ldots, J)$, in which the outcomes are modeled as a function of Q predictor variables. The outcomes or dependent variables in the regression on Level 1, such as, students' achievement or attendance, are denoted by w_{ij} $(i = 1, \ldots, n_j, j = 1, \ldots, J)$. The Q explanatory variables at Level 1 contain information on students' characteristics (e.g., gender and age), which are measured without error. Level 1 explanatory variables can also be latent variables (e.g., socio-economic status, intelligence, community loyalty, or social consciousness). The unobserved Level 1 covariates are denoted by θ, the directly observed covariates by Λ. Level 1 of the model is formulated as

$$w_{ij} = \beta_{0j} + \beta_{1j}\theta_{1ij} + \ldots + \beta_{qj}\theta_{qij} + \beta_{(q+1)j}\Lambda_{(q+1)ij} + \ldots + \beta_{Qj}\Lambda_{Qij} + e_{ij} \quad (12.1)$$

where the first q predictors correspond to unobservable variables and the remaining $Q - q$ predictors correspond to directly observed variables. Random error $\mathbf{e}_j$ is assumed to be normally distributed with mean $\mathbf{0}$ and variance $\sigma_j^2 \mathbf{I}_{n_j}$. The regression parameters are treated as outcomes in a Level 2 model, although, the variation in the coefficients of one or more parameters could be constrained to zero. The Level 2 model, containing predictors with measurement error, ζ, and directly observed covariates, Γ, is formulated as

$$\beta_{qj} = \gamma_{q0} + \gamma_{q1}\zeta_{1qj} + \ldots + \gamma_{qs}\zeta_{sqj} + \gamma_{q(s+1)}\Gamma_{(s+1)qj} + \ldots + \gamma_{qS}\Gamma_{Sqj} + u_{qj} \quad (12.2)$$

for $q = 0, \ldots, Q$, where the first s predictors correspond to unobservable variables and the remaining $S - s$ correspond to directly observed variables.

The set of variables θ is never observed directly but supplemented information about θ, denoted as $\mathbf{X}$, is available. In this case, $\mathbf{X}$ is said to be a surrogate, that is, $\mathbf{X}$ is conditionally independent of w given the true covariates θ. In the same way, $\mathbf{Y}$ and $\mathbf{W}$ are defined as surrogates for w and ζ, respectively. For item responses, the distribution of the surrogate response depends only on the latent variable. All the information in the relationship between $\mathbf{X}$ and the predictors, θ, is explained by the latent variable. This is characteristic of nondifferential measurement error (Carroll et al., 1995, pp. 16-17). Nondifferential measurement error is important because parameters in response models can be estimated given the true dependent and explanatory variables, even when these variables (w, θ, ζ) are not directly observed. The observed variables are also called manifest variables or proxies.

12.3   Models for Measurement Error

A psychological or educational test is a device for measuring the extent to which a person possesses a certain trait (e.g., intelligence, arithmetic and linguistic ability). Suppose that a test is administered repeatedly to a subject, that the person's properties do not change over the test period, and that successive measurements are unaffected by previous measurements. The average value of these observations will converge, with probability one, to a constant, called the true score of the subject. In practice, due to the limited number of items in the test and the response variation, the observed test scores deviate from the true score. Let Y_{ijk} denote the test score of a subject ij on item k, with an error of measurement ε_{ijk}. Then $Y_{ijk} - \varepsilon_{ijk}$ is the true measurement or the true score. Further, let y_{ijk} denote the realization of Y_{ijk}. The hypothetical distribution defined over the independent measurements on the same person is called the propensity distribution of the random variable Y_{ijk}. Accordingly, the true score of a person, denoted again as θ_{ij}, is defined as the expected value of the observed score Y_{ijk} with respect to the propensity distribution. The error of measurement ε_{ijk} is the discrepancy between the observed and the true score, formally,

$$Y_{ijk} = \theta_{ij} + \varepsilon_{ijk} \tag{12.3}$$

A person has a fixed true score and on each occasion a particular observed and error score with probability governed by the propensity distribution. The classical test theory model is based on the concept of the true score and the assumption that error scores on different measurements are uncorrelated. An extensive treatment of the classical test theory model can be found in Lord and Novick (1968). The model is applied in a broad range of research areas where some characteristic is assessed by questionnaires or tests (e.g., in the field of epidemiologic studies–Freedman et al., 1991; Rosner et al., 1989).

Another class of models to describe the relationship between an examinee's ability and responses is based on the characteristics of the items of the test. This class is labelled item response theory (IRT) models. The dependence of the observed responses to binary scored items on the latent ability is fully specified by the item characteristic function, which is the regression of item score on the latent ability. The item response function is used to make inferences about the latent ability from the observed item responses. The item characteristic functions cannot be observed directly because the ability parameter, θ, is not observed. But under certain assumptions it is possible to infer information about examinee's ability from the examinee's responses to the test items (Lord & Novick, 1968; Lord, 1980). One of the forms of the item response function for a dichotomous item is the normal ogive,

$$P\left(Y_{ijk} = 1 \mid \theta_{ij}, a_k, b_k\right) = \Phi\left(a_k\theta_{ij} - b_k\right) \tag{12.4}$$

where $\Phi(.)$ denotes the standard normal cumulative distribution function, b_k is the ability level at the point of inflexion, where the probability of a correct response equals .5 and a_k is proportional to the slope of the curve at the inflexion point. The parameters a_k and b_k are called the discrimination and difficulty parameters, respectively (for extensions of this model to handle the effect of guessing or polytomously scored items, see Hambleton & Swaminathan, 1985; van der Linden & Hambleton, 1997).

The true score,

$$\sum_{k=1}^{K} P\left(Y_{ijk} = 1 \mid \theta_{ij}\right), \tag{12.5}$$

is a monotonic transformation of the latent ability underlying the normal ogive model, Equation (12.4). Every person with similar ability has the same expected number-right true score. Furthermore, the probability of a correct score is an increasing function of the ability; thus, the number-right true score is an increasing function of the ability. The true score, Equation (12.5), and the latent ability are the same thing expressed on different scales of measurement (Lord & Novick, 1968, pp. 45-46). Since the true score and the latent ability, are equivalent, the terms will be used interchangeably. Further, the context of the model under consideration will reveal whether θ represents a true score or a latent ability.

12.4   Multilevel IRT

The combination of a multilevel model with one or more latent variables modeled by an item response model is called a multilevel IRT model. The structure of the model is depicted with a path diagram in Figure 12.1. The path diagram gives a representation of a system of simultaneous equations and presents the relationships within the model. It illustrates the combination of the structural model with the measurement error models. The symbols in the path diagram are defined as follows. Variables enclosed in a square box are observed without error and the unobserved or latent variables are enclosed in a circle. The error terms are not enclosed and presented only as arrows on the square boxes. Straight single headed arrows between variables signify the assumption that a variable at the base of the arrow 'causes' variable at the head of the arrow. The square box with a dotted line, around the multilevel parameters, signifies the structural multilevel model. The upper part is denoted as the within-group regression, that is, regression at Level 1, and the lower part is denoted as the regression at Level 2 across groups. Accordingly, the regression at Level 1 contains two types of explanatory variables, observed or manifest and unobserved or latent variables and both are directly related to the unobserved dependent variable. Also Level 2 consists of observed and latent variables.

The model assumes that the latent variables within the structural multilevel model determine the responses to the items. That is, the latent variables ω, θ and ζ determine the observed responses $\mathbf{Y}$, $\mathbf{X}$ and $\mathbf{W}$, respectively. The pair of a latent variable and an observed variable enclosed in an ellipse with a dotted line defines a measurement error model. In an IRT model item parameters also determine the responses to the items.

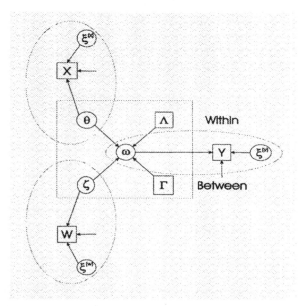

Fig. 12.1. A path diagram of a Multilevel IRT model, where item response models measure the latent variables within the structural multilevel model.

The model in Figure 12.1 is not identified. Identification of the model is possible by fixing the origin and scale of the latent variables. However, the scale is associated with several variance components. Furthermore, in multilevel modeling, one often fits various models entailing different decompositions of the ability variance, so fixing one of these components is not practical. A more convenient way is to impose identifying restrictions on the item parameters of each test. In the classical true score error model case, the measurement error variances ought to be known, or estimated properly, to identify the model. One could, for example, estimate the error variance from repeated measurements.

Handling response error in both the dependent and independent variables in a multilevel model using item response models has several advantages in comparison to the use of the classical true score model (Fox & Glas, 2000, 2001). In IRT, measurement error can be defined locally, for instance, as the posterior variance of the ability parameter given a response pattern. This results in a more realistic, heteroscedastic treatment of the measurement error. Besides, the fact that in IRT reliability can be defined conditionally on the value of the latent variable offers the possibility of separating the influence of item difficulty and ability level, which supports the use of incomplete test administration designs, optimal test assembly, computer adaptive testing and test equating. Finally, the model is identified in a natural way, without needing any prior knowledge.

12.4.1 Markov chain monte carlo (MCMC)

Analyzing the joint posterior distribution of the parameters of interest in the model in (12.1) and (12.2) is infeasible. Computing expectations of marginal distributions using, for example, Gauss-Hermite quadrature is also quite difficult (Fox, 2000; Fox & Glas, 2001). Therefore, a sampling-based approach using an MCMC algorithm to obtain random draws from the joint posterior distribution of the parameters of interest given the data is considered. MCMC is a simulation based technique for sampling from high dimensional joint distributions. From a practical perspective, the Markov chains are relatively easy to construct and MCMC techniques are straightforward to implement. They are also the only currently available techniques for exploring these high dimensional problems. In particular, the Gibbs sampler (Gelfand & Smith, 1990; Geman & Geman, 1984) is a procedure for sampling from the complete conditional distributions of all estimands.

The algorithm is described as follows. Consider a joint distribution π defined on a set $\theta \subset \mathbb{R}^k$ (θ is used as a generic parameter of π, not an ability parameter in an IRT model). The MCMC algorithm consists of specifying a Markov chain with stationary distribution π. The elements of θ are partitioned into k components $(\theta_1, \ldots, \theta_k)$, and each component of θ may be a scalar or a vector. One iteration of the Gibbs sampler is defined as an updating of one component of θ. To obtain a sample from the target distribution π, the Gibbs sampler creates a transition from $\theta^{(t)}$ to $\theta^{(t+1)}$. Updating the first component, θ_1, consists of sampling from the full conditional distribution

$$\pi\left(\theta_1 \mid \theta_2^{(t)}, \theta_3^{(t)}, \ldots, \theta_k^{(t)}\right)$$

which is the distribution of the first component of θ conditional on all other components. Subsequently, $\theta_2^{(t+1)}$ is obtained as a draw from

$$\pi\left(\theta_2 \mid \theta_1^{(t+1)}, \theta_3^{(t)}, \ldots, \theta_k^{(t)}\right),$$

and so on, until $\theta_k^{(t+1)}$ is drawn from

$$\pi\left(\theta_k \mid \theta_1^{(t+1)}, \theta_2^{(t+1)}, \ldots, \theta_{k-1}^{(t+1)}\right),$$

which completes updating the components to $\theta^{(t+1)}$.

The order of updating the different components is usually fixed, although this is not necessary. Random permutations of the updating order are acceptable. The choice of updating scheme can effect the convergence of the sampler (Roberts & Sahu, 1997). That is, a different updating strategy can make the algorithm converge faster. In some applications, a multivariate component sampler is a more natural choice. This so-called blocking of the Gibbs sampler by blocking highly correlated components into a higher-dimensional component can improve the convergence of the Markov chain (Gelman et al., 1995; Roberts & Sahu, 1997). On the other hand, updating in a block or group is often computationally more demanding than the corresponding componentwise updating scheme.

Running multiple chains reduces the variance of the parameter estimates attributable to the Gibbs sampler. This is useful in obtaining independent samples, but these are not required for estimating the parameters of interest. A very long run gives the best chance of finding new modes. However, inference from a Markov chain simulation is always problematic because there are areas of the target distribution that have not been covered by the finite chain. In practice, both methods are desirable, to check the behavior and convergence of the Markov chain. There are several methods for monitoring convergence, but despite much recent work, convergence diagnostics for the Gibbs sampler remains a topic for further research. The source of the problem is that the simulation converges to a target distribution rather than a target point. Different methods can be found in Brooks and Gelman (1998), Cowles and Carlin (1996) and Gelman (1995). In the present analysis, convergence diagnostics and multiple chains from different starting points were used to verify that the Markov chain had converged. In addition, a visual inspection of the plot of random deviates against iteration was made to decide whether the Markov chain had converged. A detailed description of the implementation of the Gibbs sampler to estimate the model in Figure 12.1 is not given here. The full conditional distributions of the parameters of interest can be found in Fox and Glas (2000, 2001). The Gibbs sampler is used to estimate parameters of the model to illustrate the effects of response error in both the dependent and independent variables of the structural multilevel model.

12.5   Ignorable and Non-Ignorable Measurement Error

This section focuses on problems associated with measurement error in the dependent and independent variables of a structural multilevel model. In certain cases, measurement error does not play a role. That is, the model for the latent variable also holds for the manifest variable with parameters unchanged, except that a measurement error variance component is added to the variance of the residuals (Carroll et al., 1995, pp. 229). An example is a structural linear regression model with measurement error in the dependent variable, where the measurement error is confounded with the residuals, resulting in greater variability of the parameter estimates. The measurement error is called ignorable in these cases. If estimates of the regression coefficients are biased because measurement error in the manifest variable is ignored, then the measurement error is called non-ignorable. For example, in a linear regression model with measurement error in a covariate, the least squares regression coefficient is biased toward zero, that is, the regression coefficient is attenuated by measurement error (Fuller, 1987, pp. 3).

Here it will be shown that response error in the dependent, independent, or both variables in a multilevel model is not ignorable. That is, the parameter estimates of a multilevel model are affected by the presence of response error in the manifest variables. It will be shown that disattenuated parameter estimates of the structural multilevel model are obtained by modeling response error in the manifest variables with a classical true score model. The generalization of the results from a multilevel true score model to a multilevel IRT model is discussed at the end of this section.

Consider the linear regression model with the independent variable measured with error,

$$\omega_{ij} = \beta_0 + \beta_1 \theta_{ij} + e_{ij}, \tag{12.6}$$

where the equation errors are independent and normally distributed with mean zero and variance σ^2. It is assumed that the distribution of true scores, θ_{ij}, in the population is standard normal, that is, the θ_{ij} are unobservable independent realizations of a standard normal random variable. For a given person, the true score is a constant, but the observed score and error term are random variables.

In the classical true score model, inferences about θ_{ij} are made from the responses x_{ijk} for $k = 1, \ldots, K$, which are related to θ_{ij} via

$$X_{ij} = \theta_{ij} + \varepsilon_{ij}^{(x)}, \tag{12.7}$$

where x_{ij} is a realization of X_{ij}, the observed total score of person ij, and $\varepsilon_{ij}^{(x)}$ an error term that is independent of θ_{ij} and e_{ij}. The superscript x denotes the connection with the observed variable X_{ij}. Further, it is assumed that $\varepsilon_{ij}^{(x)}$ are independent normally distributed with mean zero and variance φ_x, where, again, the subscript x denotes the connection with the observed variable X_{ij}. One of the consequences of the measurement error in the independent variable can be seen in the posterior expectation of the regression coefficient β_1 given the variables ω_{ij}, x_{ij} and the parameters β_0, σ^2 and φ_x. This posterior expectation is derived from the conditional distribution of θ_{ij} given x_{ij} and φ_x,

$$f(\theta_{ij} \mid x_{ij}, \varphi_x) \propto f(x_{ij} \mid \theta_{ij}, \varphi_x) f(\theta_{ij}; 0, 1), \tag{12.8}$$

where the right-hand-side consists of a product of normal densities. Due to standard properties of normal distributions (e.g., Box & Tiao, 1973; Lindley

& Smith, 1972) the full conditional posterior density of θ_{ij} given x_{ij} and φ_x is also normally distributed and is given by

$$(\theta_{ij} \mid X_{ij}, \varphi_x) \sim N \left(\frac{\varphi_x^{-1}}{1 + \varphi_x^{-1}} x_{ij}, \frac{1}{1 + \varphi_x^{-1}} \right). \tag{12.9}$$

Below, $\varphi_x^{-1}/\left(1 + \varphi_x^{-1}\right)$ is denoted by λ_x. The regression on Level 1 imposes a density $f\left(\omega_{ij} \mid \beta, \theta_{ij}, \sigma^2\right)$ that can be considered as a likelihood, and Equation (12.9) can be regarded as the prior for the unobserved θ_{ij}. Accordingly, it follows that the conditional posterior distribution of ω_{ij} is given by

$$f\left(\omega_{ij} \mid \beta, \theta_{ij}, \sigma^2, x_{ij}, \varphi_x\right) \propto f\left(\omega_{ij} \mid \beta, \theta_{ij}, \sigma^2\right) f\left(\theta_{ij} \mid x_{ij}, \varphi_x\right).$$

Due to properties of normal distributions (Lindley & Smith, 1972), the conditional distribution of ω_{ij} is also normally distributed, that is,

$$\left(\omega_{ij} \mid \beta, \sigma^2, X_{ij}, \varphi_x\right) \sim N \left(\beta_0 + \lambda_x \beta_1 x_{ij}, \sigma^2 + \beta_1^2 \left(1 - \lambda_x\right)\right). \tag{12.10}$$

In the same way it follows that, given a uniform prior for β_1, the conditional posterior of β_1 given $\omega, \beta_0, \sigma^2, \mathbf{x}$ and φ_x is normal with expectation

$$E\left[\beta_1 \mid \omega, \mathbf{x}, \beta_0, \sigma^2, \varphi_x\right] = \lambda_x^{-1} \widehat{\beta}_1, \tag{12.11}$$

where $\widehat{\beta}_1$ is the least squares estimator in the regression of $\omega - \beta_0$ on $\mathbf{x}$. Because of the measurement error in the explanatory variable, the least squares regression coefficient is biased toward zero, that is, the regression coefficient is attenuated by the measurement error. The ratio λ_x defines the degree of attenuation, which is a measure of the degree of true score variation relative to observed score variation. This ratio is commonly called the reliability of X_{ij}. From Equation (12.11) it can be seen that if the ratio λ_x is known, it is possible to construct an unbiased estimator of β_1. Several techniques for estimating this model, given λ_x, can be found in Fuller (1987). The effect of errors in variables on ordinary least squares estimators is well known (e.g., Cochran, 1968; Fuller, 1987).

Next, suppose the intercept and slope of model (12.6) are random coefficients, that is, the coefficients vary over Level 2 groups. The coefficients are treated as outcomes in a Level 2 model given by

$$\beta_{0j} = \gamma_{00} + \gamma_{01}\zeta_j + u_{0j} \tag{12.12}$$
$$\beta_{1j} = \gamma_{10} + u_{1j},$$

where the Level 2 error terms $\mathbf{u}_j$ have a multivariate normal distribution with mean zero and covariance matrix $\mathbf{T}$. It is assumed that the errors on Level 2 are uncorrelated. That is, the covariance matrix $\mathbf{T}$ consists of diagonal elements $\mathrm{var}(u_{0j}) = \tau_0^2$ and $\mathrm{var}(u_{1j}) = \tau_1^2$. Suppose that the dependent variable ω_{ij} is not observed exactly, but its error-prone version Y_{ij} is available. So

$$Y_{ij} = \omega_{ij} + \varepsilon_{ij}^{(y)}, \tag{12.13}$$

where the measurement errors $\varepsilon_{ij}^{(y)}$ are independent of w_{ij} and e_{ij}, and independent normally distributed with mean zero and variance φ_y. The superscript and subscript y emphasize the connection with the observed total score Y_{ij}. Again, the conditional posterior distribution of $\mathbf{Y}_j$, the observed scores of students in group j, given $\theta_j, \beta_j, \sigma^2$ and φ_y follows from the standard properties of normal distributions, that is,

$$f\left(\mathbf{y}_j \mid \theta_j, \beta_j, \sigma^2, \varphi_y\right) \propto f\left(\mathbf{y}_j \mid w_j, \varphi_y\right) f\left(w_j \mid \theta_j, \beta_j, \sigma^2\right),$$

where the second factor on the right-hand side defines the distribution of the true scores w_j in the population. As a result,

$$\left(\mathbf{Y}_j \mid \theta_j, \beta_j, \sigma^2, \varphi_y\right) \sim N\left(\beta_{0j} + \beta_{1j}\theta_j, \left(\varphi_y + \sigma^2\right)\mathbf{I}_{n_j}\right), \quad (12.14)$$

where $\mathbf{I}_{n_j}$ is the identity matrix of dimension n_j. Obviously, the measurement error in the dependent variable results in an extra variance component φ_y. Combining this conditional distribution of $\mathbf{Y}_j$ with the prior knowledge about β_j, in Equation (12.12), results in the conditional posterior distribution of β_j given $\mathbf{y}_j, \theta_j, \sigma^2, \gamma, \mathbf{T}, \zeta_j$ and φ_y. Define $\boldsymbol{\Sigma}_j = \left(\sigma^2 + \varphi_y\right)\left(\mathbf{H}_j^t \mathbf{H}_j\right)^{-1}$, where $\mathbf{H}_j = \left[\mathbf{1}_{n_j}, \theta_j\right]$. Then

$$\left(\beta_j \mid \mathbf{Y}_j, \theta_j, \sigma^2, \gamma, \mathbf{T}, \zeta_j, \varphi_y\right) \sim N\left(\frac{\boldsymbol{\Sigma}_j^{-1}\widehat{\beta}_j + \mathbf{T}^{-1}\mathbf{A}\gamma}{\boldsymbol{\Sigma}_j^{-1} + \mathbf{T}^{-1}}, \frac{1}{\boldsymbol{\Sigma}_j^{-1} + \mathbf{T}^{-1}}\right) \quad (12.15)$$

where $\mathbf{A}$ defines the structure of the explanatory variables on Level 2. The posterior expectation of β_j is the well-known composite or shrinkage estimator, where the amount of weight placed on the estimates depends on their precision. Notice that the usual least squares estimator, $\widehat{\beta}_j$, based on the linear regression on Level 1 given θ_j and $\mathbf{Y}_j$, is weighted by $\boldsymbol{\Sigma}_j^{-1}$, which contains the measurement error in the dependent variable. Thus, the estimator of β_j is not equivalent to the standard least squares estimator of β, and as consequence, the measurement error in the dependent variable of a structural multilevel model is not ignorable. The estimates of the random regression coefficients are attenuated when the measurement error in the dependent variable is ignored because the least squares estimator $\widehat{\beta}_j$ is attenuated by the measurement error.

Next, it is shown that the posterior expectation of β_j given the manifest variables is affected by measurement error in the explanatory variable on Level 1. From Equation (12.10) and (12.14) the conditional distribution of $\mathbf{Y}_j$ can be derived as

$$\left(\mathbf{Y}_j \mid \mathbf{X}_j, \beta_j, \sigma^2, \varphi_y, \varphi_x\right) \sim N\left(\beta_{0j} + \lambda_x \beta_{1j}\mathbf{x}_j, \left(\varphi_y + \sigma^2 + \beta_{1j}^2\left(1 - \lambda_x\right)\right)\mathbf{I}_{n_j}\right). \quad (12.16)$$

The conditional posterior distribution of β_j can be derived by considering this conditional distribution of $\mathbf{Y}_j$ as the likelihood and Equation (12.12) as the prior for its parameter vector β_j. To obtain an analytical expression for this conditional posterior distribution, it must be assumed that the variance in Equation (12.16) is known. Denote this variance, for group j, as $\mathbf{C}_j$. In practice, an empirical Bayes estimator could be used. Define $\mathbf{\Sigma}_j = \mathbf{C}_j \left(\mathbf{H}_j^t \mathbf{H}_j\right)^{-1}$, where $\mathbf{H}_j = [1, \lambda_x \mathbf{x}_j]$. Then it follows that

$$(\beta_j \mid \mathbf{Y}_j, \mathbf{X}_j, \sigma^2, \gamma, \mathbf{T}, \zeta_j, \varphi_y, \varphi_x) \sim N \left(\frac{\mathbf{\Sigma}_j^{-1} \widehat{\beta}_j + \mathbf{T}^{-1} \mathbf{A} \gamma}{\mathbf{\Sigma}_j^{-1} + \mathbf{T}^{-1}}, \frac{1}{\mathbf{\Sigma}_j^{-1} + \mathbf{T}^{-1}} \right)$$
$$(12.17)$$

where the other variables are defined as in Equation (12.15). The posterior expectation is a shrinkage estimator where $\widehat{\beta}_j = \left(\mathbf{H}_j^t \mathbf{H}_j\right)^{-1} \mathbf{H}_j^t \mathbf{y}_j$ and the variance of $\widehat{\beta}_j$ increases due to the measurement error in the dependent and independent variables. Besides the measurement error in the dependent variable, the reliability ratio λ_x further influences the least squares regression coefficients $\widehat{\beta}_j$.

Finally, assume that the explanatory variable on Level 2, ζ, is unobserved and instead a variable $\mathbf{W}$ is observed with measurement error variance φ_w, that is,

$$W_j = \zeta_j + \varepsilon_j^{(w)},$$

where the measurement errors $\varepsilon_j^{(w)}$ are independent of ζ_j and u_{0j}, and independently normally distributed with mean zero and variance φ_w. Further, it is assumed that the true scores, ζ_j, in the population are standard normally distributed. Analogous to the derivation of (12.10), it follows that

$$(\beta_{0j} \mid W_j, \gamma, \tau_0^2, \varphi_w) \sim N \left(\gamma_{00} + \lambda_w \gamma_{01} w_j, \tau_0^2 + \gamma_{01}^2 (1 - \lambda_w) \right) \qquad (12.18)$$

where $\lambda_w = \varphi_w^{-1} / \left(1 + \varphi_w^{-1}\right)$. Again, the posterior expectation of β_j can be derived by combining the prior information for β_{0j} and the standard prior information for β_{1j}, from Equation (12.12), with the likelihood in Equation (12.16). Hence the conditional posterior distribution of β_j is equivalent to Equation (12.17), except that the first diagonal-element of $\mathbf{T}$ is increased by $\gamma_{01}^2 (1 - \lambda_w)$, and the first row of $\mathbf{A} = (1, \lambda_w W_j, 0)$. Accordingly, the shrinkage estimator is a combination of two weighted estimators, where both parts are influenced by measurement error in the dependent and independent variables. As a consequence, the measurement error is not ignorable and ignoring it leads to attenuated estimates of the random regression coefficients.

Besides the effect of measurement error on the estimates of random regression coefficients, a perhaps less well-recognized effect is the increased variance of the observed dependent variable given the observed explanatory variables. Without measurement error in the explanatory variables the residual variance of Y_{ij} is

$$\text{var}\left(Y_{ij} \mid \theta_{ij}, \zeta_j\right) = \tau_0^2 + \tau_1^2 \theta_{ij}^2 + \sigma^2 + \varphi_y.$$

By taking into account the measurement error in the independent variables, the residual variance of the manifest variable, Y_{ij}, increases to

$$\text{var}\left(Y_{ij} \mid x_{ij}, w_j\right) = C_{ij} + \mathbf{H}_{ij}\mathbf{T}^{-1}\mathbf{H}_{ij}^t,$$

where $C_{ij} = \left(\varphi_y + \sigma^2 + \beta_{1j}^2\left(1 - \lambda_x\right)\right)$, $\mathbf{H}_{ij} = [1, \lambda_x x_{ij}]$ and $\mathbf{T}$ is the diagonal matrix with elements $\left(\tau_0^2 + \gamma_{01}^2\left(1 - \lambda_w\right), \tau_1^2\right)$. Notice that the response variance in the dependent variable is just an extra variance component, but the measurement error variance in the explanatory variables causes a complex variance structure. The structure gets even more complex if the variables or error terms are correlated (Schaalje & Butts, 1993).

This overview of non-ignorable measurement error is based on the classical true score model. The conditional distributions of the random regression coefficients are derived by using the standard properties of the normal distribution. If the response error is modeled by an IRT model, the conditional distributions of these parameters can be found in the same way by introducing an augmented variable $\mathbf{Z}$. Interpret the observation Z_{ijk} as an indicator that a continuous variable with normal density is negative or positive. Denote this continuous variable as $Z_{ijk}^{(x)}$, where the superscript x denotes the connection with the observed response variable X_{ijk}. It is assumed that $X_{ijk} = 1$ if $Z_{ijk}^{(x)} > 0$ and $X_{ijk} = 0$ otherwise. It follows that the conditional distribution $Z_{ijk}^{(x)}$ given θ_{ij} and $\xi_k^{(x)}$ is normal. This distribution can be used to obtain the conditional distributions of the random regression parameters in the same way as above. Expanding the two parameter normal ogive model to a three parameter normal ogive model to correct for guessing can be done by introducing an extra augmented variable (Johnson & Albert, 1999, pp. 204-205). Further, observed ordinal data can be modeled by assuming that a latent variable underlies the ordinal response (Johnson & Albert, 1999, pp. 127-133).

12.6   An Illustrative Example

In this section, the effects of measurement error in dependent and explanatory variables at different levels in a structural multilevel model are demonstrated using simulations. A numerical example is also analyzed to compare the effects of modeling measurement error in dependent and independent variables with an IRT model and a classical true score model. The model is given by

$$\omega_{ij} = \beta_{0j} + \beta_{1j}\theta_{ij} + e_{ij} \tag{12.19}$$
$$\beta_{0j} = \gamma_{00} + \gamma_{01}\zeta_j + u_{0j}$$
$$\beta_{1j} = \gamma_{10} + u_{1j},$$

where $e_{ij} \sim N\left(0, \sigma^2\right)$ and $\mathbf{u}_j \sim N\left(0, \mathbf{T}\right)$. Furthermore, it is assumed that the surrogates $\mathbf{Y}, \mathbf{X}$ and $\mathbf{W}$ are related to the latent predictors ω, θ and ζ, respectively, through a two-parameter normal ogive model.

Table 12.1. Parameter estimates of the multilevel model with measurement error in the dependent variable.

	Generated	IRT Model M_1			Classical True Score Model M_{c1}		
Fixed Effects	Coeff.	Coeff.	s.d.	HPD	Coeff.	s.d.	HPD
γ_{00}	.000	−.032	.042	[−.101, .039]	−.056	.032	[−.107, −.007]
γ_{01}	.100	.082	.026	[.040, .124]	.078	.026	[.038, .121]
γ_{10}	.100	.055	.034	[−.002, .109]	.054	.028	[.012, .103]
Random Effects	Var. Comp.	Var. Comp.	s.d.	HPD	Var. Comp.	s.d.	HPD
τ_0^2	.200	.234	.028	[.186, .287]	.200	.022	[.165, .236]
τ_1^2	.200	.201	.023	[.159, .247]	.138	.016	[.115, .167]
τ_{01}^2	.100	.169	.025	[.131, .211]	.118	.015	[.094, .143]
σ^2	.500	.513	.028	[.460, .573]	.435	.010	[.418, .450]

For the simulations, both the latent predictors, θ and ζ, were drawn from the standard normal distribution. The latent dependent variable ω was generated according to the above model. Response patterns were generated according to a normal ogive model for tests of 40 items. For tests related to the dependent and independent variables at Level 1, 6,000 response patterns were simulated. The total number of groups was $J = 200$, each group or class consisting of 20 and 40 individuals. For the test related to the latent covariate ζ at Level 2, 200 response patterns were generated. The generated values of the fixed and random effects, γ, σ^2 and $\mathbf{T}$, are shown under the label "Generated" in Table 12.1.

12.6.1   Explanatory variables without measurement error

In the first simulation study, no response error in the explanatory variables on Level 1 and Level 2 was present, that is, the latent predictors θ and ζ were observed directly without an error. The dependent variable was unobserved but information about ω, denoted as $\mathbf{Y}$, is available. The data were simulated by the multilevel IRT model. The structural multilevel model with measurement error in the dependent variable was estimated with the Gibbs sampler, using the normal ogive model and the classical true score model as measurement error models. Noninformative priors were used for the fixed effects and variance components in the multilevel model (Fox & Glas , 2000; 2001). Also, the methods for computing starting values can be found there. After a burn-in period of 1,000 iterations, 20,000 iterations were made to estimate the parameters of the structural model with the two-parameter normal ogive model.

For the classical true score model, 500 iterations were necessary as a burn-in period and 5,000 iterations were used to estimate the parameters. Convergence of the Gibbs sampler was investigated by running multiple chains from different starting points to verify that they yielded similar answers and by plotting the MCMC iterations to verify convergence (for a comprehensive discussion of convergence of the Gibbs sampler, see Cowles & Carlin, 1996).

In Table 12.1, the expected a posteriori estimates of the parameters of the multilevel IRT model obtained from the Gibbs sampler are given under the label "IRT Model", denoted as Model M_1. Parameter estimates of the structural multilevel model using the classical true score model are given under the label "Classical True Score Model", denoted as Model M_{c1}. The multilevel IRT model M_1 was identified by fixing a discrimination and a difficulty parameter to ensure that the latent dependent variable was scaled the same way as in the data generation phase. The structural model with the classical true score model as measurement error model was identified by specifying the parameters of the measurement error distribution. Therefore, the group specific error variance was a priori estimated. The unbiased estimates of the error variances of individual examinees were averaged to obtain the group specific error variance (Lord & Novick, 1968). The group specific error variance relating to the unweighted sums of item responses or test scores Y_{ij}, φ_y was .118, for every individual ij. The observed sum scores were scaled in the same way as the true latent dependent variable ω_{ij}. The reported standard deviations are the posterior standard deviations. The 90% highest posterior probability (HPD) intervals for parameters of interest were computed from a sample from their marginal posterior distribution using the Gibbs sampler (Chen & Shao, 1999).

The true parameter values were well within the HPD intervals obtained from the multilevel IRT model, M_1, except for the covariance of the Level 2 residuals, τ_{01}^2, which was too high. Further, the fixed effect, γ_{10}, was not significantly different from zero. The parameter estimates of the random and fixed effects are given under the label "Classical True Score Model", Model M_{c1}. Here, more parameter estimates differed from the true parameter values. Specifically, the variance at Level 1 and the variance of the residuals of the random slope parameter were too low. As a result, the estimates of the slope parameters corresponding to the different groups were more alike in comparison to the corresponding estimates resulting from the multilevel IRT model and the true simulated values. In the fit of Model M_{c1}, the slope parameter estimates varied less across groups. The estimates of the variance components affected the estimate of the intraclass correlation coefficient. This is the proportion of the total residual variation that is due to variation in the random intercepts, after controlling for the Level 1 predictor variable. The simulating values implied an intraclass correlation coefficient of $\rho = .286$, the multilevel IRT estimate was $\rho = .313$, and the Model M_{c1} estimate $\rho = .314$.

Table 12.2. Parameter estimates of the multilevel model with measurement error in both the dependent and independent variables.

	Observed Scores M_o		IRT Model M_2			Classical True Score Model M_{c2}		
Fixed Effects	Coeff.	s.d.	Coeff.	s.d.	HPD	Coeff.	s.d.	HPD
γ_{00}	−.057	.032	−.048	.045	[−.120, .027]	−.058	.034	[−.112, .000]
γ_{01}	.058	.026	.081	.030	[.032, .130]	.058	.026	[.018, .103]
γ_{10}	.050	.026	.055	.034	[.000, .110]	.049	.026	[.005, .091]
Random Effects	Var. Comp.	s.d.	Var. Comp.	s.d.	HPD	Var. Comp.	s.d.	HPD
τ_0^2	.201	.023	.233	.030	[.184, .278]	.200	.023	[.165, .238]
τ_1^2	.126	.015	.200	.027	[.157, .241]	.138	.014	[.098, .144]
τ_{01}^2	.110	.015	.167	.024	[.128, .204]	.118	.015	[.083, .131]
σ^2	.560	.010	.515	.035	[.454, .562]	.435	.010	[.416, .450]

These estimates were based on iterates of the variance components and were not based on the posterior means of the variance components.

12.6.2   Explanatory variables with measurement error

In the second simulation, both the dependent and independent observed variables had measurement error. Table 12.2 presents the results of estimating the parameters of the multilevel model using observed scores, denoted as Model M_o, using a normal ogive model as measurement error model, denoted as Model M_2, and using the classical true score model as measurement error model, denoted as Model M_{c2}, both for the dependent and independent variables. In the estimation procedure, all uncertainties were taken into account, where the group specific error variances for the sum scores relating to the Level 1 and Level 2 predictors, φ_x and φ_w, were .103 and .109, respectively. The multilevel IRT model, where measurement error in the covariates was modeled by a normal ogive model, Model M_2, was identified by fixing a discrimination and a difficulty parameter of each test. Model M_{c2} was identified by specifying the response variance of the observed scores. The true parameters were the same as in Table 12.1. The true parameter values were well within the HPD regions of the multilevel IRT estimates, Model M_2. That is, the parameter estimates were almost the same as the parameter estimates resulting from Model M_1, where the true parameter values were used for the predictor variables instead of modeling the variables with an IRT model. The same applied to the parameter estimates of Model M_{c2} which were comparable to the estimates of Model M_{c1}. Subsequently, the deficiencies of the fit of model M_{c1} also applied to the fit of Model M_{c2}. The posterior variances of the estimates of Model M_2 and M_{c2} were slightly higher in comparison to Model M_1 and M_{c1} because the measurement errors in the predictor variables were taken into account, but the differences were rather small. The estimates given under the label "Observed Scores" resulted from estimating the multilevel model using observed scores for both the dependent and independent variables, ignoring measurement error in all variables. It was verified that taking account of measurement error in the observed variables resulted in different parameter estimates, especially for the variance components.

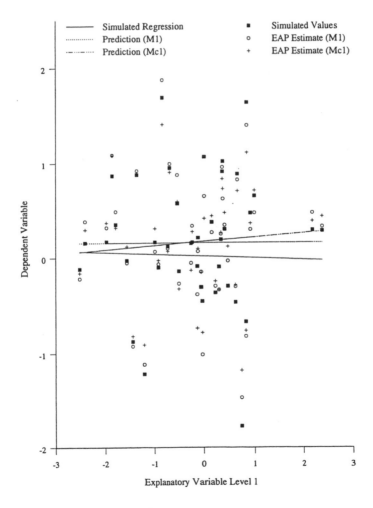

Fig. 12.2. Expected a posteriori estimates and predictions of the dependent values given the true independent variables.

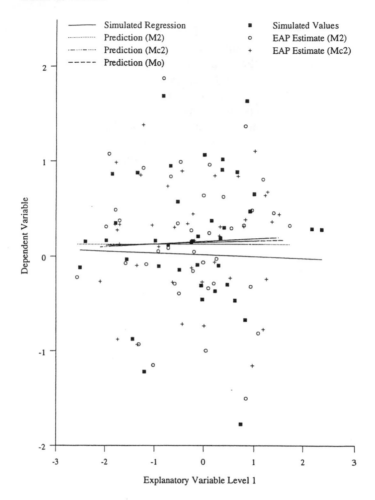

Fig. 12.3. Expected a posteriori estimates and predictions of the dependent values given that the explanatory variables at Level 1 and Level 2 are measured with an error.

Tables 1 and 2 show that the estimates of the variance components were attenuated because the measurement error was ignored. As seen in the preceeding section, the estimates of the random intercept and random slope parameters were strongly influenced by the variance components. The effects of measurement error in the dependent and independent variables were also reflected in the estimates of the random regression parameters. Figure 12.2 shows the expected a posteriori estimates of the dependent values in an arbitrary group using Model M_1 and M_{c1}. There was no horizontal shift in the estimates because both models used the true independent variables. The estimates of both models were quite close to the true values, but the more extreme values were better estimated by Model M_1, where the normal ogive model was the measurement model. The regression predicted by Model M_1 resulted in a higher intercept, the slope parameter nearly equaled the true slope parameter. The regression lines were based on posterior means of the random regression coefficients. The predicted regression slope, using Model M_{c1}, was of opposite sign and resulted in different conclusions. In the same group as in Figure 12.2, the expected a posteriori estimates of the dependent values based on dependent and independent variables measured with an error, using the classical true score model and the normal ogive model, are given in Figure 12.3. The horizontal shifts in the expected a posteriori estimates, in relation to the estimates in Figure 12.2, were caused by the measurement error in the independent variables. The estimates were shrunk towards the mean of both variables. The estimates following from Model M_2 were closer to the more extreme true values. As a result, the predicted regression according to Model M_2 had a wider range, and was closer to the true regression. As in Figure 12.2, the slope estimate of the predicted regression of Model M_{c2} was positive, even though the true parameter slope was negative. In this group, the predicted regression based on observed scores, Model M_0, followed the regression of Model M_{c2}, and seemed to follow the true regression better. Notice that the predictions are slightly better in Figure 12.3, where the explanatory variables were modeled with the classical true score model or the normal ogive model. It seemed that the more complex model, which takes measurement error in all variables into account, was more flexible, resulting in a better fit of the model. Both figures indicate that the normal ogive model for the measurement error model yielded better estimates of the outcomes, especially, in case of the more extreme values. Further, the estimates of the random regression coefficients depended on the values of the variance components and were sensitive to measurement error in the variables. As shown in Figures 12.2 and 12.3, measurement error in the dependent and independent variables may lead to incorrect conclusions.

12.7 Discussion

Errors in the dependent or independent variables of a multilevel model are modeled by an item response model or a classical true score model. The Gibbs sampler can be used to estimate all parameters. Other estimation procedures, such as error calibration methods (Carroll et. al., 1995), do not take all parameter variability into account.

A fully Bayesian approach accommodates both covariate and response measurement error, and provides more reliable estimates of the variability of the model parameters. On the other hand, the Bayesian approach is computer intensive and still unrecognized in many working environments. Besides, the lack of programs for handling measurement errors in major statistical computer packages further impedes the use of structural multilevel models.

In this chapter, the consequences of ignoring measurement error were examined to evaluate estimation methods that are able to handle measurement error in both the explanatory and dependent variables of a structural multilevel model. It was shown that the estimates of the variance components and random regression coefficients are sensitive to measurement error in both the dependent and explanatory variables. Simulations were used to exemplify the impact of the measurement error. Other forms of measurement error can be handled similarly, but information concerning the probability structure is necessary. Notice that the classical true score error model requires a priori estimates of the group specific error variances. These estimates strongly affect the parameter estimates (Fox & Glas, 2000). That is, a small change in the a priori estimates can lead to different conclusions (a detailed description of the Bayesian estimation procedure can be found in Fox & Glas, 2000, 2001). The procedure is flexible in the sense that other measurement error models, and other priors can be used. This supports a more realistic way of modeling measurement error. Also, the estimation procedure can handle multilevel models with three or more levels. It takes the full error structure into account and allows for errors in both the dependent and independent variables.

References

Aitkin, M., & Longford, N. (1986). Statistical modelling issues in school effectiveness studies. *Journal of the Royal Statistical Society, Series A, 149*, 1-43.

Baltagi, B. H. (1995). *Econometric analysis of panel data*. Chichester: Wiley.

Bernardinelli, L., Pascutto, C., Best, N. G., & Gilks, W. R. (1997). Disease mapping with errors in covariates. *Statistics in Medicine*, 16, 741-752.

Bock, R. D. (Ed.) (1989). *Multilevel analysis of educational data*. San Diego, CA: Academic Press, Inc.

Box, G. E. P., & Tiao, G. C. (1973). *Bayesian inference in statistical analysis*. Reading, MA: Addison-Wesley Publishing Company.

Brooks, S. P., & Gelman, A. (1998). General methods for monitoring convergence of iterative simulations. *Journal of Computational and Graphical Statistics*, 7, 434-455.

Bryk, A. S., & Raudenbush, S. W. (1987). Applying the hierarchical linear model to measurement of change problems. *Psychological Bulletin*, 101, 147-158.

Buonaccorsi, J. P. (1991). Measurement errors, linear calibration and inferences for means. *Computational Statistics & Data Analysis*, 11, 239-257.

Buonaccorsi, J. P., & Tosteson, D. (1993). Correcting for nonlinear measurement errors in the dependent variable in the general linear model. *Communications in Statistics, Theory & Methods*, 22, 2687-2702.

Burstein, L. (1980). The analysis of multilevel data in educational research and evaluation. *Review of Research in Education*, 8, 158-233.

Carroll, R., Ruppert, D., & Stefanski, L. A. (1995). *Measurement error in nonlinear models*. London: Chapman & Hall.

Chen, M. -H., & Shao, Q. -M. (1999). Monte Carlo estimation of Bayesian credible and HPD intervals. *Journal of Computational and Graphical Statistics*, 8, 69-92.

Cochran, W. G. (1968). Errors of measurement in statistics. *Technometrics*, 10, 637-666.

Cowles, M. K., & Carlin, B. P. (1996). Markov chain Monte Carlo convergence diagnostics: A comparative review. *Journal of the American Statistical Association*, 91, 833-904.

Dempster, A. P., Laird, N. M., & Rubin, D. B. (1977). Maximum likelihood from incomplete data via the EM algorithm (with discussion). *Journal of the Royal Statistical Society, Series B*, 39, 1-38.

Fox, J.-P. (2000). *Stochastic EM for estimating the parameters of a multilevel IRT model*. Technical Report RR 00-02, Enschede: University of Twente.

Fox, J.-P., & Glas, C. A. W. (2000). *Bayesian modeling of measurement error in predictor variables using Item Response Theory models*. Technical Report RR 00-03, Enschede: University of Twente.

Fox, J.-P., & Glas, C. A. W. (2001). Bayesian estimation of a multilevel IRT model using Gibbs sampling. *Psychometrika*, 66, 269-286.

Freedman, L. S., Carroll, R. J., & Wax, Y. (1991). Estimating the relation between dietary intake obtained from a food frequency questionnaire and true average intake. *American Journal of Epidemiology*, 134, 310-320.

Fuller, W. A. (1987). *Measurement error models*. New York, John Wiley & Sons, Inc.

Gelfand, A. E., & Smith, A. F. M. (1990). Sampling-based approaches to calculating marginal densities. *Journal of the American Statistical Association*, 85, 398-409.

Gelman, A. (1995). Inference and monitoring convergence. In W.R. Gilks, S. Richardson, & D.J. Spiegelhalter (Eds.), *Markov Chain Monte Carlo in practice* (pp. 131-143). London: Chapman & Hall.

Gelman, A., Carlin, J. B., Stern, H. S., & Rubin, D. B. (1995). *Bayesian data analysis*. London: Chapman & Hall.

Geman, S., & Geman, D. (1984). Stochastic relaxation, Gibbs distribution, and the Bayesian restoration of images. *IEEE Transactions on Pattern Analysis and Machine Intelligence*, 6, 721-741.

Goldstein, H. (1986). Multilevel mixed linear model analysis using iterative generalized least squares. *Biometrika*, 73, 43-56.

Goldstein, H. (1987). *Multilevel models in educational and social research* (2nd ed.). Griffin/New York: Oxford University Press.

Goldstein, H. (1989). Models for multilevel response variables with an application to growth curves. In R.D. Bock (Ed.), *Multilevel analysis of educational data* (pp. 107-125). San Diego, CA: Academic Press, Inc.

Goldstein, H. (1997). Methods in school effectiveness research. *School Effectiveness and School Improvement*, 8, 369-395.

Goldstein, H., Rasbash, J., Plewis, I., Draper, D., Browne, W., Yang, M., Woodhouse, G., & Healy, M. (1998). *A user's guide to MLwiN.* London, Multilevel Models Project, Institute of Education, University of London.

Hambleton, R. K., & Swaminathan, H. (1985). *Item response theory: Principles and applications.* Boston: Kluwer Nijhoff Publishing.

Heck, R.H., & Thomas, S.L. (2000). *An introduction to multilevel modeling techniques.* Mahwah, NJ: Lawrence Erlbaum Associates.

Hox, J. J. (1995). *Applied multilevel analysis* (2nd ed.). Amsterdam: TT-Publikaties.

Hüttner, H. J. M., & van den Eeden, P. (1995). *The multilevel design: A guide with an annotated bibliography 1980-1993.* Westport: Greenwood Press.

Johnson, V. E., & Albert, J. H. (1999). *Ordinal data modeling.* New York, Springer-Verlag, Inc.

Kreft, I. G. G., & De Leeuw, J. (1998). *Introducing multilevel modeling.* London: Sage Publications.

Lindley, D. V., & Smith, A. F. M. (1972). Bayes estimates for the linear model. *Journal of the Royal Statistical Society, Series B*, 34, 1-41.

Longford, N. T. (1990). *VARCL. Software for variance component analysis of data with nested random effects (maximum likelihood).* Princeton, NJ: Educational Testing Service.

Longford, N. T. (1993). *Random coefficient models.* New York, Oxford university press, Inc.

Lord, F. M. (1980). *Applications of item response theory to practical testing problems.* Hillsdale, New Jersey: Lawrence Erlbaum Associates, Inc., Publishers.

Lord, F. M., & Novick, M. R. (1968). *Statistical theories of mental test scores.* Reading, MA: Addison-Wesley.

Mallick, B. K., & Gelfand, A. E. (1996). Semiparametric errors-in-variables models: A Bayesian approach. *Journal of Statistical Planning and Inference*, 52, 307-321.

Mason, W. M., Wong, G. Y., & Entwisle, B. (1983). Contextual analysis through the multilevel linear model. In S. Leinhardt (Ed.), *Sociological methodology* (pp. 72-103). San Francisco: Jossey-Bass.

Müller, P., & Roeder, K. (1997). A Bayesian semiparametric model for case-control studies with errors in variables. *Biometrika*, 84, 523-537.

Muthén, K. L., & Muthén, B. O. (1998). *Mplus. The comprehensive modeling program for applied researchers.* Los Angeles, CA: Muthén & Muthén.

Raudenbush, S. W., Bryk, A. S., Cheong, Y. F., & Congdon, R. T., Jr. (2000). *HLM 5. Hierarchical linear and nonlinear modeling.* Lincolnwood, IL; Scientific Software International, Inc.

Richardson, S. (1996). Measurement error. In W.R. Gilks, S. Richardson, & D.J. Spiegelhalter (Eds.), *Markov Chain Monte Carlo in practice* (pp. 401-417). London: Chapman & Hall.

Roberts, G. O., & Sahu, S. K. (1997). Updating schemes, correlation structure, blocking and parametrization for the Gibbs sampler. *Journal of the Royal Statistical Society, Series B*, 59, 291-317.

Rosner, B., Willett, W. C., & Spiegelman, D. (1989). Correction of logistic regression relative risk estimates and confidence intervals for systematic within-person measurement error. *Statistics in Medicine*, 8, 1051-1069.

Schaalje, G. B., & Butts, R. A. (1993). Some effects of ignoring correlated measurement errors in straight line regression and prediction. *Biometrics*, 49, 1262-1267.

Scheerens, J., & Bosker, R. J. (1997). *The foundations of educational effectiveness.* Oxford: Pergamon.

Snijders, T. A. B., & Bosker, R. J. (1999). *Multilevel analysis.* London: Sage Publications Ltd.

van der Linden, W. J., & Hambleton, R. K. (Eds.) (1997). *Handbook of modern item response theory.* New York: Springer-Verlag.

Wakefield, J., & Morris, S. (1999). Spatial dependence and errors-in-variables in environmentol epidemiology. In J.M. Bernardo, J.O. Berger, A.P. Dawid, & A.F.M. Smith (Eds.), *Bayesian statistics 6* (pp. 657-684). New York: Oxford University Press, Inc.

Zellner, A. (1971). *An introduction to Bayesian inference in econometrics.* New York: John Wiley & Sons, Inc.

Author Index

A

Äyras, M., 160, *193*
Agresti, A. 42, 56, *60*
Agulló, J. 156, *191*
Aitkin, M., 63, 64, 66, *83*, 246, 248, *266*
Aizen, I., 85, *102*
Akey, T. M., 86, *103*
Albanese, M. T., 15, *39*, 76, *83*
Albert, J. H., 259, *268*
Allison, P. D., 107, 109, *118*
Anderson, T. W., 3, 4, *12*
Arbuckle, J. L., 105, 106, 107, *118*, 228, *242*
Arminger, G., 4, *12*, 121, 131, *133*

B

Baltai, B. H., 245, *266*
Bartholomew, D. J., 4, 5, 7, 8, 10, 11 *12*, 21, *39*, 63, 65, 66, *83*, 195, 198, 201, 212, *222*, 241, *242*
Basilevski, A., 157, *191*,
Bates, D. M., 137, 18, 139, 148, *150*, *151*
Becker, C., 170, *194*
Bentler, P. M., 86, 87, 95, 97, *102*, *103*, 107, *119*, 135, 138, 141, 143, 147, *150*, *151*,
Bernadinelli, L., 247, *266*
Best, N. G., 247, *266*
Birnbaum, A., 2, *12*, 57, *60*, 63, *83*
Bloomfield, P., 169, *191*,
Blozis, S. A., 227, *242*
Bock, R., 63, 66, *83*
Bock, R. D. 246, *266*
Boehning, D., 64, *83*
Bogatyrev, I., 160, *193*
Bolck, A., 209, 220, 222, *220*
Bollen, K. A., 85, *102*, 121, 122, 124, 131, *133*,
Bolt, D.M., 121, 131, *133*
Boomsma, A., 108, *119*, 230, *243*
Borgen, O., 172, *193*

B (cont.)

Bosker, R. J., 245, 248, *269*
Box, G. E. P., 255, *266*
Boyd, R., 160, *193*
Bradshaw, S., 30, *40*,
Brooks, S. P., 254, *266*
Browne, M. W., 86, *102*, 135, 137, 147, *151*, 227, 235, 241, *242*, 245, *268*
Bryk, A. S., 245, 246, *266*, *268*
Buonaccorsi, J. P., 246, 247, *266*
Burdick, R. K., 135, *151*
Burr, E. J., 202, *223*
Burstein, L., 245, *266*
Butler, R. W., 156, *191*
Butts, R. A., 259, *269*

C

Cameron, B., 227, *242*
Carlin, B. P., 254, *267*
Carlin, J. B., 254, *267*
Carroll, R., 170, *193*, 246, 247, 249, 250, 254, 265, *267*
Casella, G., 197, 203, *223*
Chekushin, V., 160, *193*
Chen, M. -H., 261, *267*
Chen, Z., 185, 191, *193*
Cheong, Y. F., 245, *268*
Christoffersson, A., 87, *102*
Chung, C. -M., 3, *12*
Clogg, C. C., 64, *84*, 85, *102*, 195, 200, *222*, *223*
Cochran, J. A., 207, *222*
Cochrand, W. G., 256, *267*
Coenders, G., 87, *102*
Congdon, R. T., 245, *268*
Cornwell, J. M., 199, *222*
Cowles, M. K., 254, 261, *267*
Cressie, N., 64, *83*
Croon, M. A., 54, *60*, 208, 209, 220, 222, *222*
Croux, C., 156, 158, 159, 164, 172, 173, 174, 175, 176, 183, 184, 185, 186, 190, 191, *191*, *192*, *193*

Subject Index

Robustness, 154